The Role of Human Factors in Home Health Care

Workshop Summary

Steve Olson, *Rapporteur*

Committee on the Role of Human Factors in Home Health Care

Committee on Human-Systems Integration

Division of Behavioral and Social Sciences and Education

NATIONAL RESEARCH COUNCIL
OF THE NATIONAL ACADEMIES

THE NATIONAL ACADEMIES PRESS
Washington, D.C.
www.nap.edu

THE NATIONAL ACADEMIES PRESS 500 Fifth Street, N.W. Washington, DC 20001

NOTICE: The project that is the subject of this report was approved by the Governing Board of the National Research Council, whose members are drawn from the councils of the National Academy of Sciences, the National Academy of Engineering, and the Institute of Medicine. The members of the committee responsible for the report were chosen for their special competences and with regard for appropriate balance.

This study was supported by Contract No. HHSP23320042509XI, task order HHSP233200800004T, between the National Academy of Sciences and the U.S. Department of Health and Human Services. Any opinions, findings, conclusions, or recommendations expressed in this publication are those of the author(s) and do not necessarily reflect the views of the organizations or agencies that provided support for the project.

International Standard Book Number-13: 978-0-309-15629-5
International Standard Book Number-10: 0-309-15629-7

Additional copies of this report are available from the National Academies Press, 500 Fifth Street, N.W., Lockbox 285, Washington, DC 20055; (800) 624-6242 or (202) 334-3313 (in the Washington metropolitan area); Internet, http://www.nap.edu.

Printed in the United States of America

Suggested citation: National Research Council. (2010). *The Role of Human Factors in Home Health Care: Workshop Summary*. Steve Olson, Rapporteur. Committee on the Role of Human Factors in Home Health Care, Committee on Human-Systems Integration. Division of Behavioral and Social Sciences and Education. Washington, DC: The National Academies Press.

THE NATIONAL ACADEMIES

Advisers to the Nation on Science, Engineering, and Medicine

The **National Academy of Sciences** is a private, nonprofit, self-perpetuating society of distinguished scholars engaged in scientific and engineering research, dedicated to the furtherance of science and technology and to their use for the general welfare. Upon the authority of the charter granted to it by the Congress in 1863, the Academy has a mandate that requires it to advise the federal government on scientific and technical matters. Dr. Ralph J. Cicerone is president of the National Academy of Sciences.

The **National Academy of Engineering** was established in 1964, under the charter of the National Academy of Sciences, as a parallel organization of outstanding engineers. It is autonomous in its administration and in the selection of its members, sharing with the National Academy of Sciences the responsibility for advising the federal government. The National Academy of Engineering also sponsors engineering programs aimed at meeting national needs, encourages education and research, and recognizes the superior achievements of engineers. Dr. Charles M. Vest is president of the National Academy of Engineering.

The **Institute of Medicine** was established in 1970 by the National Academy of Sciences to secure the services of eminent members of appropriate professions in the examination of policy matters pertaining to the health of the public. The Institute acts under the responsibility given to the National Academy of Sciences by its congressional charter to be an adviser to the federal government and, upon its own initiative, to identify issues of medical care, research, and education. Dr. Harvey V. Fineberg is president of the Institute of Medicine.

The **National Research Council** was organized by the National Academy of Sciences in 1916 to associate the broad community of science and technology with the Academy's purposes of furthering knowledge and advising the federal government. Functioning in accordance with general policies determined by the Academy, the Council has become the principal operating agency of both the National Academy of Sciences and the National Academy of Engineering in providing services to the government, the public, and the scientific and engineering communities. The Council is administered jointly by both Academies and the Institute of Medicine. Dr. Ralph J. Cicerone and Dr. Charles M. Vest are chair and vice chair, respectively, of the National Research Council.

www.national-academies.org

COMMITTEE ON THE ROLE OF HUMAN FACTORS IN HOME HEALTH CARE

David H. Wegman (*Chair*), School of Health and Environment, University of Massachusetts–Lowell
Sara Czaja, College of Engineering and Department of Psychiatry and Behavioral Sciences, University of Miami Miller School of Medicine
K. Eric DeJonge, Washington Hospital Center, Washington, DC
Daryle Jean Gardner-Bonneau, Bonneau & Associates, Portage, Michigan
Michael Christopher Gibbons, Johns Hopkins University Urban Health Institute, School of Medicine, and Bloomberg School of Public Health
Laura N. Gitlin, Jefferson Center for Applied Research on Aging and Health, Thomas Jefferson University
Judith Tabolt Matthews, Department of Health and Community Systems, University of Pittsburgh School of Nursing
Misha Pavel, Division of Biomedical Engineering, Department of Science and Engineering, Oregon Health and Science University
P. Hunter Peckham,[1] Donnell Institute of Biomedical Engineering and Orthopaedics, Case Western Reserve University
Jon Pynoos, Ethel Percy Andrus Gerontology Center, Davis School of Gerontology, University of Southern California
Robert M. Schumacher, User Centric, Inc., Oakbrook Terrace, Illinois
Mary Weick-Brady,[2] Food and Drug Administration, Rockville, Maryland
Jennifer L. Wolff, Johns Hopkins University Bloomberg School of Public Health and School of Medicine

Susan B. Van Hemel, *Study Director*
Barbara Wanchisen, *Director, Committee on Human-Systems Integration*
Renée L. Wilson Gaines, *Senior Program Assistant*

[1]Resigned from the committee in March 2010.
[2]Resigned from the committee in May 2010.

COMMITTEE ON HUMAN-SYSTEMS INTEGRATION

William S. Marras[1] (*Chair*), Institute for Ergonomics, Ohio State University
Deborah A. Boehm-Davis, Human Factors and Applied Cognition Program, George Mason University
Pascale Carayon, Department of Industrial and Systems Engineering, Center for Quality and Productivity Improvement, University of Wisconsin–Madison
Don Chaffin,[1] Industrial and Operations Engineering and Biomedical Engineering, University of Michigan
Nancy J. Cooke, Department of Applied Psychology, Arizona State University
Mary (Missy) Cummings, Department of Aeronautics and Astronautics, Massachusetts Institute of Technology
Jonathan Grudin, Microsoft Research, Redmond, Washington
Waldemar Karwowski, Department of Industrial Engineering and Management Systems, University of Central Florida
Steven W.J. Kozlowski, Department of Psychology, Michigan State University
Arthur Kramer, Beckman Institute, University of Illinois
Matthew Rizzo, Department of Neurology, University of Iowa Hospitals and Clinics
Thomas F. Sanquist, Pacific Northwest National Laboratory, Seattle
Thomas B. Sheridan,[1] Massachusetts Institute of Technology (*Emeritus*)
Philip J. Smith, Institute for Ergonomics, Ohio State University
David H. Wegman, University of Massachusetts–Lowell (*Emeritus*)
Howard Weiss, Department of Psychological Sciences, Military Family Research Institute, Purdue University

Barbara Wanchisen, *Director*
Mary Ellen O'Connell, *Associate Director*
Matthew McDonough, *Senior Program Assistant* (through December 2009)
Christie R. Jones, *Program Associate* (from December 2009)

[1]Member, National Academy of Engineering.

Preface

In the United States, health care devices, technologies, and care practices are rapidly moving into the home. This transition, which is likely to accelerate in the future, has raised a host of issues that have received insufficient attention in the past. Care recipients and caregivers have particular capabilities and limitations that can shape home health care processes and procedures. Very few homes have been designed for the delivery of health care, yet the aging of the population and changes in medical practice and health care reimbursement are leading to greater reliance on care at home. Medical equipment and technologies that are designed for hospitals and clinics can be ill-suited for use in the home. The community environment can support or detract from home health care.

As stated earlier, the rapid growth of home health care has raised many insolved issues and will have consequences that are far too broad for any one group to analyze in their entirety. Yet a major influence on the safety, quality, and effectiveness of home health care will be the set of issues encompassed by the field of human factors research—the discipline of applying what is known about human capabilities and limitations to the design of products, processes, systems, and work environments. For that reason, the Agency for Healthcare Research and Quality (AHRQ) asked the Committee on Human-Systems Integration of the National Research Council to conduct a wide-ranging investigation of the role of human factors in home health care. In response, the multidisciplinary Committee on the Role of Human Factors in Home Health Care was formed to examine a diverse range of behavioral and human factors issues resulting from the increasing migration of medical devices, technologies, and care practices into the home. Its goal is to lay the groundwork for a thorough integration of human factors research with the design and implementation of home health care devices, technologies, and practices.

As part of its work, the committee conducted a workshop on the role of human factors in home health care on October 1-2, 2009, in Washington, DC. The workshop and this report represent the culmination of the first phase of the study. The second phase will culminate in a consensus report containing the committee's conclusions and recommendations concerning the best use of human factors in home health care. In addition, the committee is overseeing the preparation of a designers' guide for the use of health information technologies in home care.

The landmark report *To Err Is Human: Building a Safer Health System*, published in 2000 by the Institute of Medicine, found that illness, injuries, and other adverse health consequences often result from poor interactions between care recipients and the health care delivery system. By highlighting the importance of human factors in the inpatient hospital setting, that report led to a broad array of reforms aimed at improving the quality of health care delivery.

The committee's hope is that this workshop report and its consensus report will motivate similar reforms for home health care, even as the terrain of the health care delivery system is undergoing dramatic changes. In the future, individuals will play a greater role in managing their own health care needs and those of their family members at home and in the community. The extent to which human factors research is incorporated into home-based devices, technologies, and practices will have a big influence on whether greater reliance on home health care proves to have beneficial or detrimental effects on people's lives.

The committee members identified presenters, organized the agenda, introduced presentations, and facilitated discussion, although they did not participate in the writing of this report. This summary reflects their diligent efforts, the excellent presentations by other experts at the workshop, and the insightful comments of the many workshop participants.

The planning efforts of the committee were greatly assisted by the interest and support of Kerm Henriksen, AHRQ human factors advisor for patient safety, and Teresa Zayas-Caban, senior manager, Health IT at AHRQ, which are much appreciated. Henriksen also provided some very helpful introductory remarks and closing comments at the workshop.

The workshop included discussions led by Paul Crawford of Intel, Margaret Quinn of the University of Massachusetts–Lowell, and Carol Raphael of the Visiting Nurse Service of New York. Their contributions are greatly appreciated.

This workshop summary has been reviewed in draft form by individuals chosen for their diverse perspectives and technical expertise, in accordance with procedures approved by the Report Review Committee of the National Research Council. The purpose of this independent review is to provide candid and critical comments that will assist the institution in making its published report as sound as possible and to ensure that the report meets institutional standards for objectivity, evidence, and responsiveness to the charge. The review comments and draft manuscript remain confidential to protect the integrity of the process. We thank the following individuals for their review of this report and the attached papers: Jane Behr-Lehman, Steinhardt Department of Occupational Therapy, New York University; Deborah A. Boehm-Davis, Human Factors and Applied Cognition Program, George Mason University; R. Paul Crawford, Product Research and Innovation, Digital Health Group, Intel Corporation; Steven Landers, Center for Home Care and Community Rehabilitation, Cleveland Clinic; Suzanne Mintz, President and Chief Executive Officer, National Family Caregivers Association, Kensington, MD; Marcia Nusgart, Nusgart Consulting, Bethesda, MD; Terrance J. O'Shea, Digital Health Group, Intel Corporation; Denise C. Park, Center for Vital Longevity, University of Texas at Dallas; Richard W. Pew, BBN Technologies, Cambridge, MA; Eduardo Salas, Institute for Simulation and Training, University of Central Florida; Susan Stark, Program of Occupational Therapy, Department of Therapy and Neurology, Washington University School of Medicine; and Bernadette Wright, The Lewin Group, Falls Church, VA.

Although the reviewers listed above provided many constructive comments and suggestions, they were not asked to endorse the content of the report, nor did they see the final draft of the report before its release. The review of this report was overseen by Matthew Rizzo of the University of Iowa. Appointed by the National Research Council, he was responsible for making certain that an independent examination of this report was carried out in accordance with institutional procedures and that all review comments were carefully considered. Responsibility for the final content of this report rests entirely with the author and the institution.

Contents

Part I:
Workshop Summary

1

Introduction

On October 1 and 2, 2009, a group of human factors and other experts met to consider a diverse range of behavioral and human factors issues associated with the increasing migration of medical devices, technologies, and care practices into the home. The Committee on the Role of Human Factors in Home Health Care organized the event to gather information on a topic on which relatively little has been established empirically, although it is increasingly clear that more and more health care is being delivered in homes. Part I of this volume is a summary of the presentations and discussions that took place at the Workshop on the Role of Human Factors in Home Health Care.

THE ROLE OF HUMAN FACTORS IN HOME HEALTH CARE[1]

A standard textbook definition characterizes the field of human factors research as "the discipline that takes into account human strengths and limitations in the design of interactive systems that involve people, tools and technology, and environments to ensure their safety, effectiveness, and ease of use." This definition can easily be modified to apply to human factors in home health care said Kerm Henriksen during his opening remarks at the workshop:

[1]This section is based on remarks at the workshop by Kerm Henriksen, human factors advisor for patient safety in the Agency for Healthcare Research and Quality.

> The field of human factors in home health care takes into account provider and recipient capabilities in the design of interactive home care systems of people, devices and technology, and environments to ensure their safety, effectiveness, and ease of delivering care.

Figure 1-1 provides a more detailed characterization of the role of human factors in home health care. From the perspective of the care recipient, the ultimate goal is to ensure the delivery of high-quality care in the home and to avoid preventable adverse events, as shown at the bottom of the figure. A host of factors must come together for this objective to be achieved, Henriksen observed. The factors closest to the recipient that can cause adverse events are the characteristics of the provider and the recipient. (These are labeled as "active errors" in the figure.) Factors more distant from the recipient (labeled "latent conditions") can also result in deficiencies in care. These factors include the nature of home health care tasks and the characteristics of the physical environment, of medical devices and technologies, and of the social or community environment. Exerting an even broader influence are factors in the external environment, including demographic, economic, and political factors. Thus, recipients and providers "inherit the sins of omission and commission of everybody else who has played a role in the design of the greater sociotechnical system," said Henriksen.

Human factors research has a long track record of addressing challenging issues in demanding environments, particularly when it is able to address issues in the context of integrated systems. But systems thinking has not come easily to home health care, Henriksen said. Homes are not designed for health care, and considerable variation exists in what constitutes a home. Recipients and providers, whether formal or informal, have considerable variation in knowledge and skills. Many lay providers are themselves care recipients, as the provider workforce ages. Hazards in the home are often unrecognized, and home health care providers have limited experience with medical devices and medical information technologies. Home and community culture and environments are extremely variable. And health care reform often tends to mean doing more with less.

A comprehensive study of the role of human factors in home health care faces a challenging set of goals:

- Achieve an in-depth understanding of the human factors challenges underlying safe and high-quality home health care.
- Specify critical gaps in understanding.
- Develop an integrated framework to guide research across the major components and disciplines relevant to safe delivery of care in the home.

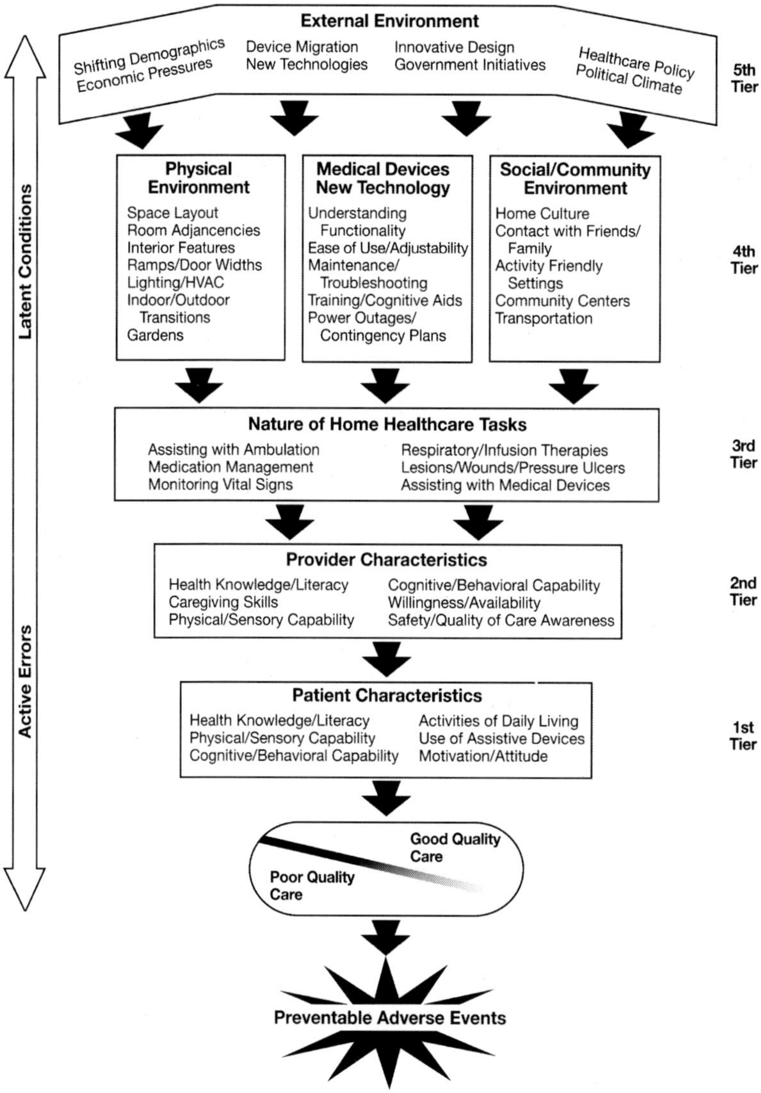

FIGURE 1-1 Factors that influence the safety, quality, and effectiveness of home health care range from the immediate characteristics of recipients and providers (Tiers 1 and 2) to aspects of home health care tasks, technologies, and environments (Tiers 3, 4, and 5).
SOURCE: K. Henriksen, Anjali, J., and Zayas-Caban, T. (2009). The human factors of home health care: A conceptual model for examining safety and quality concerns. *Journal of Patient Safety, 5*(4), 229-236. Reprinted with permission of Wolters Kluwer Health.

- Develop guidelines for those involved in the design, development, and implementation of health information technology in the home.
- Provide a roadmap for needed research.

Given the rapid increases in home health care that have already occurred and will continue to occur, the overall goal, said Henriksen, must be to "provide a wake-up call for home health care policy."

WORKSHOP THEMES

Nine presentations, given in three half-day sessions, summarized the main conclusions of the background papers prepared for the workshop by experts in human factors and home health care. The first session covered the people who receive and provide home health care. The second session looked at the tools and technologies involved in the delivery of home health care, and the third session focused on the physical and social environments in which home health care occurs. At the end of each session, a discussant highlighted important points, fielded questions, and moderated an exchange among the presenters, committee members, and workshop participants on the topics covered during the session. At the end of the workshop, the committee chair, David Wegman, moderated a final discussion of the most important observations and conclusions to emerge from the workshop as a whole.

ORGANIZATION OF THE REPORT

Part I is a summary of the workshop event. This chapter gives the context in which the workshop took place. Chapters 2, 3, and 4 summarize the presentations and discussions that occurred during each of the three sessions. Chapter 5 describes the main points made in the final wrap-up session.

Part II contains individually authored papers written for the workshop and consists of Chapters 6 through 12. The Appendix presents the workshop agenda and list of participants.

It is important to be specific about the nature of the workshop summary (Part I), which documents the information presented in the workshop presentations and discussions. Its purpose is to lay out the key ideas that emerged from the workshop, and it should be viewed as an initial step in examining the research and applying it in specific policy circumstances. The report is confined to the material presented by the workshop speakers and participants. Neither the workshop nor this summary is intended as a comprehensive review of what is known about human factors in home health care, although it is a general reflection of the literature. The presentations and discussions were limited by the time available for the workshop. A more comprehensive review and synthesis of relevant research knowledge will have to await the committee's consensus report.

This report was prepared by a rapporteur and does not represent findings or recommendations that can be attributed to the planning committee. Indeed, the report summarizes views expressed by workshop participants, and the committee is responsible only for its overall quality and accuracy as a record of what transpired at the workshop. Also, the workshop was not designed to generate consensus conclusions or recommendations but focused instead on the identification of ideas, themes, and considerations that contribute to understanding of human factors in home health care. The insights of the presenters and workshop participants constitute extremely useful input for the committee's continuing work.

2

The People Who Receive and Provide Home Health Care

FITTING PEOPLE TO HEALTH CARE IN THEIR HOME ENVIRONMENTS[1]

About one-sixth of the U.S. gross domestic product is currently being spent on health care—about $7,000 annually per U.S. resident. Almost 90 percent of those expenditures involve people with chronic conditions—treating either their chronic diseases or acute conditions that they develop, said Neil Charness. Chronic diseases, according to a definition adopted by the Centers for Disease Control and Prevention, are "noncommunicable illnesses that are prolonged in duration, do not resolve spontaneously, and are rarely cured completely." The most costly chronic conditions include heart conditions, cancer, trauma-related disorders, mental disorders, and asthma plus chronic obstructive pulmonary disease (COPD). The percentage of people with chronic conditions increases with age, to the point that more than 90 percent of people older than 85 have one or more chronic conditions.[2]

The bulk of health care expenditures is spent on hospital care and physician services, Charness observed. "If I were trying to cut costs in this very costly system, I would try to eliminate as much as possible unnecessary visits to hospitals and unnecessary visits with physicians, because those are

[1]This section is based on the presentation by Neil Charness, William G. Chase professor of psychology at Florida State University. For more information and for references to the information cited in this presentation, see Chapter 6.

[2]Tables and figures illustrating this and other statistics cited here can be found in the papers in Part II.

the two biggest slices of the pie." Home health care has the potential to reduce both of those costs.

Assessing Efficacy

The efficacy of much of the current health care that takes place in homes is unknown. For example, some assistive devices have high abandonment rates. "Something like 30 to 50 percent of people who adopt or are fitted for a hearing aid will put it in a drawer and not use it at some point," said Charness. Yet many people also express a preference to be treated in their homes. As one measure of this preference, in Canada from 1994 to 2004 the percentage of total deaths that occurred in hospitals declined from 78 to 61 percent.

In analyzing home health care technologies and practices, Charness and his colleagues often assess the fit of capabilities and demand. Health care devices, technologies, and practices can make many demands on a person's capabilities. A videoconferencing system, for example, might have a software interface that a care recipient has to understand in order to use the technology. But users differ greatly along many dimensions, including their age, their education, their health literacy, their technical experience, and their perceptual, cognitive, and psychomotor capabilities. These factors affect outcomes like efficiency, efficacy, and safety. Thus, the outcomes of home health care depend on the fit between a device, technology, or practice and a person's capabilities.

Charness used as an example an older person who has just been diagnosed with adult-onset diabetes. Such a person might be told to monitor blood sugar levels, inject insulin, and modify diet and exercise. All of these tasks can be difficult for many people. They may not like to use a glucose meter or inject insulin. They may also have unrealistic expectations, thinking that changes in diet or exercise will immediately improve their condition. "If you don't have appropriate expectations, that can lead to inappropriate adherence to the routine that you have been asked to engage in," Charness said.

The Diversity of Home Health Care Users

Home health care is an extremely diverse enterprise. It encompasses people with very different illnesses and capabilities, from children with diabetes to young adults with mental illnesses to middle-aged adults who might be taking medication for hypertension to older adults with dementia or renal failure. The home environment also exhibits tremendous diversity. About 27 percent of all the households in the United States have single members, rising from a low of 17 percent for adults under age 20 to as high as about 57 percent for people over age 75. The proportion of people with disabilities increases greatly with age as well. However, because the population of younger people is larger, the absolute numbers of people with disabilities are higher among people ages 21 to 64 than among those over age 64. On average, men tend to become disabled earlier in their lives than do women.

Veterans represent an important subset of the disabled population. According to the U.S. Department of Veterans Affairs, about 2.6 million veterans were considered disabled and were being compensated in 2007. The most prevalent types of disabilities are musculoskeletal and mental disorders, including posttraumatic stress syndrome. Hearing problems and diabetes are also fairly common and can have an influence on home health care.

The U.S. population is itself exceedingly diverse along many dimensions, such as language, financial resources, attitudes, insurance coverage, Internet access, and media exposure. Minority groups are growing as a portion of the population, including the elderly population. Many different languages are spoken at home in the United States—not only English and Spanish but also Slavic languages, Asian languages, and many others. In addition, an estimated 11 million U.S. residents have below basic literacy skills, which limit their ability to perform even relatively simple tasks.

Although access to the Internet has been growing for all populations, including the elderly, only about 40 percent of people over age 65 had Internet access in 2008. Interestingly, almost 50 percent of them report using a cell phone. Differing minority groups also have different levels of access to the Internet and cell phones.

As people get older, their hearing and vision often decline, to the point that medication instructions that younger people can make out easily are difficult for many older people to read. Similarly, medical devices, such as oxygen concentrators, may need both visual and auditory warnings to alert older users to potential hazards when the equipment is failing.

The learning rate slows with age, so that it can take an older adult between 50 and 100 percent longer to learn new material. As a result, device designers, for example, need to take learning time into account so that people don't become frustrated and give up on a device.

Finally, attitudes toward health care differ greatly. For example, people generally have to believe that a medication is going to improve their condition to stick to a prescription regimen. The opinions of family and friends can also be an important predictor of someone's willingness to engage in a particular behavior. Some people comply with societal norms, and some do not. People also differ in their beliefs about their own ability to follow a routine or engage in a behavior.

Privacy Concerns

As home health care expands, increasing amounts of health care information will be transmitted to and from the home. For example, vital signs or activity can be monitored through home-based devices, with reminders for people to engage in particular activities. "Aware homes" or robots could serve as health care coaches.

Such developments raise concerns about privacy and confidentiality. For example, care recipients may have greater concerns for confidentiality with regard to telemedicine than in face-to-face exchanges with a health care provider. Internet users also express a strong preference for privacy, although their online behavior does not always accord with this preference.

More impaired care recipients are more willing to cede some degree of privacy and confidentiality regarding such issues as toileting, medications, movement in the home, cognitive abilities, and driving. But they often are unwilling to share that information with insurance companies or government agencies.

Human Factors Tools

Human factors research has produced a number of tools that can be used in the analysis of home health care, Charness said. Focus groups and questionnaires, task analysis, usability testing, and modeling and simulation can all contribute to the design and implementation of home health care devices, technologies, and practices. As an example of how these tools might be applied to an older adult with newly diagnosed adult-onset diabetes, focus groups and questionnaires might uncover a gap in expectations regarding the results of diet and exercise. Task analysis and usability testing could lead to better equipment design and instructional materials. And better health instruction earlier in the life span might have led to a lifestyle that prevented adult-onset diabetes.

Improving the Use of Human Factors Research in Home Health Care

Charness had a number of ideas for furthering the use of human factors research in home health care:

- Promote usability testing for more home health care devices, including smart phones, webcams, cognitive training systems, and even videogames that could be used in rehabilitation programs.
- Assess home health care efficacy and efficiency through randomized trials.
- Examine attitudes to such issues as technology adoption and abandonment through tools like the Current Population Survey.

- Conduct research on instructional and training principles, especially for older users, disabled users, non-English-speaking users, and users with low health literacy.
- Promote secure, high-speed Internet access to all households.
- Develop more detailed knowledge about the home, including such features as electrical wiring and access to wireless and broadband communications. This is particularly important in the homes of disadvantaged people, who are less likely to be represented in trials of home health care systems.

Responses to Questions

Charness was asked how the designers of home health care systems can accommodate the very broad range of users of such systems. He acknowledged that "the entire U.S. population, from small children to older adults, are potential home health care users," which makes the problem of design very difficult. Part of the solution is to have good data on what the differences are. For example, in what ways do women differ from men? How should variations in language or age affect the design of home health care devices? "Chances are, for certain types of devices, you can define who the user population is reasonably narrowly," he said.

Charness also described potential variations in the level of trust that different groups may hold toward home health care providers or technologies. These levels of trust can vary by age, ethnicity, or other factors. In some cases, people trust health care devices too much, even when a device is unreliable or needs to be checked. Similarly, the providers of home health care may trust or mistrust different categories of care recipients to different extents.

One questioner discussed the use of social networking technologies to advance home health care, both by providing information to care recipients and by allowing recipients with conditions such as depression to connect with each other. Charness pointed out that virtual groups, even if they include large numbers of people living alone, can be large and geographically extended.

INFORMAL CAREGIVERS: FAMILY, FRIENDS, OTHERS[3]

Many of the people who provide home health care are not paid professionals but family members, friends, and other lay providers, said Richard Schulz. Most people will play this role at one time or another in their life, but estimating the prevalence of informal caregiving is complicated by the

[3]This section is based on the presentation by Richard Schulz, professor of psychiatry and director of the University Center for Social and Urban Research at the University of Pittsburgh. For more information and for references to the information cited in this presentation, see Chapter 7.

absence of a standard definition for either a family or an informal caregiver. Other countries have formal definitions of what it means to be a family caregiver, and those definitions are used to shape policy, but no such definition exists in the United States. "Getting a handle on this problem requires, to some extent, that we achieve consensus and apply a good definition of what we mean by family caregiving," Schulz said.

The largest category of people receiving informal home health care consists of adults with chronic health problems or disabilities, and their providers tend to be middle-aged and older parents and spouses. The second largest category is children with chronic health problems or disabilities. An estimated 22 percent of households with children fall into this category, and their caregivers are typically young to middle-aged parents and sometimes grandparents.

A large group about which relatively little is known is people who are discharged from hospitals. Roughly 40 million hospital discharges occur each year, and these individuals generally are cared for by adults of all ages. This group overlaps with the other two, but they have different kinds of needs for home health care. After hospitalization, needs tend to be more acute, and informal caregivers can be required to provide highly specialized and technical assistance.

There are interesting subgroups within these larger populations, Schulz observed. For example, about 2.5 million grandparents in the United States provide care to children. In another reversal of expectations, about 1.5 million children provide health-related care to their parents. These two situations present very different challenges, even though both groups would be characterized as family caregivers.

Roles and Responsibilities of Caregivers

Given that much caregiving is provided to older individuals, a typical caregiver is likely to be female, middle-aged, and somewhat more educated than the population at large, often with at least some college education. Although they typically spend more than 20 hours per week providing this care, informal caregivers also may be employed in other jobs full or part time. They typically have been providing care for about four years, although of course some caregivers have quite different experiences and characteristics.

Among the adult recipients of care, approximately 80 percent are age 50 or older and have mostly age-related disabilities. Another relatively large group consists of adults ages 18 to 49, often with mental illness. War veterans with chronic diseases and disabilities are a smaller group that can have lifelong and very intensive needs.

The most common disabilities occurring in children are learning disabilities; attention deficit disorders; other mental, emotional, and behavioral problems; intellectual disabilities; developmental disabilities; asthma; speech or language problems; and diseases such as cancer and diabetes. These problems tend to vary with the age of the child. Speech problems are common early in life but tend to recede later, and learning disabilities are more likely to arise later in childhood.

The most common forms of care provided by informal caregivers are assistance with activities of daily living (ADLs) or instrumental activities of daily living (IADLs),[4] medication management, and care coordination, which involves figuring out what kind of care is needed, where to find care, and how to arrange for care. Informal caregivers also may need to negotiate among family members. "This is particularly an issue with elderly caregiving," said Schulz, "where adult children may have different opinions about what should be done, and the primary caregiver plays the role of negotiating and settling disputes within families." Informal caregivers provide companionship and emotional support. In some cases, they perform very complex medical and nursing tasks, such as infusion therapies or tube feeding.

Care coordination can be particularly challenging. Even seasoned health professionals who need to coordinate care for a parent or sibling can find it extremely difficult to access complex and fragmented health and social service delivery systems. In response to this difficulty, some systems have been organized that provide essentially one-stop shopping for caregivers looking to coordinate care. Schulz cited as examples Child's Way and the Program of All-Inclusive Care for the Elderly (PACE).

PACE, a Medicare program for older adults and people over age 55 living with disabilities, provides community-based care and services through local centers to people who otherwise need nursing home level of care. "At least from my limited perspective, [these systems] have been very successful in achieving that goal." But these two programs have strict eligibility criteria and are not widely used.

All of the tasks undertaken by informal caregivers are amenable to training. A small industry has taken shape in the United States focused on how to teach caregivers to provide home care services. A variety of technology-based strategies are also available, such as telehealth—that is, the delivery of health-related services and information via telecommunications technologies—or computer-based communication systems, that enable a caregiver to be in touch with a professional provider who can guide them through issues that they are facing.

---

[4]Activities of daily living are activities performed for self-care, work, or leisure, such as eating, bathing, or grooming. Instrumental activities of daily living are activities that allow an individual to live independently in a community, such as preparing meals, shopping, or using the telephone.

The Ability to Provide Care

Caregiving can have adverse effects on individual providers and undermine their ability to provide care. A large research literature links the stress of caregiving to a variety of physical and psychological stress conditions. Physiological indicators, such as stress hormones, neurotransmitters, cardiovascular measures, and metabolic measures, all show a worsening on average for caregivers, although the effects tend to be relatively small. Health habits, such as sleep, diet, self-care, and medical adherence, also suffer, although, again, the effects are not large. However, several methodological issues in these studies may cause the relationship between caregiving and health effects to be underestimated. For example, recent work suggests that the effects of caregiving in terms of both health and economic costs may not show up until later, after a person is no longer in that role.

The evidence of effects on mental health is stronger, according to Schulz. Depression, anxiety, stress, and other mental conditions are associated with taking on and moving through the caregiving role. However, it can be difficult to unravel cause and effect in these studies. What is needed, said Schulz, are prospective studies in which people are tracked as they move into and out of the caregiving role.

Caregiving tends to evolve over time, from assistance with instrumental activities of daily living to more intensive forms of caregiving. For elderly caregiving, the progression can continue into some kind of institutional placement and then death. When caregivers are followed prospectively through this progression, strong evidence emerges that the middle phase, in which caregiving responsibilities are very intense, produces the most profound health-related effects. There is some evidence of increased risk of mortality in this population of caregivers.

Institutional placement does not relieve many of these stressors, in part because caregivers remain involved in providing care. Death, paradoxically, does provide relief. Caregivers can recover quite well after the death of the person that they have been caring for, even if it has been an intensive caregiving experience.

Laboratory studies have demonstrated that exposure to stress can reduce executive functioning, prospective memory, working memory, speed of processing, and other mental capabilities. This raises the question of how stress in caregivers affects their performance. "I'm not aware of any literature that has directly tested this, but my best guess would be that those effects would be profound, particularly with older individuals where reserve capacities are limited due to aging," said Schulz.

Depression, which is highly prevalent among caregivers, can also have major effects on motivation, performance, and functioning. Depression can erode informal support and isolate the individual from valuable sources of information that is needed for caregiving. There is even some evidence that severe depression is associated with elder abuse.

Sociodemographic factors also play into the effects of home health care on caregivers. Informal caregivers tend to have lower socioeconomic status, and this status might be affected by the caregiving experience itself. Evidence indicates that some caregivers leave the workforce in order to provide care, which may have long-term consequences with respect to pensions and other kinds of economic indicators, particularly for women.

Older caregivers are more subject to developmental declines, such as hearing loss, visual impairment, and decreasing strength and mobility. "Lifting an individual who weighs 200 pounds out of a bed or out of a chair, when you weigh 90 pounds, is a potentially formidable task," said Schulz. Declines in cognitive function also affect the ability to acquire skills and provide complex care. Assessments of family members caring for someone at home often uncover disability and cognitive declines in the person providing the care. Furthermore, these declines tend to be more similar than dissimilar in the providers and the recipients of care. People tend to select each other based on disability, Schulz observed. They also have similar lifestyle and environmental exposures. "If they have been married for 40 years, they have been doing the same things, eating the same foods, so they end up with the same disabilities."

The Mismatch Between Demand and Capability

The need and demand for home health care are going to increase dramatically in the future. The aging of the baby boom generation, increased survival of infants and children with disabilities, an increase in such disabling health conditions as obesity and diabetes, and new populations of disabled people, such as veterans of recent wars, are all going to increase the need for home health care. Meanwhile, fewer children of baby boomers to provide care, fragmented and geographically dispersed families, the high costs of formal care, and a lack of appropriately prepared health care providers create a dire picture on the supply side.

Schulz had several ideas for easing the mismatch between demand and capability:

- Identify the stressors in the caregiving experience. Studies should differentiate among such factors as the functional disability of the care recipient, the care demands, the coordination of care, and the suffering of the care recipient. Policy should then be based on an in-depth understanding of the caregiving experience.
- Coordinate formal and informal health care. The task demands of informal care should be known in order to assess the capacity

of caregivers. Caregiver performance and recipient status should be monitored, and training and tools should be provided to health and social service providers.

- Adopt a standard definition of caregiving. This definition could be used to assess the prevalence of informal caregiving and its public health burden in terms of what kinds of care are being provided, for how long, and at what cost. This definition should be applied consistently in national surveys, such as the decennial census, Schulz said.
- Fast-track technology options. Emerging technologies could be very useful in training care providers, monitoring caregivers and recipients, and enhancing functioning and autonomy. More emphasis needs to be placed on implementation as opposed to developmental research, and privacy concerns need to be addressed.

Many people in America today are unprepared to provide or to receive care, said Schulz. Two-thirds of U.S. adults expect to be a caregiver in the future, but most admit to being unprepared. "We need campaigns to educate adults about the likelihood of their becoming caregivers, the likelihood of their being care recipients, and how to plan for those eventualities," said Schulz.

Responses to Questions

Schulz observed that assessing the need for home health care should be a factor in the ongoing debate over health care reforms. Many medical societies have advocated that when a person comes to a clinic for treatment, health care providers should assess the family members who are involved with care of that individual in the home. But these efforts are currently splintered, poorly funded, and in need of coordination.

A person's needs for home health care also vary over time. In the early stages of a disability or disease, preventive activities may be important. Later in a caregiving experience, technologies that make individuals more independent can have a big impact. Today, human factors research tends to focus on the later and more intensive caregiving period and slight the early-stage opportunities for prevention, along with the transitions that occur toward the end of the caregiving experience.

In response to a question about remote caregiving, Schulz observed that this is likely to become more important given the geographic dispersal of families. A large private-sector market is emerging to facilitate remote caregiving—for example, by facilitating communication via computer and video. These activities are likely to increase, which will raise questions about how to do them best. For example, an ideal system might be triangular among the care recipient, the family, and the health care team.

When asked about the motivations of caregivers, Schulz replied that many caregivers provide care not because they want to but because they have to. Their reasons for providing care may vary, and data show that these reasons can make a difference. For example, people who are forced into the role tend to do worse than people who perform it voluntarily.

New technologies offer considerable potential for enhancing the functioning and capabilities of older persons. Many such technologies are ready to be deployed but have not yet been implemented on a large scale. Federal agencies need to devote more attention to the translation of technologies into the community and into homes.

One-stop care coordination can make a huge difference to care providers and recipients. But services and care providers tend to be fragmented, making it difficult to achieve such coordination. The basic problem, said Schulz, is cost. Programs like PACE do a good job, but they are expensive to implement on a wide scale. "There must be a middle ground somewhere. Maybe it requires a radical reorganization of the health care system in order to achieve. But the current system is clearly not sustainable."

FORMAL CAREGIVERS[5]

Paula Milone-Nuzzo defined formal caregivers as clinicians and trained individuals who receive compensation to provide intermittent or continuous in-home services. These services can be provided by a traditional home care agency, a community or social service agency, or for-profit providers. The vast majority of in-home formal caregiving is provided by personnel from traditional home-visiting programs, such as home care, hospice, and maternal/child health services. The remainder is provided by diverse community-based organizations, such as PACE, area aging programs, and organizations that support independent living by persons with physical, cognitive, psychiatric, and developmental disabilities.

Even though formal caregivers are paid employees, they can develop deep and significant relationships with care recipients, Milone-Nuzzo said. As a result, they can experience the same psychological and physical impact of caregiving as informal caregivers.

It is impossible to discuss formal home health care deliverers without also discussing Medicare and Medicaid, said Milone-Nuzzo. Together, Medicare and Medicaid represent by far the largest funder of home care services, and they influence how other organizations pay for them.

---

[5]This section is based on the presentations by Paula Milone-Nuzzo, dean of the School of Nursing at the Pennsylvania State University, and Carolyn Humphrey, an independent consultant specializing in administrative and management operations, regulatory compliance, and education for home health care nurses.

Reimbursement rules, set by both government agencies and insurance companies, dictate the parameters of care. Similarly, the paperwork burden that accompanies something as simple as an admission to a home care agency strongly affects professional caregivers.

The Centers for Medicare & Medicaid Services, the federal agency that administers Medicare and Medicaid, has many new and ongoing initiatives under way that support best practices in the provision of Medicare services. It also has initiated a new focus on comparative effectiveness research.

Characteristics of Formal Caregivers

Formal caregivers can be divided into two categories: (1) professionals include nurses, physicians, therapists (including physical therapists, speech and language therapists, and occupational therapists), dieticians, and social workers; and (2) direct-care workers include home health aides, homemakers, companions, and patient care attendants. Typically, formal providers work in interdisciplinary teams of professionals and direct-care workers to assist care recipients to achieve their health and daily living goals. While physicians generally have the formal responsibility for ordering home care services, home care nurses or physical therapists often develop the plan of care, based on their knowledge and expertise, and send it to the physician for approval. Other professional caregivers and direct-care workers become part of the team as needed.

Other providers that are important to the home care delivery system include medical equipment providers, oxygen providers, and organizations that provide medical supplies; for-profit organizations that provide housekeeping, personal care, rehabilitation, and companion care; and community-based programs such as Meals on Wheels, care management programs, and well-baby care. The organizations that provide these kinds of services often offer a discrete service to particular age groups. For example, oxygen providers very often offer just oxygen. For-profit care tends to be focused on meeting unmet needs for care recipients who can afford to pay privately.

The largest group of professional home care employees is made up of registered nurses and licensed practical nurses, representing 21 percent of all home care employees and more than 80 percent of professional home care workers. In contrast, speech and language therapists, physical therapists, occupational therapists, social workers, and dieticians together represent just 5 percent of all home care employees.

Physicians should also be included in a list of professional home caregivers, although the number of people who provide these services is unknown. Fewer than 1,000 physicians belong to the National Association for Physicians in Home Care, and only about 1,500 are in the American Academy of Physicians in Home Care. Furthermore, these proxy measures of physicians who provide home care also include physician assistants, nurse practitioners, and home care administrators, "so we really didn't get a good number for the number of physicians who are practicing in home care," said Milone-Nuzzo.

The competencies of professional home care workers are defined both by the scope of practice, which varies from state to state and from one professional discipline to another, and by health care regulations. For example, the responsibilities of a licensed practical nurse differ from the responsibilities of a registered nurse in home care.

While the complexity of care has increased over the years, the educational preparation of professional nurses has remained relatively stable. In 2000, 60 percent of the nurses practicing in home care had either a baccalaureate or an associate's degree. Nursing has multiple entries into practice, and home care is the most autonomous setting for practice. These factors lead to a lower level of education and professional development among home care providers than in most clinical care settings. "There may be an impact on patient outcomes," Milone-Nuzzo said.

The use of advanced-practice nurses[6] in home care has lagged behind their involvement in other practice settings. The reasons for this disparity include a lack of well-defined roles for them in home care, restrictive reimbursement mechanisms, and regulatory challenges pertaining to the scope of practice. In addition, only a few research programs have looked at the use of advanced-practice nurses in home care.

Direct-care workers, who represent a large proportion of the home care workforce, include home health aides, companions, homemakers, and personal-care attendants. Their responsibilities include personal care, housekeeping, companionship, and assistance with activities of daily living. In 2006, approximately 42 percent of the estimated 3 million direct-care workers in the United States cared for individuals in their homes. "Being knowledgeable, skilled, and culturally competent is just as important for the direct-care worker group as it is for the professional care worker group."

In traditional home care systems, direct-care workers are supervised by professional caregivers in the home setting. A plan of care is defined by the professional, and regular supervisory sessions provide a way to determine the quality of care that is being provided. But consumer-driven models of care are also common in the direct-care workforce. These models, often supported by states, use direct-care workers who are employed by the recipient of care, with payment to the worker made directly by the program or through reimbursement of the care recipient. While these direct-care workers

[6]Advanced-practice nurses are nurses with master's degrees who are qualified, and often licensed or certified, to practice in such roles as nurse practitioner, nurse anesthetist, nurse midwife, and other specialties.

may have some supervision and direction from a home care professional, they typically do not have the amount of supervision or regular contact with a health care professional required by traditional home care agencies.

A third group of home care providers consists of people hired by individuals in the home to do health care. They are the least supervised of all the direct-care workers. Sometimes referred to as occupants of the gray zone of direct-care workers, they often work off the books, are hired without background checks, and arrive with unknown skill levels. They are not eligible for workers' compensation if they should get hurt and very often do not pay Social Security. "It's a market that is highly unregulated," said Milone-Nuzzo.

Direct-care workers, even those in formal home care agencies, often receive little formal training before beginning employment. Home health aides who work in Medicare- and Medicaid-certified home care agencies are required to have a minimum of 75 hours of training, including classroom content and clinical experience, and they are required to pass a test. Aides are allowed to work up to four months before getting that training. Subject areas covered in the training include communication skills, reading and recording vital signs, infection control, assistance with bodily functions and changes in bodily functions, mobility transfers, and basic nutrition. Homemakers and companions require no formal training.

As the overall population ages, so do the populations of nurses and other professional caregivers. Approximately 50 percent of the registered nurse workforce will reach retirement age in the next 15 years. At the same time, the number of physical therapists and occupational therapists who graduated in 2003 and 2004 was significantly smaller than the number who graduated in 1998 and 1999. Primary care physicians are another group of providers currently experiencing shortages that are expected to become more severe in the future.

Cultural values can have an impact on the quality of care provided. Income and socioeconomic status are variables that affect how professional caregivers interact with care recipients. The caregiver and the care recipient are often not of the same culture or socioeconomic status. Direct-care workers tend to have a high school diploma or less education. Half are nonwhite, and most are married with children; 20 percent live below the poverty line; and almost half are on public assistance. Potential differences in culture and socioeconomic status require cultural competence of both the provider and the recipient of care.

Challenges for Formal Caregivers

Carolyn Humphrey elaborated on the challenges facing formal caregivers, who have great responsibility and great autonomy in their work.

They generally work alone and cannot easily consult with colleagues. They may be the only person who sees a care recipient. Or, in other situations, such as a newborn coming home with complex needs, they may be part of a team of nurses, physicians, therapists, and aides working together.

Formal home care providers experience several issues associated with reimbursement policies. Most reimbursement structures pay either by the visit or by the hour but do not pay for interactions with other professionals, which can further increase the isolation of home care providers. Also, if a medical device is not approved by Medicare, then it will not be reimbursed by either the government or insurance companies. This can also be an issue when a device needs to be tailored to an individual. If the needed device is not reimbursed, then recipients often just do without. "They will get the one that maybe doesn't fit them best," said Humphrey. "That's a very big human factors issue."

Professional organizations serving home care providers are minuscule. The nurses' association under the National Association for Home Care has only about 100 members. Home health care recently lost its ability to be certified by the American Nurses Credentialing Center because not enough people were being encouraged to be credentialed. According to Humphrey, "There is no financial incentive, surely not by insurance companies and not by the federal government, to have that kind of qualification." Likewise, the American Physical Therapy Association and the Occupational Therapy Association have special interest groups for home care, but they are small work committees that look at specific home care issues. The American Speech-Language-Hearing Association does not have such a group.

Education in home health care is lacking in most of the curricula of professional disciplines. As a result, such care providers as doctors or discharge planners often have little idea of what it is like to provide care in the home. "That can result in some unrealistic expectations, unrealistic orders for treatments, [or] things that aren't applicable to the home environment."

There are no federal ergonomic guidelines for home care. Yet the transport of equipment and supplies is a responsibility that causes many injuries for home care providers. About two-thirds of U.S. adults are overweight or obese, yet home care providers often need to move these individuals by themselves. Assistive devices are often recommended, but their use is usually assessed relative to the needs of the recipient, not the care provider.

Professional care providers often have a mobile office, performing clinical documentation in the home, the employee's car, or the employee's home. Human factors issues, such as noise, distractions, and poor light can be critical in such settings.

Formal home providers also encounter violence in neighborhoods and homes. Caregivers can be targets of attack, or they can be bystanders during other instances of violence.

Many technologies, such as clinical documentation systems, affect formal caregivers directly. For example, many home care providers have point-of-care devices, such as laptops or tablet devices, that they use in their care and their documentation of care. But many times these devices have been created by simply putting traditional paperwork in electronic format, so the care provider is just checking off forms and doing repetitive work. The same can be true for various medical devices, including both new devices and older ones that a provider or recipient already owns.

In addition, every device has environmental parameters that must be considered. For example, Humphrey pointed out that temperatures in individual homes may vary from 60 to 120 degrees. This can be an issue not only for the operation of devices but also for the caregivers themselves.

Telemedicine and remote monitoring of care recipients in their homes similarly raise many human factors issues. Many home care providers say that they left jobs in institutions because they did not have enough manual dexterity to perform particular tasks. Care providers both in institutions and in homes can also be very anxious that they will lose their jobs if technology becomes too efficient. "There are some built-in issues about not wanting the devices to work."

Humphrey offered some suggestions related to formal home care providers. In the area of policy, she suggested the following:

- Better entries into practice for nurses at the baccalaureate level.
- An improved role for direct-care workers.
- Involvement by the Food and Drug Administration with manufacturers and formal caregivers on medical devices used in the home.
- Involvement by the Occupational Safety and Health Administration in issuing home care guidelines.
- Raising consciousness of human factors issues in the home health care community and among the recipients of care.
- Exploring formal relationships between home health care providers and nursing education.
- Communication between home health care technology manufacturers and human factors engineers.

In the area of research, she suggested the following:

- Effective strategies to educate formal caregivers on ways to improve care delivery and outcomes.
- Human factors and home health care research in the field to optimize shared goals.
- Human factors approaches for vulnerable care recipients and formal caregivers.

Responses to Questions

Humphrey identified the technologies used by home care providers as the number-one issue needing attention. "The point-of-care devices that they use are very unfriendly to the user." For example, six different glucose monitors can have six different plugs, she observed. Improving such technologies would save time, improve the accuracy of the data gathered, improve the care plans developed from those data, and enhance the monitoring and reporting of home health care.

When asked what she saw as the most important issue affecting formal home care providers, Milone-Nuzzo replied that it is the amount of education required for nurses in home care. Humphrey added that web-based education models hold considerable promise for delivering ongoing professional education for working providers. In addition, continuing education done online and/or on demand could provide home care workers with information that they need when they need it.

Care coordination is another critical factor, said Humphrey. Home care providers have often done this coordination, even when they were not reimbursed for it. But it can be very difficult to find enough time, given today's reimbursement policies, to perform coordination tasks.

DISCUSSION

Margaret Quinn, professor in the Department of Work Environment at the University of Massachusetts–Lowell, began the discussion by reviewing some of the most important points to emerge from the session and the connections among those points. Many factors are contributing to rapid increases in the provision of home health care. Elderly populations in the United States are increasing rapidly, although the populations that traditionally have provided care are undergoing almost no increase. The 30 percent of people who need home care but are not elders have important needs that can differ from those of the elderly population. The home is not consistently or systematically considered as a care or work environment, which can have important human factors implications. Meanwhile, public opinion is disconnected from this confluence of factors, with many adults unprepared to deliver care and believing that they will not need care.

Quinn noted that informal caregivers are often limited in their ability to provide care, partly because of a lack of training and social support. Home caregiving disproportionately affects women, racial and ethnic minorities, and those with low incomes, often at the peak of their own ability to earn wages outside the home. There also are significant psychological and health impacts on informal caregivers, such as musculoskeletal strains caused by lifting and ambulation. "I heard a nurse recently highlight that if in [another industry] a worker is asked to lift a 200-pound object, they say, 'Sure, I'll go do that right away.' They go get a forklift, and they drive it over and they move it." The health and well-being of the informal caregiver and the care recipient are linked, Quinn said.

With regard to formal caregivers, home health care is the fastest growing segment of health care and one of the fastest growing industries in the United States. Personal and home care aides and home health aides are among the top 10 fastest growing jobs in the United States. However, shortages and high turnover in the workforce, especially among aides, are creating a crisis of care, leading to reduced care quality and increased costs.

The heterogeneity of the home health care workforce has several human factors consequences. The direct-care workforce in home health care is relatively invisible. Many formal caregivers are not prepared for health care crises, such as pandemic flu, and many do not have health insurance. Little formal research has been done on formal caregivers and the human factors involved in their health and safety. Although many human factors issues are similar for formal and informal caregivers, there are differences that are not well understood.

Quinn offered some suggestions in the areas of practice, research, policy, and education and training. In the area of practice, she suggested the following:

- Create systems to coordinate formal and informal caregiving.
- Expand and update the availability and quality of training to account for new technologies, procedures, and complexity.
- Broaden the skill base of paraprofessionals.
- Adopt a standard definition of home caregivers, especially for informal caregiving.

Regarding research, she suggested the following:

- Identify the full range of human factors stressors for care recipients and informal and formal caregivers.
- Identify the extent to which the health and safety of care recipients and of caregivers are linked in order to develop comprehensive solutions for quality care.
- Evaluate human factors risks and prioritize interventions.
- Identify, develop, implement, and evaluate interventions with the input of care recipients and caregivers, including studies that compare home settings with institutional ones.
- Fast-track technology options emphasizing usability for care recipients and caregivers.

- Identify effective methods to recruit and retain the home health care workforce.

In the area of policy, she suggested the following:

- Evaluate federal and state programs that affect home health care and identify the role that human factors play in supporting agencies' programs related to home health care.
- Coordinate programs across jurisdictions and settings.
- Provide health care services for caregivers as well as care recipients.
- Encourage efforts to provide improved social support for informal caregivers.
- Preserve and enhance meaningful, dignified, caring relationships.

In the areas of education and training, she suggested the following:

- Improve the education and training of formal caregivers, including nurses, physicians, other clinicians, paraprofessionals in agencies, and paraprofessionals hired privately.
- Improve training for informal caregivers.
- Prepare all of society for caregiving, including young people.

In the discussion that followed Quinn's remarks, Humphrey elaborated on the difficulties involved in point-of-care documentation systems. There has been a lack of clinical input into the design and deployment of these technologies, she said. Many decisions are framed by reimbursement policies rather than focusing on the needs of caregivers. From her perspective, the findings of human factors research have not had much of an influence on these systems. For example, the systems are not "smart," in that they do not cue the user easily, point out things that were missed, or notify the user of conflicts. As a result, other people laboriously need to check a caregiver's documentation to make sure nothing has been missed.

Several presenters described issues involving the coordination of care. Schulz observed that the Department of Veterans Affairs has conducted several experiments to coordinate care but that they have mostly been on a small scale. Milone-Nuzzo pointed out that health care reform could lead to new policies on care coordination and that the National Academies of Practice are preparing a paper on the subject. Humphrey said that the Centers for Medicare & Medicaid Services are also working on the issue and is developing a communication system to be used during transitions in care.

Milone-Nuzzo observed that caregivers who are in a home on a day-to-day basis are in the best position to identify threats to a care recipient's safety. She has been involved in research on smart homes (discussed in Chapter 3), and this research needs to take into account the experiences of direct-care workers, and especially paraprofessionals like home health aides, companions, and homemakers who are in homes for longer periods of time than are nurses, therapists, or dieticians.

As part of an exchange on the educational requirements for nurses, Milone-Nuzzo observed that research has demonstrated that health outcomes improve as the education of nurses increases. "I say this in the most kind and gentle way: we need to increase the education [level] of nurses," she remarked. Humphrey pointed out that other caregiver disciplines, such as physical therapists, are increasing their educational requirements. A lack of attention to both education and certification will have a negative impact on home health care, she said.

In response to a question about whether human factors research considers the positive aspects of systems, Charness observed that this research looks to optimize not only efficiency and safety but also comfort. Schulz added that there is a positive side to informal family caregiving "in that individuals do report positive benefits." Quinn reported on a survey with which she has been involved of 1,200 home health care nurses working with AIDS patients, in which a majority responded that they are satisfied with their work. The nurses particularly cited the autonomy of their work and the relationships they formed. "When they can have meaningful ongoing relationships, . . . that is the most rewarding to them, and that's why they are doing it."

Committee chair David Wegman asked whether distinguishing between formal and informal caregivers is the proper frame of reference or whether a distinction between more and less intense levels of involvement may be preferable. Milone-Nuzzo agreed that there is a great deal of overlap between formal and informal caregivers, especially in terms of the relationships that develop, the physical tasks involved, and the use of medical equipment. Yet distinguishing between these two groups does offer a "lens to begin the conversation." Schulz added that informal caregivers also rely on formal caregivers for various services, creating a back-and-forth dynamic between the two groups. Humphrey pointed to some of the complications in the distinction. For example, a home health aide could work for a Medicare-certified agency during the week and for a private-duty agency on the weekends, providing care in different environments to different individuals.

3

Home Health Care Tasks and Tools

HOME CAREGIVING TASKS[1]

Home caregiving tasks are extremely diverse, including help with activities of daily living, transportation, interaction with medical personnel and a care recipient's family or social group, use of medical devices, negotiation with insurance carriers, and use of the Internet and other information sources, said Colin Drury. These tasks call on the physical, cognitive, social, and emotional abilities of caregivers. Relating these task-derived demands to actual caregiver capabilities is one aspect of the discipline known as task analysis.

The errors committed during the delivery of home health care can range from the trivial to the deadly, said Drury. Because the task demands made of home caregivers can exceed human capabilities, these tasks need to be carefully analyzed.

Care recipients and care providers are extremely diverse, and all are under more stresses than in the past. Many people, including home care providers, are working harder than they have in the past, Drury said. "There are more people doing a lot of small part-time jobs, and there are people working large hours of overtime on one job. The good old 40-hour week . . . is disappearing."

A standard finding from human factors research is that, as task demands exceed human capabilities, error rates increase. Errors may occur occasion-

[1]This section is based on the presentation by Colin Drury, distinguished professor emeritus of industrial and systems engineering and director of the Research Institute for Safety and Security in Transportation at the State University of New York, Buffalo.

ally when a caregiver is distracted, sick, or otherwise incapacitated. But as the diversity of tasks and the diversity of people increase, the potential for errors grows.

To bring task demands in line with capabilities, there are five things that can be changed:

1. the task,
2. the person providing or receiving care,
3. the technology being used,
4. the environment surrounding the task, and
5. the social system surrounding the task.

Making changes in these five areas implies better procedures, better training, better equipment design, better home environment design, and better social interactions. In this context, "better" means fitting tasks to people, Drury said.

Task Analysis

Task analysis has two parts. First, assessing the demands of a task requires a task description—a detailed and hierarchical breakdown of every step involved in the task. Second, assessing human capabilities draws on the literature on human factors plus contributions from other disciplines, such as psychology and biomechanics, supplemented with professional judgment.

In addition, there are two methods of understanding tasks, and both are needed for error-proof designs. The first is to analyze errors or system failures in existing systems, as was done in the 2000 report on medical errors by the Institute of Medicine, *To Err Is Human: Building a Safer Health System*, National Academy Press, Washington, DC. The second is to analyze the functioning of a system, starting with its objectives and then focusing on the task elements for existing and proposed systems.

A common pitfall of task analysis is to assume that everyone looks like you, Drury said. Avoiding this false assumption requires that the people performing the task be involved along with someone who can integrate the various tasks being analyzed. As an example, Drury cited the transport of a care recipient, whether from the bed to a chair, from the home to a hospital, or from the hospital to a care facility. Each of these overall tasks requires planning to tie its constituent tasks together. The job is simple if the constituent tasks are lined up in a logical and linear order. "You just go down the checklist and you do them. But lots of them have branches. If it says this, you do this. It may not be that. This may be blocked. You may have to do something else." Because of this complexity, task analyses generally involve multiple levels of detail.

Drury also drew an analogy with task analysis in aviation, in which he has done considerable work. The task of inspecting the safety of airplanes has many built-in safeguards, Drury said. It often involves both humans and technologies. It is designed to discover possible errors and identify good practices that lead to error reduction. It leads to advice for the people running the systems—something that "adds to your knowledge, not just your rule base."

Drury listed some important components of task analysis.

First, task analyses begin by specifying what has to be done rather than focusing on specifically who does what, since different parts of a task can be done by different individuals or even by technology. Once tasks have been identified, the appropriate person or technology to do each part of a task can be identified (task allocation).

Task analyses are the basis for design recommendations in the form of good practices for general use and specific design changes for specific tasks. There is a well-developed methodology for task analysis that can be adapted for home caregiving, and other domains also demonstrate how to format the results for maximum impact and how to use the results in a design or redesign context.

Task analysis needs both human factors practitioners and subject matter experts to be successful. "You need people who have been doing the job. You need the potential users and the real users."

Finally, for any new equipment or procedure, a task analysis is the start of the design to reduce future user errors. These analyses are best performed by a team with knowledge of both human factors and the subject matter.

Responses to Questions

In response to a question about how to make task analysis a more standard practice in home health care, Drury replied that the practitioners of task analysis need to describe its benefits to the individuals who are in a position to use it. Technology manufacturers and designers of the built environment in particular can be approached, as well as the professional organizations that support home health care. "You need to go to those communities and say that this ought to be done."

Task analysis in health care is somewhat different than in many other areas because of the communications, social, and emotional issues involved. Greater understanding of the dimensions of human capabilities is needed, such as the human subsystems likely to be overstressed by caregiving.

In response to a question about the kinds of tasks involved in home health care, Drury cited the high-level division of physical/cognitive needs, psychological/emotional needs, and social needs. "That may not be an exhaustive list. . . . But that struck me, from what I have read, as an appropriate starting point." Drury also observed that a taxonomy of the kinds of errors that occur in home health care could be a useful precursor to a more generic task analysis.

MEDICAL DEVICES AND EQUIPMENT[2]

According to the Center for Devices and Radiological Health of the Food and Drug Administration (FDA), a medical device is "an instrument, apparatus, implement, machine, contrivance, implant, or *in vitro* reagent or other similar article that is . . . intended for use in the diagnosis of disease or other conditions, or in the care, mitigation, treatment, or prevention of disease." Similarly, the Home Health Committee of the center has defined a home medical device as "a device intended for use in a nonclinical or transitory environment [that] is managed partly or wholly by the user, requires adequate labeling for the user, and may require training for the user by a health care professional in order to be used safely and effectively."

These definitions lay out the three dimensions that must be considered in applying human factors research to the design of home medical devices: (1) the device itself, (2) the people who use it, and (3) the environment in which it is used, said Molly Story. These dimensions, in turn, become more complex as the complexity of medical devices used in the home increases. Today, such devices as ventilators, infusion pumps, and dialysis machines are frequently being used outside the hospital or clinic, often by lay users, even though many of these devices were not designed for and were not specifically labeled for this use, Story said.

Devices used in the home are not always the same models used in health care facilities. They may be older or lower in quality. Professionals who encounter them in the home or in a clinic may not be familiar with their operation. Consumers are giving these devices to each other and are selling and buying them on the Internet. Such devices are less likely to be appropriate, to be properly operated or maintained, or even to come with complete instructions.

Many different people use medical devices in the home, including physicians, nurses, nurse practitioners, various therapists, workers, home care aides, independent contractors, family members, friends, neighbors, care recipients, or even someone who gets pulled in from the street in an emergency. These users may be of any age, may have various kinds of disabilities, or may be sick themselves. A person's ability to use a home health device depends on many factors, including

[2]This section is based on the presentation by Molly Story, president of Human Spectrum Design. For more information and for references to the information cited in this presentation, see Chapter 8.

- physical capabilities, such as their size, strength, stamina, dexterity, flexibility, and coordination;
- sensory capabilities, including not only vision and hearing but also sometimes touch;
- cognitive abilities, including their memory, literacy, language skills, knowledge, and experience base;
- general health;
- mental and emotional state;
- cultural background;
- personal history and experience with home health care and medical care in general; and
- ability and willingness to learn how to use new devices and adapt to having new devices in the home.

Many environmental factors also affect a person's ability to use a medical device. Space issues can be very important, especially if there are obstacles in a home or if the device needs to be moved. Floor surfaces can make a difference, such as wood versus carpeting. Lighting, noise levels, temperature, and humidity can be very high or very low. "All of these can make devices misbehave," Story said.

The activity level in the environment can be confusing and can conflict with the operation of a device. The environment may not be clean. Animals—pets, service animals, vermin—can affect devices. Electromagnetic interference can come from other devices in the environment, such as computer gear or videogames. "You have heard that beeping that your cell phone makes on the radio when you are in the car? It does the same to your medical devices in the home." In addition, the electrical power may go out for a variety of reasons and an emergency backup system may be needed, especially if a device is keeping a person alive.

If a device needs to move into and out of a home, other questions arise. How portable is the device? What does it weigh? Does it have wheels? Does it have a handle? Is it discreet? If someone sees it fall out of your pocket, will you be embarrassed? How long is the battery going to last? Device durability and ruggedness are also factors when a device is taken out of a home or clinic.

Taxonomy of Home Medical Devices

Story has developed a 12-category taxonomy of home health care devices:

1. Medication administration equipment, such as syringes, cups, eyedroppers, sprays, patches, and syringes.

2. Test kits, from pregnancy and allergy kits to cholesterol and hormone tests.
3. First aid equipment, such as bandages, traction equipment, ostomy care, and defibrillators.
4. Assistive technologies, such as glasses, hearing aids, prostheses, orthotics, crutches, wheelchairs, and mobility aids.
5. Durable medical equipment, including beds, specialized mattresses, specialized chairs, lift equipment that may be either ceiling-mounted or portable, commodes, urinals, and bedpans.
6. Meters and monitors, such as thermometers, blood glucose meters, electrocardiogram monitors, and fetal monitors.
7. Treatment and therapy equipment, such as infusion pumps, dialysis equipment, transcutaneous electrical nerve stimulation equipment, and intravenous equipment.
8. Respiratory equipment, such as ventilators, forced airway devices, oxygen, masks, and suction.
9. Feeding equipment, such as feeding tubes and food pumps.
10. Voiding equipment, catheters, and colostomy gear.
11. Infant care equipment, such as incubators, warmers, bilirubin lights, and apnea monitors.
12. Telehealth equipment, such as cameras, sensors, and computers.

More technologies will move into the home in the future. Telehealth, in particular, is expected to grow vigorously in the coming years. For example, wireless technologies offer continuous monitoring and a greater range of mobility for care recipients. Remote monitoring allows for long-term monitoring, encourages adherence to treatment regimens, and provides for reminder alerts to perform certain acts, such as taking medication or scheduling an appointment.

Future technological advances will bring new types of medical devices into the home, like improved pacemakers, cochlear implants, corneal implants, and artificial retinas. Nanotechnology will be embedded into devices, allowing for much more sophisticated biosensing. Smart fabrics will detect events happening in the body. Heads-up displays with pattern recognition software will help people with vision impairments or cognitive impairments recognize objects and faces. Skin surface mapping can keep track of things like moles on the skin to see if they are changing. Other types of biosensors will be embedded in all kinds of familiar objects, such as toothbrushes. And many other kinds of devices are on the way, including "things that we can't yet imagine," said Story.

Design Considerations

Good designers of medical devices understand the needs of both average users and users who have capabilities far from the average. Device designers also need to give attention to the positive or negative aspects of using the device and the potential individualization of the device. "Once people's needs for safety, functionality, and usability are satisfied, designers should address their needs for pleasure and self-actualization."

These considerations are factors in the concept known as universal design, which has seven basic principles:

1. Equitable use, so that everyone can use the same device. "Just as we are not going to have the accessible MRI machine and the regular MRI machine, the same should hold true for all home health care devices as well."
2. Flexibility in use, so that the design accommodates the full range of individual preferences and abilities. "We need to accommodate individual operational styles, as well as learning styles, such as using things left-handed."
3. Simple and intuitive use, so that the design is easy to understand regardless of the user's experience, knowledge, language skills, or current concentration level. "Keep it simple. Remember that not everyone reads or understands English."
4. Perceptible information, so that the design communicates necessary information effectively to the user, regardless of ambient conditions or the user's sensory abilities. "Everything that is visible on the device also should be auditory—and vice versa."
5. Tolerance for error, so that the design minimizes hazards and the adverse consequences of accidental or unintended actions. "We need to minimize the risk of injury to both the user and the device."
6. Low physical effort, so that the device can be used efficiently, comfortably, and with a minimum of fatigue. "It needs not to wear you out just to turn it on."
7. Size and space for approach and use, regardless of the user's body size, posture, or mobility. "There has to be sufficient space available for whatever body parts may be involved, as well as whatever assistive technologies—wheelchairs, crutches, service dogs, or personal assistants—may be present."

Less tangible factors may also come into play. Users may have powerful emotions knowing that they or their loved ones are seriously ill. They may be overwhelmed by the critical new responsibilities they have had to take on. They may be acutely aware of the potential for harm to the equipment, to their loved ones, or to themselves. They may be confused by the new terminology that they have to master in a hurry. They may be confused by the care instructions and the device instructions. They may not have the personal or institutional support that they need.

Standards

National and international standards play an important role in medical device development. A U.S. human factors engineering process standard, referred to as ANSI/AAMI HE74 and published in 2001, is for use in fulfilling user interface design requirements in the development of medical devices and systems, including hardware, software, and documentation. An international human factors engineering process standard, referred to as ISO/IEC 62366 and published in 2007, specifies a process for a manufacturer to analyze, specify, design, verify, and validate usability as it relates to the safety of a medical device.

In addition, a guidance document published by the FDA in 2000, *Medical Device Use-Safety: Incorporating Human Factors Engineering into Risk Management* (see http://www.fda.gov/downloads/MedicalDevices/DeviceRegulationandGuidance/GuidanceDocuments/ucm094461.pdf [accessed August 2010]), describes how the agency wants hazards related to medical device use to be addressed during device development, noting that they should be addressed in the context of a thorough understanding of how a device will be used.

Finally, a committee with which Story has been involved is working on the standard ANSI/AAMI HE75, scheduled to be released in 2010, which provides detailed human factors engineering design guidance to those who are responsible for human factors engineering work in medical device companies.

These documents provide information, guidance, and models of best practices to designers and manufacturers. They also enable manufacturers to show that they are aware of the processes in the guidance and that they have followed them. "Standards are helpful," said Story, "but you still have to know what you are doing with them."

Instructions and Training

Device labeling and user instructions are important for home health care, and Story said they get too little attention. These resources for users include the packaging, the graphics and text on the box, the printed instructions, user manuals, quick-start guides, user brochures, leaflets, advertisements, and all other forms of information, including video and audio files that may be offered on DVD or on Internet websites. "These things have to be written for lay users," said Story. "They are too often written for health care professionals—that is, to the education and knowledge levels of people who know about medical technology in general and the subject device in particular." Written procedures and diagrams need to be user-tested and offered in alternative modes and formats, not just print, because not everybody can read print. "Put it on a disk. Put it on the Internet. Even if the person doesn't have Internet access themselves, they may know someone who can get it for them."

Training for home users may have deficiencies, including being presented too quickly, using jargon, not providing enough practice for the user, or not providing enough explanation of the problems that may arise if the required steps are not done correctly. Training has to be designed for lay users and needs to be available in multiple modes. "Hands-on training is far and away the best way to do this. Have people practice using the device—there is no substitute." A lot of people may use a device just occasionally, so designers need to minimize the need for long-term memory.

Information needs to be provided where and when it is needed. "Stick it to the device itself. Embed it in the user interface. Don't make me go find the manual. I have no idea where it is." And some form of user support should be available 24 hours a day, 365 days a year.

Voice output in a device offers many benefits. It reinforces the visual messages. It reduces misinterpretation of visual information. It is especially helpful for infrequent users. It improves user confidence and trust in the device. It reduces the burden of customer support for health care professionals. And it is vitally important for people with vision impairments.

Many different human factors methods can be used to assess device safety, functionality, and usability, including task analysis, risk assessment of potential errors and their consequences, evaluation by a group of testers against a set of heuristics or general principles, expert review, and formative and summative user testing. "It's really important to identify the people who are at highest risk. Those are the people you need to be testing on the risk-critical tasks that are identified through your task analysis. By doing that, you can identify the sources and the nature of difficulties that they are having and develop design solutions to mitigate the risks."

Improving the Use of Human Factors Research in Medical Devices and Equipment

Story had a number of ideas for action, research, and development. In the area of action, she suggested the following:

- Professional caregivers, lay caregivers, and home care recipients need better mechanisms to provide feedback about a device to designers.

In the area of research, Story highlighted some questions to be addressed:

- For users, what factors influence people's ability and willingness to follow their doctors' recommendations and adhere to treatment regimens?
- For manufacturers, what factors influence their ability and willingness to address the human factors needs of their users and customers?
- For purchasers, what factors influence the medical device purchasers and what factors influence prescribers to consider the needs of their end-users when they choose a device?

In the area of development, she suggested the following:

- For users, tools are needed to improve people's ability and willingness to follow doctor's orders and adhere to treatment regimens.
- For health care providers, assessment tools and mechanisms are needed to gauge whether a medical device is appropriate for a specific user.
- For manufacturers, higher standards are needed for home health devices in such areas as safety, accuracy, and ease of use for more diverse user populations.

Users need to be more demanding of the devices they use to provide care in the home, Story concluded. "People seem reluctant to blame the devices. . . . Lay users tend to blame themselves when they have trouble. I think we need to turn that around and blame the device."

Responses to Questions

Committee member Mary Weick-Brady added that the availability of clean water is an environmental factor that can affect the use of a home medical device. She also urged designers to design the errors out of a device rather than just adding warnings to a flawed one. And she noted that users often are being required to purchase rather than rent some of the devices they use, even though they then become responsible for maintenance and upgrades.

Committee member Jon Pynoos reminded the workshop participants of one of the most feared phrases in the English language: Assembly required. "If you can't even get it together, you can't use it."

In response to a question about the difficulty of using some devices, Story speculated that some engineers may design devices for themselves. "They think, if I can use it, then anybody can." User testing is essential to discover the problems in a design. "I have been doing user testing for 16 years, and real people always teach me things I didn't expect."

There was some discussion of how considerations of good design can be integrated into the education of students, including the possibility of infusing human factors education into the basic engineering curriculum. Story agreed that such education is critically needed, and not just for engineers. "In medicine it's critical, [and] you certainly need it in lots of other professions, too. . . . The question is, where is it, who does it, how do you do it? It is a complicated project."

Story also noted that many of the technologies used for home health care would not necessarily be defined as medical devices by the FDA. For example, software used in various contexts is not necessarily a device but can make a critical difference in home health care applications.

INFORMATION TECHNOLOGY[3]

Several factors have greatly increased interest in the use of information technology in home health care, including the need to reach people in rural and underserved areas, a clinical workforce shortage, and technological advances, such as social networking. In addition, said George Demiris, there is great potential for new technologies to empower care recipients and involve them more actively in health care delivery.

Active Monitoring and Management

Demiris divided the use of information technology into two categories: (1) active monitoring and management and (2) passive monitoring.

Active monitoring implies that the end user is involved with and, in most cases, operates the equipment. Technologies falling into this category include telehealth applications, social networking systems, and personal health record systems.

Telehealth technologies are a diverse set of devices that collect and transmit data over phone lines or other communications media, so that care providers or others can access data remotely. These technologies also

---

[3]This section is based on the presentation by George Demiris. associate professor of biobehavioral nursing and health systems at the University of Washington. For more information and for references to the information cited in this presentation, see Chapter 9.

include video devices, including low-cost videoconferencing solutions and videophones that are currently available. These can enable home care recipients and their families to communicate with care providers remotely. Video technologies can also link home care recipients with distant caregivers, such as family members, friends, or other parts of a social network.

Some systems integrate video with monitoring devices or have other components to allow for self-report. For example, they might have built-in screens on which people can respond to predetermined questions. Kiosks that are publicly accessible can be used by multiple users, with each user entering a password or swiping a card so that the system knows who the person is.

Research on telehealth applications has focused on care recipients with chronic conditions, including asthma, diabetes, chronic obstructive pulmonary disease, congestive heart failure, stroke rehabilitation, wound care, oncology, and post-transplant care. This research has produced several important findings with human factors implications:

- In most cases a significant component of end-user training is involved. The end-user may be the care recipient or, in many cases, the family caregiver, the spouse, or other caregivers who are entering the data or learning how to use the equipment.
- The residential infrastructure can be critical. Technologies that rely on phone lines are becoming less usable as people give up their landlines. Technologies that rely on broadband Internet service cannot be used in regions, or individual homes, without such access.
- Storing and managing data raises issues associated with security and privacy. These issues also come up in considering how to allow health care providers to process new large data sets gathered from telehealth applications.
- Users have to accept and be comfortable with the use of such systems or devices in their homes.
- A growing body of literature deals with the effectiveness of those systems on clinical outcomes. However, most of the studies have had small sample sizes and have been focused on feasibility. "We don't have a very solid evidence base as of yet in terms of these types of telehealth systems reducing rehospitalization rates or improving other specific clinical outcomes," Demiris said.

Web-based communities, often referred to as virtual communities, are groups of people with a common purpose and common interests who communicate without meeting face to face. They use telecommunications, the Internet, or other technologies to bridge geographic distances. For example, they may use web applications to link care recipients remotely with family members, with health care providers, or with peer-to-peer communities. In other cases, virtual communities may link health care teams to each other or to groups of domain experts.

Again, not enough evidence exists to demonstrate that these communities improve clinical outcomes. Some individual applications do seem to improve specific clinical outcomes. However, peer-to-peer or web-based communities generally are parts of larger interventions that may include other aspects, such as education or cognitive therapy, making it difficult to attribute positive outcomes solely to the use of peer-to-peer communities.

A relatively new use of web technologies is to create social networks that do not require registering with a website but instead use readily available social networking systems. Early studies have looked at Facebook, for example, in which people link to peers and seek feedback on their progress. Some web-based applications use synchronous communications in which people have to be present virtually at the same time, such as a chat room. Others rely on asynchronous communications, in which people can use discussion boards or other tools to communicate at their discretion. Some of these applications are moderated to control communications and make sure that rules are followed. Other applications do not have a moderator.

Finally, a personal health record is an individual's electronic medical record that is managed, shared, and controlled by the individual. People own their own data and decide who will have access to them, creating care that is more patient- than institution-centered. Many vendors have shown an interest in personal health records. The Department of Veterans Affairs has implemented an early prototype of a personal health record, called MyHealtheVet, which allows patients to log in and access health-related information, notes and comments about their well-being, and records of health care transactions. Google has been investing in a platform called Google Health that allows users to store health-related data and choose to export data from the application to health care providers or other third parties. In addition, Microsoft has introduced Health Vault as a personal health record platform, with an emphasis on chronic conditions and people who frequently use multiple health care providers.

Although much effort has been invested in the design of personal health records, they have not been tested extensively to see how they affect the quality of home health care, Demiris said.

Passive Monitoring

With passive monitoring, the end-user does not have to operate any equipment and continues with daily activities. Technologies in the environment collect information and direct it to health care providers and other recipients.

"Smart homes" are equipped with an infrastructure allowing passive monitoring of residents to improve their quality of life. For example, the Aware Home developed by the Georgia Institute of Technology provides a display of a resident's well-being that can be accessed remotely by family members. Another smart home developed in Florida, GatorTech, includes technologies like a smart mirror that provides reminders to residents. TigerPlace, a smart home designed for an independent retirement community, has motion sensors, heat sensors, stove sensors, and bed sensors to track such things as sleep quality, activity in the home, and time outside the home.

Smart homes are a relatively new technology and for the most part have not been systematically evaluated. Existing studies have looked mostly at safety monitoring and assistance, cognitive and sensory assistance, cognitive aids, and overall wellness. As with other technologies, an extensive body of evidence on clinical effectiveness is lacking. Furthermore, clinical trials of smart homes are even more costly than for traditional telehealth or virtual communities.

Privacy and Confidentiality

With any technology involving the collection and movement of information, privacy and confidentiality are concerns.

The Health Insurance Portability and Accountability Act (HIPAA) plays a major role in telehealth applications and web-based applications in which individuals transmit personal health information over the Internet. However, HIPAA cannot address some of the new and emerging trends in health information technology. For example, many of the vendors introducing personal health records are not covered entities according to HIPAA. "There is a debate about whether we need to actually rethink what it means to be a covered entity and how we would deal with a vendor who collects personal health record information for other purposes," said Demiris.

Interoperability is a major consideration for different information systems that can be employed in the home setting. An infrastructure needs to be in place that will enable data sets to be transmitted among different systems, such as a remote monitoring system and a personal health record. Vocabulary and workflow standards, along with provisions to address security issues, will be needed to make interoperability possible.

Information technologies need to be accessible for people with diverse physical or cognitive limitations. This will require usability testing among users with various limitations. A major problem with information technology systems in the past is that end-users have not been involved in their design and development. Device development often has been driven by what a technology can do rather than by clinical needs. Human factors research offers a variety of methods, such as prototyping, sketching, or cognitive walkthroughs, to solicit end-user feedback and assess how users interact with a technology.

Policy Considerations

Several important policy issues will influence the future use of information technologies in home health care.

Technologies can improve access to care, yet they can also be associated with barriers to access. For example, they may be too expensive for some people to afford, the infrastructure may be missing to access a technology in all locations, or some people may lack the education and training to use a technology.

Reimbursement for health information technologies will heavily influence their use. "Who is going to pay for those types of systems, and how are health care providers going to be reimbursed for their time to use the systems or to process data that are resulting from these systems?" asked Demiris.

Data streams may include large quantities of information that are difficult to interpret. "We don't want to burden health care providers with too much information that may not even be significant, but rather find the right ways to display the data in aggregate form to allow them to identify trends or patterns and detect emergencies in an effective and efficient way."

Ensuring the safety and efficacy of information technology devices becomes especially complex when additional software or hardware can be added to a system to enhance functionality but is perhaps not subjected to the same scrutiny as the earlier system. In addition, telehealth often will involve delivering care across state borders, raising issues bearing on liability and accreditation.

Finally, introducing information technology in the home environment can have ethical impacts, such as creating dependence on automation, dehumanizing interpersonal relationships, reducing social interaction, generating stigma associated with the use of technology, or being overly intrusive.

Demiris made several suggestions:

- Integrate usability, interoperability, and human factors considerations in all phases of the design, implementation, and evaluation of information technology systems.
- Explore technical and clinical guidelines proposed by different groups that inform the reimbursement debate.

In the area of research, he suggested the following:

- Move away from small pilot studies of technical feasibility toward wide-scale implementation of technologies with clinical studies to assess their effectiveness.
- Focus on clinical outcomes and on current gaps in the literature.
- Define and assess the empowerment of care recipients and shared decision making.
- Enlist the expertise of an interdisciplinary group to conduct translational research that will inform users.
- Examine both processes and outcomes.

Responses to Questions

When asked about the human factors issues involved in the use of personal medical records, Demiris observed that commercial vendors claim that their systems will be intuitive to most end-users who are familiar with their other products. Vendors also claim that work focused on human factors has been done on their systems because they are patient-centered systems, not electronic medical records that are focused on clinical encounters. "People are recognizing that human-factors considerations need to inform the design. But it remains to be seen if indeed it will become the case." An additional challenge will be interactions between personal health records and electronic medical records, especially if multiple entities desire access to those records.

Demiris also said that the category of applications with the best evidence for efficiency and efficacy is telehealth technologies, with clinical trials of web-based virtual communities also showing some effects. Studies tend to be difficult to do because people in a test group cannot be deprived of a standard of care, so they often receive standard care plus additional virtual visits. "The argument there is that you are obviously increasing the attention you are paying to your patients, and it's not necessarily the technology that is doing great things; it's just that they get to talk to the health care provider more frequently." Even if a test group forgoes some in-person visits, the equipment being used may greatly increase their contact with care providers.

In response to a question about the ethical effects of information technologies, Demiris observed that no evidence is yet available showing a detrimental effect on human relationships. However, he pointed to people who sometimes refuse to carry wearable devices when they interact with each other. Making devices less visible, such as making them part of jewelry, might lessen such stigma. In some cases, technologies will have the positive effects of increasing communication and a sense of community. But designers must also try to anticipate unexpected reactions to new technologies. For example, he cited the case of an elderly resident of a smart home who mistakenly believed that sensors were capturing images of residents.

A discussion began that continued during the session wrap-up about the value of the information being collected by information technologies. Demiris stated that "the verdict is still out in terms of whether it's really useful to know all the things we are now capturing with sensors." Case studies have demonstrated successful applications, such as sensors that detect large amounts of wandering, falls, or long periods of inactivity. "The challenge is to have the right infrastructure to respond to [emergencies], because we can detect an emergency, but if there is no plan in terms of how to address it or who would go and check that somebody has indeed fallen, then the system won't really work."

DISCUSSION

Paul Crawford, director of research in the Digital Health Group at the Intel Corporation, led a discussion of some of the most important points and missing elements in the session. In the area of task analysis, risk-based systems engineering approaches have not been widely adopted in health care, he said. Also, a larger research infrastructure than currently exists will allow people to build on each other's work.

The regulation and surveillance of home-based medical devices need to be reexamined. "We can't just force-fit what we have been using in the institutional-care setting into the home health care setting." For example, different standards may be needed for regulatory clearance of home health care devices. Such devices are subject to different demands and expectations and move from person to person in different ways. As a specific example, should medical devices controlled by mobile phones be subject to the same regulatory standards as other devices?

Finally, information technology offers "game-changing possibilities," but its effects must be better understood and its benefits clinically validated for usage to increase. "How can you identify effectively those characteristics and attitudes that will allow your [technology] solution to flourish as opposed to fail?" Crawford asked. Executives of the companies developing these technologies want to see returns on investments, while regulatory agencies want to see proof of efficacy.

In all three areas, said Crawford, an important step will be to establish priorities. It also is important to determine what legacies of the existing health care system will extend into the future and which can be discarded and reimagined. For example, "Do we need to build a whole separate workforce and education system . . . as home health care grows at the expense of institutional health care?" A cohesive community and leading journal—equivalent to the *New England Journal of Medicine*, but for home health care—"would obviously be productive."

Committee member Christopher Gibbons said that reimagining the delivery of health care requires asking what recipients want and need, not just doing what others think they want or need. Crawford agreed, saying "there is certainly a lot of interesting feedback out there that is not obvious." Taking such steps requires a sound infrastructure for regulation, technology development, and reimbursement, said committee member Laura Gitlin. "It's not developing the same infrastructure we have for [institutional] settings but what a new infrastructure is going to look like."

In response to a question about incompatibilities caused by technology upgrades, Crawford said that Intel has emphasized backward compatibility, so that capabilities are not lost when a system is upgraded. The issue also arose of incorrect data entry into home health care technologies by users, whether a care recipient or a formal or informal provider. The possibility of erroneous data entry requires both user testing and safeguards built into technologies that could cross-check entries. But full capabilities in this area will require that systems be integrated across different devices and technologies, which will require even greater attention to human factors issues.

Committee member Judith Matthews raised the issue of trust. "Does the system do what it's intended to do?" Airplanes rely on redundant systems, which increase the level of trust among fliers. "It's not just a matter of the information being put in or the output at the other end to the recipient of that information. It's also knowing that the system is working, that it's calibrated, that it's good to go."

Carolyn Humphrey observed that a large number of formal caregivers have had extensive experience with home health care devices and technologies. These individuals could inform discussions about user needs and trust. She also mentioned that current reimbursement structures do not necessarily lend themselves to the widespread adoption of particular medical devices, including telehealth applications. "If we do get telehealth for a patient while they are on formal home care, we most of the time don't have a way to get it continued after their discharge from home care." And the removal of equipment can be traumatic for people who have learned to trust it. "We had people crying, literally, when their systems were leaving," said Crawford.

Several physician participants at the workshop questioned the value of at least some of the data generated by new technologies. Much of this information is simply discarded by physicians too busy to consult or use it. The data need to be filtered and analyzed. Gibbons said, "This is why health care has to change. There are some things we do now that we shouldn't do, that we don't need to do. But there are some things that we are not doing that we should do."

4

The Environments of Home Health Care

THE PHYSICAL ENVIRONMENT AND HOME HEALTH CARE[1]

The physical environment can create demands on people's abilities, said Jon Sanford. If environmental demands are either too strong or too weak, maladaptive behavior can result. "We want to find the zone where the demands equal our abilities."

In its International Classification of Functioning, the World Health Organization made the environment an integral part of the domain of health. The environment helps determine what people *can* do—based on their body function and structure—and what they *do* do—their activities and participation. However, the classification does not emphasize that the environment also affects health, Sanford observed. "They talk about it, but they don't really have it in the model."

Environmental Modifications to Improve Activity and Health Outcomes

To make environmental modifications that improve the ability to carry out activities and tasks, assessments need to be made of the fit among a person's abilities, the demands of activities and tasks, and the attributes of the environment. This information about abilities, activities, and attributes then needs to be analyzed and translated into appropriate interventions.

[1]This section is based on the presentation by Jon Sanford, director and senior research scientist in the Center for Assistive Technology and Environmental Access at the Georgia Institute of Technology. For more information and for references to the information cited in this presentation, see Chapter 10.

Not all assessments are the same, said Sanford. Some look at the expected performance of an individual, and others look at actual performance. Assessments of expected performance look at the anticipated performance of activities based on ability and environmental attributes. They do not accurately reflect differences between what individuals can do and what they actually do.

Assessments of actual performance focus on activities rather than abilities or attributes of the environment. These kinds of assessments then require additional assessments of the environment to determine what needs to be modified and how. For example, one assessment asks people if they are satisfied with what they are able to do in terms of dressing, bathing, feeding, and so on. If they are not satisfied, the next question is how the situation can be modified to allow them to do what they want to do.

By linking assessments of abilities, activities, and attributes, designers of the physical environment can develop best-fit solutions. These solutions should be individualized, customized, and personalized, Sanford said, to fit the functional needs of the individual. Still, best-fit solutions are situational. A number of confounding factors can mediate and influence decisions about modifications. Examples of these factors include the personal tastes or preferences of individuals in the home, the social constraints of the living situation, the structure of the home, building and zoning codes, and cost.

The majority of the modifications that are typically made relate to getting into and out of the home, safe movement within the home, and safe transfers and greater independence in self-care activities. For getting into and out of a home, ramps and lifts can obviate the need for stairs. Chair lifts and architectural modifications, such as wider doors, can facilitate movement within the home. And safe transfers and greater independence can involve modified toilets, sinks, and baths; grab bars and other devices in bathrooms and kitchens; and other modifications designed to facilitate daily activities.

A wide variety of organizations and individuals support and provide these modifications, including government agencies, nongovernmental organizations, private contractors, remodelers, builders, occupational therapists, home health nurses, and social service providers, some of whom are trained and certified for their jobs and others of whom are not. Overall, the system is complex and fragmented, said Sanford. "Imagine people trying to get into the system and figure it out."

Most home modifications are paid for by the recipient of care or someone associated with the recipient. From one perspective, this makes sense, since disability can be seen as a life-cycle event comparable to having a baby or building a home office. But modifications could also be seen as part of the health care system. In some countries, the government subsidizes home modifications throughout the life span. "Whatever you need you get, and if you need it again or if your situation changes, you can get the house remodified or new modifications brought in."

In those cases in which government does pay for home modifications in the United States, many different agencies and organizations can be involved, including state agencies, private insurers, social service organizations, and volunteer organizations. "Again, it's a patchwork, and it's fragmented," Sanford commented.

Products and Technologies to Improve Health Management and Treatment

Products and technologies can facilitate both caregiver tasks and access to caregivers. For example, a wide variety of products can aid in mobility and transfer, such as ceiling track lifts, portable lifts, wall boom lifts, and rolling lifts. However, some lifts can require major modifications to a home, which can lessen their appeal to homeowners. They can also be expensive. A regular bathtub costs a few hundred dollars, whereas a walk-in tub can cost about $3,000, plus installation.

Within a bathroom, devices for transfer include tub seats, transfer benches, lifts, raised toilet seats, and grab bars. All can be very useful, although some products can create obstacles and clutter for people who do not need them.

Various products and technologies can reduce safety hazards by turning off stove burners, maintaining water temperatures, adjusting lighting levels, detecting smoke, or setting off an alarm if an individual wanders. Monitors and communication devices can connect individuals with broader networks of formal and informal caregivers and peer communities.

One problem, Sanford pointed out, is "Where do we put all this stuff?" Homes can get "obese" if too many products and technologies are crammed into them. Also, builders are very reluctant to build larger houses to accommodate these devices. Builders have even resisted building stair steps that are seven inches high and have eleven inches of run because steeper but more dangerous stairs take up less room.

To integrate health care products and technologies into the environment in a better way, devices can be combined so they take up less room. Another option is to rethink where and how activities take place in the home.

Another approach is to adopt the principles of universal design (see the section on medical devices and equipment in Chapter 3). Universal design differs from either accessible design or assistive technology. Assistive technology consists of add-on devices and specialized equipment to improve accessibility for an individual or small cohort of people with specific needs. Accessible design is added to everyday design to reduce demands on groups of people with similar types of impairments.

Universal design is everyday design, Sanford said, not specialized or add-on design. It reduces the demands of the environment on everyone, not just people with functional limitations, reflecting the fact that everyone has different degrees of ability. Universal design makes access the norm rather than the exception. It is part of the environment so that it is not obtrusive or obvious. Design features are easier to use and learn by both health care recipients and providers. Universal design can also eliminate the need for many assistive technologies and home modifications.

Barriers to Housing Innovations

There are numerous barriers to the adoption of housing innovations, on both the supply side and the demand side. Providers with expertise in environmental interventions are few. Certification programs are weak and are specific to only certain of the professions that provide modifications. A few universities and occupational therapy schools have classes and programs in environmental intervention, but they usually depend more on individual faculty members who are interested in the topic rather than a group that supports them.

Although the principles of universal design have been widely disseminated, they have not been tested or validated. Some specific policies also create disincentives for universal design. For example, assistive technology may be eligible for reimbursement, but universal design is very unlikely to be reimbursed precisely because it is for everyone rather than for a specific person. "Our system cannot reimburse something that is basically usable by everyone because it is a system that is geared toward disability, not ability."

On the demand side, consumers are generally unaware of universal design and of many potential interventions. Modifications can look industrial and institutional rather than residential. Consumers see devices and technologies in homes and react negatively to them. "It's a vicious cycle. Instead of coming up with new ideas, we just keep using the old ideas and recycling them over and over again."

Universal design does not have to be more expensive than other designs, Sanford said, especially if it is built into a home from the beginning. Wider hallways and doors do not add greatly to the cost. Appliances and other products can be more expensive, but that is usually because they are higher quality devices, which is a manufacturing and marketing issue.

Improving the Use of Human Factors Research in the Physical Environment of Home Health Care

Sanford described several policy changes that might increase the adoption of housing innovations:

- Overcoming policy barriers to interventions in housing. Both governments and private insurers are reluctant to put money into people's homes because they have no control over those homes. But modifications to local building and zoning codes could help modify the environment. For example, the zoning codes in single-family neighborhoods often dictate how many people who are not related can live in a house. This can make it hard to bring in care providers who may need to be in a home continuously. Similarly, by regulating other aspects of the physical environment, codes can assist individuals who provide health care in a home environment.
- Creating incentives for universal design by recognizing it as a health care intervention. In part, this can be done by "medicalizing" environmental interventions. Physicians, nurse practitioners, and the many professionals who see people with health care needs can be educated about the importance of these interventions. "Prescribing medications or prescribing a medical device is great, but what about prescribing how those medications are going to be taken in the home if you don't have lights to read the labels or you don't have a place for the medical device in the home? The home has to support all of the other health care interventions that we do."
- Certifying environmental service providers in the same way that other professionals are certified. To affect legislation and regulatory policy, the efficacy and effectiveness of interventions need to be demonstrated for care recipients, for providers, and for society as a whole. Today, thinking about environmental interventions and universal design is based more on practice-based evidence than evidence-based practice. "If we cannot even define universal design and validate what designs will work, then it is all based on our practice."

Sanford also had ideas regarding a research agenda:

- Quasi-experimental pre-/post-modification designs can be used to compare the effects of interventions with the effects of not having them.
- Naturally occurring situations can be used in cases in which funders already have programs that are making modifications.

- Good outcomes are defined so as to be relevant to individuals, programs, and agencies on both the supply and demand sides of the equation.
- Experts in the physical environment are essential to research studies and review panels.

The high initial cost of environmental interventions makes randomized controlled trials very difficult. Crossover designs are less expensive, but the disruption of installing interventions is burdensome to the subjects. Epidemiological studies often lack a basic understanding of environmental factors. And there is a lack of mutually agreed-upon outcomes and measures. Clinical significance may be more important than statistical significance, and small changes may equate to big gains in the quality of people's lives.

Responses to Questions

Sanford observed that he does not draw a sharp distinction between devices to overcome environment obstacles and modifications of the environment itself. "It is not an either/or. If the environment were designed more appropriately in the first place, we would need fewer devices. Given that the environment is never going to obviate the need for all devices, then we need to better design the devices that will then fit within the environments we have." The interchangeability between the two categories makes trade-offs inevitable. Devices may be so expensive as to be equivalent in cost to extensive environmental changes.

In response to a question about whether houses with environmental modifications are harder to sell, Sanford labeled such an idea a misperception. The actual effect depends on the attributes of the modification. "I can show you ramps that the only way that house would be bought is if it was the right price and somebody just needed to get in there. I can show you other houses where the ramps are lovely, and it looks like part of the house, even if it isn't a sloping lot." The crucial determinant is how a feature looks and fits in with the rest of the house.

Because subsidized and public housing often have higher percentages of disabled individuals than in the general population, the U.S. Department of Housing and Urban Development has an interest in environmental modification, Sanford said. The building and zoning codes governing the construction of such housing have important effects on accessibility and usability. As Jon Pynoos observed, the Section 202 Supportive Housing for the Elderly Program requires 5 to 10 percent of units to be basically accessible with walk-in showers. "But the most future-looking developers of that housing are putting walk-in showers in *all* their units and finding that it works much better and gives people many more choices of where to stay in the buildings. So there is some response from the market end." Sanford added that modifications to existing housing provide opportunities to do pre-/post-modification studies in which people can act as their own controls.

In response to a question about the best outcome measures for such studies, Sanford said that defining and agreeing on appropriate measures is a difficult task. Outcomes that might be dismissed as statistically insignificant could actually be making a major difference in people's lives. "We don't have a really good measure of what it means to the individuals who are getting these modifications."

Accessibility in the physical environment surrounding a house or apartment can be just as important as accessibility to and within it, Sanford said. Without an accessible environment, such as navigable sidewalks, people are "imprisoned in their homes, and that just doesn't work. You can't get to work, you can't get to a place of worship, you can't get to the market, you can't get to the doctor, you can't get anywhere. Our community environments are less than accessible." Furthermore, the Americans with Disabilities Act exerts little control over the community environment.

Many of the issues affecting people with physical disabilities apply with even greater force to people with cognitive disabilities. As people enter into a cognitive decline, more caregiver assistance is necessary and independence diminishes. The need for assistance then shifts as much to the caregiver as to the care recipient.

Sanford also pointed out that builders tend to be extremely conservative and have few incentives to change. "Before the bust, they sold everything that they had. They sold it no matter how bad it was. They sold it as fast as they could build it. What is the incentive to do anything different? There was none." As a result, making changes to support universal design or health and wellness is "a difficult sell."

Finally, incorporating design changes from hospitals and other institutional settings can be a good idea. "But it has to be residential in scale. It cannot just be translated from hospital to home."

THE IMPACT OF CULTURAL, SOCIAL, AND COMMUNITY ENVIRONMENTS ON HOME HEALTH CARE[2]

Steven Albert began his talk by describing two care settings that he encountered in his first job, at the Philadelphia Geriatric Center. In the first, a middle-aged African American woman was caring for her mother,

[2]This section is based on the presentation by Steven Albert, professor and associate chair for research and science in the Department of Behavioral and Community Health Sciences of the University of Pittsburgh. For more information and for references to the information cited in this presentation, see Chapter 11.

who had Alzheimer's disease, in a northern Philadelphia home. She had placed the hospital bed in the living room right by the front door, where everyone who came into the home had to see and interact with her mother. Over the hospital bed hung a mobile with photos and family keepsakes attached to help orient her mother. The shelves around the living room held supplies, including adult diapers, wipes, and everything else needed for Alzheimer's care, and there was a commode right next to the bed. The daughter said to him, "'This is the best-looking lady with Alzheimer's disease in Philadelphia. Touch her skin. Touch her hair.' That, as a very young man, left a very good impression on me."

That same week he went to another home where a person with similarly profound Alzheimer's disease, mostly confined to a hospital bed, lived upstairs in an isolated, poorly maintained room that few people entered. "What is involved in this sort of contrast?" asked Albert. "Is it a cultural factor? Is it social or family factors? Is it community factors, since these were different communities? . . . Many, many things go into what kind of adaptation families think is reasonable in the case of severe chronic disease care."

The Social-Ecological Model

One approach Albert uses to analyze these issues is a social-ecological model that places the individual in successively broader family, community, and policy contexts. This model makes it possible to see how definitions of challenges and resources at each level may be linked or depend on processes at a different level. For example, a home care challenge may require disruption of home routines and the home environment. This decision may be informed by a strong filial obligation, social traditions of home care, or an expansive cultural definition of "home." All of these factors can affect the choice to adapt the home for intensive medical care.

Similarly, a family decision to disrupt family relations may depend on a supportive division of labor within the family, family networks that allow appropriate information gathering, the willingness to include home health care staff as family, or perhaps modification of a home. At the level of the community or neighborhood, the challenge might be the availability of home health care providers, and relevant resources might include neighborhood support of medical technology in the home, reliable services, and an appropriate infrastructure for home medical equipment. And at the policy level, eligibility for services might depend on linkages between providers, the quality of home technology, the reputation of providers, and waiting times. "The basic idea in social ecology is that what happens at one level may be relevant for decisions at another level. . . . We can go up and down levels and see additional layers of complexity."

Home Care Culture

A model used to analyze the culture of home health care defines culture as shared beliefs, knowledge, feelings, and expectations that carry motivational force. Albert draws on ideas from cognitive anthropology to elicit cultural expectations about home care that are relevant for decisions about the use of services. In particular, he has used cultural consensus theory to determine the degree to which ideas are shared and the extent to which individual expectations are consonant with a group consensus.

An example would be asking family members and caregivers to consider what changes in a home would be appropriate when a family member is seriously ill and may die. People would then generate lists of changes to their homes or their own behaviors that they think would be appropriate. Another question might be: What changes in your household would you need to make in order to provide quality care for a family member receiving home health care services? Not much research has been done in this area, but Albert speculated that studies of family caregivers would show differing preferences for such interventions as home hospice services, infusion technologies, hospital beds, the placement of commodes, telemonitoring, places to store supplies, or more reliable utilities. By generating lists of this type, researchers could calculate the extent to which lists overlap and the degree of consensus surrounding any given intervention.

It may be possible, Albert said, to identify subcultures of people based on lists of what is appropriate and correlate those subcultures with caregiving choices. For example, a list may demonstrate a commitment to family care originating in filial piety. This in turn may be linked to choices about the use of formal providers or receptivity to an in-home medical technology. These kinds of decisions could be linked to caregiver training, communication with health care providers, exposure to health information, and perceptions of stigma associated with disability.

Social and Family Relationships

Familism—the subordination of individual interests to family concerns—can affect decisions about home health care in many different ways. It may reinforce individual cultural expectations for home care. It may also place such great stress on families to provide this care that it interferes with the care. Families "differ in their consensus about care and their willingness to divide the labors of care," said Albert.

Preferences for dignity, privacy, comfort, choice, and autonomy may not take precedence over more basic decisions about care. "Once someone achieves a certain level of chronic care need, families seem to be more willing to compromise on these." An interesting natural experiment related to these issues is the Cash and Counseling Demonstration Project conducted by the Centers for Medicare & Medicaid Services in Alabama, Arkansas, and New Jersey.[3] It allowed people who qualify for home care to hire their own caregivers, work out scheduling, and influence the training of a caregiver rather than being assigned a home care paraprofessional and a package of services. Results suggested some positive outcomes.[4] "This [was] a very nice experiment, because we can see whether greater consumer direction leads to different outcomes." For example, will people use their funds to purchase medical assistive equipment? How will they use home paraprofessionals? "One of my hypotheses might be that with greater consumer direction we might see more effective use of home care technologies," said Albert.

Community and Neighborhood Factors

At the community and neighborhood levels, safety, access, the infrastructure of neighborhoods, the physical features of homes, social networks, and the degree of linkage between home care agencies servicing a community all need to be considered. For example, neighborhoods with greater linkages among home care providers diffuse innovations and share information better, which benefits consumers who need such help. "We don't normally think about that as being a health resource, but it most likely is."

Social networks can also have properties that are protective of health. Many studies have shown that neighbors checking on each other or common spaces in a neighborhood where people can go can be important health resources.

Improving the Use of Human Factors Research in Cultural, Social, and Community Environments

Albert had several ideas for action:

- Expanding consumer direction–type demonstrations (like Cash and Counseling) to include not only greater control over hiring and scheduling but also greater control over the adoption of in-home medical technologies.
- Establishing cultural competence training and certification for allied health home care providers. In New York City, some agencies have reported that the racial/ethnic cultures of the home care

[3]The Cash and Counseling Demonstration Project has ended, and similar programs have since been implemented in multiple states.

[4]See Chapter 12 for a description of these outcomes.

paraprofessional and the care recipient are different 80 percent of the time, and in a third of those cases the care provider and the recipient do not even speak the same language.

In the area of research, he suggested the following:

- Studies of home care culture to assess intracultural variation and cross-cultural differences. Such studies may lead to better tools for assessment of cultural expectations for home care.
- Cross-level investigations of the choices people make to modify homes, use home care paraprofessionals, adopt advanced home care technologies, or some combination of the three. Such studies could help clarify the results of inconsistent studies that have focused on a single level.

Albert also presented several research hypotheses that could be investigated. One is that familism probably will be a poor predictor of home adaptation unless a broader perspective and a more sophisticated approach are adopted. Another is that greater consumer direction in home care may lead to better use of home care technologies. And a third is that families in areas with fewer resources, who often are forced to accept greater standardization of services, experience greater conflict and poorer outcomes.

Responses to Questions

Albert observed that the model he described applied to the decision to let a care provider into the home or make environmental modifications. But the model can also be applied to the relationship between a care provider and a care recipient. Many care providers are appalled, Albert said, at the lack of concern families show to a person who needs help. This is an example of a culture clash that can be exacerbated, for example, by the personalities of the people attracted to work in the field of home health care. "[Professionals] think care to a frail person or a disabled person is the most important thing in the world," Albert remarked. Lessening this clash requires that families be educated, but it also requires that care providers learn to maintain a proper professional distance. "They often feel they have to buy food for a person, for example, or they get in the middle of conflicts between family and the disabled person who needs help." These kinds of conflicting expectations can produce very difficult situations.

In response to a question about training and certification of home care providers from cultures different from that of a care recipient, Albert called attention to the boredom that such jobs can entail. "They get very good at what they're doing. They can cook, clean, do the personal assistance care in 45 minutes, and then they have another three hours in the home, and they end up watching television with the elder. We have squandered a wonderful opportunity for activity programming and other sorts of things that these paraprofessionals could learn and enhance their skills." The same observation applies to many other kinds of caregivers, whether formal or informal.

An important issue is deciding which types of care are done better by a human and which are more appropriate for technologies. Home caregivers provide social support and forms of monitoring that cannot be achieved with technology. Many of these forms of support and monitoring may not appear on a task analysis, but human support can be extremely flexible and valuable.

In response to a question about ethnic and racial differences in perceptions of home health care, Albert acknowledged that there are broad differences among groups. Minorities are less likely to use nursing homes, for example. African Americans, however, are more likely to prefer hospital care and more aggressive care at the end of life rather than hospice care. Hispanics are more reluctant to have paraprofessional caregivers in the home. These differences are not well understood. They could come from familism or from some other factors. It also is difficult to determine how much is due to a cultural orientation or expectation and how much is due to lack of knowledge. These questions need to be studied rather than presuming causes for such differences.

FINANCE, REGULATION, AND CLINICAL MODELS[5]

The current system of delivering health care to the elderly is not sustainable, said Peter Boling. The Medicare Trust Fund, which pays for hospitals, nursing homes, and home health care, will run out of money in 2018, with obligations for publicly funded health care continuing to grow dramatically after that point. "We're sailing on a massive ship," said Boling. "It has hit an iceberg, and we have to do something or it is going to sink."

Spending on individual Medicare beneficiaries varies greatly across states, from a maximum of $16,000 in 2006 to a minimum of $5,000. Yet spending is not associated with quality of care. "People are looking at these numbers and saying we need to really change what we're doing."

According to the National Health Interview Survey, 2 to 3 percent of people age 65 and older say they cannot walk, stand, or sit by themselves,

[5]This section is based on the presentation by Peter Boling, director of long-term care and geriatrics in the Medical College of Virginia Hospital at Virginia Commonwealth University. For more information and for references to the information cited in this presentation, see Chapter 12.

and about 15 percent of this population cannot stand or walk without help. The survey also shows that about 2 million people in the United States have deficits in three or more activities of daily living, including about 1.1 million people age 65 and older. These numbers are expected to grow dramatically as the baby boom generation starts to reach retirement age.

Home Care Silos

Home health care, which represented about 4 percent of the $484 billion Medicare budget in fiscal year 2009, is broken into a variety of separately funded categories—called "silos" in the field of health care financing—based partly on payment sources and regulations. ("Silo" is a metaphorical term often used to describe artificial boundaries among domains of expertise, services, jurisdiction, or interest that serve to discourage communication, interaction, or cooperation.) Medical equipment and supplies are paid for largely by Medicare Part B and Medicaid. Home health agency care is paid mostly by Medicare Part A, by Medicaid, and privately. Personal care is paid mostly by Medicaid and out of pocket but not at all by Medicare. Pharmacy benefits are paid by "an enormous, complex panoply of organizations" under Medicare Part D, private coinsurance, and Medicaid. Medical care is paid for mostly by Medicare Part B and Medicaid.

These silos are not coordinated with each other, and hospitals and physicians often work in their own separate silos. The system does not have a way of considering care across time or institutions. "This is not patient-centered care in any way, shape, or form," said Boling. "And we have good evidence that it's dangerous."

About 5 percent of Medicare beneficiaries account for 43 percent of the Medicare budget, with the next 5 percent using 18 percent. The top 5 percent of beneficiaries consumed an average of $63,000 in 2005, the next 5 percent consumed $27,000, and the bottom 50 percent just $550. Thus, three-fifths of the Medicare budget is consumed by 10 percent of the population, whereas the bottom half uses only 4 percent of the budget.

This concentration of resources in a small portion of the Medicare population presents a great opportunity, said Boling, if much better care management can be targeted to this group. This group is typically chronically ill. Among members of this group followed for 60 months from 1997 through 2001, health care expenditures were high in 22 of those months. "That's a person who is intermittently chronically ill. No one can stay critically ill for 22 months in the hospital. These are people who go in and out of the hospital, in and out of health care, using the system a lot, and don't die, and we do a terrible job of taking care of them."

Categories of Care

Boling divided the general population into six categories requiring different levels of care:

A. No illness (acute or chronic).
B. Ambulatory, independent; some chronic conditions.
C. Function limited, need support for activities of daily living (ADLs); younger, not in ill health.
D. Older, cognitive or functional impairment; not acutely ill very often.
E. Postacute rehabilitation; returning to independence.
F. High comorbidity and illness burden.

Groups A and B are essentially healthy. They need public health information, prevention, episodic care, and self-care. Some of them have chronic diseases, such as hypertension, diabetes, or asthma, for which they can be tested and monitored. They are mobile and can use a doctor's office.

Groups C and D are function limited for various reasons that can vary by age. They are not medically ill often, but they need considerable long-term care support.

Groups E and F are chronically sick and are often in the health care system. Many, particularly in Group F, need lifelong care and highly individualized health care plans that change according to their needs.

Long-Term Care

The U.S. health care system needs reform both in the area of community-based long-term care and in the area of chronic illness care for seriously ill people, said Boling.

In the first category, many people in Groups C and D need personal care for ADL support, which can be provided by home health aides, family, or friends. Many also need assistive technology, ranging from supplies to the wide range of technologies being tested in smart homes. If these individuals have access to Medicaid, they have access to much more assistance. But that depends on their income and where they live. The federal poverty level in 2009, often used as a qualifier for Medicaid, was just $10,830 for a family of one, $14,570 for a couple, and $22,050 for a family of four. State funding of Medicaid as a percentage of gross state product ranges from less than 1 percent in three states to over 4 percent in two states. "That is a big range, and that is a problem. That is going to influence whether people stay in the state where they've been living or . . . move to a state where their family members are."

Paying privately can be done through an agency, which extracts overhead from the payment, or through an individual care provider. Direct employment can be highly beneficial, but it is not easy to arrange and is not the prevalent mode of home health care (see discussions above of the variety of home care arrangements).

A variety of new models have been tested for the delivery of long-term care. For example, the Centers for Medicare & Medicaid Services Cash and Counseling demonstration project has shown improvement in caregiver satisfaction and decreases in measures of caregiver strains. A recent survey, the Consumer Assessment of Health Care Providers and Systems, has also been evaluating the quality of care from a consumer perspective.

Chronic Illness Care

For the seriously ill people in Groups E and F, programs of postacute care paid for by Medicare Part A work reasonably well for at least a portion of the population. But weaknesses are common in transitional care, in which people are moving between care environments.

Largely missing from health care services for seriously ill people is long-term ADL support, unless a recipient is poor, on Medicaid, or has an advanced chronic illness. ADL care may be provided only for short, predetermined periods. In the Medicare model, prospective payments have been available since 2008 for 60-day episodes with case mix adjustments. This has resulted in a decrease in the frequency of visits and a more focused care model. However, 29 percent of the recipients are hospitalized within 60 days, and one in seven is hospitalized within 2 weeks of the end of the care period. "Most folks would say that this is really a mediocre track record," said Boling. Several recent attempts to reform long-term care for the chronically ill have failed. The Medicare Coordinated Care demonstration, which basically assigned nurses to talk with patients, had an average net increase in costs and was marginally effective in only 2 of 13 sites. The Medicare Advantage plans have had a 13 percent net increase in cost, with a decrease in service and a decrease in perceived quality by enrolled individuals. Interim results from the Medicare Disease Management program indicate that commercial disease management does not deliver short-term medical cost savings.

Other programs have had more success. A program based on having nurses serve as health coaches, along with an enhanced health record, helped individuals become their own advocates as they moved through the posthospital period, and it saved about $500 per person. Another program has suggested that cost savings may result by putting a nurse in the doctor's office and having that nurse coordinate care. In a third program, nurses saw patients in the hospital, got to know them, and then followed them for a month to 6 weeks at home. The nurses coordinated care, changed care plans, and interacted with the doctors, with a net savings of about $3,000 to $5,000 per patient. And the Department of Veterans Affairs has found that putting a comprehensive home-based primary care model in place produced a 24 percent reduction in overall cost and a 60 percent reduction in hospital use.

Home Visits

When people are concerned about their health or the health of a family member or friend, they want access to a team led by somebody who is able to make medical decisions, provide good advice about complex problems, and be accessible and available. "This is not what we have for this population," said Boling. One solution to this problem is "old-fashioned medicine with a new twist" based on house calls. To take good care of chronically ill people, providers need to go to their homes. New technologies and devices make it possible to do timely diagnoses and direct treatment in homes. "In the past you had to be kind of a wizard and intuit what was wrong with the patient. [Now] we can measure most of the stuff that you need to know right there on the spot."

A few such programs supported by Medicare Part B exist across the United States, although on very thin margins. "We built our health care system around a model that was dependent on bricks and mortar and fixed overhead that is very expensive. It was done for good reasons. It wasn't a bad idea. It works quite well for certain types of people. [But] for some other people, who happen to be the ones who cost most of the money, it really doesn't work very well."

The costs of drugs, hospitalization, and nursing homes are exorbitant and could cover a large number of home visits and the involvement of a team of health care providers. Based on this observation, Boling has been working on a piece of health care legislation, called Independence at Home,[6] that calls for interdisciplinary teams that would use house calls, electronic health records, other forms of technology, and their own expertise to deliver care where and when people need it. Any net savings would flow both to Medicare and to the Independence at Home program. Candidates for the program would be people with multiple chronic diseases or functional deficits. "We want high-cost patients, the higher the better, the sicker the better. That's what we do best. . . . This is really what patient-centered health care is supposed to be." Estimated savings from the program could be as high as $50 billion per year.

---

[6]The 2010 health care reform act includes provisions for an Independence at Home demonstration project.

Boling closed by emphasizing two points. A national policy is needed for long-term care that does not impoverish people and encourages community-based care. And there is a great need for interdisciplinary, comprehensive, in-home health care for people with multiple frailties.

Responses to Questions

In response to a question about how much of health care expenditures go to bureaucratic, regulatory, and legal paperwork, Boling agreed that doing paperwork is "what we all remember the least favorably of our experiences as providers." But he added that it is necessary to document how care is being delivered and how it affects the care recipient. Much paperwork has been created to make sure that value is provided in exchange for dollars. "There has to be some mechanism of documenting the impact, . . . because funds are not unlimited."

Boling was also asked whether the states, which have different populations with differing needs, should be allowed to have more control over how they use their health care monies. A good case can be made for states having control over services that are a public good, he replied, but too many differences between states can have serious negative effects. People cannot move from one state to another without major disruptions in services and funding, which may restrict freedom of movement or how people and families organize their lives. "We have to strike a balance there as well. That's one of the reasons why the [health care reform] process has been so enormously complicated."

The parts of the Independence at Home legislation that he views as most important are attracting talented people to the field, creating teams that can go to care recipients, and aligning financial incentives with objectives. "If the objective is comprehensive care with less dependence on hospitals and nursing homes, you need to structure the financial parameters in such a way that you are paying to obtain those results." In addition, research has shown that home visits yield marked improvements in detection of and intervention in significant health problems. People who make home visits are also more adept at obtaining the resources needed and making appropriate referrals.

DISCUSSION

Discussant Carol Raphael, president and chief executive officer of the Visiting Nurse Service of New York, began the discussion by articulating three messages:

1. The physical environment, including the philosophy behind housing design, can enable or diminish the ability to live independently, perform ADLs, and manage health.
2. An individual's cultural expectations, social supports, neighborhood, and community all have effects on openness to home health care, interaction with caregivers, and subsequent outcomes.
3. The current state of financing, regulation, and delivery of home health care limits its potential contribution to making the health care system more effective and efficient.

She also pointed out a number of common themes that emerged from the discussion, including the issues of silos versus integration, downstream versus upstream interventions, misalignment or lack of incentives, the need for engagement of care recipients, and the potential of technology as a virtual integrator and enabler of health care.

Many of these themes are apparent in the work of the Visiting Nurse Service, which sees 30,000 people a day in home settings. "When you walk into a home, you never know what you are going to find," said Raphael. "It ranges from no heat, no food in the refrigerator, a very poorly kept apartment, pets (the second-largest cause of workers' compensation in my organization is dog bites), and a remarkable range of family constellations, from very, very supportive families to families who have 'checked out.' So it is not at all a monolithic picture."

The home care population is remarkably diverse, not only in age and background but also in the capacity to lead independent, autonomous lives. Most people want to hold on to their privacy and independence to the greatest extent possible. People can also vary along a continuum of needs over time, which highlights the need for fluidity and flexibility in home care.

One way to achieve these objectives is to incorporate family caregivers into the home care community. For example, in its hospice and palliative care programs, the Visiting Nurse Service defines the client as not only the care recipient but also the recipient's family. Families are trained as part of the care team, they receive satisfaction surveys, and the nurse service continues to work with the family for more than a year after a death.

The Visiting Nurse Service has also done considerable work on aging in place programs to help residents stay in their homes and communities. The service becomes part of the fabric of communities, performing screenings, assessments, and group health education and providing certified home care services if needed. It also works in 31 of the 44 naturally occurring retirement communities in New York, including a new one in Chinatown that extends over a large area. "We're looking at that as a model for suburban communities where we have to [work] across many blocks."

Some models used by the program incorporate medical management. The Visiting Nurse Service of New York is licensed as a health maintenance organization in New York state and has a Medicare Advantage Special Needs Plan. In addition, a new program imported from the United Kingdom, called the Community Connections TimeBank, matches the skills and assets of individuals in the community with the needs of community members. "We have had an enormous response in terms of the number of people, often living alone, who have been able to feel comfortable taking a service because they feel they are also making a contribution."

Finally, Raphael noted that she is the head of the Health Information Technology Board in New York state and is very interested in how technology can be an integrator in health care. "The promise here is enormous [and] untapped. We can do a lot more to share information at point of care as well as to transform environments."

In response to a question about the lack of geriatricians in health care, Boling pointed out that the rewards for physicians and nurse practitioners in geriatrics are modest when compared with specialties with similar levels of professional development. Yet geriatricians provide care for people with complex problems and should be paid well. The Independence at Home program would create an incentive structure to pay geriatricians what they are worth. "We need more people who have that as a focus, and we have to create an incentive structure that rewards it."

Boling also agreed with a comment made about providing care in a variety of settings, such as schools, community centers, and senior centers. "I am not at all a fan of people having to come to a hospital or to a medical center for chronic illness care, because I don't think that for the majority of those folks we are doing them any good by making them do that."

David Wegman emphasized the importance of human factors research in the discussion, to which Sanford responded that occupational therapists could be trained and encouraged to be part of home health care teams. They could bring new attention to the influence of the built environment, even as physicians, nurse practitioners, and other clinicians are trained to be more observant of that environment.

In response to a question about passive monitoring, Raphael described a test in which 400 people with congestive heart failure were telemonitored while 400 comparable people were not. After one year, the telemonitored group had reduced emergency room visits and hospitalizations and other positive indicators. "It is definitely something that needs to be looked at very seriously. We had much better patient acceptance than we thought we would."

Albert observed that the responsibility for accessing medical devices in the home is not always clear. In some cases, families are expected to research and purchase equipment. In other cases, physicians are expected to prescribe it. Or allied health professionals or vendors may introduce devices into the home and train families in how to use them. This issue, he said, "needs to be explored more carefully."

In response to a question about the logistics of home visits, Boling observed that traveling to care recipients has advantages over recipients traveling to care providers because most recipients are always at home, so people can be added to a schedule at the last minute. "I could see them within hours of the time that they need to be seen, not days or weeks. They don't have to make an appointment. I go. If I can't go, somebody else on my team goes." With a good dispatch office and communications network, logistical problems are less severe than with traditional health care, and recipients are more satisfied. "You don't see as many patients per day," Boling admitted. But "those who are counting widgets and thinking in that way need to think differently about how this whole things works, because how many patients you see per day [is] really not the sole agenda."

Sanford added that the use of interactive teleconferencing can bring health care providers into the home virtually. In that way, providers can see someone engaged in an activity in the place where they actually perform that activity.

5

Concluding Discussion

In the final session of the workshop, David Wegman led a general discussion of the core concepts and concerns raised by the speakers and invited participants to comment on issues not yet discussed.

Paula Milone-Nuzzo raised the issue of violence associated with home health care and the problems it creates for providers to get to people's homes. It may not be possible to go into certain communities at particular times or without a police escort.

Mary Weick-Brady observed that coordination of regulations is needed in addition to coordination of care. Medical devices, reimbursement issues, transportation, housing, and even the bandwidths used for medical monitoring are all important factors in home health care, and in an ideal world the regulations governing these domains would work together rather than at cross purposes. George Demiris added that software platforms for disease management or telemonitoring need to be coordinated to avoid problems with interoperability, vocabulary, and communications. Christopher Gibbons made the same point for medical information that directly targets consumers. Jon Sanford observed that a similar situation exists with regard to building regulations. Although a national standard exists, it is model code that is not enforceable, and many thousands of municipalities adopt their own codes. The original intent of the codes was for public health, safety, and welfare, but that is not necessarily the principal concern today.

Molly Story observed that the principal message she took away from the workshop was that "it's a mistake to . . . take the medical care of health care and try to cram it into the house." Health care needs to understand the home much better and make changes based on that understanding.

Changes in the education of health care professionals can help establish this new emphasis, said Judith Matthews. The focus of education in the past has been acute care, but that does not equip people to practice in a community setting.

Neil Charness called attention to the challenge very low population densities pose to home health care. Technology may provide a way to do virtual visits in such settings, but technology does not necessarily offer full access to a person's home.

More than half of the older population lives alone, which highlights the need for supportive technologies that can help these individuals remain independent in their communities. In many cases, family members do not live nearby, exacerbating the problem of providing effective health care.

For caregivers who visit homes, these homes are their workplace, said Margaret Quinn. In addition, for many paraprofessionals, who are predominantly female and members of minority groups, their work and social positions are largely invisible in the larger society. Effective models of care recognize that home care is patient- and home-centered while simultaneously acknowledging the home as a workplace.

Committee member Daryle Jean Gardner-Bonneau observed that care recipients and care providers are part of a single system. Both groups will have a major effect on the way the system is designed and structured. The system needs to be flexible enough to enable a wide variety of choices by both care recipients and providers, and, she said, "I am not sure we always do that."

COMMITTEE PERSPECTIVE

Wegman summarized some of the messages he heard at the workshop.

- Better definitions can inform interdisciplinary analyses of home health care.
- Funding practitioners and knowledge in separate silos restricts the construction of more comprehensive and coherent systems for the delivery of home health care.
- Thinking longitudinally over the life course can help to meet the needs of care recipients in a home or community.
- New approaches can improve education and training, ranging from specific training in the use of a device to general interdisciplinary professional education.
- Care providers and care recipients always operate together as a dyad, and productive policy discussions will consider this dyad as a unit.

- Models from abroad can inform future discussions and work in home health care.
- Devices can be designed for the full range of the population, not just for the median of the population.
- Formal and informal markets for home health care devices can be a powerful influence on how these devices are used.
- Implementation of new programs and approaches ideally will be accompanied by studies of their efficacy and effectiveness.
- The principles of universal design can provide a foundation for thinking comprehensively about home health care.
- Reimbursement is "a glorious mess" in need of concerted attention.
- Good care management emphasizes teams of care providers.
- Existing models of effective home care can be implemented elsewhere and studied.

SPONSOR PERSPECTIVE

Kerm Henriksen commented on some of the main messages he absorbed from the discussion.

- The knowledge in people's heads can be translated into knowledge in the world to address such issues as the personnel shortage in home health care.
- Examples of very effective home health care can be studied to draw lessons from experience and existing expertise.
- Assessment methods used in inpatient care could have beneficial applications in home health care.
- Human factors techniques, such as root cause analyses or failure modes and effects analyses, could provide useful insights in the home health care setting.
- Quasi-experimental designs and evaluation techniques could be used to spur interest in research and applications.
- Aesthetics in design can play an important role with respect to home assistive technologies.
- Home health care has a dark side, as evidenced by violence in the community, abuse in the home, and frustration because of dementia.
- The problems of transitional care are ripe for human factors research.
- Training in silos is antithetical to working in teams, yet teamwork is essential in home health care.

- Health care may not be a unified system, but systems analysis can be applied to the role that health care plays in people's lives.
- Health care needs change over time, and human factors research can consider the ways in which these changes affect the delivery of health care.

Part II: Workshop Papers

6

The Health Care Challenge: Matching Care to People in Their Home Environments

Neil Charness

My tasks in this chapter are to (1) review the demographics concerning current and future home health care users; (2) examine data on their capabilities; (3) assess their attitudes and how these might be expected to impact successful interaction with current and future home health care technology; (4) provide some examples of how user characteristics may influence the ability to perform home health care tasks, particularly involving technology; and (5) identify important gaps in the understanding of these relationships and make some recommendations. I stress a human factors perspective in attempting to address these issues.

THE SHIFT TO HOME HEALTH CARE

Justification for concern with these issues lies in the remarkable shift in the way in which health care has been delivered to individuals in the past century in the United States. The major changes include the diversity in the population being treated and in their attitudes about health care, who pays for treatment, what type of health conditions are treated, where people are treated, and the demands made on those who are treated by current technology products. As one example of change in treatment locale, today about 99 percent of children in the United States are born in hospitals or clinics (DeClercq, Paine, and Winter, 1995), whereas home births probably predominated before 1900. In contrast, place of death has begun to shift away from hospital settings (dropping from 78 to 61 percent from 1994 to 2004 in a Canadian study; Wilson et al., 2009) to homes and hospice facilities. Finally, except for occasional programs that cater to housebound older adults (e.g., Beck et al., 2009), one travels to an office or clinic to see a health care professional today or is taken by ambulance to a hospital in an emergency. (The author can remember a childhood visit by a physician to diagnose and schedule an emergency appendectomy.) Perhaps the greatest change is the treatment of patients with serious health conditions at home instead of in hospitals, a trend being driven in part by treatment cost considerations.

A motivator for such treatment locale changes is the rapidly rising cost of health care coupled with a shift in the burden of payment. Individuals now pay directly for less than half their medical care expenses, with public and private insurance entities picking up the bulk of the payment, whereas as few as 50 years ago these relationships were reversed. Finally, people a century ago came in contact (sparingly) with medical care providers to address acute health concerns, such as communicable illnesses and injuries. In contrast, it was estimated that about 78 percent of health care expenditures in the United States in 1996 were made to treat people with chronic conditions (Anderson and Horvath, 2002). By 2005 that figure had risen to 90 percent (Machlin, Cohen, and Beauregard, 2008), in part because of the high prevalence of these conditions in the population. About 60 percent of adult civilian noninstitutionalized people have at least one chronic condition, although only about half of total medical care expenditures were for treatment of them. (Those with chronic conditions also experience disproportionate treatment for acute conditions.) The definition of chronic diseases by the Centers for Disease Control and Prevention is that they are "noncommunicable illnesses that are prolonged in duration, do not resolve spontaneously, and are rarely cured completely." The five most costly ones in 2006 were (1) heart conditions, (2) cancer, (3) trauma-related disorders, (4) mental disorders, and (5) asthma that includes chronic obstructive pulmonary disease (Soni, 2009). Many of these disorders are experienced throughout the life course (trauma-related, such as auto accidents), although some are more strongly associated with childhood (asthma), some are associated more with young adulthood (mental disorders, such as schizophrenia), and some are most associated with old age (heart disease, cancer, Alzheimer's disease). I focus primarily on older adult health care examples because that part of the population bears the greatest burden from chronic diseases.

Given the aging of the population, the percentage of health care cost expended to treat chronic diseases will undoubtedly rise because of the strong relation between age and chronic disease prevalence (see Figure 6-1). The Government Accountability Office projected a quadrupling of spending on older adult long-term care alone between 2000 and 2050 (Allen, 2005). There is also concern that other trends, such as increased prevalence of diabetes, which is variously projected to increase from 11 million in 2000

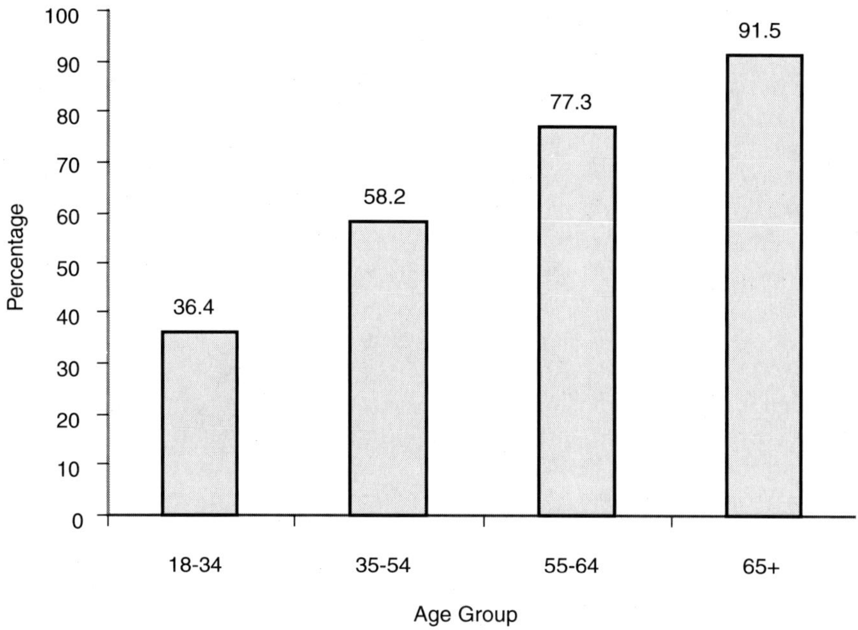

FIGURE 6-1 Relation between age and prevalence of a chronic condition.
SOURCE: Based on data from Machlin, Cohen, and Beauregard (2008).

to 29 million in 2050 (Boyle et al., 2001) or to 38 million in 2031 (Mainous et al., 2007), coupled with improved survival from traumas that used to lead to death (e.g., traffic crashes and battlefield injuries), will also increase demands on the health care system.

The future population of home health care users is already in place: it is the current U.S. population ranging from young to old and living with a variety of ailments whose treatment regimen makes a variety of demands on themselves and their caregivers. Examples are prematurely born infants on ventilators, children with diabetes requiring insulin injections, young adults with AIDS who must adhere to complicated medication regimens, middle-aged adults with "silent" hypertension that requires medication with unpleasant side effects, older adults with sleep apnea who must use uncomfortable equipment to maintain continuous positive airway pressure, and people with renal failure who use home dialysis to avoid costly kidney transplants (with comparable outcomes; Pauly et al., 2009). As well, children and adults also experience acute conditions, such as infections (influenza) and injuries (broken bones), that make demands of shorter duration on their capabilities and those of their caregivers but are typically treated mostly at home.

What will change is that today's relatively healthy children and young adults will, as they age, develop chronic conditions in addition to the acute conditions that affect health for shorter periods of time. In addition, many of those who have chronic conditions now (e.g., spinal cord injuries, diabetes) will continue to consume home health care services as their general health deteriorates and as comorbidities develop. The changing ethnic composition of the population, coupled with differential susceptibility to some diseases, means that one can also anticipate a change in the mix of morbidities, such as diabetes, whose incidence tends to be greater in minority groups (Mainous et al., 2007).

Given the enormous expenditures made on health care in the United States (discussed below), the model of providing continuing care through the traditional hospital and physician system is being questioned. One can expect to see more and more health care migrating into the home, with increased monitoring of health status being accomplished through technological systems, such as remote vital sign monitoring equipment. The goal is that such systems will provide more efficient health care delivery. However, designers of technology systems need to consider human factors in their design and deployment, because a badly designed system may fail to accomplish the goal of efficient delivery of health care and can even lead to fatal errors (e.g., Leveson and Turner, 1993; Institute of Medicine, 2000). Another example is assistive devices such as hearing aids, which have a high rate of abandonment (e.g., 30-50 percent) despite their potential benefit to users (Fuhrer, 2001). Some of the problems that arise may be the result of a poor fit between a device and the abilities and expectations of a specific user. Human factors and ergonomics specialists can offer insights into how best to design better health self-care systems.

THE HEALTH CARE ENVIRONMENT

People in the United States consumed $2.1 trillion of health care in 2006, that is, $7,026 per capita, representing 16 percent of gross domestic product (National Center for Health Statistics, 2008). About 84 percent of the expenditures were on personal health care and about 16 percent were on administrative costs, government public health activities, research, structures, and equipment. The highest percentage of those personal expenditures was for in-hospital care, followed by physician services (see Figure 6-2).

As many have noted (e.g., Schoen et al., 2006), Americans pay more than citizens of most other developed countries for their health care, yet by most health outcome measures, they fail to obtain benefits commensurate with these expenditures. Thus, using the figure above as a guide, in order

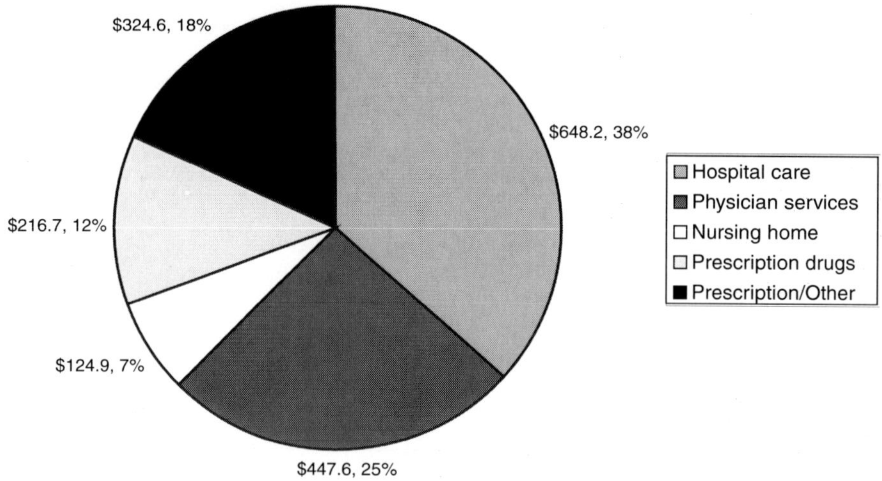

FIGURE 6-2 U.S. health care expenditures, 2006.
SOURCE: National Center for Health Statistics (2008).

to cut health care costs, the most likely candidates would be to diminish unnecessary contacts with hospitals and physicians and to consume fewer unnecessary over-the-counter and prescription drugs. Deployment of home health care technologies may reduce some of these expenditures by enabling people to be monitored from home by less skilled health care workers (in some cases, the user and family members) and by identifying health care problems before they require expensive treatments.

THE PERSON-ENVIRONMENT FIT FRAMEWORK

I consider health care somewhat broadly to include not only treatment of acute or chronic disorders but also such processes as information seeking and advice provision for health-related activities (e.g., exercise and diet) that might occur through a search of the Internet.[1] A useful framework for envisioning how best to match care to people in their home environments is that of capability-demand fit. A sample framework, based on Czaja et al. (2001), is presented in Figure 6-3, one that exemplifies demands for a telehealth tool, such as a videoconferencing system used in telemedicine interventions. The person would be asked to use this device at home (e.g., to receive therapy for a mental health disorder). The device presents challenges

[1]A 2008 Pew study indicated that 61 percent of adults in the United States had sought health information from the Internet (Fox and Jones, 2009).

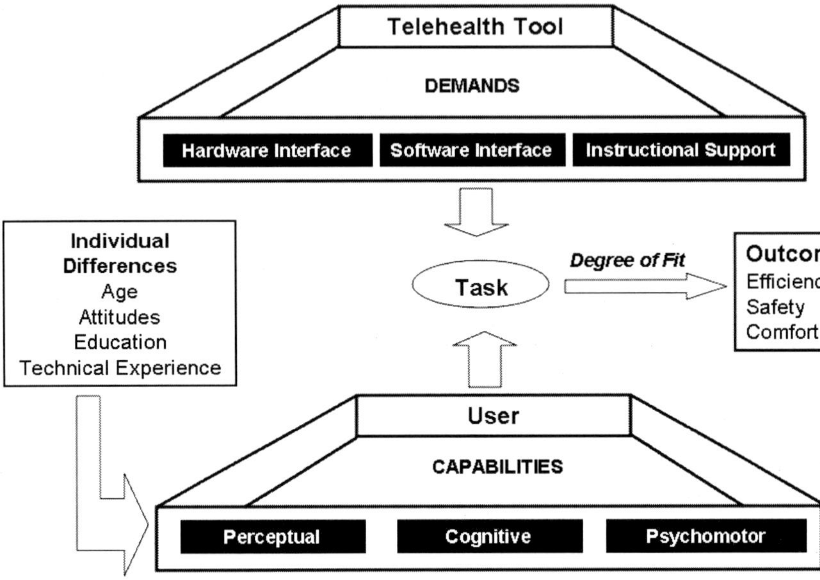

FIGURE 6-3 Capability-demand fit framework.
SOURCE: Adapted from Czaja et al. (2001).

in the form of its hardware interface, software interface, and instructional support. The user brings a range of abilities to bear, including perceptual, cognitive, and psychomotor capabilities. In short, systems make demands on users and the capabilities of the users will determine whether there is an adequate fit, which can affect acceptance and use of the system. Use of the (health care) system may in turn determine whether someone has a positive or negative health outcome.

As another example, think of some of the demands made by newer mobile vital sign monitoring devices now entering the home health care market. Consider a wristwatch-like device that, in the presence of a wireless network in the home, streams information, such as the user's temperature, location, and potential falls (via an embedded accelerometer), to a remote server. The information is aggregated, filtered through an intelligent program that tests for out-of-bounds values for vital sign parameters, and is presented to a health care provider via a password-protected website. However, the watch is battery-operated and needs to be recharged once a week on a charging station. If the user is somewhat cognitively impaired or simply forgetful, it is possible for the watch to fail based on a too-low battery state. Worse yet, the charging station may require precise placement of the watch within the station for effective charging to take place. If the older adult has a tremor, he or she may fail to align the watch with the charging contacts. Although the watch can signal its low-battery state to the server and present an alarm (via the web-based interface, or with an alert sent through the cellular phone system), unless someone is monitoring for the low-battery alarm, a fall could be missed before the user is alerted and reminded to recharge the watch (or the fall could occur while the watch is being charged). Even if the watch puts out a low-battery warning on the watch face, unless the user is carefully monitoring the watch and remembers what the low-battery icon means, that signal could be missed. Thus, user perceptual, cognitive, and psychomotor capabilities set a limit on how effectively the tool can function, despite the presence of a sophisticated hardware and software interface and instructional support.

As an example of how user characteristics, such as attitudes, can affect degree of fit for technology, consider a newly diagnosed older adult diabetic who is told to monitor blood sugar levels and inject insulin accordingly,[2] as well as to change diet and exercise levels. Blood glucose meters are relatively easy (although somewhat painful) to use with appropriate instruction (e.g., Mykityshyn, Fisk, and Rogers, 2002), but they may come with inadequate instructions, hobbling both cognitively fit young adults and less fit older adults (Rogers et al., 2001). Similarly, advice to change diet and to increase exercise levels may not yield adherence if the senior sees little linkage between glucose meter readings and short-term diet or exercise changes. The user may have unrealistic expectations and attitudes at the outset, which are reinforced by difficulties and unpleasantness associated with glucose meter use and the injection of insulin. All these difficulties may lead to poor adherence to diet, exercise, and monitoring/injection schedules. Better instructional materials, the training of expectations, quick access to skilled health care professionals for troubleshooting with equipment (e.g., through videoconferencing), and better designed equipment (e.g., noninvasive glucose measurement, automated insulin pumps) could lead to superior outcomes by making the treatment demands better match user capabilities and attitudes. One could also argue that having better health instruction earlier in the life span might have led to a lifestyle that would have avoided adult-onset diabetes.

For most health self-care, the proximal environment includes the home, its residents, and health care devices. In the United States, some relevant characteristics of households for the noninstitutionalized civilian population are shown in Table 6-1 and Figure 6-4. Of the roughly 117 million households in 2008, about two-thirds are family households, although composition varies with age of householder. For those ages 20-24, about half dwell

[2]This is admittedly an extreme case, as most forms of Type 2 diabetes are managed through diet and exercise changes and typically don't require insulin injections.

TABLE 6-1 U.S. Households by Type and Age, 2008 (numbers in thousands)

		Age of Householder			
U.S. Households	Total	Under 20 Years	20-24 Years	25-29 Years	30-34 Years
Total all households	116,783	862	5,691	9,400	9,825
Family households					
Total	77,873	535	2,824	5,869	7,384
Married couple	58,370	58	1,166	3,753	5,240
Male householder	22,972	361	2,124	2,724	2,140
Female householder	35,442	443	2,401	2,923	2,444
Proportion family households	*0.67*	*0.62*	*0.50*	*0.62*	*0.75*
Nonfamily households					
Total	38,910	327	2,867	3,531	2,440
Male householder	17,872	147	1,521	2,074	1,595
Female householder	21,038	180	1,346	1,457	845
Size of household					
One member	32,167	143	1,507	2,167	1,764
Two members	38,737	269	1,992	2,966	2,340
Three members	18,522	215	1,230	1,934	1,988
Four members	15,865	121	611	1,394	2,133
Five members	7,332	63	222	597	1,062
Six members	2,694	29	80	222	383
Seven+ members	1,467	22	50	120	155
Proportion one-member households	*0.28*	*0.17*	*0.26*	*0.23*	*0.18*

SOURCE: Based on data from U.S. Census Bureau (2009).

with family members, and that percentage increases to a high of 78 percent by ages 35-39 and then declines to a low of 42 percent by age 75+.

Household composition is likely to affect the willingness (and ability) of another household member to provide help with activities of daily living (ADLs) and instrumental activities of daily living (IADLs) and, more specifically, with health technology products. Research on problem solving suggests that two heads are sometimes better than one (Hinsz, Tindale, and Volrath, 1997), although 28 percent of all households have single members, and the proportion by age rises from 17 percent for those under age 20 to 56 percent for those over age 75. Also, as seen in Figure 6-4, women are

35-39 Years	40-44 Years	45-49 Years	50-54 Years	55-64 Years	65-74 Years	75+ Years
10,900	11,548	12,685	11,851	19,909	12,284	11,829
8,605	8,996	9,438	8,511	13,218	7,503	4,990
6,406	6,583	7,105	6,737	11,144	6,365	3,813
1,956	2,113	2,363	2,163	3,457	1,765	1,804
2,537	2,852	3,217	2,951	5,308	4,153	6,213
0.79	*0.78*	*0.74*	*0.72*	*0.66*	*0.61*	*0.42*
2,295	2,552	3,247	3,340	6,690	4,781	6,839
1,442	1,567	1,766	1,696	2,944	1,568	1,552
853	985	1,481	1,644	3,746	3,213	5,287
1,760	2,040	2,702	2,877	5,995	4,542	6,671
1,974	2,152	3,183	3,954	9,307	6,243	4,358
2,060	2,280	2,494	2,350	2,535	915	521
2,803	2,790	2,593	1,707	1,248	310	156
1,465	1,503	1,102	645	473	129	70
557	522	406	187	210	68	29
281	262	205	131	140	76	24
0.16	*0.18*	*0.21*	*0.24*	*0.30*	*0.37*	*0.56*

much less likely to be living in family households than are men at advanced ages. By age 85+, of those not institutionalized, about 64 percent of men compared with 39 percent of women live in family households. Particularly when it comes to managing and maintaining complex technology, having help accessible may be the difference between succeeding or failing with a task. Technology can provide access to such support when it does not reside in the household.

A more inclusive definition of the health care environment would consider other providers outside the home (physicians, nurses, formal and informal caregivers), including health care staff or advisors associated with schools and workplaces as well as other service providers who enter the home (e.g., to prepare meals, help with bathing). Thus, it is also likely that home health

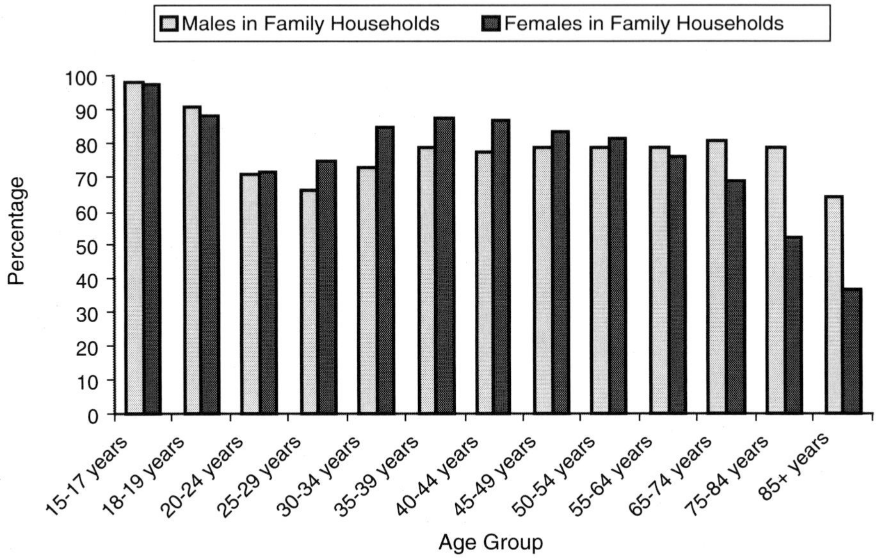

FIGURE 6-4 Male and female percentages for living with a family member, by age and sex.
SOURCE: U.S. Census Bureau (2009).

care will resemble a team environment, one in which team members will vary widely in their skills. Communication skills are central to expert team performance. Team environments also place a high premium on training members for their roles (Salas and Cannon-Bowers, 2001), a usually neglected aspect of home health care settings. I restrict consideration mainly to noninstitutionalized dwellings (apartments, detached and semidetached houses) rather than congregate housing (e.g., assisted living and chronic care institutions), primarily because the vast majority of Americans live in such dwellings for most of their lives, spending only a few years in assisted living or other chronic care residences. For example, for people ages 65+, only about 5 percent live in congregate housing settings, although percentages rise steeply with age.

DEMOGRAPHICS OF HEALTH CARE USERS

Every member of the population is a potential home health care user. So, for example, knowing the palm-down press and twist strength of children, young adults, and older adults is helpful for designing the cap mechanisms on prescription drug containers. One needs to ensure that opening requirements are too great for toddlers but not for older adults with arthritic hands. There are good sources of ergonomic information for different subsets of the population (e.g., Kroemer, 2005), although chronicling user capabilities for the entire population (e.g., some disabled veterans have lost limbs and use prostheses) is beyond the scope of this chapter. However, given that those with chronic conditions incur about 90 percent of the health care expenditures, they are the primary focus of this review.

Although it is difficult to predict trends for home health care utilization (or cost; Manton, Lamb, and Gu, 2007), given current promising trends of increasing disability-free longevity (e.g., Manton, Gu, and Lowrimore, 2008), one relatively safe prediction is that those already suffering from impairments are candidates to reach old age with fewer financial resources and with disabilities that will complicate treatment of other chronic conditions likely to arise. Those with disabilities are much less likely to be employed full time. For example, the unemployment rate in May 2009 for those ages 16 and over who were not institutionalized in the United States was 8.9 percent for persons without a disability and 13.7 percent for those with one (see http://www.bls.gov/cps/cpsdisability.htm [accessed June 2010]). Thus, at least for expected income levels, which strongly influence health care consumption, the life chances for those with a disability are likely to be poorer. There are two obvious subgroups for disability: civilians and wounded veterans who are classified as disabled.

Disability

According to the American Community Survey (ACS), in 2006 there were approximately 41.3 million people in the United States who reported some form of disability. Disability rises with age, particularly after age 65. Figure 6-5 shows percentage data for men and women derived from the 2006 ACS. (Data were downloaded as an Excel spreadsheet for a Factfinder query based on the U.S. population.) Disability is defined in that survey as "a long-lasting sensory, physical, mental, or emotional condition or conditions that make it difficult for a person to do functional or participatory activities such as seeing, hearing, walking, climbing stairs, learning, remembering, concentrating, dressing, bathing, going outside the home, or working at a job."

Percentages can be misleading, so Figure 6-6 shows the numbers in millions from the ACS. Although percentage of disability rises with age past 65, the majority of disabled individuals are in their working years. Assuming that a moderate percentage of them reach old age (mortality can be expected to be higher than in the general population, e.g., three times higher for those with an intellectual disability; Tyrer, Smith, and McGorther, 2007), they will constitute a very large cohort that will need significant assistance with self-care activities, and many others in the nondisabled segments of the population can be expected to transition into their ranks as they age.

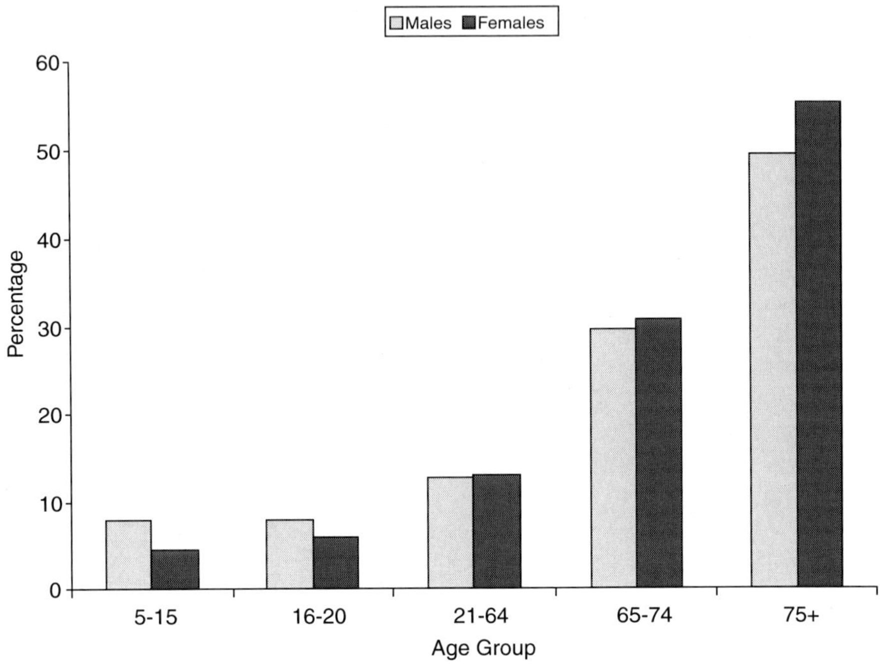

FIGURE 6-5 Percentage of the U.S. civilian noninstitutionalized population reporting any disability, 2006.
SOURCE: Based on data from U.S. Census Bureau (2010).

Veterans

According to a recent report sponsored by the Veterans Administration (VA), approximately 2.6 million veterans were receiving disability compensation benefits in September 2007 (Economic Systems Inc., 2008). Disabled veterans include those from World War II onward, including Korea, Vietnam, and more recent conflicts in Iraq and Afghanistan.

The types of service-connected disability classifications that are most prevalent are musculoskeletal (45 percent) and mental disorders, including posttraumatic stress disorder (PTSD) (15 percent), with other categories comprising less than 10 percent each. For recent disability compensation enrollees in the period 2001-2007 (approximately 776,500 individuals), the most common disorders reported were tinnitus (215,000 cases, 8.3 percent) and defective hearing (171,000 cases), followed by diabetes (143,000 cases) and PTSD (113,000 cases).

Note that not all veterans with impairments apply for and receive

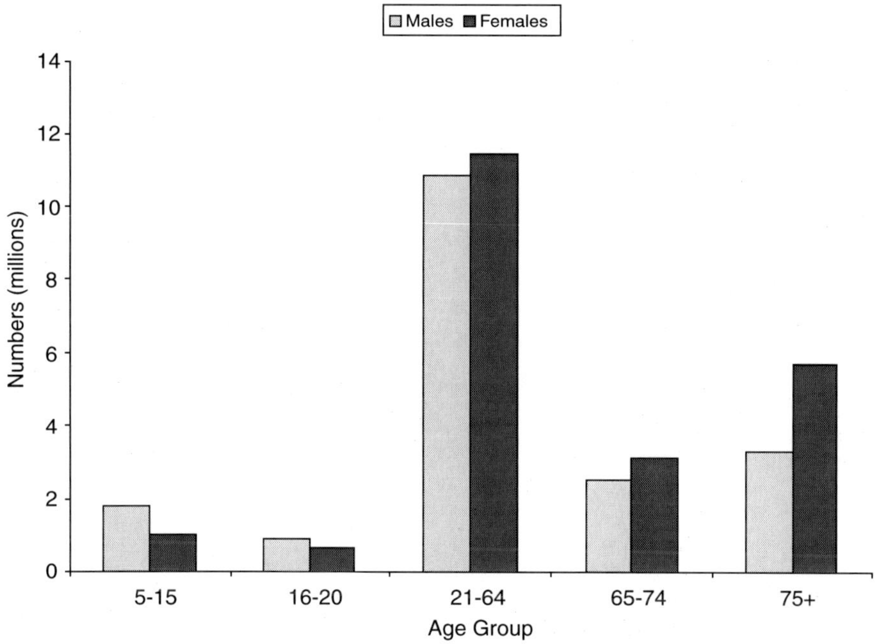

FIGURE 6-6 Numbers of the U.S. civilian noninstitutionalized population reporting any disability, 2006.
SOURCE: Based on data from U.S. Census Bureau (2010).

disability compensation from the VA, so the number of uncompensated cases in the general population could be significant (although presumably they would be captured in ACS data sets). Also, one article (http://www.nytimes.com/2009/07/13/us/13backlog.html?hpw [accessed July 2009]) suggests that there is a significant backlog for processing VA disability claims of about 400,000 cases. Nonetheless, even if one assumed that a significant proportion of disabled veterans are in institutional settings not counted in the ACS survey, disabled veterans represent about 6 percent of the total disabled population in the United States. However, one should note that the VA definition of disability and the definition in surveys such as the ACS are quite different.

Finally, the types of disability in veteran populations are likely to differ from those in the civilian population and have implications for home health care system design. Given the very high prevalence of musculoskeletal and hearing problems, health care device manufacturers need to pay heed to ease of manipulation (for example, permit one-handed operation of devices similar to requirements for keyboard use in Section 508 of the Rehabilitation Act) and provision of instruction through text rather than through voice. Similarly, for these veteran populations, vision rather than audition should be the preferred channel for providing information about system states and warnings.

Diversity in Users of Home Health Care

The U.S. population, like that of many other nations, is changing. And the changes encompass characteristics that relate to health status, such as age, gender, education level, and ethnicity. I briefly review some of those changes, at the general population level, as they pertain to health care utilization and, when information is available, to health technology use. What becomes obvious for each category is that there is enormous diversity in the United States, making the tasks of designing home health care devices and training challenging ones.

Age

The U.S. population continues to age because of its relatively low birth rates coupled with declining death rates. The population pyramid is also "lumpy" because of the very large cohort of babies (baby boom generation) born between 1946 and 1964, although it is expected to become more rectangular by 2050.

Assuming that war or natural disasters (such as epidemics) do not suddenly increase mortality rates in the United States, the projected population pyramids indicate that there will be greater than a doubling in the size of the group ages 65 and older (from about 35 million in 2000 to 80 million in 2050) and a quadrupling in the size of the group ages 85 and older (from about 5 to 20 million). These age ranges are associated with high consumption of health care, in part because chronic conditions show strong age-related increases, and some dementing diseases, such as Alzheimer's, occur very rarely before the age of 50. An example of age-related increases in serious health conditions can be seen in Figure 6-7, showing moderate or severe memory impairment. Advanced age is a strong negative predictor of information technology use for current elders (Czaja and Lee, 2008). This trend of lower use with age goes back at least a quarter of a century (e.g., the 1981 survey of technology use reported in Brickfield, 1984) and can be expected to hold in future older cohorts.

Gender

The older population, now and somewhat less so in the future, is likely to be predominantly female, and hence women living alone are likely targets

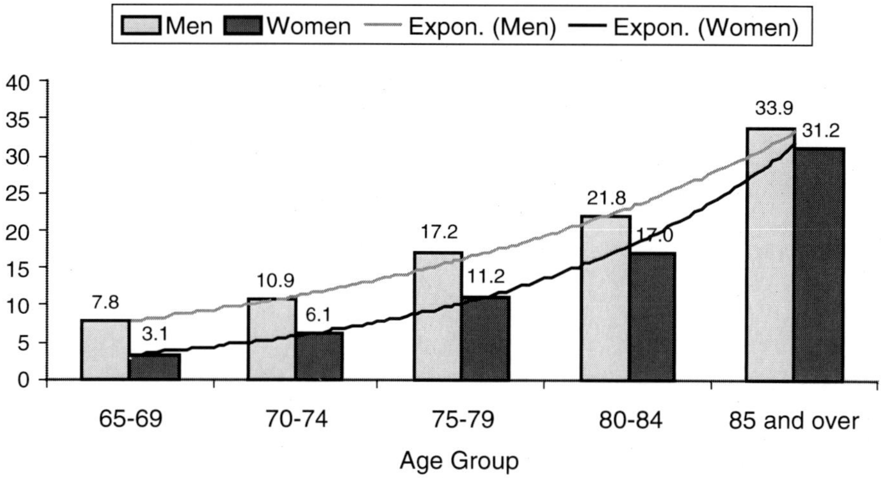

FIGURE 6-7 Percentage of the elderly with moderate or severe memory impairment, 2006.
NOTE: The definition of "moderate or severe memory impairment" is four or fewer words recalled (out of 20) on combined immediate and delayed recall tests.
SOURCE: National Institute on Aging, National Institutes of Health, and U.S. Department of Health and Human Services (2007).

of home health care in old age. Although there were early indications that women were less likely than men to be technology adopters (particularly computer and Internet users), this has changed (Cooper and Kugler, 2008). There are still gender-related differences in types of use, however. As an example, the author's 84-year-old mother uses e-mail and instant messaging as well as some web browsing, and his 86-year-old father primarily uses stock market software and a fax machine, relying on a telephone to communicate with relatives and friends. However, as discussed below, use of such technology is sharply lower in today's elders.

Education

In general, there has been a remarkable increase in educational achievement over the past 70 years in the United States. The percentage of the population ages 25 and older with four years of high school has risen from less than 40 percent in 1940 to nearly 90 percent in 2008. For four or more years of college, there was a sixfold increase, from 5 to over 30 percent. Part of the increase in attainment may be attributed to a concomitant increase in cognitive ability worldwide (measured with intelligence tests, such as the Army Alpha administered to military draftees), known as the Flynn effect (Flynn, 1987). Higher educational attainment is associated with higher income, better health, and greater longevity. These education and cognitive increases bode well for the ability of future generations to cope with complex health care equipment, with the caveat that as people age, such "fluid" abilities can show dramatic declines (Salthouse, 2010).

Ethnicity

There are also going to be marked changes in the ethnic composition of the United States over the coming decades, particularly in the older population (see Figure 6-8). The non-Hispanic white population of seniors is expected to increase about 80 percent, whereas blacks will increase about threefold, and Hispanics, Asians, and American Indians will increase nearly sevenfold in total. There are health status disparities across ethnic groups. Also, with respect to technology generally, such as computer and Internet use, nonwhites currently show less use than whites. Also, as discussed below, attitudes toward health care issues vary with ethnicity.

Language Use

A critical issue for providing instructions to home health care technology users is determining people's language comprehension abilities, particularly in English. Data from the American Community Survey for 2005-2007 show that, of those who report that they do not speak English at home, about 37 percent report that they speak English less than "very well." For the largest language group, Spanish, 16 million speak English less than "very well." An earlier (2003) assessment of adult basic English reading skills (Baer, Kutner, and Sabatini, 2009) yielded similar findings, showing about 11 million Americans with below basic literacy skills (reading letters, numbers, words, and comprehending simple texts, such as one from a medicine container). So, for example, when meeting with a health care professional, Spanish-speaking Americans may not easily express themselves (speaking skills), comprehend complex instructions when given in English (listening comprehension skills), or be able to use a health care device like a glucose meter when provided with written English instructions (reading comprehension skills). Translators (human or computer) may be needed in some instances, although current language translation software cannot compete with skilled human translators. However, the Internet does provide free and convenient access to short-passage written language translation in many common languages (e.g., http://babelfish.yahoo.com/ [accessed May 2010]).

Thus, it is obvious that for a significant number of people their English language skills will be weak (and their education level is likely to be low),

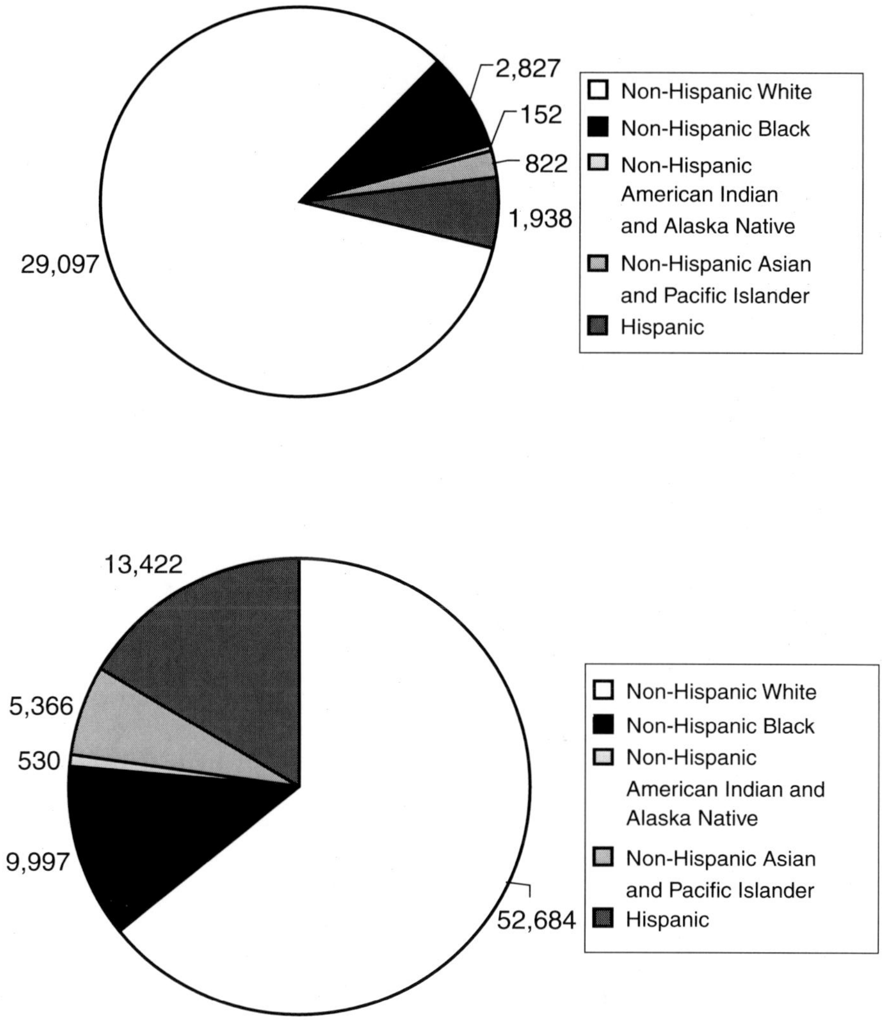

FIGURE 6-8 Ethnic composition of the U.S. population ages 65+ in 2000 and projections for 2050.
SOURCE: U.S. Census Bureau, Population Projections of the United States by Age, Sex, Race, Hispanic Origin, and Nativity: 1999 to 2100. Available: http://www.census.gov/population/www/projections/natproj.html and http://www.census.gov/population/projections/nation/detail/np-d2.txt [accessed August 2010].

and English-only instructions will not be adequate to ensure accurate comprehension. Whether such barriers as weak language or cognitive skills can be surmounted by having instructional materials that make greater use of symbols, diagrams, or video is not yet well understood (e.g., Morrell and Park, 1993) although video demonstrations of the use of some health care devices are already available on the Internet in languages other than English (e.g., a glucose meter with Spanish instructions on YouTube). At present, people with weak comprehension skills are likely to have lower socioeconomic status and hence be less likely to have fast, convenient access to the Internet.

Home Health Care Use

There are few good sources for assessing home health care use, simply because people do not typically provide records of minor injuries or short-term illnesses that are typically treated at home. As an example, the author's spouse broke her ankle in 2008 and became quite disabled while confined for a month in a nonwalking cast, having significant initial difficulty performing ADLs. There are few if any public records of this incident, aside from an application filed with the state of Florida for a handicapped parking sticker. However, once people (older or low income) use public funding for medical care, such as the Medicare/Medicaid system, records are available to track such incidents.

Medicare tracks home health expenditures through the Medical Expenditures Panel. The cost of such usage is increasing, although policy changes implemented in 1997 reduced expenditures from 1997 to 1999, more so for the lowest income groups and the frailest patients (Zhu, 2004). Expenditures for home health care since 1999 have continued to increase, although not as fast as for nursing home care (see Figure 6-9). Such patterns suggest that if health care could be delivered more effectively in the home, chronic care treatment costs for older adults could be significantly curtailed. There is evidence through meta-analysis that home care modestly reduces hospital use/cost (Hughes et al., 1997). There is considerable interest in updating technology in the home to produce so-called smart homes or aware homes; however, a recent report looking at smart home technology failed to find a single study suitable for inclusion in the analysis of the efficacy of such homes (Martin et al., 2008).

There is no lack of imagination for how to supply home health care devices and systems (e.g., Dishman, Matthews, and Dunbar-Jacob, 2004; Horgas and Abowd, 2004). However, there is reason to be cautious about seeing this brave new world any time soon, in part because those who would provide and use such systems have not been fully involved in their design and sometimes have unrealistic expectations about ease of use or

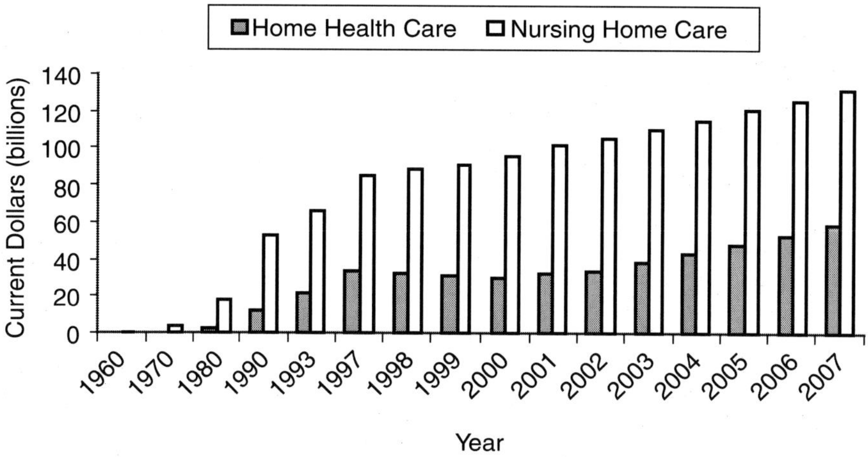

FIGURE 6-9 Expenditures (in constant dollars) on nursing home care and home health care.
SOURCE: Centers for Medicare & Medicaid Services, Office of the Actuary, National Health Statistics Group. Available: http://www.cms.gov/NationalHealthExpendData/downloads/tables.pdf [accessed August 2010].

cost. Thus, one must consider the person-environment fit for any home health care device and system, and this leads to the first commandment of human factors and ergonomics, sometimes phrased as "Honor thy user" or "Know thy user."

PERCEPTUAL, COGNITIVE, AND PSYCHOMOTOR CAPABILITIES OF USERS

I now briefly review some of the normative changes with age (and disability) that can affect interactions with home health care technology, giving some examples for such abilities as perception, cognition, and psychomotor ability, and anthropometrics.

Perception

In order for a user to interact with a home health care device, it must be perceived in some way. That information channel could be visual, haptic (touch), aural (smell or taste is less likely), or some combination of these modalities. The disabled population and the older population typically have impairments in some or all of these sensory and perceptual systems. Even the general population above the age of 45-50 is highly unlikely to be able to focus the lens of the eye on fine visual details without corrective lenses.

Thus, text should minimally be about 12 points (x-height) and shown with high contrast (e.g., black on white), and diagrams with fine visual details should be magnified in any materials provided to instruct or train the user. Such guidelines are often violated with printed medication information, as seen in Figure 6-10, in part due to constraints of packaging. Prescription drug containers are now often accompanied by page-sized instruction sheets that do use larger print (although that information may easily become separated from the pill container). As well, lighting in homes generally needs to be increased, although glare should be avoided, given changes to the eye that result in less effective transmission of light through to the retina. There is also some loss of color sensitivity at short wavelengths, making violet-blue-green discrimination more difficult. Given that a significant percent of males in the general population have defective color vision (about 5-8 percent), signaling important information solely through color cues (e.g., red versus green) should be avoided.

Furthermore, particularly for aging men, audition is likely to be impaired, meaning that sounds need to be more intense and environmental noise needs to be minimized to permit adequate comprehension of speech or perception of auditory warnings. For example, alarms on home health care equipment, such as oxygen concentrators, follow standards set by the U.S. Food and Drug Administration and international bodies (e.g., ISO standard IEC 60601-1-8) that specify details, such as the number of frequencies pres-

Drug Facts

Active ingredient (in each tablet) **Purpose**
Aspirin 325 mg..Pain reliever/fever reducer

Uses ■ temporarily relieves:
■ headache ■ pain of colds ■ toothache pain ■ menstrual pain
■ muscle aches and pains ■ minor aches and pains of arthritis
■ temporarily reduces fever

Warnings
Reye's syndrome: Children and teenagers should not use this drug for chicken pox or flu symptoms before a doctor is consulted about Reye's syndrome, a rare but serious illness reported to be associated with aspirin.
Allergy alert: Aspirin may cause a severe allergic reaction which may include: ■ hives ■ facial swelling
■ asthma (wheezing) ■ shock
Alcohol warning: If you consume 3 or more alcoholic drinks every day, ask your doctor if you should take aspirin or other pain relievers/fever reducers. Aspirin may cause stomach bleeding.
Do not use ■ if you have ever had an allergic reaction to any other pain reliever/fever reducer ■ if you are allergic to aspirin

FIGURE 6-10 Scanned image (actual size) of medication information for an aspirin bottle. Print size is too small for older adults with presbyopia and those with visual impairments.

ent in the warning sound, but apparently not the decibel level for the alarm, relying on "the experience of medical equipment designers." For users who are hard of hearing, such audible alarms may not be very audible, although the devices also use flashing light indicators. See Fisk et al. (2009) for a review of older adult capabilities and a guide to design.

Cognition

Some aspects of cognition improve with age, particularly the accumulation of knowledge tapped by tests of certain aspects of intelligence and, in young children, the ability to hold and manipulate information in working memory (e.g., as indexed with memory span measures; Dempster, 1981). Thus, particularly when considering adherence to routines that require prospective memory (i.e., remembering to carry out future actions), young children are likely to be disadvantaged. An example might be medication adherence, for which a caregiver would be required to assist the child in taking prescription drugs. Another case would be remembering to carry an inhaler to school to treat potential asthma attacks (see American Academy of Pediatrics, 2009, for general advice about home health care for children).[3]

In adulthood, the usual pattern is for abstract problem-solving skills (fluid abilities) to decline sharply, with a drop of about 1.5 to 2 standard deviations between the 20s and the 80s (Salthouse, 2010). Such declines are likely to have an impact on the ability to troubleshoot new malfunctioning health care devices. A particularly striking change in cognition is slowing in the learning rate. An older adult may require twice as much time as younger adults to learn to use software (e.g., Charness et al., 2001). Thus, when needing to learn to use a new home health care device from instructional materials, both very young children and older adults are likely to be disadvantaged, as will be those with poor English comprehension skills and veterans with closed head injuries (increasingly common for recent veterans because of roadside bomb incidents). Maximizing ease of comprehension by ensuring that instructional prose is at a grade 8 or lower level, coupled with providing some indication of training time needed (to provide realistic expectations), could help less cognitively able users. See Charness and Czaja (2006) for an overview of issues in training older workers that has relevance to the use of health care devices.

Normal aging is likely to impair working memory capacity (ability

[3]Although the guidelines are aimed primarily at pediatricians, much of the advice revolves around ensuring that caregiver teams be properly trained to administer treatment for the specific condition, with little concrete advice on how to conduct the training or how to assess its efficacy and cost-effectiveness.

to store and manipulate cognitive representations) and speed of processing generally—and even more so for abnormal aging or dementia (see Jastrzembski and Charness, 2007, for information processing parameters for younger and older adults). Such cognitive changes could, for example, make it difficult to learn and remember the step-by-step procedure needed for blood glucose monitoring (which might be 50-60 steps long; Rogers et al., 2001). Thus, users need better "environmental support" (Morrow and Rogers, 2008), by having relevant cues to procedures out in the environment (e.g., having the device provide prompts to the user for tasks), rather than stressing working memory capacity by requiring memory for a long procedure.

Although knowledge tends to increase with age, there are major individual differences in knowledge in the population (e.g., as a function of education) and particularly in knowledge about health, termed health literacy (e.g., in the ability to comprehend written health instructions, see Benson and Forman, 2002; measured in national surveys, see National Center for Education Statistics, 2006). However, this construct may overlap substantially with general cognitive ability (Morrow et al., 2006; Levinthal et al., 2008).

Cognitive changes associated with normal aging, with a dementing illness, and with closed head injuries may also have effects on health care decision making. In some cases—for example, for breast cancer and prostate cancer treatment—there can be considerable uncertainty about the best course of action (e.g., see decision making by younger and older adults in Meyer, Talbot, and Ranalli, 2007). For a review of the heuristics involved in decision making under uncertainty, see Kahneman and Tversky (1979) and Gigerenzer and Goldstein (1996). A recent meta-synthesis outlines some of the factors involved in shared decision-making processes among patients and health care providers (Edwards, Davies, and Edwards, 2008). Factors involved in the information exchange process during health consultations were broken into practitioner influences, patient influences, and joint influences. Practitioner factors included receptiveness to informed patients and patient choice, knowledge of cultural differences, and degree of patient centeredness or stereotyping. Patient factors included motivation to seek information, appraisal of information (particularly before the interview), cultural identity, and how risk was managed for poor information. Joint influences included differing illness notions, role expectations, and language. Health literacy was identified as an important mediator. Diminished cognition in a health care recipient will obviously affect most facets of joint decision making.

Psychomotor Ability

The slowing in basic information processing speed in middle adulthood mentioned above is also accompanied by less precision in physical movements, such as moving a cursor with a mouse or moving from one key to another on an input device. Accurate movement involves making microcorrections at the end of movement trajectories, as people undershoot or overshoot on their approach to a target, and general slowing will impact such corrections. Older adults need larger targets (e.g., large, well-spaced keys on keyboard devices) or shorter distances to move to ensure fast, accurate movement. Good design of input devices for home health care systems becomes even more important when considering those with limb tremor or movement initiation disorders (e.g., Parkinson's disease).

Older adults often also have slower walking speeds and experience negative changes to the vestibular system that make balance less stable, increasing the risk of injury when performing caregiver tasks, such as helping a spouse with transfers from bed or toilet, although help is coming from robotics advances.

Anthropometrics

The size, shape, and flexibility of the human body set important constraints on the way that people interact with tools and environments. One important variation in anthropometric capabilities involves gender. Women are about five inches shorter and two-thirds as strong, on average, as men (for age-related values for anthropometric capabilities, see Steenbekkers and van Beijsterveldt, 1998; Kroemer, 2005). This can affect IADLs, such as cooking (e.g., retrieving and opening jars), caregiver activities, such as assisting a mobility-impaired spouse, and even opening a childproof prescription drug container. As well, there are normative changes in height (people shrink in size) as well as in strength (which diminishes) as people age. However, one of the concerns with population-based approaches to design is that the average capability may describe no member of the sample particularly well. For example, a classic guideline is to design for the 85th percentile capability of a population, but this tends to have an adverse impact on important population subgroups, such as women and children.

USER AND PROVIDER ATTITUDES TOWARD HEALTH CARE AND HEALTH CARE TECHNOLOGY

Attitudes are frequently invoked as an important factor in health care utilization, although most studies provide associations. General attitudes toward health and health care may constrain utilization and treatment adherence no matter what a person's cognitive, perceptual, or psychomotor capabilities. An individual's social network may also play an important role in the process. As an example, a national survey of health care professionals treating child and adolescent obesity found that health care providers cited as barriers to successful treatment both parental involvement and patient motivation (Story et al., 2002).

The well-known observation that men consume less health care than women has prompted considerable speculation about whether attitudes may play a role, such as greater reluctance on the part of men to seek help for health conditions. However, after adjusting for reproductive-related care and age-specific mortality rate differences, there are no sex differences in per capita expenditures when universal health care coverage is available (Mustard et al., 1998). There is evidence consistent with the view that cultural differences in attitudes toward seeking help might underlie ethnic differences in health care utilization (e.g., underutilization by Vietnamese Americans; Thang, Patrick, and Nash, 2009).

Attitudes That Influence Use of Home Health Care Technology

There is not enough space to describe the vast literature on the role of attitudes in health behavior.[4] Chapter 11, on social and cultural environments, addresses some key issues; see Cameron (2009) for an overview of major models of persuasion that involve attitude effects. Probably the most popular framework is the theory of planned behavior (Ajzen, 1991), which postulates that behavioral intentions (e.g., for health this might involve diet, exercise, medication adherence, safe sex practices) are best predicted from attitudes toward the behavior, subjective norms about the behavior (e.g., family and friend opinions), willingness to comply with those norms, as well as beliefs about one's ability to engage in the behavior (control beliefs, such as self-efficacy). Here I focus primarily on the narrower case of attitudes that may influence home health care technology use. Both user and prescriber attitudes are potential barriers to adoption. Attitudes can be differentiated as general (e.g., feelings of self-efficacy approaching any new device) or specific (e.g., feeling inadequate about computer troubleshooting, trusting that a device will work safely or reliably).

As noted in an Institute of Medicine report (1996), demands on health care personnel to learn and deploy telemedicine systems (which are increasingly being used for home health care) are a sticking point for adoption. Similarly, unfamiliarity with technology may be a barrier to adoption. Technology adoption in the United States has accelerated over the past century

[4]A search in PsycINFO for "attitudes" and "health" as keywords turned up nearly 40,000 references.

(Charness, 2008a) in part because of falling prices, the presence of infrastructure to support deployment, and the exponential increase in wealth. To take the iconic case of the digital computer, there has been a major shift in the public's perceptions and attitudes toward the computer (e.g., from being seen as scary or threatening; Lee, 1970) as it downsized from a huge, vacuum-tube-laden mass of hardware to a compact consumer product. Still, a Pew Internet and American Life survey (Charness, 2008b) showed that older adults and those with less education were less likely to endorse an item that "technology provides more control over life" and that this control belief was a significant predictor of technology use.

One barrier to widespread delivery of health care information and telehealth services to the home is lack of access to high-speed communication channels, and particularly the Internet, for older adults and low-income users. As Figure 6-11 shows for a recent data set, although Internet access has nearly quadrupled in the past decade for those ages 65 and older, this age group (with chronic health conditions) was still at very low levels of Internet use, 40 percent. Use dropped strikingly with age if this age group was divided into more typical young-old, middle-old, and old-old

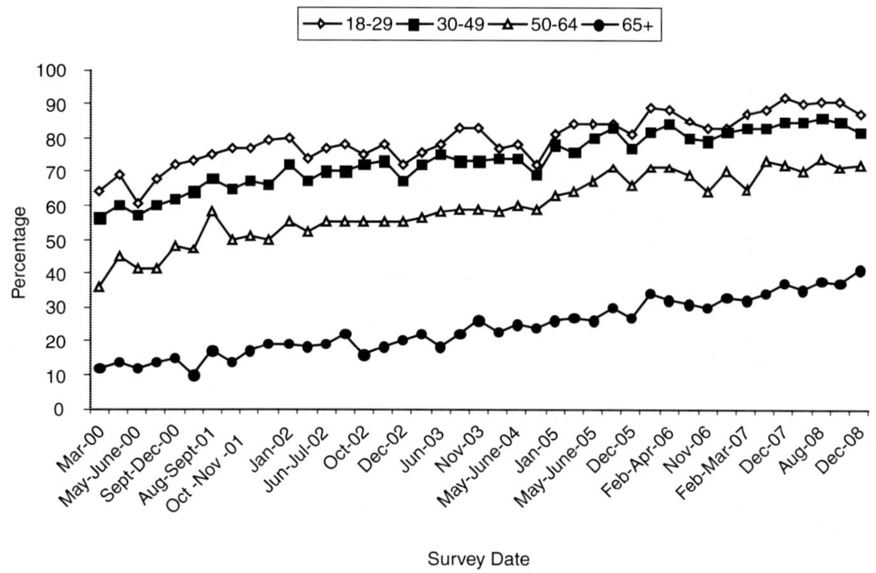

FIGURE 6-11 Percentage of Internet use by age group from March 2000-December 2008.
SOURCE: Pew Internet and American Life Project trend data for "usage over time." Available: http://www.pewinternet.org/Trend-Data/Usage-Over-Time.aspx [accessed August 2010].

age categories (39, 24, and 8 percent, respectively, for March 2007 data; Charness and Boot, 2009). Furthermore, a significant predictor of computer and Internet use is education and income (Kaiser Family Foundation, 2005); economically disadvantaged groups, who are also the most likely to be in poorer health (e.g., Marmot and Shipley, 1996; Crimmins, Kim, and Seeman, 2009), are the least able to access health care information and services in this way.[5]

Survey research suggests that attitudes toward health care and health care technology are related to a number of factors, including age, gender, and ethnicity. Katz and Rice (2009) gathered survey data (n = 1,106) that was representative of the U.S. population on interest in getting new or existing services on mobile devices, and particularly radio-frequency identification (RFID) devices attached to the arm or mobile phone. Medical information, such as a hotline to a doctor or notices about health information on mobile devices, was rated less highly on a 1-5 scale (2.2-2.3) than having those devices provide television programs or ads about services (3.7-3.8). There was more interest in monitoring health on the mobile phone (3.1 rating) and very little concern about privacy threat (ratings 2.0-2.5) or privacy rights (rating of 1.5).

In a qualitative analysis of focus groups with congestive heart failure and chronic obstructive pulmonary disease (Rahimpour et al., 2008), low self-efficacy and anxiety were factors identified as affecting perceptions and potential acceptance of a home telecare system (shown in a video). Those with lower self-efficacy and greater anxiety about the video expressed more negative attitudes about intention to use the system.

Blackhall and colleagues (1999) examined general and personal attitudes toward the use of life-sustaining technology (with such questionnaire items as "If life prolonging technology exists, it should always be used") in a diverse sample of 200 older adults in Los Angeles County. They found greater acceptability of such technology use in Korean American than in African American and Mexican American, and least in European American groups. Men were more accepting than women. Income (less acceptable for higher income than lower) and personal experience with illness (those with more experience about withholding care were less accepting) also played a role in acceptability.

When the question was, "If you were in a coma, and your physicians felt that there was a small but uncertain chance of regaining full awareness and function but a greater chance of surviving with severe mental dis-

[5]Although current young cohorts will be more computer and Internet literate when they reach old age, technology will continue to advance, and they too can expect to fall behind the technology curve because of slowing in the learning rate with aging (Charness and Boot, 2009).

abilities, would you want: (a) cardiopulmonary resuscitation; (b) mechanical ventilation?"—the significant factors associated with acceptance were ethnicity, gender, and access to health care, all operating in the same direction as above. In general, people tended to be more accepting of the use of life support technology on others than on themselves. This fits with models of attitudes being differentiable so that general tendencies are less associated with actions to be taken than are specific attitudes (Ajzen and Fishbein, 1977).

A sparsely researched topic in attitudes is the role of religion or religiosity in health care practice. The research literature has found that religiosity is associated with better health (e.g., Krause, 2008), perhaps through the mediating effects of belonging to a close-knit social group and the sense of meaning in life that religious beliefs support. Religiosity can play a major role in home health care when congregants of a religious organization provide services to people who are ill at home. Although some religious beliefs directly affect willingness to accept certain treatments—for example, blood transfusions, or to permit autopsies to be carried out to diagnose causes of death—there are undoubtedly also subtle influences from beliefs, such as what constitutes God's will, that will affect willingness to seek or to accept home health care treatment. There are also not so subtle effects of religious/political attitudes when political authorities such as a state intervene to enforce medical treatment.[6]

Another sparsely investigated area of research is individual differences in trust about home health care. For example, trust may play a role in whether someone will seek or accept (care recipient) or offer (provider) help. General trust in medical advice may vary with ethnicity (Krakauer, Crenner, and Fox, 2002).

With respect to attitudes toward technology and computer anxiety, the older adult literature has shown that rather than attitudes predicting people's performance when trained with that technology, their attitudes change as a function of success with training (e.g., Czaja and Lee, 2008). So there is reason to be optimistic that those with negative attitudes toward health care technology might change in a positive direction if the equipment is well designed and well supported.

Privacy and Confidentiality

Privacy and confidentiality are often cited as concerns for those hoping to provide remote monitoring in homes (or even just for entry of home health care workers), and several frameworks for distinguishing and

[6]Perhaps the most famous recent case of state and federal religiously motivated intervention was the Terry Schiavo case concerning removal of a feeding tube (Quill, 2005).

understanding these concerns have been advanced (Caine, Fisk, and Rogers, 2006; Hensel, Demiris, and Courtney, 2006). However, data are scarce, with early studies being based on very small focus group samples (Demiris et al., 2004; Mynatt et al., 2004). Fox (2000) looked at a large (n = 2,117) representative sample of Americans in the Pew Internet and American Life Project and found that, although Internet users have a strong stated preference for privacy when they go online, their risky behavior online does not match their stated concerns (19 percent reported credit card or identity theft, although only 8 percent of those cases involved online theft). If anything, older Americans were more concerned than younger ones with privacy (concern was reported as "notably higher" in Fox's report). One randomized controlled study found greater concern with confidentiality (item was "I was worried that others were listening or watching") between patients in a telemedicine intervention compared with face-to-face treatment (Chua et al., 2001).

Aside from the Katz and Rice (2009) study mentioned above, which did not have privacy as the sole focus, one large-sample privacy study, Beach et al. (2009), used a web-based survey (hence unlikely to be representative of the older adult population) and was unique in its focus on both older and disabled populations. The critical finding in that study was that more impaired people (older, more disabled) were more willing to share health information (about toileting, medications, movement in the home, cognitive ability, driving behavior) with family members and health care workers, although not with insurance companies or government entities, for the expectation of better care. Curiously, there were few age differences in privacy concerns in this sample, with older adults slightly more willing to share (age ranges: 45-64, 65+). It appears that privacy issues (that is, who has access to what information) are not a strong barrier to home monitoring or mobile monitoring, any more than they have been to electronic commerce.[7] As long as perceived usefulness and ease of use (benefits) outweigh perceived costs, people, including older adults (Melehnorst, Rogers, and Bouwhuis, 2006), are willing to adopt technology (e.g., the technology acceptance model of Venkatesh and Davis, 2000).

Nonetheless, it is apparent that different user subgroups exist in the general population with respect to familiarity with, positive attitudes toward, and ability to use home health care technology, and the design community needs to keep this in mind.

---

[7]Two purveyors of database systems for industry and government were perhaps prescient a decade ago in their comments. Larry Ellison, chief executive officer of Oracle, said "The privacy you are concerned about is largely an illusion." (http://valleywag.gawker.com/152187/larry-ellisons-privacy-is-largely-an-illusion [accessed May 2010]). And Scott McNealy, chief executive officer of Sun Microsystems, said "You have zero privacy. Get over it." (http://www.wired.com/politics/law/news/1999/01/17538 [accessed May 2010]).

Joint Influences on Technology Adoption

Although it is challenging enough to study the simple effects of cognition, perception, and attitudes on home health care use, it is even more challenging to look at joint effects. A salient study that looked at how attitudes, age, and cognitive factors affected technology use, including computer and Internet use, is Czaja et al. (2006). They found that measures of cognitive ability, either fluid or crystallized ones, were strong independent predictors of technology use, including computer and Internet use. Other predictors were attitudes toward technology (computer anxiety, computer self-efficacy) and age.

Thus, it is not surprising that technology use clearly declines with age in nationally representative samples (e.g., Pew Internet and American Life studies of computer and Internet use; Mobilate study in Europe: Tacken et al., 2005). Although this is discouraging from the perspective that older adults (who have chronic conditions) are the most likely to be in need of health care information and access to the Internet might help, it is not the case that they are averse to adopting all health-related technology. As Figure 6-12 illustrates, in contrast to Internet and computer use, mobile phone adoption is relatively high, even in older age categories (50 percent at ages 75-84). Thus, use of mobile phones in telemedicine interventions (e.g., Quinn et al., 2009) is feasible for that group, assuming that people can be convinced to adopt smart phone technology and adopt data plans that provide Internet access from the phone. However, at present, such devices represent a small percentage of overall mobile phone use in the United States (about 25 percent of mobile phone users; see http://news.cnet.com/8301-10787_3-10157264-60.html [accessed May 2010]). Communication devices are central to remote delivery of health care, the burgeoning field of telehealth.

Telehealth Technology

Some of the most promising approaches to supplying home health care come from the field of telemedicine or, as it is also known, telehealth (or e-health). Human factors aspects of telehealth are discussed in Demiris et al. (in press). The practice of supplying health care advice at a distance dates back at least to the 17th century, when plague-stricken English villages would post warning signs at the village entrance (Darkins and Cary, 2000). The next big source of remote health care advice and delivery was the wired line telephone. There is evidence that offering advice through phone conversations leads to better mortality outcomes for Medicare-managed settings (e.g., Alkema et al., 2007). Today we take for granted such services as the ubiquitous 9-1-1 emergency number in the United States and

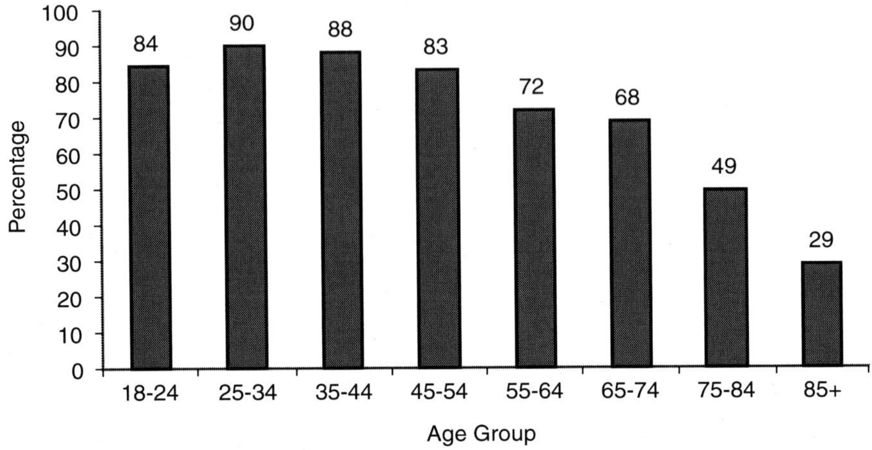

FIGURE 6-12 Mobile phone use by age group.
SOURCE: Pew Internet and American Life Project data for "usage over time." Available: http://www.pewinternet.org/Trend-Data/Usage-Over-Time.aspx [accessed August 2010].

elsewhere, except for controversies over how to access such services with mobile phone technology. Today, websites on the Internet are a potentially important source of health information for those with Internet access, despite expressed concerns with the accuracy of information on some sites. However, even reputable sites are not necessarily easy to navigate to find relevant information (e.g., the Medicare website; Czaja, Sharit, and Nair, 2008).

An important area for home health care is the monitoring of chronic conditions. Many telehomecare (remote home care) interventions attempt to monitor and treat such conditions as diabetes, congestive heart failure, and hypertension. Monitoring can take many forms, from question-administering devices that report back daily over telephone lines, to sensor sets deployed through the home to track activity and communicate over Internet connections, to complex wearable devices that monitor pulse, temperature, blood oxygen, location, and falls and can report back over wireless channels. In some cases, an instrumented ("aware") home (Mynatt et al., 2004) can become a coach.

As an Institute of Medicine (1996) report indicated, it is difficult to evaluate clinical applications of telemedicine for a number of reasons, including rapid advances that render some technologies obsolete, infrastructure that is not user-friendly and distracts from practical projects, and high demands on reluctant health care providers. Field and Grigsby (2002) noted that advances in remote monitoring seem to be driven by work with astronauts and elite athletes. Also, better technology was beginning to lower costs for transmitting information. These trends have continued with deployment of cellular (mobile phone) technologies that are increasing bandwidth, so-called third- and fourth-generation (3G, 4G) networks, although monthly bandwidth caps by providers make them impossible to use for videoconferencing at the moment (author's 2009 inquiry in Tallahassee, Florida). Together with changes in the subscription to high-speed wired connections in homes (copper wire for DSL, coaxial and fiber optic cable), there is now a better opportunity to transmit data to and from homes.

One can evaluate the impact of an intervention from such perspectives as clinical benefit and cost.[8] I use the term "efficacy" to refer to whether the treatment or intervention is better than no treatment or a placebo in a typical clinical trial. A more rigorous test of the intervention would be comparative clinical effectiveness: whether the new intervention is better than the current best clinical practice, also assessed with a clinical trial. However, clinical trials are typically carefully planned interventions with select populations and blinding, and some have argued that regular clinical practice situations may vary in important ways, suggesting the need for "pragmatic trials" (Macpherson, 2004) that use normal clinical settings without blinding. One could argue that human factors approaches can play an important role in ensuring that ideal interventions be implemented successfully in typical clinical settings. Finally, cost-effectiveness refers to the clinical benefit in the context of its cost. For example, if a telemedicine intervention has the same clinical benefit (efficacy or comparative clinical effectiveness) but costs less than a usual treatment, it would be more cost-effective.

An early review (Currell et al., 2000) was equivocal about the cost savings and clinical benefit of telemedicine. A later review was more positive (Hersh et al., 2001), showing significant clinical benefits for management of chronic conditions, including hypertension and AIDS, with less evidence of efficacy for diabetes. A quick review by the author of studies conducted subsequent to those reports indicates that cost-effectiveness was shown for management of congestive heart failure, although in a very small sample (Lehmann, Mintz, and Giacini, 2006) and in a randomized trial for controlling blood pressure (Parati et al., 2009) but not for rehabilitation in a large, quasi-experimental VA study (Bendixen et al., 2009). One can conclude that clinical efficacy for telemedicine is comparable to usual treatment and that patient satisfaction is usually very high. Cost-effectiveness is

[8]There does not appear to be complete agreement on terminology in this area. See http://www.hhs.gov/recovery/programs/cer/draftdefinition.html [accessed May 2010] for a framework on comparative effectiveness research.

generally unproven, except for cases in which costly transportation expense can be bypassed via videoconferencing.

Telehealth technology has been used for all phases of medical care, from diagnosis to treatment. Telehomecare has been shown to be cost-effective (Bowles and Baugh, 2007). A recent example in the area of mental health is diagnosis of dementia remotely through the use of a screening tool, the mini-mental state examination (Ciemins et al., 2009). Nonetheless, few evaluations have been made of the demands that such systems make on users with chronic conditions or on the willingness of users and their insurers to pay for this form of care.

EXAMPLES OF CONSTRAINTS IN TECHNOLOGY USE: HANDHELD DEVICES

The trend toward miniaturizing devices threatens to exclude potential users with diminished vision, hearing, or touch, although this may pose less of a problem for children. Portable device technology is now being introduced to get information to and from home health care users. Personal digital assistants for medication reminding (Mayhorn et al., 2005) and smart phones employed as part of a wireless communication system (Varshney, 2007) are somewhat handicapped by poor legibility (small screens with tiny fonts) and awkward input capabilities (small, closely spaced buttons or touchable icons). Although such systems are usable by those without significant impairments and can be improved for those with low vision when designed with appropriate tactile and audio feedback for key presses, they are not ideally suited for an aging or disabled health care-using population. Many devices are moving from stylus and button to touch screen input in the expectation that natural gestures will improve usability. But so-called natural gestures, such as a pinching movement on a touchscreen, could prove difficult or impossible for those with movement disorders or prosthetic limbs. Speech recognition may be a viable alternative to requiring fine motor movements (although only in quiet environments). See Lewis and colleagues (2008) for a discussion of human factors issues in designing handheld digital devices.

Personal anecdotes also underline the need for a better person-environment fit for mobile phone use at the level of device design and particularly for instructional support (which is often sparse for mobile phones). Take the case of two nonusing seniors being taught to use mobile phone technology following an acute health problem. When a woman more than 80 years old was in rehabilitation following an auto accident and out of touch (no telephone access could be quickly arranged in the facility), family members brought her a mobile phone and tried to instruct her to use it. However, given her background (high school education, limited technology experience), disabilities in cognition (mild dementia), pain (broken back), and poor vision (prior unsatisfactory cataract surgery), she was unable to use it effectively. Another similarly elderly woman coming from a more advantaged background (university education, computer user), when hospitalized with an acute gastric incident, was able to learn to use a mobile phone; however, her cognition and eyesight were very good, and the phone was a less complicated, large button model with carefully designed step-by-step instructions (courtesy of the author).

HUMAN FACTORS TOOLS FOR ASSESSING AND DESIGNING PERSON-ENVIRONMENT FIT

In order to assess and design for person-environment fit, the discipline of human factors and ergonomics has developed a number of tools, including task analysis, usability testing, modeling and simulation, questionnaires, and focus group techniques.

Task Analysis

A basic tool for assessing fit is a task analysis (based on Drury's presentation). This involves breaking down a complex task into a sequence of component operations, usually in a hierarchical fashion corresponding to the goals and subgoals that need to be achieved in order to complete the task successfully. The level of decomposition depends on the goals of the analysis as well as the type of device or environment. For an example, see the task analysis of using a blood glucose meter by Rogers and colleagues (2001). The idea behind such analyses is to uncover components of a task that are difficult to perform or error prone in order to redesign the device or its operating procedures (e.g., to make fewer demands on the user's limited-capacity working memory or speed of performance) or design better training materials to enable people to perform the task successfully (see the redesign of training materials for a glucose meter by Mykityshyn, Fisk, and Rogers, 2002).

Usability Testing

Often in conjunction with task analysis a usability test will be designed. Here the goal is to observe people attempting to perform representative tasks with the device under realistic conditions (e.g., in a home) in order to identify design and instructional flaws that can be remediated before the device is made available to a targeted user population. Depending on the level of detail needed for assessing performance, an experimenter may simply observe the user by taking notes with the aid of a checklist, make video recordings, ask the person to think aloud and record their voice while performing the task to reveal the problem-solving processes that they engage in, make eye movement recordings, and perhaps monitor the user with EEG or neuroimaging equipment if records of brain activity are needed. The device may be a working prototype, or a "Wizard of Oz" technique might be used, in which a human substitutes for some function in a device under development. An example of the latter might be having a human listener substitute for a speech comprehension module in a computer coaching system for a smart home that is not yet fully capable of speech comprehension. The human would type the words, which appear on the user's screen.

Modeling and Simulation

Either as an adjunct to usability testing or as an independent technique, models (e.g., mathematical) and simulations (e.g., computer models) can be used to predict typical human performance without the expense of bringing a user into a laboratory or following their activities in a home environment. Often this involves making use of preexisting simulation environments (e.g., for handheld medical devices, there is Bonnie John's CogTool; http://cogtool.hcii.cs.cmu.edu/ [accessed May 2010]) or using task analysis in combination with model human processor parameters (Card, Moran, and Newell, 1983) to predict how long tasks would take for different user groups or different devices. Such simulation techniques can uncover design flaws in devices (e.g., inadequate time-out intervals for input on some mobile phones; Jastrzembski and Charness, 2007) without the need for expensive usability testing and can do so for different populations (e.g., younger and older adults) when parameter estimates are available. Typically, a task, such as accessing a health message on a mobile phone, is decomposed into unit tasks (e.g., basic cognitive, perceptual, and motor operations) for which there are estimates of the unit task time or probability of error. The times (or errors) are then summed to estimate total task completion time (or error). Such analysis takes into account technology demands and user capabilities (see Figure 6-3) with degree of fit being determined by the time to complete the task or the probability of making an error.

Questionnaires and Focus Groups

Questionnaires can be an efficient way to assess some of the dimensions of person-environment fit, for either a high-tech or a low-tech device (e.g., an illuminated magnifying lens to help those with low vision to read health care instructions). Either standard instruments (e.g., that assess ease of use and perceived usefulness) or tailored ones can quickly probe user attitudes, satisfaction, and degree of workload experienced for a device. Similarly, focus group studies with transcription and coding of user discussion can uncover concerns and preferences in a reasonably cost-effective manner. For tutorials on these techniques, see Fisk et al. (2009).

GAPS IN KNOWLEDGE

Research is needed to fill in gaps about user attitudes, knowledge about the home environment, and knowledge about what home health care interventions are cost-effective.

Knowledge of User Attitudes

There is a lack of representative data on attitudes toward health care technologies (e.g., privacy concerns and trust), health care technology adoption, and, more importantly, technology abandonment. Surveys could be commissioned to address these issues as part of the U.S. Census Bureau's Current Population Survey. In general, there are few population-representative studies about health care technology attitudes and health care technology adoption. Few studies investigate the influence of potentially important mediators or moderators, such as ethnicity, gender, education/income, and age.

There are relatively well-developed models about factors that influence technology adoption that might be adapted to studying home health care technology adoption (e.g., the technology acceptance model). Technologies (and attitudes toward technologies) change rapidly, which makes knowledge acquisition a moving target. A related gap is knowledge about factors influencing abandonment of health care technology. It is evident that maintenance of technology is not simple or easy, so maintenance and repair are important issues to address, particularly for users with low income and education. Mass adoption of home telehealth technology is not likely until there is widespread, competent, and relatively inexpensive technical support available to users.

Knowledge of the Home

Recall that person-environment fit depends on characteristics of both the person and the environment. One reason for the rise of specialized environments for health care delivery, such as hospitals and clinics, is that, in theory, they provide standardized environments for tending to those in ill health. They can provide well-lit, quiet, clean, well-equipped rooms for treatment of patients with fast access to highly trained health care specialists. How does the typical home or apartment environment compare?

There are no systematic surveys of the home health care environment. How many households have access to modern telecommunications links (wireless, broadband)? How many homes have adequate wiring to support modern equipment?[9] Something as simple as lighting (which influences legibility of written instructions) varies enormously in homes, partly as a function of the age of the homeowner (Charness and Dijkstra, 1999). I would recommend incorporation of such questions into health care surveys (see as well Chapter 10 on the physical environment).

Knowledge of Home Health Care Efficacy and Cost-Effectiveness

What are the risks and benefits of treating chronic (and acute) conditions in the home? Cochrane reports indicate that there are too few randomized trials to assess efficacy (or cost-effectiveness) of telemedicine with much confidence. Undoubtedly, clinical trials are under way and further meta-analyses are being prepared, but given the unique features of each study from the perspective of population sampled and intervention chosen and also what constitutes usual care for the control group, it will be some time before there are definitive answers to the question of what form of home health care works best. One promising way to proceed is to abandon usual treatment as a comparison point and replace it with currently recognized best treatment.

RECOMMENDATIONS

In order to have successful deployment of home health care, there must be access, sound design, and appropriate training to ensure good person-environment fit. I make three recommendations to promote successful deployment.

1. Promotion of Secure High-Speed Internet Access to Households. Given the importance of access to health care information, coupled with the rapid movement of such information to the Internet, having high-speed Internet access in households is becoming more of a necessity than a luxury. Telehealth applications to homes, including diagnosis, treatment, and rehabilitation, would be facilitated by such access. However, such televisits will depend on having secure communication channels to comply with regulations (e.g., the Health Insurance Portability and Accountability Act, HIPAA, in the United States), as well as on having standardized protocols

[9]The author recalls having to buy an adapter for a three-pronged plug to use computer equipment at his mother-in-law's home, which had wiring to support only two-pronged outlets.

and interfaces for home health care equipment (e.g., stethoscopes, scales, vital sign monitoring equipment) to minimize cost and training difficulty. Whether such access should be mandated in the same way as basic wired phone service or electricity and provided (with government subsidies if necessary) by current wired cable and phone connections (often unavailable in rural communities) or by soon-to-be-deployed wireless networks is open to debate. However, I recommend that the Federal Communications Commission carry out studies to advise Congress about the best way to bring secure, high-speed access to U.S. households capable of hosting telehealth services, such as videoconferencing.

2. Promotion of Usability Testing for Home Health Care Devices. It is not wise to design and then deploy a health care device or system in a home and expect it to work well for an increasingly diverse population of users. Usability testing should be encouraged with relevant user populations. *Universal design* (see Chapter 9) is a potential solution, by designing so that anyone, from a child to an impaired adult, could use a device, but it is unrealistic given the range of abilities/disabilities in the population. So *inclusive design* is the more sensible goal, making it ever easier to use devices, based on a cycle of design, testing, and redesign. Ideally, users of devices would fall into a few well-defined categories so that manufacturers could target them efficiently for testing. Simulation and modeling may prove to be a viable option to potentially expensive usability testing, as models are extended to cover people with more diverse abilities. The Food and Drug Administration currently requires manufacturers of medical devices to attend to human factors concerns. However, many devices not specifically classified as medical devices either could be or are now used to provide information about health care or delivery of home health care services (e.g., mobile phones, computers equipped with webcams for videoconferencing, videogame systems intended to promote physical and mental exercise). I recommend that manufacturers of such products and system integrators be strongly encouraged to provide evidence of efficacy through usability testing (or modeling) of the device with likely user populations.

3. Researching and Promoting Sound Instructional and Training Principles. Too little is known about the most effective techniques to instruct and train the use of home health care devices and how to search for and evaluate health care information (e.g., from the web) in the increasingly diverse population of home health care users. A good example is the recent *Guidelines for Pediatric Home Health Care* (American Academy of Pediatrics, 2009), which highlights, in chapter after chapter, the need to train caregivers but offers few if any suggestions for how to do this training or how to assess its efficacy. What are the optimal training principles and techniques for those with low health literacy, those with poor English comprehension skills, those from minority ethnic communities? Although guidelines have been proposed for training older adults (e.g., Fisk et al., 2009), the empirical support behind such recommendations is relatively weak (e.g., being based on those who volunteer for lab-based experiments rather than representative samples). Thus, I recommend that further research be conducted into potential ability-by-treatment interactions for training diverse populations of health care users, emphasizing the use of representative sampling. That is, studies need to assess whether and how ability levels for such variables as literacy, ethnicity, education, and age moderate the effectiveness of different training techniques.

ABOUT THE AUTHOR

Neil Charness is William G. Chase professor of psychology and an associate in the Pepper Institute on Aging and Public Policy at Florida State University. His research interests include understanding relations between age and technology use, expert performance, and work performance.

REFERENCES

Ajzen, I. (1991). The theory of planned behavior. *Organizational Behavior and Human Decision Processes, 50*, 179-211.

Ajzen, I., and Fishbein, M. (1977). Attitude-behavior relations: A theoretical analysis and review of empirical research. *Psychological Bulletin, 84*, 888-918.

Alkema, G.E., Wilber, K.H., Shannon, G.R., and Allen, D. (2007). Reduced mortality: The unexpected impact of a telephone-based care management intervention for older adults in managed care. *Health Services Research, 42*, 1,632-1,650.

Allen, K.G. (2005). *Long-term care financing: Growing demand and cost of services are straining federal and state budgets.* GAO Testimony Before the Subcommittee on Health, Committee on Energy and Commerce, House of Representatives. GAO-05-564T. Available: http://www.gao.gov/new.items/d05564t.pdf [accessed July 2009].

American Academy of Pediatrics. (2009). *Guidelines for pediatric home health care* (2nd ed.) Elk Grove Village, IL: Author.

Anderson, G., and Horvath, J. (2002). *Chronic conditions: Making the case for ongoing care.* Baltimore, MD: Johns Hopkins University Press.

Baer, J., Kutner, M., and Sabatini, J. (2009). *Basic reading skills and the literacy of America's least literate adults: Results from the 2003 National Assessment of Adult Literacy (NAAL) supplemental studies (NCES 2009-481).* Washington, DC: National Center for Education Statistics, U.S. Department of Education. Available: http://nces.ed.gov/pubs2009/2009481.pdf [accessed August 2009].

Beach, S.R., Schulz, R., Downs, J., Matthews, J., Barron, B., and Seelman, K. (2009). Disability, age, and informational privacy attitudes in quality of life technology applications: Results from a national web survey. *ACM Transactions on Accessible Computing (TACCESS), 2*(1), 1-21.

Beck, R.A., Arizmendi, A., Purnell, C., Fultz, B.A., and Callahan, C.M. (2009). House calls for seniors: Building and sustaining a model of care for homebound seniors. *Journal of the American Geriatric Society, 57*(6), 1,103-1,109.

Bendixen, R.M., Levy, C.E., Olive, E.S., Kobb, R.F., and Mann, W.C. (2009). Cost effectiveness of a telerehabilitation program to support chronically ill and disabled elders in their homes. *Telemedicine and e-Health, 15*, 31-38.

Benson, J.G., and Forman, W.B. (2002). Comprehension of written health care information in an affluent geriatric retirement community: Use of the Test of Functional Health Literacy. *Gerontology, 48*, 93-97.

Blackhall, L.J., Frank, G., Murphy, S.T., Michel, V., Palmer, J.M., and Azen, S.P. (1999). Ethnicity and attitudes towards life sustaining technology. *Social Science and Medicine, 48*, 1,779-1,789.

Bowles, K.H., and Baugh, A.C. (2007). Applying research evidence to optimize telehomecare. *Journal of Cardiovascular Nursing, 22*, 5-15.

Boyle, J.P., Honeycutt, A.A., Venkat Narayan, V.M., Hoerger, T.J., Giess, L.S., Chen, H., and Thompson, T.J. (2001). Projection of diabetes burden through 2050: Impact of changing demography and disease prevalence in the United States. *Diabetes Care, 24*, 1,936-1,940.

Brickfield, C.F. (1984). Attitudes and perceptions of older people toward technology. In P.K. Robinson and J.E. Birren (Eds.), *Aging and technological advances* (pp. 31-38). New York: Plenum.

Caine, K.E., Fisk, A.D., and Rogers, W.A. (2006). Benefits and privacy concerns of a home equipped with a visual sensing system: A perspective from older adults. *Proceedings of the Human Factors and Ergonomics Society*, 50th Annual Meeting, pp. 180-184. Available: http://awarehome.imtc.gatech.edu/publications/Caine-Fisk-Rogers-2006P.pdf [accessed May 2010].

Cameron, K.A. (2009). A practitioner's guide to persuasion: An overview of 15 selected persuasion theories, models and frameworks. *Patient Education and Counseling, 74*, 309-317.

Card, S.K., Moran, T.P., and Newell, A. (1983). *The psychology of human-computer interaction*. Hillsdale, NJ: Lawrence Erlbaum Associates.

Centers for Disease Control and Prevention. (2008). Self-reported falls and fall-related injuries among persons aged > 65 years—United States, 2006. *Morbidity and Mortality Weekly Report, 57*, 225-229. Available: http://www.cdc.gov/mmwr/preview/mmwrhtml/mm5709a1.htm [accessed July 2009].

Charness, N. (2008a). Technology as multiplier effect for an aging work force. In K.W. Schaie and R. Abeles (Eds.), *Social structures and aging individuals: Continuing challenges* (pp. 167-192). New York: Springer.

Charness, N. (2008b). Computer and Internet use in the United States of America: Influence of age, attitude, employment status, and education. *International Society for Gerontechnology Proceedings*, June 4, Pisa, Italy.

Charness, N., and Boot, W.R. (2009). Aging and information technology use: Potential and barriers. *Current Directions in Psychological Science, 18*, 253-258.

Charness, N., and Czaja, S.J. (2006). *Older worker training: What we know and don't know.* AARP Public Policy Institute #2006-22. Washington, DC: AARP. Available: http://assets.aarp.org/rgcenter/econ/2006_22_worker.pdf [accessed June 2010].

Charness, N., and Dijkstra, K. (1999). Age, luminance, and print legibility in homes, offices, and public places. *Human Factors, 41*, 173-193.

Charness, N., Kelley, C.L., Bosman, E.A., and Mottram, M. (2001). Word processing training and retraining: Effects of adult age, experience, and interface. *Psychology and Aging, 16*, 110-127.

Chua, R., Craig, J., Wootton, R., and Patterson, V. (2001). Randomized controlled trial of telemedicine for new neurological outpatient referrals. *Journal of Neurology, Neurosurgery, and Psychiatry, 71*, 63-66.

Ciemens, E.L., Holloway, B., Coon, P.J., McClosky-Armstron, T., and Min, S-J. (2009). Telemedicine and the mini-mental state examination: Assessment from a distance. *Telemedicine and e-Health, 5*, 476-478.

Cooper, J., and Kugler, M.B. (2008). The digital divide: The role of gender in human computer interaction. In A. Sears and J.A. Jacko (Eds.), *The human-computer interaction handbook: Fundamentals, evolving technologies, and emerging applications* (pp. 763-775). Boca Raton, FL: CRC Press.

Crimmins, E.M., Kim, J.K., and Seeman, T.E. (2009). Poverty and biological risk: The earlier "aging" of the poor. *Journals of Gerontology Series A: Biological and Medical Sciences, 64A*, 286-292.

Currell, R., Urquhart, C., Wainwright, P., and Lewis, R. (2000). Telemedicine versus face to face patient care: Effects on professional practice and health care outcomes. *Cochrane Database of Systematic Reviews, 2*, CD002098. DOI: 10.1002/14651858.

Czaja, S.J., and Lee, C.C. (2008). Information technology and older adults. In J.A. Jacko and A. Sears (Eds.), *The human-computer interaction handbook: Fundamentals, evolving technologies, and emerging applications* (pp. 777-792). New York: Lawrence Erlbaum Associates.

Czaja, S.J., Charness, N., Fisk, A. D., Hertzog, C., Nair, S. N., Rogers, W. A., and Sharit, J. (2006). Factors predicting the use of technology: Findings from the Center for Research and Education on Aging and Technology Enhancement (CREATE). *Psychology and Aging, 21*, 333-352.

Czaja, S.J., Sharit, J., and Nair, S.N. (2008). Usability of the Medicare health web site. *Journal of the American Medical Association, 300*, 790-792.

Czaja, S.J., Sharit, J., Charness, N., Fisk, A.D., and Rogers, W. (2001). The Center for Research and Education on Aging and Technology Enhancement (CREATE): A program to enhance technology for older adults. *Gerontechnology, 1*, 50-59.

Darkins, A.W., and Cary, M.A. (2000). *Telemedicine and telehealth: Principles, policies, performance and pitfalls.* New York: Springer.

Declercq, E.R., Paine, L.L., and Winter, M.H. (1995). Home birth in the United States, 1989-1992: A longitudinal descriptive report of national birth certificate data. *Journal of Nurse-Midwifery, 40*, 478-481.

Demiris, G., Charness, N., Krupinski, E., Ben-Arieh, D., Washington, K., and Farberow, B. (in press). Human factors and telehealth: A white paper of the ATA human factors SIG. Submitted to *Telemedicine and E-health.*

Demiris, G., Rantz, M.J., Aud, M.A., Marek, K.D., Tyrer, H.W., Skubic, M., and Hussam, A.A. (2004). Older adults' attitudes towards and perceptions of "smart home" technologies: A pilot study. *Informatics for Health and Social Care, 2*, 87-94.

Dempster, F.N. (1981). Memory span: Sources of individual and developmental differences. *Psychological Bulletin, 89*, 63-100.

Dishman, E., Matthews, J., and Dunbar-Jacob, J. (2004). Everyday health: Technology for adaptive aging. In National Research Council, *Technology for adaptive aging* (pp. 179-208). Steering Committee for the Workshop on Technology for Adaptive Aging. R.W. Pew and S.B. Van Hemel (Eds.). Board on Behavioral, Cognitive, and Sensory Sciences, Division of Behavioral and Social Sciences and Education. Washington, DC: The National Academies Press.

Economic Systems Inc. (2008). *A study of compensation payments for service-connected disabilities: Volume I, executive report.* (2008). Available: http://www1.va.gov/op3/docs/ProgramEvaluations/CompPaymentStudy/DS_VOLUME_I_Executive_Report.pdf [accessed April 2009].

Edwards, M., Davies, M., and Edwards, A. (2008). What are the external influences on information exchange and shared decision-making in healthcare consultations? A meta-synthesis of the literature. *Patient Education and Counseling, 75*, 37-52.

Field, M.J., and Grigsby, J. (2002). Telemedicine and remote patient monitoring. *Journal of the American Medical Association, 288*, 423-425.

Fisk, A.D., Rogers, W.A., Charness, N., Czaja, S.J., and Sharit, J. (2009). *Designing for older adults: Principles and creative human factors approaches* (2nd ed.). Boca Raton, FL: CRC Press.

Flynn, J.R. (1987). Massive gains in 14 nations: What IQ tests really measure. *Psychological Bulletin, 101*, 171-191.

Fox, S. (2000). *Trust and privacy online: Why Americans want to rewrite the rules.* Washington, DC: Pew Internet and American Life Project. Available: http://www.pewinternet.org/~/media//Files/Reports/2000/PIP_Trust_Privacy_Report.pdf.pdf [accessed July 2009].

Fox, S., and Jones, S. (2009). *The social life of health information: Americans' pursuit of health takes place within a widening network of both online and offline sources.* Washington, DC: Pew Internet and American Life Project. Available: http://www.pewinternet.org/~/media//Files/Reports/2009/PIP_Health_2009.pdf [accessed August 2009].

Fuhrer, M.J. (2001). Assistive technology outcomes research: Challenges met and yet unmet. *American Journal of Physical and Rehabilitation Medicine, 80*, 528-535.

Gigerenzer, G., and Goldstein, D.G. (1996). Reasoning the fast and frugal way: Models of bounded rationality. *Psychological Review, 103*, 650-669.

Hensel, B.K., Demiris, G., and Courtney, K.L. (2006). Defining obtrusiveness in home telehealth technologies: A conceptual framework. *Journal of the American Informatics Association, 13*, 428-431.

Hersh, W.R., Helfand, M., Wallace, J., Kraemer, J., Patterson, P., Shapiro, S., and Greenlick, M. (2001). Clinical outcomes resulting from telemedicine interventions: A systematic review. *BMC Medical Informatics and Decision Making, 1*, 1-5. Doi:10.1186/1472-6947-1-5.

Hinsz, V.B., Tindale, R.S., and Vollrath, D.A. (1997). The emerging conceptualization of groups as information processors. *Psychological Bulletin, 121*, 43-64.

Horgas, A., and Abowd, G. (2004). The impact of technology on living environments for older adults. In National Research Council, *Technology for adaptive aging* (pp. 230-252). Steering Committee for the Workshop on Technology for Adaptive Aging. R.W. Pew and S.B. Van Hemel (Eds.). Board on Behavioral, Cognitive, and Sensory Sciences, Division of Behavioral and Social Sciences and Education. Washington, DC: The National Academies Press.

Hughes, S.L., Ulasevich, A., Weaver, F.M., Henderson, W., Manheim, L., Kubal, J.D., and Bonarigo, F. (1997). Impact of home care on hospital days: A meta analysis. *Health Services Research, 32*, 415-418.

Institute of Medicine. (1996). *Telemedicine: A guide to assessing telecommunications in health care.* Committee on Evaluating Clinical Applications of Telemedicine, M.J. Field (Ed.). Division of Health Care Services. Washington, DC: National Academy Press.

Institute of Medicine. (2000). *To err is human: Building a safer health system.* Committee on Quality of Health Care in America, L.T. Kohn, J.M. Corrigan, and M.S. Donaldson, Eds. Washington, DC: National Academy Press.

Jastrzembski, T.S., and Charness, N. (2007). The model human processor and the older adult: Parameter estimation and validation within a mobile phone task. *Journal of Experimental Psychology: Applied, 13*, 224-248.

Kahneman, D., and Tversky, A. (1979). Prospect theory: An analysis of decision under risk. *Econometrica, 47*, 263-292.

Kaiser Family Foundation. (2005). E-health and the elderly: How seniors use the Internet for health information. Report #7223. Menlo Park, CA: Author. Available: http://www.kff.org/entmedia/7223.cfm [accessed June 2010].

Katz, J.E., and Rice, R.E. (2009). Public views of mobile medical devices and services: A U.S. national survey of consumer sentiments towards RFID healthcare technology. *International Journal of Medical Informatics, 78*, 104-114.

Krakauer, E.L., Crenner, C., and Fox, K. (2002). Barriers to optimum end-of-life care for minority patients. *Journal of the American Geriatric Society, 50*, 182-190.

Krause, N. (2008). *Aging in the church: How social relationships affect health*. West Conshohocken, PA: Templeton Foundation Press.

Kroemer, K.H.E. (2005). *"Extra-ordinary" ergonomics: How to accommodate small and big persons, the disabled and elderly, expectant mothers, and children*. Boca Raton, FL: CRC Press.

Lee, R.S. (1970). Social attitudes and the computer revolution. *Public Opinion Quarterly, 34*, 53-59.

Lehmann, C.A., Mintz, N., and Giacini, J.M. (2006). Impact of telehealth on healthcare utilization by congestive heart failure patients. *Disease Management and Health Outcomes, 14*, 163-169.

Leveson, N., and Turner, C.S. (1993). An investigation of the Therac-25 accidents. *IEEE Computer, 25*, 18-41.

Levinthal, B.R., Morrow, D.G., Tu, W., Wu, J., and Murray, M.D. (2008). Cognition and health literacy in patients with hypertension. *Journal of General Internal Medicine, 23*, 1,172-1,176.

Lewis, J.R., Commarford, P.M., Kennedy, P.J., and Sadowski, W.J. (2008). Hand-held digital devices. In C. Melody Carswell (Ed.), *Reviews of Human Factors and Ergonomics, 4*, 105-148. Santa Monica, CA: Human Factors and Ergonomics Society.

Machlin, S., Cohen, J. and Beauregard, K. (2008). *Health care expenses for adults with chronic conditions, 2005*. Statistical brief #203, May. Rockville, MD: Agency for Healthcare Research and Quality. Available: http://www.meps.ahrq.gov/mepsweb/data_files/publications/st203/stat203.pdf [accessed September 2009].

Macpherson, H. (2004). Pragmatic clinical trials. *Complementary Therapies in Medicine, 12*, 136-140.

Mainous, A.G., Baker, R., Koopman, R.J., Saxena, S., Diaz, V.A., Everett, C.J., and Majeed, A. (2007). Impact of the population at risk of diabetes on projections of diabetes burden in the United States: An epidemic on the way. *Diabetalogia, 50*, 934-940.

Manton, K.G., Gu, X., and Lowrimore, G.R. (2008). Cohort changes in active life expectancy in the U.S. elderly population: Experience from the 1982-2004 National Long-Term Care Survey. *Journal of Gerontology: Social Sciences, 63B*, S269-S281.

Manton, K.G., Lamb, V.L., and Gu, X. (2007). Medicare cost effects of recent U.S. disability trends in the elderly: Future implications. *Journal of Aging and Health, 19*, 359-381.

Marmot, M.G., and Shipley, M.J. (1996). Do socioeconomic differences in mortality persist after retirement? 25-year follow up of civil servants from the first Whitehall study. *British Medical Journal, 313*, 1,177-1,180.

Martin, S., Kelly, G., Kernohan, W.G., McCreight, B., and Nugent, C. (2008). Smart home technologies for health and social care support. *Cochrane Database of Systematic Reviews, 4*, CD006412. DOI:10.1002/14651858.CD006412.pub2.

Mayhorn, C.B., Lanzolla, V.R., Wogalter, M.S., and Watson, A.M. (2005). Personal digital assistants (PDAs) as medication reminding tools: Exploring age differences in usability. *Gerontechnology, 4*, 128-140.

Melenhorst, A., Rogers, W.A., and Bouwhuis, D.G. (2006). Older adults' motivated choice for technological innovation: Evidence for benefit-driven selectivity. *Psychology and Aging, 21*, 190-195.

Meyer, B.J.F., Talbot, A.P., and Ranalli, C. (2007). Why older adults make more immediate treatment decisions about cancer than younger adults. *Psychology and Aging, 22*, 505-524.

Morrell, R.W., and Park, D.C. (1993). The effects of age, illustrations, and task variables on the performance of procedural assembly tasks. *Psychology and Aging, 8*, 389-399.

Morrow, D.G., and Rogers, W.A. (2008). Environmental support: An integrative framework. *Human Factors, 50*, 589-613.

Morrow, D., Clark, D., Tu, W., Wu, J., Weiner, M., and Steinley, D. (2006). Correlates of health literacy in patients with chronic heart failure. *The Gerontologist, 46*, 669-676.

Mustard, C.A., Kaufert, P., Kozyrskyj, A., and Mayer, T. (1998). Sex differences in use of health care services. *New England Journal of Medicine, 338*, 1,678-1,683.

Mykityshyn, A.L., Fisk, A.D., and Rogers, W.A. (2002). Learning to use a home medical device: Mediating age-related differences with training. *Human Factors, 44*, 354-364.

Mynatt, E.D., Melenhorst, A.S., Fisk, A.D., and Rogers, W.A. (2004). Aware technologies for aging in place: Understanding user needs and attitudes. *IEEE Pervasive Computing, 3*, 36-41.

National Center for Education Statistics. (2006). *The health literacy of America's adults: Results from the 2003 National Assessment of Adult Literacy* (NCES 2006-483). M. Kutner, E., Greenberg, Y. Jin, and C. Paulsen, Eds. Washington, DC: U.S. Department of Education.

National Center for Health Statistics. (2008). *Health, United States, 2008 with chartbook.* Available: http://www.cdc.gov/nchs/data/hus/hus08.pdf [accessed April 2009].

National Institute on Aging, National Institutes of Health, and U.S. Department of Health and Human Services. (2007). *Growing older in America: Health and retirement study.* Institute for Social Research, University of Michigan. Available: http://hrsonline.isr.umich.edu/index.php?p=dbook [accessed August 2010].

Parati, G., Omboni, S., Abini, F., Piantoni, L., Giuliano, A, Revera, M., Illyes, M., and Mancia, G. (2009). Home blood pressure telemonitoring improves hypertension control in general practice. The TeleBPCare study. *Journal of Hypertension, 27*, 198-203.

Pauly, R.P., Gill, J.S., Rose, C.L., Asad, R.A., Chery, A., Pierratos, A., and Chan, C.T. (2009). Survival among nocturnal home haemodialysis patients compared to kidney transplant recipients. *Nephrology Dialysis Transplantation, 24*, 2,915-2,919.

Quill, T.E. (2005). Terri Schiavo—A tragedy compounded. *New England Journal of Medicine, 352*, 1,630-1,633.

Quinn, C.C., Gruber-Baldini, A.L., Shardell, M., Weed, K., Clough, S.S., Peeples, M., Terrin, M., Bronich-Hall, L., Barr, E., and Lender, D. (2009). Mobile diabetes intervention study: Testing a personalized treatment/behavioral communication intervention for blood glucose control. *Contemporary Clinical Trials, 30*, 334-346.

Rahimpour, M., Lovell, N.H., Celler, B.G., and McCormick, J. (2008). Patient's perceptions of a home telecare system. *International Journal of Medical Informatics, 77*, 486-498.

Rogers, E.M. (2003). *Diffusion of innovations* (5th ed.). New York: Free Press.

Rogers, W.A., Mykitshyn, A.L., Campbell, R.H., and Fisk, A.D. (2001). Analysis of a "simple" medical device. *Ergonomics in Design, 9*, 6-14.

Salas, E., and Cannon-Bowers, J.A. (2001). The science of training: A decade of progress. *Annual Review of Psychology, 52*, 471-499.

Salthouse, T.A. (2010). *Major issues in cognitive aging.* Oxford: Oxford University Press.

Schoen, C., Davis, K., How, S.K., and Schoenbaum, S.C. (2006). U.S. health system performance: A national scorecard. *Health Affairs, 25*, W457-W475.

Soni, A. (2009). *The five most costly conditions, 1996 and 2006: Estimates for the U.S. civilian noninstitutionalized population.* Statistical brief #248, July. Rockville, MD: Agency for Healthcare Research and Quality. Available: http://www.meps.ahrq.gov/mepsweb/data_files/publications/st248/stat248.pdf [accessed September 2009].

Steenbekkers, L.P.A., and van Beijsterveldt, C.E.M. (Eds.). (1998). *Design-relevant characteristics of ageing users.* Delft, The Netherlands: Delft University Press.

Story, M.T., Neumark-Stzainer, D.R., Sherwood, N.E., Holt, K., Sofak, D., Trowbridge, F.L., and Barlow, S.E. (2002). Management of child and adolescent obesity: Attitudes, barriers, skills, and training needs among health care professionals. *Pediatrics, 110,* 210-214.

Tacken, M., Marcellini, F., Mollenkopf, H., Ruoppila, I., and Széman, Z. (2005). Use and acceptance of new technology by older people. Findings of the international MOBILATE survey: "Enhancing mobility in later life." *Gerontechnology, 3,* 126-137.

Thang, L., Patrick, L., and Nash, S.G. (2009). Help-seeking attitudes among Vietnamese Americans: The impact of acculturation, cultural barriers, and spiritual beliefs. *Social Work in Mental Health, 7,* 476-493.

Tyrer, F., Smith, L.K., and McGrother, C.W. (2007). Mortality in adults with moderate to profound intellectual disability: A population-based study. *Journal of Intellectual Disability Research, 51,* 520-527.

U.S. Census Bureau. (2009). *Current population survey, 2008 annual social and economic supplement.* Available: http://www.census.gov/population/socdemo/hh-fam/cps2008/tabH2-all.xls [accessed June 2009].

U.S. Census Bureau. (2010). *American community survey, 2006.* Available: http://www.census.gov/acs/www/ [accessed July 2010].

Varshney, U. (2007). Pervasive healthcare and wireless health monitoring. *Mobile Network Applications, 12,* 113-127. DOI 10.1007/s11036-007-0017-1.

Venkatesh, V., and Davis, F.D. (2000). A theoretical extension of the technology acceptance model: Four longitudinal case studies. *Management Science, 46,* 186-204.

Wilson, D.M., Truman, C.D., Thomas, R., Fainsinger, R., Kovacs-Burns, K., Forggatt, K., and Justice, C. (2009). The rapidly changing location of death in Canada, 1994-2004. *Social Science and Medicine, 68,* 1,752-1,758.

Zhu, C.W. (2004). Effects of the balanced budget act on Medicare home health utilization. *Journal of the American Geriatric Society, 52,* 989-994.

Suggested General Readings

Carayon, P., and Friesdorf, W. (2006). Human factors and ergonomics in medicine. In G. Salvendy (Ed.), *Handbook of human factors and ergonomics* (3rd ed., pp. 1,517-1,537). Hoboken, NJ: Wiley.

Fisk, A.D., Rogers, W.A., Charness, N., Czaja, S.J., and Sharit, J. (2009). *Designing for older adults: Principles and creative human factors approaches* (2nd ed.). Boca Raton, FL: CRC Press.

Jacko, J.A., and Sears, A. (Eds.). (2008). *The human-computer interaction handbook Part V: Designing for diversity* (2nd ed.). New York: Lawrence Erlbaum Associates.

Krupinski, E., Dimmick, S., Grigsby, J., Mogel, G., Puskin, D., Speedie, S., Stamm, B., Wakefield, B., Whited, J., Whitten, P., and Yellowlees, P. (2006). Research recommendations for the American Telemedicine Association. *Telemedicine and e-Health, 12,* 579-589.

7

Informal Caregivers in the United States: Prevalence, Caregiver Characteristics, and Ability to Provide Care

Richard Schulz and Connie A. Tompkins

Informal caregivers are a critical resource to their care recipients and an essential component of the health care system in the United States, yet their role and importance to society as a whole have only recently been appreciated. An informal caregiver, often a family member, provides care, typically unpaid, to someone with whom they have a personal relationship.[1] For the last two decades, investigators have endeavored to identify who informal caregivers are, what roles they play in providing care, what needs they have, and what strategies might best support their efforts.

This chapter has three broad goals. One is to describe the prevalence of informal caregiving in the United States by identifying who provides care and to whom that care is provided. The roles and responsibilities of caregivers are discussed next, with a special emphasis on challenges of coordinating care across multiple social and health service organizations to access needed services. This is followed by a discussion of factors that affect the ability to provide care, including the effects of caregiving itself on the ability to perform this role as well as sociodemographic and developmental factors that compromise the ability to provide care. We conclude with a look to the future, which poses formidable challenges to informal caregivers as well as formal health care systems, and we suggest ways in which these challenges might be met.

[1]We realize that some prefer the term "family caregiver" to "informal caregiver." We are using the term to contrast informal unpaid caregiving with formal paid caregiving.

DIMENSIONS OF INFORMAL CAREGIVING

Prevalence of Caregiving

Rosalyn Carter is often quoted for her observation that "there are only four types of people in the world: (1) those who have been caregivers, (2) those who currently are caregivers, (3) those who will be caregivers, and (4) those who will need caregivers." There are three distinct groups of informal caregivers, roughly defined by the age of the people they care for: (1) children with chronic illness and disability are typically cared for by young adult parents, (2) adult children with such conditions as mental illness are cared for by middle-aged parents, and (3) older individuals are cared for by their spouses or their middle-aged children. Because the nature of caregiving differs substantially for children and adults, we describe each of these groups separately. We begin with adults, who are by far the largest group of people receiving health-related caregiving.

Caregiving for Adults

There are no exact estimates of the number of informal caregivers in the United States. Prevalence estimates vary widely depending on the definitions used and the populations sampled. At one extreme are estimates that 28.5 percent of the U.S. adult population, or 65.7 million people, provided unpaid care to an adult relative in 2009, with the majority (83 percent) of this care being delivered to people age 50 or older (National Alliance for Caregiving and American Association of Retired Persons, 2009). This number, based on the Behavioral Risk Factor Surveillance System survey (Centers for Disease Control and Prevention, 2006), approximates the estimated 59 million adults with a disability in the United States. At the other extreme, data from the National Long-Term Care Survey suggest that as few as 3.5 million informal caregivers provided instrumental activities of daily living (IADLs) or activities of daily living (ADLs) assistance to people ages 65 and over (not to all adult care recipients). Intermediate estimates of 28.8 million caregivers ("persons aged 15 or over providing personal assistance for everyday needs of someone age 15 and older") are reported by the Survey of Income and Program Participation (National Family Caregivers Association and Family Caregiver Alliance, 2006). A recent national survey of individuals ages 45 and older yielded a caregiving rate of 12 percent or 14.9 million adults in that age group (Roth et al., 2009).

These differences are in part attributable to the period of data collection, the age range of the population sampled, the populations targeted, and, most importantly, the definition of caregiving. Thus, the high-end estimates are generated when broad and inclusive definitions of caregiving are used—for example, "unpaid care may include help with personal needs or household chores. It might be managing a person's finances, arranging for outside services, or visiting regularly to see how they are doing" (National Alliance for Caregiving and American Association of Retired Persons, 2009). Low-end estimates are generated when definitions require the provision of specific ADL or IADL assistance (e.g., Wolff and Kasper, 2006). A related issue is that definitions of caregiving do not clearly distinguish caregiving for chronic disability from caregiving for acute care episodes that might follow a hospitalization event. However, most definitions emphasize chronic disability; intermittent episodes of caregiving are not well represented in the existing data.

Although there are some encouraging signs that age-related disability is declining in the United States, this will be offset by the rapid growth of the senior population to an estimated 70 million in 2035. It is projected that the number of older adults with functional deficits will grow from 22 million in 2005 to 38 million by 2030, assuming no changes in disability rates from current levels (Institute of Medicine, 2007). The challenges posed by this demographic shift will be exacerbated by the decreasing ability of existing formal care systems to care for older adults because of a shortage of nurses and other health care workers and increasing costs of hospitalization and long-term care (Talley and Crews, 2007). Changes in family size and composition and the increased labor force participation of women will make informal caregivers less available. Thus, the convergence of three factors in the decades ahead—increased need for care, decreased availability of formal care, and decreased number of adult children to provide care—have the makings of a perfect storm that will challenge policy makers in the decades ahead.

Finally, recent historical events have added one additional unanticipated caregiving challenge. Young adults are returning from our ongoing wars with multiple, interacting injuries, or polytrauma, which they may be coping with for the rest of their lives. Posttraumatic stress is a common sequel of service in wartime as well. The need for sustained informal caregiving for these young veterans is potentially immense, and the nature of the challenges for their informal caregivers warrants thorough investigation.

Caregiving for Children

All children are care recipients under a broad definition of caregiving. Human beings require nearly two decades to acquire the necessary knowledge and skills to function independently. Throughout this developmental period, virtually all children also experience multiple acute illnesses that require support and care from their parents. More extraordinary levels of care occur when a child suffers from a chronic disability that requires intensive and long-term support from their parents. The 2005-2006 National Survey of Children with Special Health Care Needs estimates that 13.9 percent of children under age 18 have special health care needs, defined in terms of use of services, therapies, counseling, or medications or functional limitations of at least a year in duration (U.S. Department of Health and Human Services, 2008). According to this survey, 21.8 percent of U.S. households with children include a child with special needs. In some cases, grandparents are the primary caregivers of these children. According to 2000 census data, approximately 2.4 million individuals over age 30 were grandparent caregivers, defined as people who had primary responsibility for coresident grandchildren younger than 18, although it is not known what proportion of these grandchildren had special needs. The prevalence of grandparent caregiving is particularly high among African Americans (4.3 percent age 30 or older) and American Indians and Alaska Natives (4.5 percent) compared with whites (1.1 percent) and Hispanics (2.9 percent) (Simmons and Dye, 2003).

The most prevalent chronic health conditions reported as causing activity limitations among children under age 18 include learning disabilities; attention deficit or hyperactivity disorder; other mental, emotional or behavioral problems; mental retardation or other developmental problems; asthma or breathing problems; and speech or language problems (Institute of Medicine, 2007). These conditions have developmental trajectories such that speech problems are more prevalent at young ages and learning disabilities at later ages. Not included in this list are illnesses or such conditions as childhood cancers, diabetes, heart disease, and cerebral palsy, which are less common among children than adults but create high caregiving demands when present. Other examples of conditions with low prevalence and outsized demands for care and particularly high levels of family stress are autism spectrum disorder and cystic fibrosis.

With the exception of a few selected health conditions, such as spina bifida and neurodevelopment problems resulting from lead exposure, the overall trend in recent decades has been for increased chronic illness, associated disabilities, and the need for sustained care from parents (Zylke and DeAngelis, 2007). These trends have important repercussions for future adult health, as their effects will be felt throughout the remaining life of the affected individual and involved informal caregivers. Multiple factors have contributed to the increased rates of chronic illness and disability in children, including (a) medical advances enabling higher rates of survival of high-risk infants, the increase in multiple births associated with fertility treatments, and the number of infants born prematurely and with low birth weights; (b) increases in diagnosis rates for conditions that cause childhood disability; and (c) increased reporting of disability as a result of enhanced knowledge among health, education, and social service professionals as well as the general population.

Many children with a disability will carry the burden of chronic illness and disability into middle and old age and require support from informal care providers throughout their lives. This means that some individuals will spend their entire adult lives as caregivers. The ability to survive with disability into late life will add to the already growing number of people who acquire disability as adults, increasing demands for support and care. The growing prevalence of obesity and related disorders among both children and adults in the United States is expected to further raise disability rates and increase the demand for care.

Episodic Caregiving

Because most caregiving data are based on care for chronic illness and disability, little is known about the prevalence of episodic care. Episodic caregiving is typically provided after discharge from an acute care hospital for such events as hip fracture, stroke, cancer, or trauma. In 2007 the United States had nearly 40 million hospital discharges (Agency for Healthcare Research and Quality, 2007), and many of these individuals were likely to require care from a family member following discharge. Little is known about the intensity, duration, or type of care provided or about the characteristics of informal caregivers in this instance. Because episodic events are often characterized by acute onset without warning, they entail different challenges than chronic caregiving. Episodic caregivers have to quickly acquire skills related to performing in-home medical procedures, operating medical equipment, monitoring patient status, and coordinating care. Caregivers with limited experience and training may find these challenges overwhelming.

Long-Distance Caregiving

Approximately 15 percent of caregivers to older adults live at least an hour away from their relative and provide care at a distance. Long-distance caregivers tend to be more educated and affluent and are more likely to play a secondary helper role when compared with in-home caregivers. Distant caregivers spend on average 3.4 hours per week arranging services and another 4 hours per week checking on the care recipient or monitoring care. One-third of long-distance caregivers visit at least once a week and provide on average 34 hours of IADL/ADL assistance per month (National Alliance for Caregiving, 2004).

Because distance and time are limiting factors to providing direct support to the recipient, long-distance caregivers have the added challenges of identifying relevant resources in the recipient's local environment from a distance, hiring individuals to provide needed care, and monitoring the care providers' performance as well as the status of the care recipient. From a human factors perspective, performing these tasks requires sophisticated search skills, the ability to screen and evaluate professional care providers, and systems for monitoring care recipient status, which may range from contact via telephone to sophisticated electronic monitoring and communication devices. These caregivers also may have to be able to cope with psychological distress associated with being unable to do more for their distant loved ones who need care.

Characteristics of Informal Caregivers

Nearly everyone serves as an unpaid caregiver at some point in life, and some individuals enact this role over extended periods of time lasting months and often years. Providing care to an individual with chronic illness and disability is generally viewed as a major life stressor, and its effects on the health and well-being of the caregiver have been intensively studied over the last three decades. Because informal caregivers are often called on to provide highly demanding and complex care over long periods of time, the question inevitably arises: Who ends up in this role and how able are they to address care recipients' needs?

Relatively few population-based studies have been carried out to characterize the population of caregivers. One of the most comprehensive national caregiving studies to date (National Alliance for Caregiving and American Association of Retired Persons, 2009) estimates that among adults ages 18 and over, 28.5 percent, or 65.7 million individuals, provide unpaid care in any given year to an adult family member or friend who is also age 18 or older. The typical caregiver in the United States is a 48-year-old woman, has some college education, works, and spends more than 20 hours per week providing unpaid care to her mother. And 66 percent of caregivers are women, and most work either full or part-time (59 percent). The education level of caregivers is slightly higher than that of the U.S. adult population, with more than 90 percent having completed high school and 43 percent being college graduates (compared with 85 percent and 27 percent, respectively) (Stoops, 2004).

Although caregivers are predominantly middle-aged or older, there is growing recognition that even children can be cast in the caregiver role. As many as 1.4 million children in the United States between the ages of 8 and 18 provide care for an older adult. These caregiving children are more likely to come from households with lower incomes, are less likely to live in a two-parent home, and are more likely to experience depression and anxiety when compared with their noncaregiving counterparts (Levine et al., 2005).

Care recipients are typically female (66 percent) and older (80 percent are age 50 or older), and their main presenting problems or illnesses are "old age" (12 percent) followed by Alzheimer's disease or other dementia (10 percent), cancer (7 percent), mental/emotional illness (7 percent), heart disease (5 percent), and stroke (5 percent). Among younger care recipients (ages 18-49), the primary health problem requiring assistance is mental illness or depression (23 percent). Caregivers provide assistance with a wide range of IADLs, including help with transportation (83 percent), housework (75 percent), grocery shopping (75 percent), and preparing meals (65 percent). And 56 percent of all caregivers also provide ADL assistance, primarily helping the care recipient to get into and out of bed (40 percent), dress (32 percent), and bathe (26 percent). The average length of time caregivers report providing care is 4.6 years (National Alliance for Caregiving and American Association of Retired Persons, 2009).

Much less is known about the informal caregivers of children. The National Survey of Children with Special Health Care Needs indicates that 10 percent of family caregivers spend more than 11 hours each week arranging, coordinating, and providing care and that 24 percent of caregivers either quit working or cut back their hours at work, creating financial problems for their families. The most common types of assistance provided to children with special needs include monitoring the child's condition (85 percent); ensuring that others (e.g., child's teachers) know how to deal with the child (84 percent); advocating on his or her behalf to schools, government agencies, or other care providers (72 percent); performing emotional or behavioral treatments or therapies (6 percent); and giving medications (64 percent) (National Alliance for Caregiving and American Association of Retired Persons, 2009).

ROLES AND RESPONSIBILITIES OF CAREGIVERS

The delivery of effective health-related care in the home requires caregivers to play multiple roles. To varying degrees, caregivers must communicate and negotiate with family members about care decisions, provide companionship and emotional support, interact with physicians and other health care providers about patient status and care needs, drive care recipients to appointments, do housework, shop, complete paperwork and manage finances, hire nurses and aides, help with personal care and hygiene, lift and maneuver the care recipient, and assist with complex medical and nursing tasks (e.g., infusion therapies, tube feedings, medication monitoring) necessitated by the care recipient's health condition. In addition, caregivers are also called on to coordinate services from health and human service agencies, to make difficult decisions about service needs, and to figure out how to access needed services. Inasmuch as caregiving tasks are physically, cognitively, and emotionally demanding, individuals who are cast in the caregiving role who are older, have low income, and are chronically ill or disabled will be particularly vulnerable to adverse outcomes.

Figure 7-1 illustrates a typical caregiving trajectory involving an older individual with disability living in the community. Caregiving often begins when that individual is no longer able to perform IADL tasks, such as cooking, cleaning, or managing finances, because of a chronic health condition. Thus, the early stages of a caregiving career involve such tasks as monitoring symptoms and medications, helping with household tasks and finances, providing emotional support, and communicating with health professionals. As the health condition of the care recipient worsens and disabilities increase, the caregiver typically provides assistance with ADL tasks, such as dressing, bathing, ambulating, and toileting. Caregivers may also be required to closely monitor the care recipient's activity in order to ensure his or her safety.

It is important to note that the tasks performed by caregivers are cumulative. Thus, at this stage in a caregiving career, caregivers typically help with ADL tasks in addition to the tasks they performed earlier. For some caregivers, the need for care exceeds their ability to provide it, resulting in the placement of the care recipient into a long-term care facility, but even under these circumstances, caregiving does not end. Many caregivers continue to provide high levels of ADL assistance (e.g., feeding, grooming) to their institutionalized relative, and they must in addition acquire new

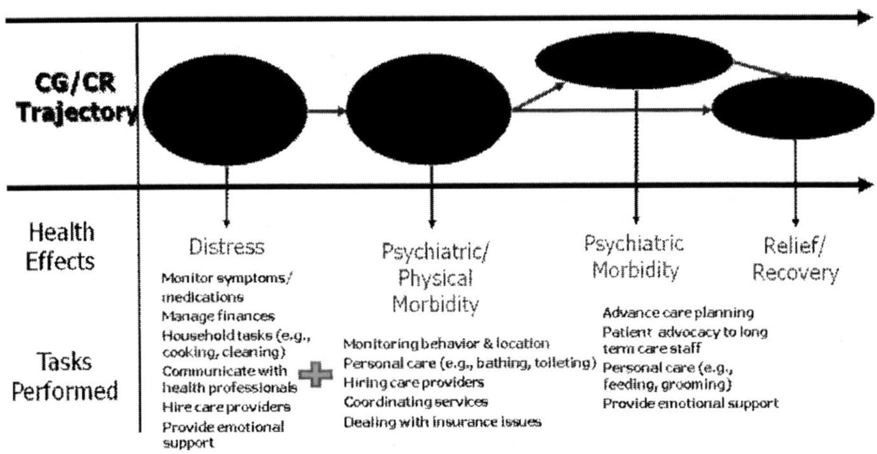

FIGURE 7-1 Caregiver health effects and task demands at different stages of the caregiving career.

skills associated with navigating long-term care systems. Given the demands and duration of long-term caregiving, it should come as no surprise that some caregivers may experience relief when the care recipient dies (Schulz et al., 2003).

Effective caregiving requires skills in multiple domains that vary as a function of the underlying illness or chronic condition, type of disability, and age of the care recipient. Both generic and disease-specific caregiving task lists are reported in the literature (Chen et al., 2007; Pakenham, 2007; Horsburgh et al., 2008; Wilkins, Bruce, and Sirey, 2009). From a human factors perspective, the level of specificity in describing these tasks is limited. For example, a typical list might describe tasks broadly, such as monitoring symptoms, providing emotional support, helping with transportation, assisting the patient with body cleaning routines, and so on (Chen et al., 2007; Wilkins et al., 2009). A few researchers have attempted to decompose these global descriptions into constituent components. For example, bathing subtasks might include obtaining supplies, taking off clothes, adjusting water, helping into the tub, getting into bathing position, washing body, leaving bathing position, helping out of the tub, drying body, and getting dressed (Naik, Concato, and Gill, 2004). Even more fine-grained analyses to task decomposition, characteristic of human factors approaches to task analysis, are relatively rare in this literature (e.g., Clark, Czaja, and Weber, 1990). Such human factors analyses of caregiving tasks could greatly benefit the development of robotic and other technologies to assist individuals with disabilities.

Coordinating Care

One of the biggest difficulties facing informal caregivers is the coordination of services to support care recipients in the home or as they transition from one care setting to another. Caregivers may need to negotiate roles among family members who disagree on care options, identify relevant available services, assess eligibility requirements, and communicate and negotiate with health professionals and insurance companies. Even seasoned health professionals with detailed knowledge of and experience with health care systems find care coordination for care recipients a formidable challenge.

Coordinating care is particularly problematic for caregivers providing support to older individuals. The spectrum of formal support options available to care recipients and caregivers is broad, complex, and disorganized, with different access points and eligibility criteria. Access to information about options for care, such as respite services, adult day care, support groups, meals on wheels, transportation services, and financial help, is one of the major unmet needs of informal caregivers (National Alliance for

Caregiving and American Association of Retired Persons, 2004). This is particularly problematic among African American, Asian American, and Hispanic caregivers, who are much more likely than white caregivers to say they need help obtaining, processing, and understanding health information (National Alliance for Caregiving and American Association of Retired Persons, 2004).

Low-health literacy—that is, deficiencies in the ability to obtain, process, and understand basic health information and service needs in order to make appropriate health decisions—is associated with poverty, limited education, minority status, immigration, and older age. Results from a recent national survey in the United States suggest that 36 percent of the adult population have limited health literacy skills (National Center for Education Statistics, 2006), which have been consistently associated with poorer health outcomes (i.e., poorer disease management) and increased rates of hospitalization and mortality (Kripalani et al., 2006; Hironaka and Paasche-Orlow, 2008).

The magnitude of care coordination challenges was recently demonstrated in a study to evaluate the ability of relatively well-educated adults with computer experience to use the Medicare.gov website to make decisions about eligibility for services and prescription drug plans (Czaja, Sharit, and Nair, 2008). Participants were asked to determine eligibility for home health care services, select a home health agency to meet specified needs, make decisions about enrollment in Medicare Part D, and select a drug plan and determine associated costs based on a specified medication regime. Most participants were unable to specify all eligibility criteria for home health services (68.8 percent), choose the correct home health agency (80.4 percent), or execute computation procedures needed for making a plan enrollment decision (83.9 percent).

To help address the need for coordinated and comprehensive care, one-stop service programs, such as Child's Way and the Program for All-Inclusive Care for the Elderly (PACE), have been developed to provide integrated and seamless total care, including both social and medical services. These programs, however, have eligibility criteria that make them inaccessible to the majority of individuals with chronic disability and their caregivers (e.g., for Child's Way a participant must be age 8 or younger, have a chronic illness with long-term medical needs, and qualify for in-home services; for PACE the participant must be age 55 or older and meet criteria for nursing facility level of care). Thus the need in this area remains great.

In sum, the complexity of identifying and accessing health and social service options that might be useful to caregivers is daunting even to experienced health professionals cast in an informal caregiving role. The average lay person has little chance of optimizing formal support services to minimize the burdens of caregiving.

Assessment, Training, and Monitoring of Caregiver Performance

Systematic assessment of individuals with chronic health conditions or disability occurs routinely in medical, health, and social service settings. However, assessment of informal caregivers' needs and capabilities is rare. Caregiver assessment is an essential requisite for optimizing care recipient functioning and caregiver well-being. There is strong consensus among community service providers, clinicians, and researchers that caregivers should be assessed, not only to determine eligibility for services but also to gauge their capacity to provide the care required by the care recipient. Although this view is widely endorsed, its implementation is highly variable in the United States. Few federal or state home- or community-based services programs uniformly assess the informal caregiver's well-being and needs for support. To help address these gaps, the National Center on Caregiving at the Family Caregiver Alliance convened a national consensus development conference in 2005 to generate principles and guidelines for caregiver assessment (Family Caregiver Alliance, 2006a, 2006b). The resulting guidelines address the methods and goals of caregiver assessment in detail, including the recommendation that government and other third-party payers should recognize and pay for caregiver assessment as a routine part of care for older people and individuals with disability. To date, few of the conference recommendations have been implemented, although issues of informal caregiving have become part of the health care reform debate in the United States.

Turning to caregiver training, knowledge about chronic illness and disability, how to provide care, and how to access and utilize services is another requisite to effective caregiving. Caregivers who do not know the difference between stroke and Alzheimer's disease, for example, and the differential trajectories of these conditions, are unlikely to know which types of services are appropriate and available, or how to access them.

Interventions designed to diminish caregiver burden invariably include education and training to help the caregiver understand the nature of a particular disease, its symptoms, and its progression. Such education is often complemented with referral resources that provide additional information and services relevant to a particular health condition. Numerous intervention studies have shown that the ability to cope with the challenges of caregiving in chronic illness is enhanced by skills training that helps the caregiver to better monitor the care recipient's behavior and the progression of the disease and to provide appropriate assistance.

One recent randomized clinical trial demonstrated the efficacy of a caregiver psychoeducational intervention on quality of life in multiple domains among white, African American, and Hispanic caregivers of individuals with dementia (Belle et al., 2006). Other psychoeducational intervention studies, focusing on environmental modifications (Gitlin et al., 2009), found that providing caregiver counseling (Mittelman et al., 2007) can reduce burden and delay institutionalization of the care recipient. Finally, there is increasing recognition that caregivers and care recipients reciprocally affect each other. This perspective has led to the development of interventions that simultaneously treat the caregiver and the care recipient, with the aim of showing that dual treatment psychoeducational approaches are superior to treatments that focus on the caregiver only (Schulz et al., 2009a). In sum, recent studies demonstrate that education and training are valuable tools in enhancing caregiver functioning, but they have not yet been widely implemented in community settings. Efforts are currently under way to translate this research into community applications (see Burgio et al., 2009).

Monitoring of caregiver performance is a neglected area among both researchers and clinicians. With few exceptions (Gitlin et al., 2003), intervention studies that provide skills training to caregivers rarely assess the extent to which the intended skills are effectively implemented outside the treatment sessions, whether the learned skills are useful for newly emerging caregiver challenges, or how long skills learned as part of an intervention are used after the intervention is terminated. Similarly, clinicians who educate caregivers about how to provide care to the recipient rarely assess quality and appropriateness of caregiving outside the training session. For some types of care, patient status may be used as a proxy for caregiver performance, but this does not guarantee that the care provided by the caregiver was delivered as intended or was effective.

Technology has the potential of improving both the training and monitoring of caregivers. Websites that provide information about medical conditions and caregiving have become valuable resources to the discerning consumer who can filter the vast amounts of information available. Computers have also been used to deliver training programs and provide individualized support to caregivers (Smith, 2008). Numerous web-based support programs are available for caregivers. For example, the Comprehensive Health Enhancement Support System (CHESS) advises caregivers by e-mail, conducts assessments by web camera, and models caregiving procedures in video clips (Glasgow, 2007; Comprehensive Health Enhancement Support System, 2008). To be effective, the available information has to be accessible in its organization and layout, the complexity of language and visual images, and ease of interface.

Monitoring technologies that provide remote access to care recipient status have become important aids to caregivers and clinicians. What has not yet been realized is the use of online monitoring devices, such as embedded sensor systems and video cameras that would enable clinicians to infer or observe the delivery of care to the care recipient and provide real-time corrective guidance as needed. Although episodic monitoring is currently used in some telehealth systems that enable a care recipient–caregiver dyad to remotely check in with a health care professional, more continuous monitoring of caregiver performance and provision of real-time instruction or guidance have not been implemented. Many such technologies raise privacy concerns that may make them difficult to put into practice. Recent research in this area suggests that with increasing levels of disability, individuals receiving care become more willing to relinquish privacy for increased functioning and independence (Beach et al., 2009). However, little is known about caregivers' willingness to be monitored and remotely guided by health care professionals.

ABILITY TO PROVIDE CARE

What factors affect caregivers' ability to provide care? The answer to this question requires keeping in mind both who occupies the caregiving role and how the experience of caregiving itself affects the ability to provide care, especially over the long haul. One can anticipate that the increasingly compromised health status of chronically stressed caregivers diminishes their capacity to provide care. In addition, subgroups of individuals defined by race, economic status, education, and age vary in their capacity to provide care.

Health Effects of Caregiving

Several recent reviews document the link between caregiving and health (Pinquart and Sörensen, 2003b, 2007; Vitaliano, Zhang, and Scanlan, 2003; Gouin, Hantsoo, and Kiecolt-Glaser, 2008). For example, Vitaliano and colleagues (2003) reviewed 23 studies to compare the physical health of dementia caregivers with demographically similar noncaregivers, and across 11 health categories caregivers exhibited a least a slightly greater risk of health problems than did noncaregivers. Tables 7-1 and 7-2 summarize the wide range of outcome variables represented in the literature. Each of these variables has been linked to such stressors as the duration and type of care provided and functional and cognitive disabilities of the patient, as well as secondary stressors, such as finances and family conflict. As a result of these stressors, providing care has been shown to affect psychological well-being, health habits, physiological responses, psychiatric and physical illness, and mortality (Quittner, Glueckauf, and Jackson, 1990; Schulz, Visintainer, and Williamson, 1990; Schulz et al., 1995; Schulz and Quittner, 1998; Schulz and Beach, 1999; Pinquart and Sörensen 2003a, 2003b, 2007; Vitaliano et al., 2003; Epel et al., 2004; Christakis and Allison, 2006).

TABLE 7-1 Physical Health Effects of Caregiving

Type of Measure	Specific Indicators	Comments
Global Health	Self-reported health (current health, health compared with others, changes in health status) Chronic conditions (chronic illness checklists) Physical symptoms (Cornell Medical Index) Medications (number and types) Health service utilization (clinic visits, days in hospital, physician visits) Mortality	Overall, effects are small. Self-report measures are most common and show largest effects. One prospective study reports increased mortality for strained caregivers when compared with noncaregivers. Higher age, lower socioeconomic status, and lower levels of informal support related to poorer health. Greater negative effects found for dementia vs. nondementia caregivers and spouses vs. nonspouses.
Physiological	Antibodies and functional immune measures (immunoglobulin, Epstein Barr virus, T-cell proliferation, responses to mitogens, response to cytokine stimulation, lymphocyte counts) Stress hormones and neurotransmitters (ACTH, epinephrine, norepinephrine, cortisol, prolactin) Cardiovascular measures (blood pressure, heart rate) Metabolic measures (body mass, weight, cholesterol, insulin, glucose, transferin) Speed of wound healing	Effect sizes for all indicators are generally small. Stronger relationships found for stress hormones and antibodies than other indicators. Evidence linking caregiving to metabolic and cardiovascular measures is weak. Men exhibit greater negative effects on most physiological indicators.
Health Habits	Sleep, diet, exercise Self-care, medical compliance	

Measures of psychological well-being, such as depression, stress, and burden, have been most frequently studied in the caregiving literature and generally yield consistent and relatively large health effects (Schulz et al., 1995, 1997; Teri et al., 1997; Marks, Lambert, and Choi, 2002; Pinquart and Sörensen, 2003b). These effects are moderated by age, socioeconomic status (SES), and the availability of social support such that

TABLE 7-2 Psychological Health Effects of Caregiving

Type of Measures	Specific Examples	Comments
Depression	Clinical diagnosis, symptom checklists, antidepressant medication use	Most frequently studied caregiver outcomes with largest effects. Greater negative effects found for dementia vs. nondementia caregivers. Higher age, lower seociecomonic status, and lower levels of informal support related to poorer mental health.
Anxiety	Clinical diagnosis, symptom checklists, anxiolytic medication use	
Stress	Burden	
Subjective Well-Being	Global self-ratings; global quality of life ratings	
Positive Aspects of Caregiving	Self-ratings of benefit finding	
Self-Efficacy	Self-ratings	

older caregivers, with low SES and small support networks, report poorer psychological health than caregivers who are younger and have more economic and interpersonal resources (Vitaliano et al., 2003).

Detrimental physical health effects of caregiving are generally smaller, regardless of how they are measured (Vitaliano et al., 2003; Pinquart and Sörensen, 2007). Although relatively few studies have focused on the association between caregiving and health habits, researchers have found evidence for impaired health behaviors among caregivers engaged in heavy-duty caregiving (Schulz et al., 1997; Burton et al., 2003; Lee et al., 2003; Matthews et al., 2004).

While these findings are robust across many studies, one should be cautious about attributing poor health status to caregiving per se. Differences in illness rates between caregivers and noncaregivers may reflect differences that existed prior to taking on the caregiving role. For example, low-SES individuals are more likely to take on the caregiving role than high-SES ones (National Alliance for Caregiving and American Association of Retired Persons, 2004), and low SES is also a risk factor for poor health status. Higher rates of illness in spousal caregivers also may be the result of assortative mating (people tend to choose others who are similar to them) and of shared health habits (e.g., diet, exercise) and life circumstances (e.g., access to medical care, job stress).

Prospective studies that link caregiver health declines to increasing care demands provide more compelling evidence of the health effects of caregiving (Shaw et al., 1997; Schulz and Beach, 1999). A handful of studies have followed samples of noncaregivers until they become caregivers and compared them with those who do not take on the caregiving role (Lawton et al., 2000; Seltzer and Li, 2000; Burton et al., 2003; Hirst, 2005). Burton and colleagues (2003) and more recently Hirst (2005) provide compelling evidence that moving into a demanding caregiving role, defined as providing assistance with basic ADL for 20 hours or more of care per week, results in increased depression and psychological distress, impaired self-care, and lower self-reported health. Findings on the effects of transitioning out of the caregiving role because of patient improvement, institutionalization, or death help to complete the picture on the association between caregiving and health. Improved patient functioning is associated with reductions in caregiver distress (Nieboer et al., 1998), and the death of the care recipient has been found to reduce caregiver depression, enabling them to return to normal levels of functioning within a year of the patient's death (Schulz et al., 2003).

The prevalence of depressive symptoms, clinical depression, and reduced quality of life among caregivers suggests that caregiving is an important public health issue in the United States. This is particularly important because depression is the second leading cause of disability worldwide (Talley and Crews, 2007). Moreover, even if the detrimental effects of caregiving on physical health are relatively small, the large and increasing number of people affected means that the overall impact is significant. Recognition of these facts and the knowledge that caregivers represent a major national health resource has resulted in national policy, such as the National Family Caregiver Support Program. However, most advocates for caregivers feel that existing programs fall far short of what is needed (Riggs, 2003-2004).

With regard to the impact these health effects have on the ability to perform caregiving tasks, multiple factors should be considered. As noted earlier, about two-thirds of all caregivers report stress or strain associated with the caregiving role (Schulz et al., 1997; Roth et al., 2009). Decades of laboratory research have demonstrated the detrimental effects of stress on attention, memory, perceptual motor performance, and judgment and decision making (Staal, 2004). The relevance of these findings to real-world settings has been questioned, because experimental stressors typically are of short duration, are often novel, are limited in intensity, and usually do not have long-term adverse effects. Real-world stressors tend to be more severe, recurrent or continuous, and typically have long-term negative effects on the individual.

Small-sample studies on chronic stress and cognition suggest decrements in executive functioning, especially attentional control, and in prospective memory (Ohman et al., 2007), as well as slow short-term/working memory processing, especially when attention is divided (Brand, Hanson, and Godaert, 2000). The relationship between cognitive performance and the chronic stress induced by caregiving, however, is clearly multifactorial. For example, a decline in receptive vocabulary over two years in spousal caregivers of individuals with Alzheimer's disease was mediated by metabolic risk (a composite measure of obesity plus insulin use) and hostile attribution (Vitaliano et al., 2005). In another example with the same population, caregiver status alone did not account for decrements in complex attention and speed of information processing (Caswell et al., 2003). Rather, within the caregiver sample, these decrements were predicted by higher levels of distress and lower perceptions of the quantity of positive experiences in life.

Another consideration is that the effects of stress are likely to be exacerbated among individuals with limited cognitive and physical reserve, as is most likely the case with older spousal caregivers. This argues for screening strategies that would assess potential moderators of the stress response, such as education, cognitive ability, physical status, traits that may make people particularly vulnerable to chronic stress, and subjective/emotional perceptions of stress and social support, in addition to levels of stress per se. Such information could be used to decide what types of tasks can be assigned to caregivers as well as how closely to monitor caregiver performance.

Along with high levels of stress, many caregivers also report high levels of depressive symptoms. For example, among caregivers of individuals with Alzheimer's disease, nearly half of all caregivers report depressive symptoms high enough to place them at risk for clinical depression (e.g., Belle et al., 2006). Depression has both motivational and performance consequences and has been linked to impaired role functioning, particularly roles associated with work, home, social relationships, and close relations (Druss et al., 2009). Depression can erode the social support needed to provide effective care and can isolate the caregiver from important sources of emotional and informational support.

Depression in spousal caregivers is also a risk factor for potentially harmful caregiver behaviors, defined as psychological (e.g., screaming, threatening with nursing home placement) and physical mistreatment of the care recipient (e.g., withholding food, hitting or slapping, shaking) (Beach et al., 2005). Caregiver cognitive status and physical symptoms were also independent risk factors associated with care recipient mistreatment, suggesting that caregivers should be assessed on these dimensions as well. The literature does not provide clear guidelines regarding threshold values in these domains; higher levels of impairment are generally associated with higher rates of potentially harmful behaviors. In general, clinicians should be cautious about assigning caregiving responsibilities to individuals who exhibit high levels of depressive symptoms or cognitive and physical impairments that are unusually severe for their age group.

Sociodemographic Factors

As alluded to earlier, caregivers as a group, compared with non-caregivers, are characterized by sociodemographic risk factors that may affect their ability to provide effective care as well as increase their vulnerability to the detrimental health effects of caregiving. They tend to be of lower socioeconomic status, and the proportion of people involved in caregiving is higher among African Americans and Hispanics than whites (Roth et al., 2009). Caregivers tend to have fewer friends in their social networks, and older spousal caregivers tend to be physically more compromised than spouses who are not providing care (Schulz et al., 1997). In absolute terms, the magnitude of the differences between caregiver and comparable non-caregiver populations is not large, but these differences may compromise the ability to provide high levels of care over extended periods of time.

Inasmuch as health, well-being, and socioeconomic status are closely intertwined, researchers have become interested in the effects of combining employment and caregiving. Middle-aged women at the peak of their earning power, many of whom are employed, provide the majority of care to older disabled relatives (see Schulz and Martire, 2009, for a review). The increasing labor force participation of women, along with increasing demands for care, raise important questions about how effectively and at what cost the roles of caregiver and employee can be combined. Recent findings indicate that elder caregiving has both short-term and long-term economic impacts on female caregivers. Low levels of caregiving demand (e.g., 14 hours or less per week) can be absorbed by employed caregivers with little impact on labor force participation. However, heavy caregiving demands (e.g., 20 hours or more per week) result in significant work adjustment, involving either reduced hours or leaving a job altogether, and associated declines in annual incomes. Women with less than a high school education are most vulnerable to these negative effects. These short-term effects increase the probability of long-term negative impacts in the form of lower economic and health status of the caregiver. The long-term impacts may in part be attributable to the difficulty of reentering the labor force.

Developmental Declines

From a human factors perspective, developmental declines have important implications for the ability to provide care as well as the design of systems that might support caregivers. Sensory decline is common in middle-aged and older adults. For example, measured hearing loss is present in about 44 percent of adults ages 60-69, with prevalence increasing with age (Cruickshanks et al., 1998; Pratt et al., 2009). Hearing is particularly impaired in difficult listening environments, such as those with background noise or reverberation or when communication is rapid. For individuals with age-related hearing loss, attempts to comprehend spoken language can involve substantial perceptual and cognitive effort that may detract from other aspects of cognitive performance (Wingfield, Tun, and McCoy, 2005). While hearing can be improved with hearing aids or other assistive listening devices, these devices do not completely correct the typical age-related hearing loss. The devices may be abandoned because they are uncomfortable to use or perceived as ineffective. In addition, many people do not seek help for hearing loss, complaining, for example, that the people around them just talk too softly. When interacting with caregivers, it is crucial to consider their ability to perceive spoken information, and providers of that information must be aware that just talking louder will not address a speech perception problem. Visual impairment also may be a problem for older caregivers, making it difficult for them to read medication labels or other instructional materials.

Age-related declines in strength and mobility may also affect the ability to provide care. One of the hallmarks of aging is the reduction in mobility resulting in part from declining muscle mass, increased fat infiltration into muscles and decreased strength (Visser et al., 2005). As a result, older female caregivers, in particular, may be unable to carry out tasks requiring lifting heavy objects (e.g., helping their husband out of a chair) or may risk back injury or injury to the care recipient if they attempt these tasks. Essential tremor, a disorder characterized by kinetic arm tremor, is also associated with increasing age (Benito-León and Louis, 2006) and may make it difficult for caregivers to execute fine-grained motor tasks, such as giving injections or handling pills.

LOOKING TO THE FUTURE

Informal caregiving is a central feature of the health care landscape and will become even more prominent in the decades ahead. The demand and need for care will increase dramatically over the next three decades as a result of the aging of the population, infant and childhood survival, health behaviors that increase disabling health conditions such as obesity, and returning war veterans suffering from polytrauma. This will happen in a context in which the availability of informal support is declining, the costs of formal care and support are already too high and unsustainable, and there is a growing shortfall of health care professionals with relevant expertise. Resolving this supply–demand dilemma will require efficiencies in both informal and formal health care systems that greatly exceed current practice. Important research and policy issues need to be addressed before progress can be made on this agenda. We present below five recommendations that, though by no means exhaustive, should receive high priority.

1. Adopt a standard definition of what it means to be an informal caregiver and use it consistently in surveys of the U.S. population, in order to accurately assess the prevalence of caregiving, the public health burden associated with caregiving, and a full range of issues such as those discussed here. Accurate and consistent data are needed on who is providing care, what types of care are provided, for how long, at what costs to the caregiver, and the probable downstream costs to society. Having such data is an important requisite to developing policy on support programs for caregivers. The value of this recommendation is evident, for example, in Australia, Japan, and the United Kingdom, all of which have adopted standard definitions of caregiving that are linked to eligibility for caregiver and care recipient services. Variations of the standard definition may be necessary for different populations of caregivers and care recipients, and levels of care should also be consistently defined.
2. Better coordination is needed between formal and informal health care systems to ensure a close match between home care demands and the informal caregiver's ability to provide that care. This will require a clear understanding of the task demands of home care and an assessment of caregiver capabilities, including their motivation to provide care, their physical, sensory, motor, and cognitive ability to perform caregiving tasks, their levels of distress and depression, and the quantity and quality of other support available to them. Assessments of the caregiver should be a routine feature during care recipient and health care provider encounters, and these data should inform decisions about whether a caregiver is capable of taking on the caregiver role, the types of training needed, and the intensity of monitoring and external support required to ensure adequate care that does not unduly compromise the caregiver's own functioning. A related need concerns the development of decision rules for terminating caregiving responsibilities when caregivers are no longer able to carry out their assignments. Implementing these strategies will require expansion of the training of health care and social service providers to give them the skills and tools to carry out these types of assessments (Family Caregiver Alliance, 2006a, 2006b). Detailed recommendations on who should do assessments, what should be assessed, and when and where, are available from

the National Consensus Development Conference on Caregiver Assessment (Family Caregiver Alliance, 2006a, 2006b). Although intended for caregivers of older care recipients, these recommendations serve as a good starting point for developing assessment procedures and tools for all caregiving populations.

3. From a scientific perspective, there remain important unanswered questions about caregiving that have far-reaching policy implications. For example, a deeper understanding is needed of what causes distress in the caregiving experience and how best to help the caregiver. Although numerous studies point to the importance of various functional disabilities and associated care demands as causes of caregiver burden, the role that such factors as the care recipient's suffering play in the life of a caregiver may be underestimated. Making these distinctions is important because it may lead to different policy responses (e.g., providing respite to ease the burdens of care provision as well as treatments to decrease the suffering of the care recipient or to help the caregiver come to terms with the suffering of their loved one) (Monin and Schulz, 2009).
4. Technology has the potential of increasing the efficiency and effectiveness of formal and informal care providers, enhancing the functioning and autonomy of individuals with disability, preventing premature decline, and generally enhancing the quality of life of elders. Implementing technology-based solutions will require the development of user-friendly and highly reliable systems that are able to both identify needs and respond to them. Considerable progress has been made in recent years in developing and deploying sensing and monitoring technology useful in identifying individuals experiencing or at risk for adverse outcomes. Computer, sensing, and communication technologies have also been effectively used for caregiver training and performance monitoring. Research on enabling technologies that extend the functional capability of humans is still in the early stages of development and should receive high priority.
5. Because caregiving is so prevalent in U.S. society and integral to the health and well-being of the population, all adults need to be educated about the likelihood of becoming a caregiver and a care recipient, the roles and responsibilities of caregiving, and rudimentary caregiving skills. A recent survey of 1,018 adults ages 18 and over (Schulz et al., 2009b) found that adults have realistic expectations about becoming caregivers in the future but are less able to see themselves as care recipients. Nearly two-thirds of U.S. adults expect to be caregivers in the future, but nearly half believe that they won't need any care in the future. Indeed, more than one-third

of adults have never thought about needing care in the future, and few have made any preparations for future care, such as talking with family or friends about care needs in the future (34 percent), setting aside funds to cover additional expenses (41 percent), signing living wills or health care power of attorney (40 percent), or purchasing disability or long-term care insurance. When asked how prepared they are to provide care to others, the majority (56 percent) were unprepared to carry out basic caregiving tasks, such as bathing, dressing, and toileting, 35 percent said they were only somewhat or not at all (28 percent) prepared to handle health insurance matters, 56 percent said they were unprepared to assist with medications, and most worry about handling financial matters for a loved one. These data suggest that caregiving and care receiving should be a normative component of adult education. The goal of such efforts should be to inform adults about the likelihood of caregiving and care receiving, ways in which one can plan for these eventualities, and rudimentary skills needed to perform or cope in these roles.

ABOUT THE AUTHORS

Richard Schulz is director of the Center for Social and Urban Research at the University of Pittsburgh. His work has focused on social-psychological aspects of aging, including the role of control as a construct for characterizing life-course development and the impact of disabling late-life disease on patients and their families. Connie A. Tompkins is professor of communication science and disorders in the Center for the Neural Basis of Cognition at the University of Pittsburgh. Her research focuses on the cognitive and psycholinguistic bases of neurologically based communication disorders.

REFERENCES

Agency for Healthcare Research and Quality. (2007). *Acute care/hospitalization: Studies suggest ways to improve the hospital discharge process to reduce postdischarge adverse events and rehospitalizations.* Available: http://www.ahrq.gov/research/dec07/1207RA12.htm [accessed June 2010].

Beach, S., Schulz, R., Downs, J., Matthews, J., Barron, B., and Seelman, K. (2009). Disability, age, and informational privacy attitudes in quality of life technology applications: Results from a national web survey. *ACM Transactions on Accessible Computing,* 2(1), 1-21.

Beach, S.R., Schulz, R., Williamson, G.M., Miller, L.S., Weiner, M.F., and Lance C.E. (2005). Risk factors for potentially harmful informal caregiver behavior. *Journal of the American Geriatrics Society, 53*(2), 255-261.

Belle, S.H., Burgio, L., Burns, R., Coon, D., Czaja, S.J., Gallagher-Thompson, D., Gitlin, L.N., Klinger, J., Koepke, K.M., Lee, C.C., Martindale-Adams, J., Nichols, L., Schulz, R., Stahl, S., Stevens, A., Winter, L., and Zhang, S. [REACH II Investigators]. (2006). Enhancing the quality of life of dementia caregivers from different ethnic or racial groups: A randomized, controlled trial. *Annals of Internal Medicine, 145*(10), 727-738.

Benito-León, J., and Louis, E.D. (2006). Essential tremor: Emerging views of a common disorder. *Nature Clinical Practice, Neurology, 2*(12), 666-678.

Brand, N., Hanson, E., and Godaert, G. (2000). Chronic stress affects blood pressure and speed of short-term memory. *Perceptual and Motor Skills, 91*(1), 291-298.

Burgio, L.D., Collins, I.B., Schmid, B., Wharton, T., McCallum, D., and DeCoster, J. (2009). Translating the REACH caregiver intervention for use by Area Agency on Aging personnel. *The Gerontologist, 49*(1), 103-116.

Burton, L.C., Zdaniuk, B., Schulz, R., Jackson, S., and Hirsch, C. (2003). Transitions in spousal caregiving. *The Gerontologist, 43*(2), 230-241.

Caswell, L.W., Vitaliano, P.P., Croyle, K.L., Scanlan, J.M., Zhang, J., and Daruwala, A. (2003). Negative associations of chronic stress and cognitive performance in older adult spouse caregivers. *Experimental Aging Research, 29*(3), 303-318.

Centers for Disease Control and Prevention. (2006). *Disability and health state chartbook, 2006: Profiles of health for adults with disabilities*. Atlanta: Author.

Chen, H.C., Chen, M.L., Lotus Shyu, Y.I., and Tang, W.R. (2007). Development and testing of a scale to measure caregiving load in caregivers of cancer patients in Taiwan: The care task scale-cancer. *Cancer Nursing, 30*(3), 223-231.

Christakis, N., and Allison, P.D. (2006). Mortality after the hospitalization of a spouse. *New England Journal of Medicine, 354*(7), 719-730.

Clark, M.C., Czaja, S.J., and Weber, R.A. (1990). Older adults and daily living task profiles. *Human Factors, 32*(5), 537-549.

Comprehensive Health Enhancement Support System. (2008). *What is CHESS?* University of Wisconsin-Madison. Available: http://www.engr.wisc.edu/ie/research/centers/chess.html [accessed June 2010].

Cruickshanks, K.J., Wiley, T.L., Tweed, T.S., Klein, B.E., Klein, R., Mares-Perlman, J.A., and Nondahl, D.M. (1998). Prevalence of hearing loss in older adults in Beaver Dam, Wisconsin: The epidemiology of hearing loss study. *American Journal of Epidemiology, 148*(9), 879-886.

Czaja, S.J., Sharit, J., and Nair, S.N. (2008). Usability of the Medicare health web site. *Journal of the American Medical Association, 300*(7), 790-792.

Druss, B.G., Hwang, I., Petukhova, M., Sampson, N.A., Wang, P.S., and Kessler, R.C. (2009). Impairment in role functioning in mental and chronic medical disorders in the United States: Results from the National Comorbidity Survey replication. *Molecular Psychiatry, 14*(7), 728-737.

Epel, E.S., Blackburn, E.H., Lin, J., Dhabhar, F.S., Adler, N.E., Morrow, J.D., and Cawthon, R.M. (2004). Accelerated telomere shortening in response to life stress. *Proceedings of the National Academy of Sciences of the United States of America, 101*(49), 17,312-17,315.

Family Caregiver Alliance. (2006a). *Caregiver assessment: Principles, guidelines, and strategies for change*. Report from a National Consensus Development Conference (vol. I). San Francisco: Author.

Family Caregiver Alliance. (2006b). *Caregiver assessment: Voices and views from the field*. Report from a National Consensus Development Conference (vol. II). San Francisco: Author.

Gitlin, L.N., Hauck, W.W., Winter, L., Hodgson, N., and Schinfeld, S. (2009). Long-term effect on mortality of a home intervention that reduces functional difficulties in older adults: Results from a randomized trial. *Journal of the American Geriatrics Society, 57*(3), 476-481.

Gitlin, L.N., Winter, L., Corcoran, M., and Hauck, W. (2003). Effects of the home environmental skill-building program on the caregiver-care recipient dyad: Six-month outcomes from the Philadelphia REACH initiative. *The Gerontologist, 43*(4), 532-546.

Glasgow, R.E. (2007). eHealth evaluation and disseminiation research. *American Journal of Preventive Medicine, 32*(5 Supplement), S119-S126.

Gouin, J.P, Hantsoo, L., and Kiecolt-Glaser, J.K. (2008). Immune dysregulation and chronic stress among older adults: A review. *Neuroimmunomodulation, 15*(4-6), 251-259.

Hironaka, L.K., and Paasche-Orlow, M.K. (2008). The implications of health literacy on patient-provider communication. *Archives of Disease in Childhood, 93*(5), 428-432.

Hirst, M. (2005). Carer distress: A prospective, population-based study. *Social Science and Medicine, 61*(3), 697-708.

Horsburgh, M.E., Laing, G.P., Beanlands, H.J., Meng, A.X., and Harwood, L. (2008). A new measure of "lay" caregiver activities. *Kidney International, 74*, 230-236.

Institute of Medicine. (2007). *The future of disability in America*. Committee on Disability in America, Board on Health Sciences Policy. M.J. Field and A.M. Jette, Eds. Washington, DC: The National Academies Press.

Kripalani, S., Henderson, L.E., Chiu, E.Y., Robertson, R., Kolm, P., and Jacobson, T.A. (2006). Predictors of medication self-management skill in a low-literacy population. *Journal of General Internal Medicine, 21*(8), 852-856.

Lawton, M.P., Moss, M., Hoffman, C., and Perkinson, M. (2000). Two transitions in daughters' caregiving careers. *The Gerontologist, 40*(4), 437-448.

Lee, S., Colditz, G., Berkman, L., and Kawachi, I. (2003). Caregiving and risk of coronary heart disease in U.S. women: A prospective study. *American Journal of Preventive Medicine, 24*(2), 113-119.

Levine, C., Gibson Hunt, G., Halper, D., Hart, A.Y., Lautz, J., and Gould, D.A. (2005). Young adult caregivers: A first look at an unstudied population. *American Journal of Public Health, 95*(11), 2071-2075.

Marks, N.E., Lambert, J.D., and Choi, H. (2002). Transitions to caregiving, gender and psychological : A prospective U.S. national study. *Journal of Marriage and Family, 64*, 657-667.

Matthews, J.T., Dunbar-Jacob, J., Sereika, S., Schulz, R., and McDowell, B.J. (2004). Preventive health practices: Comparison of family caregivers 50 and older. *Journal of Gerontological Nursing, 30*(2), 46-54.

Mittelman, M.S., Roth, D.L., Clay, O.J., and Haley, W.E. (2007). Preserving health of Alzheimer caregivers: Impact of a spouse caregiver intervention. *American Journal of Geriatric Psychiatry, 15*, 780-789.

Monin, J.K., and Schulz, R. (2009). Interpersonal effects of suffering in older adult caregiving relationships. *Psychology and Aging, 24*(3), 681-695.

Naik, A.D., Concato, J., and Gill, T.M. (2004). Bathing disability in community-living older persons: Common, consequential, and complex. *Journal of the American Geriatrics Society, 52*(11), 1,805-1,810.

National Alliance for Caregiving. (2004). *Miles away: The MetLife Study of long-distance caregiving*. Washington, DC: Author.

National Alliance for Caregiving and American Association of Retired Persons. (2004). *Caregiving in the U.S., 2004*. Washington, DC: Author.

National Alliance for Caregiving and American Association of Retired Persons. (2009). *Caregiving in the U.S., 2009*. Washington, DC: Author.

National Center for Education Statistics. (2006). *The health literacy of America's adults: Results from the 2003 National Assessment of Adult Literacy.* (NCES 2006-483). M. Kutner, E., Greenberg, Y. Jin, and C. Paulsen, Eds. Washington, DC: U.S. Department of Education.

National Family Caregivers Association and Family Caregiver Alliance. (2006). *Prevalence, hours, and economic value of family caregiving, updated state-by-state analysis of 2004 national estimates.* Kensington, MD and San Francisco: Author.

Nieboer, A.P., Schulz, R., Matthews, K.A., Scheier, M.F., Ormel, J., and Lindenberg, S.M. (1998). Spousal caregivers' activity restriction and depression: A model for changes over time. *Social Science and Medicine, 47*(9), 1,361-1,371.

Ohman, L., Nordin, S., Bergdahl, J., Slunga Birgander, L., and Stigsdotter Neely, A. (2007). Cognitive function in outpatients with perceived chronic stress. *Scandinavian Journal of Work, Environment, and Health, 33*(3), 223-232.

Pakenham, K.I. (2007). The nature of caregiving in multiple sclerosis: Development of the caregiving tasks in multiple sclerosis scale. *Multiple Sclerosis, 13*, 929-938.

Pinquart, M., and Sörensen, S. (2003a). Associations of stressors and uplifts of caregiving with caregiver burden and depressive mood: A meta-analysis. *Journals of Gerontology, Series B, 58*, P112-P128.

Pinquart, M., and Sörensen, S. (2003b). Differences between caregivers and noncaregivers in psychological health and physical health: A meta-analysis. *Psychology and Aging, 18*(2), 250-267.

Pinquart, M., and Sörensen, S. (2007). Correlates of physical health of informal caregivers: A meta-analysis. *Journals of Gerontology, Series B, 62*(2), P126-P137.

Pratt, S.R., Kuller, L., Talbott, E.O., McHugh-Pemu, K., Buhari, A.M., and Xu, X. (2009). Prevalence of hearing loss in black and white elders: Results of the cardiovascular health study. *Journal of Speech, Language, and Hearing Research, 52*(4), 973-989.

Quittner, A.L., Glueckauf, R.L., and Jackson, D.N. (1990). Chronic parenting stress: Moderating versus mediating effects of social support. *Journal of Personality and Social Psychology, 59*(6), 1,266-1,278.

Riggs, J.A. (2003-2004). A family caregiver policy agenda for the twenty-first century. *Generations, 27*(4), 68-73.

Roth, D., Perkins, M., Wadley, V., Temple, E., and Haley, W. (2009). Family caregiving and emotional strain: Associations with quality of life in a large national sample of middle-aged and older adults. *Quality of Life Research, 18*(6), 679-688.

Schulz, R., and Beach, S.R. (1999). Caregiving as a risk factor for mortality: The Caregiver Health Effects Study. *Journal of the American Medical Association, 282*(23), 2,215-2,219.

Schulz, R., and Martire, L.M. (2009). Caregiving and employment. In S.J. Czaja and J. Sharit (Eds.), *Aging and work: Implications in a changing landscape*. Baltimore: Johns Hopkins University Press.

Schulz, R., and Quittner, A.L. (1998). Caregiving for children and adults with chronic conditions: Introduction to the special issue. *Health Psychology, 17*(2), 107-111.

Schulz, R., Czaja, S.J., Lustig, A., Zdaniuk, B., Martire, L.M., and Perdomo, D. (2009a). Improving the quality of life of caregivers of persons with spinal cord injury: A randomized controlled trial. *Rehabilitation Psychology, 54*(1), 1-15.

Schulz, R., Czaja, S.J., Belle, S.H., and Lewin, N. (2009b). *Survey of the U.S. adult population on preparedness for caregiving*. Unpublished data, University of Pittsburgh.

Schulz, R., Mendelsohn, A.B., Haley, W.E., Mahoney, D., Allen, R.S., Zhang, S., Thompson, L., and Belle, S.H. (2003). End-of-life care and the effects of bereavement on family caregivers of persons with dementia. *New England Journal of Medicine, 349*(20), 1,936-1,942.

Schulz, R., Newsom, J., Mittelmark, M., Burton, L. Hirsch, C., and Jackson, S. (1997). Health effects of caregiving, the Caregiver Health Effects Study: An ancillary study of the Cardiovascular Health Study. *Annals of Behavioral Medicine, 19*(2), 110-116.

Schulz, R., O'Brien, A.T., Bookwala, J., and Fleissner, K. (1995). Psychiatric and physical morbidity effects of dementia caregiving: Prevalence, correlates, and causes. *The Gerontologist, 35*(6), 771-791.

Schulz, R., Visintainer, P., and Williamson, G.M. (1990). Psychiatric and physical morbidity effects of caregiving. *Journals of Gerontology, 45*(5), P181-P191.

Seltzer, M.M., and Li, W. (2000). The dynamics of caregiving: Transitions during a three-year prospective study. *The Gerontologist, 40*(2), 165-178.

Shaw, W.S., Patterson, T.L., Semple, S.J., Ho, S., Irwin, M.R., Hauger, R.L., and Grant, I. (1997). Longitudinal analysis of multiple indicators of health decline among spousal caregivers. *Annals of Behavioral Medicine, 19*(2), 101-119.

Simmons, T., and Dye, J.L. (2003). *Grandparents living with grandchildren: 2000*. Washington, DC: U.S. Department of Commerce, Economics and Statistics Administration, U.S. Census Bureau. Available: http://www.census.gov/prod/2003pubs/c2kbr-31.pdf [accessed June 2010].

Smith, C. (2008). Technology and web-based support. *American Journal of Nursing, 108*(9 Supplement), 64-68.

Staal, M.A. (August 2004). *Stress, cognition, and human performance: A literature review and conceptual framework*. (NASA Technical Memorandum 2004-212824). Moffett Field, CA: NASA-Ames Research Center.

Stoops, N. (June 2004). Educational attainment in the United States: 2003. Population characteristics. *Current Population Reports*. Washington, DC: U.S. Department of Commerce, Economics and Statistics Administration, Census Bureau. Available: http://www.census.gov/prod/2004pubs/p20-550.pdf [accessed June 2010].

Talley, R.C., and Crews, J.E. (2007). Framing the public health of caregiving. *American Journal of Public Health, 97*(2), 224-228.

Teri, L., Logsdon, R.G., Uomoto, J., and McCurry, S.M. (1997). Behavioral treatment of depression in dementia patients: A controlled clinical trial. *Journals of Gerontology, Series B, 52*(4), P159-P166.

U.S. Department of Health and Human Services. (2008). *The national survey of children with special health care needs: Chartbook 2005-2006*. (Health Resources and Services Administration and Maternal and Child Health Bureau.) Washington, DC: Author. Available: http://mchb.hrsa.gov/cshcn05/ [accessed June 2010].

Visser, M., Goodpaster, B.H., Kritchevsky, S.B., Newman, A.B., Nevitt, M., Rubin, S.M., Simonsick, E.M., and Harris, T.B. (2005). Muscle mass, muscle strength, and muscle fat infiltration as predictors of incident mobility limitations in well-functioning older persons. *Journal of Gerontology, Series A, 60*(3), 324-333.

Vitaliano, P.P., Echeverria, D., Yi, J., Phillips, P.E., Young, H., and Siegler, I.C. (2005). Psychophysiological mediators of caregiver stress and differential cognitive decline. *Psychology and Aging, 20*(3), 402-411.

Vitaliano, P., Zhang, J., and Scanlan, J.M. (2003). Is caregiving hazardous to one's physical health?: A meta-analysis. *Psychological Bulletin, 129*(6), 946-972.

Wilkins, V.M., Bruce, M.L., and Sirey, J.A. (2009). Caregiving tasks and training interest of family caregivers of medically ill homebound older adults. *Journal of Aging and Health, 21*(3), 528-542.

Wingfield, A., Tun, P.A., and McCoy, S.L. (2005). Hearing loss in older adulthood: What it is and how it interacts with cognitive performance. *Current Directions in Psychological Science, 14*, 144-148.

Wolff, J.L., and Kasper, J.D. (2006). Caregivers of frail elders: Updating a national profile. *The Gerontologist, 46*(3), 344-356.

Zylke, J.W., and DeAngelis, C.D. (2007). Pediatric chronic diseases—Stealing childhood. *Journal of the American Medical Association, 297*(24), 2,765-2,766.

8

Medical Devices in Home Health Care

Molly Follette Story

As the formal health care system has become increasingly stressed, patients are being released from hospitals and other health care facilities still needing care. As a consequence, both laypeople and professional caregivers are making use of a wide variety of technologies, some of them quite complex, in noninstitutional settings to manage their own health, assist others with health care, or receive assistance with health management. These technologies provide support not only for care related to acute and chronic medical conditions but also for disease prevention and lifestyle choices.

The range of medical technologies used in nonclinical environments runs the gamut in complexity from simple materials used for administering first aid to sophisticated devices used for delivering advanced medical treatment, and in size from tiny wireless devices to massive machines. Some medical devices have been used in the home for many years; other devices are just beginning to migrate there; and emergent technologies present new opportunities for health care management in the home. While some of these devices were explicitly designed for use outside formal health care settings by professional home health caregivers as well as the general public, many devices were not. Consequently, many human factors challenges must be addressed to render these technologies, devices, and systems safe, usable, and effective for use in environments beyond the institution and for use by the much more varied population of users in these environments. This chapter discusses standalone medical devices used in home health care.

BACKGROUND

The Center for Devices and Radiological Health of the U.S. Food and Drug Administration (FDA) defines a medical device as "an instrument, apparatus, implement, machine, contrivance, implant, in vitro reagent, or other similar article that is . . . intended for use in the diagnosis of disease or other conditions, or in the cure, mitigation, treatment or prevention of disease" (Federal Food, Drug, and Cosmetic Act, 2005, Sec. 201 (h), 21 U.S.C. 321). The center's Home Health Care Committee defines a home medical device as "a device intended for use in a nonclinical or transitory environment, [that] is managed partly or wholly by the user, requires adequate labeling for the user, and may require training for the user by a health care professional in order to be used safely and effectively" (U.S. Food and Drug Administration, 2009b).

Medical devices used in home health care need to be appropriate for the people who use them and for the environments in which they are used. The people who use medical devices may be professional or lay caregivers or the care recipients themselves. As a group, these users have diverse physical, sensory, cognitive, and emotional characteristics. The environment of use may be the home, but it may also be the workplace or another destination in the community or across the globe. Environments vary in the quality and accessibility of utilities, the amount of space available, light and noise levels, temperature and humidity levels, and occupants, who may include children, pets, or vermin. All of these use factors must be considered in order to ensure that medical devices are safe and effective for people receiving home health care.

Historical Use of Medical Devices in the Home

The most common types of medical devices, found in nearly every home, are used for delivering medications or first aid. Common medication administration equipment includes dosing cups for measuring medications in liquid form, such as cough medicine, and splitting devices for reducing the size and dosage of pills. First aid equipment includes thermometers (including oral, rectal, in-ear, and forehead), bandages, ace bandages, heating pads, and snakebite kits. Other types of medical devices commonly used in the home are assistive technologies and durable medical equipment. Assistive technologies are most often either mobility aids (e.g., wheelchairs, walkers, canes, crutches) or sensory aids (e.g., glasses, hearing aids). Other common assistive technologies are prosthetic devices (e.g., artificial arms or legs) or orthotic devices (e.g., leg braces, shoe inserts). Durable medical equipment includes environmental devices, such as specialized beds, person-lifting and transferring equipment, and toileting aids.

Recently some medical devices have been produced as consumer products that enable people to manage their own health care more conveniently and independently (and inexpensively). For example, a wide variety of blood and urine testing kits are available that detect different chemicals and conditions (e.g., illegal drugs, cholesterol, pregnancy). Various types of monitors and meters are available to measure health status indicators, such as blood pressure or blood glucose levels (for people with diabetes). Newer consumer devices include ones that measure blood coagulation (prothrombin time and international normalized ratio, PT/INR) for people taking blood thinning medications, blood oxygen levels (pulse-oximeter), and sleep apnea.

Increasing Migration of Medical Devices into the Home

Climbing costs of health care services and hospital stays and shortages of health care facilities and of nurses and other skilled personnel have put pressure on the medical system to provide more care on an outpatient basis. Consequently, the range and complexity of medical devices being used outside formal health care institutions by diverse user populations are increasing. Even complex devices, such as ventilators, infusion pumps, and dialysis machines, are being used outside the hospital or clinic, often by lay users, even though many of those devices were not designed for and were not specifically labeled for this type of use. There are few regulations that limit the practice of using these devices in the home.

One of the problems associated with medical devices used in the home is that they often are not the same models as the ones used in formal health care settings. The devices may be older or of lower quality, and professionals who encounter the devices, either in the home or when patients bring them to the clinic or hospital, may not be familiar with them. Speaking on behalf of AdvaMed, Susan Morris, vice president for government affairs for Kinetic Concepts (a wound care technology firm), said, "One of the biggest concerns [of manufacturers] . . . is that legacy devices, old products that were used in the institution that may have been replaced by newer versions, are now migrating into the home because they're available . . . but they aren't products that we originally designed for use in the home" (Taft, 2007). Health care professionals sometimes send people home with medical devices, but consumers sometimes give the devices to other people or resell them, for example, through the Internet on Craigslist or eBay. Devices acquired in this manner are much less likely to be appropriate for the end-user, to be properly operated or maintained, or even to come with complete instructions.

Another challenge for medical device manufacturers is that the device user often is not the person who selected or purchased it. The device provider may be a health care professional, or it may be a distributor or supplier. In the latter cases, the device may not be the optimal choice for the end-users, and the users may not receive the education, training, or ongoing customer support they need. In turn, the device manufacturer may not understand its end-users well because it may not recognize these populations as users of its products, and its designers may never come into direct contact with them.

Users of Medical Devices in the Home

The Centers for Medicare & Medicaid Services reported that approximately 8.3 million Americans received Medicaid home care in 2004, which represents a dramatic increase over the 1.64 million who received services in 1995 (National Association for Home Care and Hospice, 2008) (see Figure 8-1). The growth trend is likely to continue.

Users of medical devices in the home are a diverse population. Some users are professional caregivers, such as physicians, nurses, nurse practitioners, physical and occupational therapists, social workers, and home care aides. These professionals are typically associated with home care organizations (e.g., home health agencies, hospices, homemaker and home care aide agencies, staffing and private-duty agencies, companies specializing in medical equipment and supplies) or they may be from registries or operate as independent providers. Other device users are lay caregivers, usually family members or friends of the person receiving care. Some care recipients operate devices themselves (while providing self-care). Lay caregivers may be of any age and may have developmental or acquired disabilities, a temporary or intermittent condition, a chronic disease, or a terminal illness (see Chapters 6 and 7).

Nonclinical Environments for Medical Devices

Medical devices are used in nonclinical environments that include homes, workplaces (which may or may not be in office buildings), schools, hotels, stores, places of worship, entertainment venues, and transportation systems (cars, buses, trains, airplanes, ships, etc.). Depending on the device and the procedure, people may use medical devices in a private space, such as a bedroom, office, or restroom, or in a public space, such as an airplane, theater, or park. The variety of use environments presents significant challenges for device and user safety.

TYPES OF HOME HEALTH CARE DEVICES

Home health care devices span a wide range, as mentioned above. Table 8-1 presents a taxonomy that uses the following major categories:

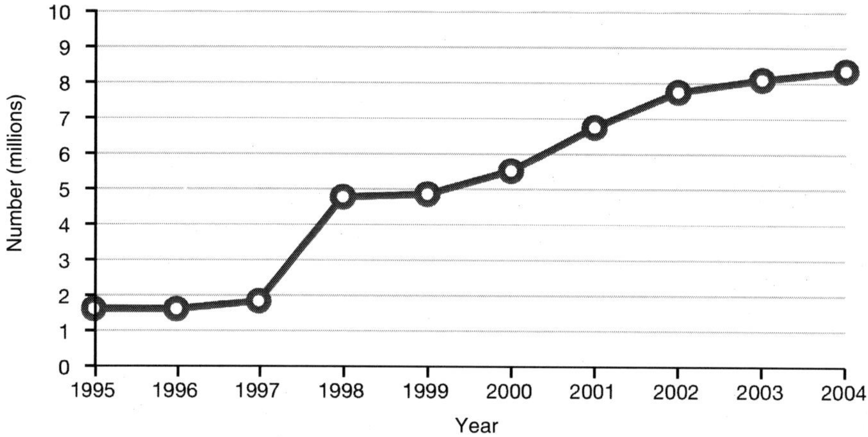

FIGURE 8-1 Medicaid home care recipients, 1995-2004.
SOURCE: Data from National Association for Home Care and Hospice (2008).

- Medication Administration Equipment—devices used to administer medications in tablet, liquid, or aerosol form.
- Test Kits—kits used for measuring the presence of various chemicals in blood or urine.
- First Aid Equipment—equipment used to care for injuries or temporary conditions.
- Assistive Technology—devices used to enhance personal capabilities, such as sensory abilities or mobility.
- Durable Medical Equipment—includes medical devices used to support performance of basic activities of daily living, such as beds, lifts, and toileting equipment.
- Meters/Monitors—includes a wide range of devices for determining health status or managing disease conditions, either one time or on an ongoing, intermittent basis.
- Treatment Equipment—equipment used to administer various medical therapies.
- Respiratory Equipment—equipment used to treat respiratory conditions.
- Feeding Equipment—devices used for feeding.
- Voiding Equipment—devices used for releasing urine or feces from the body.
- Infant Care—includes machines used to monitor and treat infants.
- Telehealth Equipment—equipment used to collect data in the home environment and transmit the data to a remote monitoring site.

TABLE 8-1 Types of Home Health Care Devices

Category	Device
Medication Administration Equipment	Dosing equipment (e.g., cups, eyedroppers, blunt syringes) Nasal sprays, inhalers Medication patches Syringes/sharps
Test Kits	Pregnancy test Male/female/stress hormone test Cholesterol test Allergy test Bladder infection test HIV test Hepatitis C test Drug, alcohol, nicotine test
First Aid Equipment	Bandages Ace bandage, compression stocking Snakebite kit Heating pad Traction Ostomy care Tracheotomy care Defibrillator
Assistive Technology	Eyeglasses Hearing aid Dentures (full or partial) Prosthetic device Orthotic device, including braces Cane or crutches Walker Wheelchair Scooter
Durable Medical Equipment	Hospital bed Specialized mattress Chair (e.g., geri-chair or lift chair) Lift equipment Commode, urinal, bed pan
Meters/Monitors	Thermometer Stethoscope Blood glucose meter Blood coagulation (PT/INR) meter Pulse oximeter Weight scale Blood pressure monitor Apnea monitor Electrocardiogram monitor Fetal monitor

TABLE 8-1 Continued

Category	Device
Treatment Equipment	IV equipment Infusion pumps Dialysis machines Transcutaneous electrical nerve stimulation systems
Respiratory Equipment	Ventilator, continuous positive airway pressure, bi-level positive airway pressure, and demand positive airway pressure equipment Oxygen cylinder Oxygen concentrator Nebulizer Masks and canulas Respiratory supplies Cough assist machine Suction machine Manual resuscitation bags
Feeding Equipment	Feeding tubes (nasogastric, gastrostomy, jejunostomy) Enteral pump
Voiding Equipment	Catheter Colostomy bags
Infant Care	Incubator Radiant warmer Bilirubin lights Phototherapy Apnea monitor
Telehealth Equipment	Cameras Sensors Data collection and communication equipment (e.g., computer) Telephone or internet connections

EMERGENT TECHNOLOGIES IN HOME HEALTH CARE

Telehealth—which is health care facilitated by telecommunications technology—has begun to transform the home care landscape and promises to grow substantially in coming years. Currently, simple technologies (e.g., e-mail, the Internet, cell phones) can be used to monitor people's health at a distance. High-resolution visual images and audio can be transmitted through telephone lines or broadband connections. In coming years, remote monitoring will increase dramatically and will involve more types of equipment in the home; technologies such as wireless electronics and digital processing will support communication between a diverse set of devices and remote health care providers. Some wireless devices, especially meters and monitors, will be wearable, which will make constant monitoring possible or intermittent testing more convenient.

Telehealth technologies can be used to support adherence to treatment regimens, facilitate self-care, and provide patient education. Cameras and sensors can be used to track patient movements and behaviors in the home. Monitors can collect and transmit a variety of data to health care providers at a distance, eliminating the need to visit a clinic or to call in. These technologies can also provide reminders to people at home, such as to take medications, measure their blood pressure, perform physical therapy, or schedule follow-up appointments.

Future technological advances will bring new devices, such as improved pacemakers, cochlear implants, and medicine delivery systems. Miniaturization of various components, including microprocessors and nanotechnology, will make possible advances to many types of medical devices used inside and outside formal health care settings. Some of the devices envisioned will be embedded in common household objects, such as a biosensing chip in a toothbrush that will check blood sugar and bacteria levels; smart bandages made of fiber that will detect bacteria or a virus in a wound and then recommend appropriate treatment; smart T-shirts that will monitor the wearer's vital signs in real time; and heads-up displays for glasses that use pattern recognition software to help people remember human faces, inanimate objects, or other data. Novel handheld devices may provide new capabilities for home health care, such as skin surface mapping, an imaging technology that will track changes in moles to detect malignancies; biosensors that will perform as portable laboratories; and alternative input devices such as eye blinks (electromyography) or brain activity (electroencephalography) that will facilitate hands-free device control, which will be especially useful for people with limited use of their hands (e.g., people with paralysis or arthritis) (Lewis, 2001).

Some people envision a future with more consumer-driven, preventive medicine in which consumers can evaluate their own bodies and communicate with health care professionals on an ongoing or as-needed basis. Other people are less optimistic that the nation will ever get to a preventive medicine model of health care, given the current business model being followed in the United States. The reality will probably fall between the two extremes, with some portion of the U.S. population making good use of new opportunities to follow good health maintenance practices. If medical devices are well-designed with appropriate and effective application of human factors principles and methods that percentage can be maximized. Chapter 9 provides more information on networked health technology for home care.

HUMAN FACTORS ISSUES FOR HOME HEALTH CARE DEVICES

User Issues

The characteristics of individuals who use medical devices in the home are not well known by many medical device designers. Indeed, some designers do not understand well even the needs of "average" users, and home device users often have capabilities that are far different from average. Particularly due to the conditions that require them to need home health care, individuals receiving care at home may have reduced physical strength or stamina (e.g., fatigue associated with chronic pain), diminished visual or hearing abilities, impaired cognitive abilities (including confusion caused by the effects of medication), or combinations of these conditions. Illness, medications, and stress can intensify the severity of any preexisting limitations in the user's physical, perceptual, and cognitive functions.

People's ability to operate a medical device depends on their personal characteristics, including the following:

- physical size, strength, and stamina;
- physical dexterity, flexibility, and coordination;
- sensory capabilities (i.e., vision, hearing, tactile sensitivity);
- cognitive abilities, including memory;
- comorbidities (i.e., multiple conditions or diseases);
- literacy and language skills;
- general health;
- mental and emotional state;
- level of education and training relative to the medical condition involved;
- general knowledge of similar types of devices;
- knowledge of and experience with the particular device;
- ability to learn and adapt to a new device; and
- willingness and motivation to use a new device.

It is important to recognize that lay users may also be affected by their own emotional states, which may be caused or aggravated by the news that they or their loved ones are seriously ill. They may be overwhelmed by new terminology and the critical responsibilities associated with home care, including awareness of the potential for harm—to the equipment, to their loved ones, or to themselves—if they make an error. Instructions may be confusing, and users may have little preparation and insufficient personal or institutional support for the tasks they must perform.

Regardless of their capabilities, individuals using medical devices in the home should be able to use the devices safely and effectively and without unintentionally making errors that could compromise the health of the person receiving care (Kaye and Crowley, 2000). This requirement has implications for medical device design, user training programs, and ongoing support. If the human factors demands of the medical device exceed the capabilities of the user, the equipment burden may be too great to manage, and the person receiving home health care may be forced to move to a long-term care facility or a nursing home.

In 2005, Hancock, Pepe, and Murphy proposed a "hierarchy of ergonomics and hedonomic needs" (see Figure 8-2). The purpose of the article was to suggest that once people's needs for safety and functionality were fulfilled, designers should address the need for pleasure.

This hierarchical structure could also represent the relationships among safety, accessibility, and usability. For individuals with any sort of physical, sensory, cognitive, or emotional disability, accessibility equates to functionality. The primary imperative is that home-use medical devices be safe; the secondary imperative is that they be functional (accessible) for the people who need to use them. Ideally, devices would satisfy all levels of the pyramid: they would be safe and functional, but also usable and pleasurable, and even offer customization to individual users' needs and preferences. There is no reason why medical devices, especially those intended for personal use, cannot be satisfying to use and aesthetically pleasing, and possibly even enable users to achieve their own health and life goals.

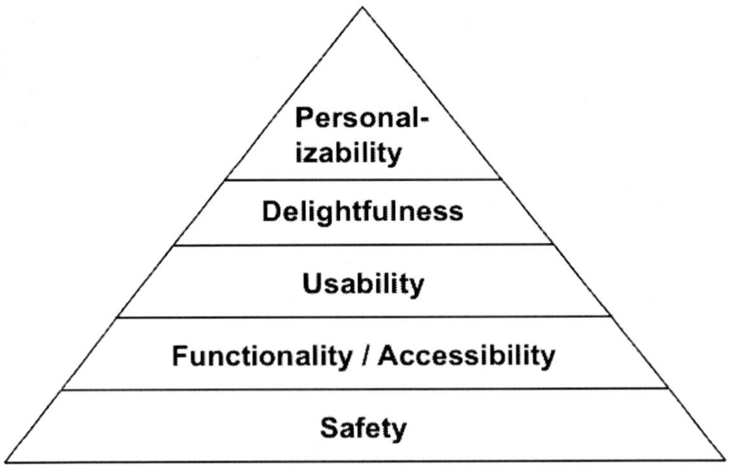

FIGURE 8-2 Hierarchy of ergonomic needs.
SOURCE: Adapted from Hancock, Pepe, and Murphy (2005).

Device Issues

Some medical devices may not be safe for all users or use environments, but medical device manufacturers have a responsibility to recognize and mitigate hazards to the greatest extent possible. In the FDA guidance document, *Medical Device Use-Safety: Incorporating Human Factors Engineering into Risk Management*, Kaye and Crowley (2000, p. 7) explain that use-related hazards occur for one or more of the following reasons:

- Devices are used in ways that were not anticipated.
- Devices are used in ways that were anticipated, but inadequately controlled for.
- Device use requires physical, perceptual, or cognitive abilities that exceed those of the user.
- Device use is inconsistent with user's expectations or intuition about device operation.
- The use environment . . . [affects] device operation and this effect is not understood by the user.
- The user's physical, perceptual, or cognitive capacities are exceeded when using the device *in a particular environment*.

The FDA's Center for Devices and Radiological Health collects data on adverse event incidents associated with medical devices. One of the FDA databases is the Medical Product Safety Network (MedSun), in which more than 350 health care facilities (primarily hospitals) currently participate and submit reports through the Internet. The database has several subnetworks that focus on specific clinical areas, including HomeNet, which focuses on medical devices used in the home environment (U.S. Food and Drug Administration, 2009b).

Another FDA database collects reports from manufacturers and health care professionals in the Manufacturer and User Facility Device Experience (MAUDE) database. The data include all voluntary adverse event reports since June 1993, user facility reports since 1991, distributor reports since 1993, and manufacturer reports since August 1996. (User facilities are defined as hospitals, nursing homes, long-term care facilities, and ambulatory and outpatient treatment facilities, including home care and hospice care.)

In evaluating reports of adverse device events in the MAUDE database between June 2008 and August 2009, the FDA found 1,059 events for which the location of the event was reported as "home." The devices involved in the greatest number of events were

- insulin infusion pump,
- implantable cardioverter defibrillator,
- automatic implantable cardioverter defibrillator with cardiac resynchronization,
- ventricular (assist) bypass device,
- mechanical walker,
- implantable pacemaker pulse generator,
- piston syringe,
- intravascular administration set, and
- continuous ventilator (facility use) (U.S. Food and Drug Administration, 2009d).

Note that this list identifies the types of devices with which *professionals* have had greatest difficulty in the home; lay users do not have access to these reporting systems, nor do they have any good mechanism for providing this type of feedback to the FDA.

Infusion pumps, the most frequently reported device on this list, are notoriously complicated to operate and put a particularly high cognitive burden on the user. This is especially problematic because the person receiving infusion tends to be sicker than the typical home health care recipient and the medications are more critical; consequently, the margin for error is small.

Three of the most common use errors when administering intravenous medications via a pump are (1) dosage miscalculation, (2) transcription data entry error, and (3) titration of the wrong medication. For home use, the first two errors (both of which result in wrong dosage) are less likely if a professional sets up the pump when it first enters the home. The third error (wrong medication) is more likely, especially if the person receiving care uses more than one type of medication. In any use scenario, the pump operator may accidently and erroneously change the rate of drug delivery. All of these types of errors can be life-threatening.

The MAUDE database contains a report of a dosing incident involving an individual who had been using an insulin pump for about 4 years. He had been using his previous pump for 2 years but had purchased a new one 3-4 months before the incident. A few hours after he arrived home one evening, he was found unconscious in his bedroom and could not be revived by paramedics. His cause of death was determined to be a severe hypoglycemic insulin reaction. The report said, "User reported having difficulties with pump outputs. No similar pump issues with older style pump" (U.S. Food and Drug Administration, 2009c). This suggests possible usability problems with the new pump.

To minimize the possibility of pump use errors, it is important that the pump clearly display the type of drug and infusion dose rate. If the pump has built-in intelligence and self-checks (e.g., bar code recognition, reference drug libraries, dosing limits, and best-practice guidelines), or transmits data to a remote health care facility, the chance of error is reduced (B. Braun Medical, Inc., 2000; Beattie, 2005; DiConsiglio, 2005).

Another example of home device user difficulty involved a home ventilator. A family member went into the patient's room one night and discovered that the patient had died and his ventilator was not functioning. The family member reported that no alarm had sounded and there was a problem with the ventilator's power cord. The police officer who arrived at the house manipulated the power cord's plug at the wall outlet, and the ventilator powered up again (Weick-Brady and Lazerow, 2006, p. 203).

Medical devices used in the home should be easy for lay users to operate and have minimal requirements for calibration and maintenance. While hospitals have departments dedicated to performing these tasks, lay users should not be expected to have this level of interaction with equipment. Devices should be self-calibrating whenever possible. Maintenance should generally be limited to only the most basic, routine functions, such as simple cleaning and battery replacement. Depending on the device involved, however, some home care providers will need to sterilize components or dispose of used supplies, and the device system should be designed so that these tasks are easy to perform.

Human Factors Standards and Guidance

U.S. and international standards provide guidance to industry on the importance of and methods for applying human factors to medical device design. Standards offer companies models for including various processes in corporate operating procedures and allow them to utilize bodies of knowledge about best design practices without having to conduct their own research. Following standards enables companies to demonstrate to the FDA (and other regulatory bodies) that they have applied best practices.

One of the key U.S. standards is referred to as ANSI/AAMI HE74:2001, *Human Factors Design Process for Medical Devices*. The document describes "a recommended human factors engineering process for use in fulfilling user interface design requirements in the development of medical devices and systems, including hardware, software, and documentation." The standard includes an overview and a discussion of the benefits of human factors engineering, a review of the human factors engineering process and its analysis and design techniques, and a discussion of implementation issues.

One of the most important international standards is ISO/IEC 62366:2007, *Medical Devices—Application of Usability Engineering to Medical Devices*, which refers to and builds on HE74. Its abstract says that the document:

> Specifies a process for a manufacturer to analyze, specify, design, verify and validate usability, as it relates to safety of a medical device. This usability engineering process assesses and mitigates risks caused by usability problems associated with correct use and use errors, i.e., normal use. It can be used to identify but does not assess or mitigate risks associated with abnormal use. If the usability engineering process detailed in this International Standard has been complied with and the acceptance criteria documented in the usability validation plan have been met, then the residual risks, as defined in ISO 14971, associated with usability of a medical device are presumed to be acceptable, unless there is objective evidence to the contrary.

ISO/IEC 62366 incorporates HE74 as an informative appendix (with the exception of a description of the relationship between HE74 and the FDA Quality Systems Regulation). These two documents describe human factors methods that may be applied to assess device safety and performance.

A new standard, ANSI/AAMI HE75:2009, *Human Factors Engineering—Design of Medical Devices,* supplements these process documents with design guidelines. The recommended practice is approximately 500 pages long and is organized into 25 sections, including one explicitly on home health care. In an interview in August 2008, shortly before his retirement as the FDA's human factors team leader, Peter Carstensen praised the document but cautioned against applying its contents without judgment (Swain, 2008, p. 52):

> HE75 is a very comprehensive handbook describing almost everything a designer needs to know. It's a one-stop shopping text with most all the information a designer would need to design a good user interface and validate it. But it still requires intelligent interpretation. It's like someone could write a detailed text on how to perform brain surgery, but careful study and practice will be needed to pull it off. HE75 is a very good start but it's not a substitute for expertise in the field.

HE75 is massive and may be difficult to apply for engineers and designers who are unfamiliar with human factors and do not know how to prioritize the recommendations for a particular device or how to choose among the inevitable trade-offs that must be made when guidelines conflict. Human factors engineering is an art as well as a science and must be practiced differently for every application.

To complement national and international standards, guidance associated with the concept of universal design provides useful information related to the needs of lay users. Universal design considers the needs of the broad spectrum of potential design users, which is relevant when designing medical devices (Story, 2007), especially for home use.

In 1995 a group of architects, product designers, engineers, and environmental design researchers convened to articulate the fundamental concepts that underlie universal design. The purpose of the resulting document, called *The Principles of Universal Design* (see Table 8-2), was to support evaluation of existing designs, inform development of new designs, and educate both designers and consumers about the characteristics of more usable products and environments (Connell et al., 1997; Story, Mueller, and Mace, 1998). Implicitly, their purpose was to integrate accessibility into as much of the built environment as possible in order to make it more usable by people of all ages and abilities or disabilities.

Below are examples of how the principles can be applied to medical devices for home health care.

- Principle 1. Equitable Use—i.e., *design for all.* Optimizing universal accessibility can increase the number of people for whom a medical device, such as a dialysis machine, is appropriate and therefore extend the option of home health care to more people.
- Principle 2. Flexibility in Use—i.e., *design for each.* A bed control can accommodate users' personal characteristics, abilities, and preferences if it can be operated with a variety of switches that can be activated with a variety of body parts (e.g., hand, foot, cheek).
- Principle 3. Simple and Intuitive Use—i.e., *design for the mind.* User interfaces for pumps (e.g., infusion, insulin, enteral) should be easy to understand and intuitive and logical to use.
- Principle 4. Perceptible Information—i.e., *design for the senses.* A blood coagulation (PT/INR) meter should transmit information in multiple sensory modes in order to maximize communication. It could allow users to enlarge the size of the information on the display (for people with vision impairments) and offer voice output (for people who are blind or who understand auditory information better than visual). The voice output should have a volume control (for people with different hearing abilities) that can be turned off (for people who cannot or do not want to hear it).
- Principle 5. Tolerance for Error—i.e., *design for error.* Having the device's user interface request confirmation of irreversible or potentially critical operations can reduce the chance of inadvertent actions. Having devices that revert to benign settings when the operator takes no action for a period of time, or that automatically shut off in case of a power surge (such as by using a ground-fault interrupter), can reduce the level of hazard.
- Principle 6. Low Physical Effort—i.e., *design for limited strength and stamina.* Buttons that activate in response to body heat require no force (however, they are unusable for people with limb pros-

TABLE 8-2 The Principles of Universal Design

Principle	Definition and Guidelines Associated with Principle
1. Equitable Use	The design is useful and marketable to people with diverse abilities.
1a.	Provide the same means of use for all users: identical whenever possible; equivalent when not.
1b.	Avoid segregating or stigmatizing any users.
1c.	Make provisions for privacy, security, and safety equally available to all users.
1d.	Make the design appealing to all users.
2. Flexibility in Use	The design accommodates a wide range of individual preferences and abilities.
2a.	Provide choice in methods of use.
2b.	Accommodate right- or left-handed access and use.
2c.	Facilitate the user's accuracy and precision.
2d.	Provide adaptability to the user's pace.
3. Simple and Intuitive Use	Use of the design is easy to understand, regardless of the user's experience, knowledge, language skills, or current concentration level.
3a.	Eliminate unnecessary complexity.
3b.	Be consistent with user expectations and intuition.
3c.	Accommodate a wide range of literacy and language skills.
3d.	Arrange information consistent with its importance.
3e.	Provide effective prompting and feedback during and after task completion.
4. Perceptible Information	The design communicates necessary information effectively to the user, regardless of ambient conditions or the user's sensory abilities.
4a.	Use different modes (pictorial, verbal, tactile) for redundant presentation of essential information.
4b.	Maximize "legibility" of essential information (in all sensory modes).
4c.	Differentiate elements in ways that can be described (i.e., make it easy to give instructions or directions).
4d.	Provide compatibility with a variety of techniques or devices used by people with sensory limitations.
5. Tolerance for Error	The design minimizes hazards and the adverse consequences of accidental or unintended actions.
5a.	Arrange elements to minimize hazards and errors: most used elements, most accessible; hazardous elements eliminated, isolated, or shielded.
5b.	Provide warnings of hazards and errors.
5c.	Provide fail-safe features.
5d.	Discourage unconscious action in tasks that require vigilance.
6. Low Physical Effort	The design can be used efficiently and comfortably and with a minimum of fatigue.
6a.	Allow user to maintain a neutral body position.
6b.	Use reasonable operating forces.
6c.	Minimize repetitive actions.
6d.	Minimize sustained physical effort.

TABLE 8-2 Continued

Principle	Definition and Guidelines Associated with Principle
7. Size and Space for Approach and Use	Appropriate size and space is provided for approach, reach, manipulation, and use regardless of user's body size, posture, or mobility.
7a.	Provide a clear line of sight to important elements for any seated or standing user.
7b.	Make reach to all components comfortable for any seated or standing user.
7c.	Accommodate variations in hand and grip size.
7d.	Provide adequate space for the use of assistive devices or personal assistance.

SOURCE: Connell et al. (1997).

theses or cold hands). Some devices may be controlled with voice commands.

- Principle 7. Size and Space for Approach and Use—i.e., *design for body sizes and postures.* A medical device should provide clearance for people who use it. The diameter of a cylindrical handhold can be tapered to allow users to place their hands along whichever section best suits the size of their hands as well as their needs and preferences for the specific task.

These universal design principles can help improve accessibility and usability (and safety) for laypeople who operate medical devices in the home.

Device Labeling and User Training Issues

Device labeling, instructions, and training can all affect the occurrence of use errors. Use errors may be categorized as either active or latent. Active errors have immediate and potentially serious consequences, such as from an incorrect medication dose or an injection in an incorrect site. Latent errors occur on an ongoing basis and can be much more difficult to identify, such as failure to replace the code key on a blood glucose meter or placing old test strips into a vial of new strips that have a different code (Patricia Patterson, Agilis Consulting Group, personal communication, 2004).

Instructions and labeling that accompany medical devices used in the home must also be designed for lay users. Too often, medical device documentation and labeling are written not for novice users but for health care professionals—that is, to the education and knowledge levels of people who know about medical technology in general and the subject device in particular. Poor labeling increases the likelihood that users will need to call either the doctor's office or the device manufacturer's customer service line, which is expensive and may not answer all the user's questions. User confusion can lead to use errors or product abandonment, either of which compromises quality of care.

All home caregivers, whether professional or lay, must be adequately trained to use and maintain the medical devices that they will use in the home. All household residents who are capable should learn how to interact with the medical equipment. Some residents should be taught about the limits of their involvement, such as children who may be taught to get help if an alarm sounds.

Home users may have multiple problems with training. As described by Fisk and colleagues (2004, p. 131):

> The training may be provided under the stressful and emotional context of being newly diagnosed with an illness. Training provided by a health care professional may be presented too quickly, using jargon, with little practice by the patient, and without adequate explanation of the difficulties that may arise if the steps are not followed properly. When users are at home attempting to use a system, they may forget the details of the steps, have no idea about what to do if the system does not operate as expected, and have no immediate access to help.

Lack of ongoing training and support is a particular challenge when device users are faced with purchasing a device when the reimbursement period ends. When a device, such as oxygen therapy equipment, is used under reimbursement, the distributor or supplier usually sets it up, services and maintains it, and delivers any necessary supplies. However, at the end of the reimbursement period, patients must purchase the device if they want to continue using it, but if they do, they lose the supports that the distributor or supplier used to provide. The home user typically has not been trained to service or maintain the device and may not know what supplies they will need or where to procure them, which can lead to serious problems.

Training should be provided in multiple formats, including visual and auditory information, because individuals have different capabilities, learning styles, and preferences. Some people understand information better when it is delivered in visual format, and others understand the spoken word better. Some device users have limited education or are illiterate. Some people do not understand English well or at all. Hands-on training is generally most effective.

Patricia A. Patterson, president of Agilis Consulting Group, is an expert in performance-based training and labeling systems for medical devices. She warns (Patterson, 2004, p. 145):

> Getting information into people's long-term memory so that they can recall it when needed—accurately and consistently—is like walking on thin ice: it's risky, and when we're talking medical, it's dangerous. And it has less to do with the media (a.k.a. video) and more to do with the instructional design. . . . If the user needs information to perform a task—where is that information going to be stored: in their head (long-term memory) or someplace else? We try to opt for someplace else whenever appropriate for obvious reasons. . . . What labeling can do is to minimize the need for memory by making it accessible to the user when and where needed—like stuck to the device, in the [user interface] itself, etc.

In addition to clear device labeling and effective training, home caregivers need to have access to ongoing support, always by telephone but also through e-mail, on the Internet, or via telehealth connection. Ideally, some form of help should be available 24 hours a day, 365 days a year.

Environmental Issues

Residential environments vary considerably and can present a range of complexities for introduction of medical devices (see Chapter 10). Medical devices may be used under variable conditions involving such environmental attributes as space, lighting, noise levels, and activity:

- Rooms may be physically crowded or cluttered, making it difficult for the person providing or receiving care to maneuver in the space.
- Carpeting or stairs may hinder device portability or maneuverability.
- The lighting level may be low, making it hard to see device displays and controls.
- The noise levels may be high, making it difficult to hear device prompts and alarms.
- The temperature may be very high (e.g., in Florida) or very low (e.g., in Alaska), which can cause equipment to overheat or stall out.
- The humidity may be very high (e.g., in Louisiana), which can cause condensation, or very low (e.g., in Arizona), which can produce static electricity.
- The home may not be clean.
- The household may be busy with other residents and activities, providing distractions that may confuse people while they use medical devices.

- Children, unauthorized users, pets, or vermin in the home can cause damage to themselves (e.g., playing with syringes), cause damage to devices (e.g., chewing on tubing), or change device settings, which may not be noticed before the unit is used again.
- Electromagnetic interference from other equipment in the home (e.g., computer gear, such as Gameboys and Wii sets) can affect medical device functions.

These environmental influences can have a significant impact on how safe or risky a device is in the home. An example of electromagnetic interference in the home involved a motorized wheelchair. One day when the patient was at home in the wheelchair, it began spontaneously spinning around, out of control. The patient tipped backward in the chair and fell out, sustaining an injury. After the incident the patient reported that someone had been using a cell phone nearby, which may have contributed to the event (Weick-Brady and Lazerow, 2006, p. 203).

Not all medical devices stay at home. People who work may take their device along with them to the workplace. This situation has implications for device portability (size and weight) and appearance, particularly with regard to discretion. People may also take their device with them when they go out in their communities or when they travel away from home. In this case, battery life, durability, and ruggedness also matter.

A home dialysis patient who liked to travel offers an example of traveling with a significant medical device. After receiving dialysis in medical centers in 19 countries on 5 continents for 11 years, he began home dialysis and now takes a dialysis machine with him when he travels. He dialyzes himself five nights a week, unassisted, using a relatively compact, "portable" machine that weighs 99 pounds (Taylor, 2008).

The utilities available must be taken into consideration when selecting a medical device for nonclinical use. For example, for treatments that involve water (such as home dialysis), it will be important to have a clean and reliable source of tap water. For devices powered by electricity, the room will need a sufficient electrical supply (including outlets and circuit capacity). For foreign travel, this may require outlet or power adapters. The device or room will also need a source of backup power, such as a battery or generator, in case of power failure or other emergency (e.g., after a hurricane or earthquake). Some care recipients cannot survive long without the medical devices on which they depend.

APPLICATION OF HUMAN FACTORS TO HOME HEALTH CARE DEVICES

The history of medical devices used in the home is filled with stories, some successful and some cautionary. Among the successful stories, blood glucose meters with voice output are useful for a variety of users. Voice output is useful on many home health care devices because it

- reinforces visual messages, providing redundant cuing that improves comprehension;
- reduces misinterpretation of visual messages (including words and icons);
- is especially helpful for infrequent users who benefit from prompting and feedback as they use a device;
- improves user confidence and trust in the device; and
- reduces the burden on customer service to handle repeated contact from confused users.

In addition, speech output is vitally important for people with vision impairments who cannot perceive all the visual information provided by the device.

Among cautionary tales is the story of a patient who was receiving oxygen therapy in his home. When a pressure hose came loose from the respirator, an alarm sounded, but the alarm was not loud enough to be heard over the sounds produced by the device itself (and there was no remote monitoring system in place). The patient died (Lewis, 2001).

In a study of telemonitoring and 19 elder home health care recipients, a few participants were unable to measure their own weight using a scale, most often because they needed help to accomplish the task and no one was available at the time; at least one-third of participants could not reliably interpret their blood pressure results as being normal or abnormal, and for a significant percentage of those, even periodic retraining didn't help (Daryle Gardner-Bonneau, Bonneau and Associates, personal communication, 2009).

A study of everyday use of ventricular assist devices (to provide circulatory support before cardiac transplantation) showed that the usability of these devices affected the success and acceptance of the treatment. Of the 16 study participants, 38 percent accidentally disconnected important components of the system at least once; 38 percent reported that parts of the system rubbed against their skin (particularly the shoulder strap against the abdomen when using a bag belt); and 56 percent reported that the noises from the pump, ventilators, and alarms were annoying; however, the alarm signals were too quiet to wake 32 percent of them. Most participants (63 percent) used a carrying case other than the one supplied, and many (44 percent) overstuffed the case with additional gear, mainly medical documents, cell phones, or eyeglasses (without which the older participants had difficulty reading the messages on the device) for which space was not provided (Geidl et al., 2009).

Medical devices used in the home should be designed to be safe and easy to use by their end-users, including the people receiving care and any lay caregivers on whom they may rely. This may require that devices have fewer features in order to simplify use, such as no memory function, or have additional features, such as new alarms (which may be visual as well as auditory) or extra monitoring functions to track device usage and adherence to treatment regimens.

It is important for manufacturers to design out hazards, rather than just add warning labels or rely on training to address problems. Not everyone reads labels or instructions—indeed, not everyone can read. Training depends on good instructors and methods, which may not always be available. Both methods rely on users to interpret the information correctly and remember it when it is needed, which is difficult for some people to do. Users would be better served if devices were designed to be more error-resistant (easier to understand and operate as well as more fail-safe) irrespective of labels, instructions, or training. As psychologist and cognitive scientist Donald Norman recommended, for devices that are used infrequently, it is better to have knowledge in the world (i.e., in or on the device) so that the user need only interpret the visual cues provided by the device, rather than depend on knowledge in the head (i.e., in the user's memory) (Norman, 1980).

Medical device manufacturers should make a commitment to follow good human factors practices in the design of their products. They need to establish permanent human factors departments or identify and contract with qualified human factors consultants to perform the human factors analyses needed to ensure that medical devices will be safe and usable, reducing the likelihood of product misuse or abandonment.

HUMAN FACTORS ASSESSMENT

The Food and Drug Administration requires medical device manufacturers to demonstrate that they have addressed human factors issues during the product's development process. The FDA requires design controls for all medical devices sold in the United States. These are explained in Title 21 of the Code of Federal Regulations (CFR), Part 820 of which is the Quality System Regulation (QSR). Section 820.30, Design Controls, contains key human factors requirements in its subsections c, f, and g:

(c) *Design input.* Each manufacturer shall establish and maintain procedures to ensure that the design requirements relating to a device are appropriate and address the intended use of the device, including the needs of the user and patient. . . .

(f) *Design verification.* Each manufacturer shall establish and maintain procedures for verifying the device design. Design verification shall confirm that the design output meets the design input requirements. . . .

(g) *Design validation.* . . . Design validation shall ensure that devices conform to defined user needs and intended uses and shall include testing of production units under actual or simulated use conditions. Design validation shall include software validation and risk analysis, where appropriate.

The primary human factors guidance documents offered by the FDA are *Do It by Design: An Introduction to Human Factors in Medical Devices* (Sawyer, 1996) and *Medical Device Use-Safety: Incorporating Human Factors Engineering into Risk Management* (Kaye and Crowley, 2000). These documents include descriptions of human factors engineering methods, such as analytic and empirical approaches to identify and understand use-related hazards, methods of assessing and prioritizing hazards, strategies for mitigating and controlling hazards, and methods of verifying and validating hazard mitigation strategies. They also discuss exploratory studies and usability testing methods.

It is important that representative laypeople and caregivers be included in any user testing that is conducted in order to assess the safety of the medical device and its use by these populations. The potential user population may be very diverse, and it is vital to identify the users at highest risk. By studying their use of the device and its labeling to conduct essential tasks, the device manufacturer can ensure that any potential risks have been minimized, residual risks have been mitigated as far as possible, and the device is appropriate for home use.

Medical device manufacturers need to ensure device safety before marketing, and they also need to make a commitment to postmarket surveillance of their products to make sure that no unforeseen problems appear with long-term use. If problems are discovered, manufacturers must notify current users and address the problems by providing information and replacement parts or recalling the product, as appropriate to the severity of the issues.

FUTURE DIRECTIONS FOR THE FIELD

Critical gaps exist in the understanding of human factors issues for medical devices in the domain of noninstitutional health management and care. These include user issues, device issues, and environmental issues.

Maximizing adherence to treatment regimens is an ongoing challenge for home health care. Having a device at home may actually make people less diligent in maintaining their own health. "These risky behaviors can involve lifestyle changes, such as changes in diet or physical activity, or less attention to monitoring their health condition due to over-reliance on the device," says Ron Kaye, human factors and device use-safety team leader at the FDA's Center for Devices and Radiological Health (Lewis, 2001). Other problems with home device use, especially once the user has gotten accustomed to a device, include skipping steps rather than following proper procedures, not performing important maintenance tasks, and not communicating with health care professionals as often as they should (Lewis, 2001).

The field needs to develop methods of improving people's ability and willingness to follow their doctors' recommendations and to adhere to treatment regimens while visiting health care facilities less frequently. Medical personnel need to have good assessment tools and mechanisms to determine whether a particular individual is a good candidate to use a specific medical device. The attributes of the device, the characteristics of the user, and the expected use environments all need to be considered and should be integrated into the assessment program.

Some medical patients have comorbidities, that is, more than one disease or condition, for which they may be receiving ongoing medical treatment. The conditions and their treatments may be independent, or they may reinforce or aggravate one another. These effects must be understood and taken into consideration when treatment regimens are designed. However, concomitant conditions may also present the possibility of care efficiencies. For example, treatments (e.g., drug infusions) could be delivered simultaneously, reducing the time involved, or multiple diagnostic processes (e.g., blood glucose level and coagulation time) could be conducted on a single blood sample, reducing the number of samples and the amount of blood that needs to be drawn.

Device issues that need to be addressed include concern for accuracy of home health care devices, especially some of the more inexpensive types designed for home use. For example, the current international standard for blood glucose meters allows their measurements to be up to 20 percent inaccurate, but, in fact, the readings sometimes fall well outside even these generous limits (Harris, 2009). Standards for home devices need to be sufficiently stringent to safeguard the health of the user populations as well as engender trust in the technologies.

For people who use telehealth technologies (devices that communicate with medical professionals at a distance), it is important for the devices to be interoperable (i.e., work together using the same technology). For example, a home health care system can include multiple devices (e.g., weight scale, pulse oximeter, and blood glucose monitor) that communicate wirelessly using a common protocol (e.g., Bluetooth Medical Device Profile) to a communication device, such as a computer, a cell phone, or a dedicated standalone unit. Potentially, sets of devices designed for home use could communicate with and affect one another's operation, such as a pain medication pump that would vary dosage based on the results of patient respiration monitoring. Having communication standards for medical devices is critical and several are being developed, but the idea of interoperability continues to be controversial among device manufacturers, who do not want to share proprietary technologies with competitors. Without these standards, however, users will be limited in the selection of devices they can purchase (that will communicate with each other) and the costs are likely to be higher.

Another concern regarding home use of medical devices is the training burden on health care professionals, particularly nurses. When a device is not well designed, it falls to the medical personnel involved to train—and often retrain—users to use it, which puts a strain on the medical system that it can ill bear. Devices that are well designed can encourage use, result in better health, and reduce burdens on the medical system, including training.

The field also needs better mechanisms for home health care users to provide feedback to medical device manufacturers regarding the difficulties and hazards associated with use of devices in the home. Professional and lay caregivers and people receiving home care are rich sources of information about medical device use safety and errors, which need to be tapped. The experiences of real users in the real world need to be captured, studied, and used to inform and improve the design of the next generation of devices used in home health care.

Environmental issues that need to be addressed include surveying and documenting the range of nonclinical medical device use-environment types, situations, and conditions. The wide variation in environmental conditions is neither recognized nor taken into consideration by the designers and engineers who develop medical devices that will be used in those locations.

CONCLUSIONS

Inevitably, as medical costs continue to climb and particularly as more devices are designed with lay users in mind, more people will use medical devices for health care in their own homes and other private and public environments.

The explosion of information on the Internet has provided people with access to more data than ever before. Individuals with health concerns have resources at their fingertips that provide information about symptoms, conditions, and treatment options, which make them more informed consumers of health care services. This knowledge, in turn, enables people to be more demanding of their health care providers.

At the same time, people tend to be reluctant to blame medical devices when they have trouble using them. The professional culture in health care seems to make practitioners believe that they should be able to provide the needed care, regardless of the technology. Laypeople using medical devices tend to blame themselves if they have difficulty using a device properly, even though such difficulty often occurs because there is something wrong with the device (and not the operator). Users need to stop blaming themselves and be more demanding of medical devices. When devices are not operating correctly or are difficult or dangerous to use, users need to report those problems—to their health care providers, to their state, and to the FDA. To encourage this kind of reporting, better reporting mechanisms are needed, ones that are visible, accessible, and easy to use.

The medical industry needs to improve the health of the general public in the United States, and it also needs to reduce the cost of providing health care. Home health care promises to advance both of these goals. However, to enable good health care at home, medical devices need to be designed to be safer, more accessible and usable, and available to more people. Human factors engineering offers principles and processes that support industry to produce such devices.

ABOUT THE AUTHOR

Molly Follette Story was president of Human Spectrum Design at the time of the workshop; she is now a senior program officer at the National Research Council. Her expertise is in universal design of products and in accessibility and usability of medical instrumentation.

REFERENCES

Alliance for Home Health Quality and Innovation. (2008, May). *The future of home health care: Containing costs while serving patients' preferences.* Available: http://ahhqi.org/download/File/The_Future_of_Home_Health_Care.pdf [accessed June 2010].

American National Standards Institute and Association for the Advancement of Medical Instrumentation. (2010). *Human factors engineering: Design of medical devices* (ANSI/AAMI HE75:2010). Arlington, VA: Association for the Advancement of Medical Instrumentation.

B. Braun Medical, Inc. (2000). *Press release: B. Braun focuses on consumer education regarding infusion pump decimal and calculation errors.* Available: http://www.bbraunusa.com/index.cfm?84414D8ED0B759A1E3E55CD9354BA0C5 [accessed July 2009].

Beattie, S. (2005). Technology today: Smart IV pumps. *RNWeb,* December. Available: http://www.modernmedicine.com/modernmedicine/CE+Library/Technology-today-Smart-IV-pumps/ArticleStandard/Article/detail/254828?contextCategoryId=5763 [accessed June 2010].

Bogner, M.S. (Ed.). (2004). *Misadventures in health care.* Mahwah, NJ: Lawrence Erlbaum Associates.

Connell, B.R., Jones, M., Mace, R., Mueller, J., Mullick, A., Ostroff, E., Sanford, J., Steinfeld, E., Story, M., and Vanderheiden, G. (1997). *The principles of universal design, version 2.0.* Raleigh: Center for Universal Design, North Carolina State University.

DiConsiglio, J. (2005). Getting smart about safe infusion pump options. *Materials Management in Health Care, 14*(10), 26-30.

Fisk, A.D., Rogers, W.A., Charness, N., Czaja, S.J. and Sharit, H. (2004). *Designing for older adults.* Boca Raton, FL: CRC Press.

Geidl, L., Zrunek, P., Deckert, Z., Zimpfer, D., Sandner, S., Wieselthaler, G., and Schima, H. (2009). Usability and safety of ventricular assist devices: Human factors and design apects. *Artificial Organs, 33*(9), 691-695.

Hancock, P.A., Pepe, A.A., and Murphy, L.L. (2005). Hedonomics: The power of positive and pleasurable ergonomics. *Ergonomics in Design, 13*(1), 8-14.

Harris, G. (2009, July 18). Standards might rise on monitors for diabetics. *New York Times,* p. A14.

Jordan, M. (2008). Bringing medical devices home. *Medical Device & Diagnostic Industry Magazine, 30(*2), 62-67.

Kaufman, D., and Weick-Brady, M. (2009). HomeNet: Ensuring patient safety with medical device use in the home. *Home Healthcare Nurse, 27*(5), 300-307.

Kaye, R., and Crowley, J. (2000). *Medical device use-safety: Incorporating human factors engineering into risk management.* Food and Drug Administration, Center for Devices and Radiological Health. Washington, DC: U.S. Department of Health and Human Services.

Lewis, C. (2001). Emerging trends in medical device technology: Home is where the heart monitor is. *FDA Consumer, 35*(3), 10-15.

National Association for Home Care and Hospice. (2008). *Basic statistics about home care, updated 2008.* Available: http://www.nahc.org/facts/08HC_Stats.pdf [accessed June 2010].

Nemours Foundation/Kids Health. (2007). *Managing home health care.* Available: http://kidshealth.org/parent/system/ill/machine.html [accessed July 2009].

Norman, D.A. (1980). *The psychology of everyday things.* New York: Basic Books.

Patterson, P. (2004). Home alone: Designing information for device users. *Medical Device & Diagnostic Industry Magazine,* January, 142-147. Available: http://www.mddionline.com/article/home-alone-designing-information-device-users [accessed June 2010].

Sawyer, D. (1996). *Do it by design: An introduction to human factors in medical devices.* Food and Drug Administration, Center for Devices and Radiological Health. Washington, DC: U.S. Department of Health and Human Services.

Slater, S. (2009). Telephonic stethoscopes are used in home telehealth programs. *Cleveland Home Healthcare Technology Examiner,* July 16.

Story, M.F. (2007). Applying the principles of universal design to medical devices. In J.M. Winters and M.F. Story (Eds.), *Medical instrumentation: Accessibility and usability considerations* (pp. 101-112). Boca Raton, FL: CRC Press.

Story, M.F., Mueller, J.L., and Mace, R.L. (1998). *The universal design file: Designing for people of all ages and abilities.* Raleigh: Center for Universal Design, North Carolina State University.

Stuart, M. (2009). There's no place like the home health care market. *Start-Up,* February.

Swain, E. (2008). Q&A: Preaching the value of human factors. *Medical Device & Diagnostic Industry Magazine,* October, 48-53.

Taft, C. (2007). Home use of devices creates new challenges for FDA, manufacturers. *Medical Devices Today*, September. Available: http://www.medicaldevicestoday.com/2007/09/home-use-of-dev.html#more [accessed June 2010].

Taylor, C. (2008). Home care devices: A new challenge for the profession. *Biomedical Instrumentation and Technology,* September/October, 351-356.

U.S. Food and Drug Administration. (2009a). *About MedSun.* Available: http://www.fda.gov/MedicalDevices/Safety/MedSunMedicalProductSafetyNetwork/ucm112683.htm [accessed July 2009].

U.S. Food and Drug Administration. (2009b). *CDRH Home Health Care Committee (HHCC).* Available: http://www.fda.gov/MedicalDevices/ProductsandMedicalProcedures/HomeHealthandConsumer/ucm070198.htm [accessed July 2009].

U.S. Food and Drug Administration. (2009c). *MAUDE adverse event report: Smith Medical Md. Inc. Deltec Cosmo insulin pump insulin infusion pump.* Available: http://www.accessdata.fda.gov/scripts/cdrh/cfdocs/cfMAUDE/Detail.CFM?MDRFOI__ID=1280725 [accessed August 2009].

Weick-Brady, M. (2009). *Medical devices in the home: New devices, new risks.* Presentation at the Association for the Advancement of Medical Instrumentation's 2009 Conference and Expo, June 7, Baltimore, MD.

Weick-Brady, M., and Lazerow, R.N. (2006). Medical devices: Promoting a safe migration into the home. *Home Healthcare Nurse, 24*(5), 299-304.

9

Information Technology and Systems in Home Health Care

George Demiris

Home health care faces several challenges, such as funding limitations, large geographic distances that make such resources often more costly for rural patients, and issues of clinical workforce distribution that impose access barriers to these services. It is a general premise that information technology (IT) can address these challenges and enhance home health care services. Advances in telecommunications, web solutions, and social networking tools have the potential to support health care delivery and education. The use of IT can lead to a fundamental redesign of home care processes based on the use and integration of electronic communication at all levels. Many anticipate that IT platforms may lead to patient empowerment and a transition from a passive role, in which the patient is the recipient of care services, to an active role, in which the patient is informed, has choices, and is involved in the decision-making process. Such a transition may be possible due to the active involvement of patients in the management of their disease using home monitoring devices and software, the access to information and online communities, and the use of personal health records maintained by patients themselves.

Information technology can be introduced in home care in a multitude of ways. The following taxonomy captures the multiple levels of IT function and functionality in the context of home care:

- Active monitoring and management (requiring end-user involvement and participation)
  - Telehealth applications for home-based disease management (that link patients and their families to their health care providers)

  - Web-based communities for home care patients (that link patients and their families to health care providers, peers, and the community)
  - Personal health records (that enable patients to create and store their personal health information)
- Passive monitoring and management (for which IT implementation does not require training or operation by the end-user)
  - Robotic applications (standalone artificial intelligence applications that support home care needs)
  - "Smart homes" (in which IT based on the use of sensors becomes part of the residential infrastructure)

This chapter describes these different types of IT applications and discusses technical, practical, and ethical implications.

TELEHEALTH APPLICATIONS FOR HOME-BASED DISEASE MANAGEMENT

Telehealth applications offer a platform to support disease management for home care patients diagnosed with chronic conditions and their families. This section is organized by the disease or condition addressed by the application.

For asthma management, an example of Internet utilization is the home asthma telemonitoring system (Finkelstein, O'Connor, and Friedmann, 2001), which provides patients with continuous individualized help in the daily routine of asthma self-care and coping and alerts health care providers if specific conditions or patterns emerge. The system is operated by the patient or an informal caregiver (including family members or friends) and involves web-based questionnaires and the operation of a spirometer to assess lung capacity. The data sets (including the spirometry readings) are transmitted to health care providers.

Another example involves diabetes. As diabetes has in many cases an asymptomatic nature, the time frame between sustained hyperglycemia and observable complications can be extended, thus making a long-term program of secondary prevention an essential part of appropriate diabetes care and a suitable domain for technology-based diabetes management applications. McKay, exploring the development and feasibility of a web tool for diabetes self-management that emphasized personalized goal setting, feedback, and social support (McKay et al., 1998) found that patients were satisfied with the system and appreciated the social support and the availability of information.

Similarly, the Center for Health Services Research's Henry Ford Health System in Detroit developed the web-based Diabetes Care Management

Support System to support the provision of routine care to patients with diabetes (Baker et al., 2001). The system was evaluated in a nonrandomized, longitudinal study, and the findings indicated that web-based systems using clinical practice guidelines, patient registries, and performance feedback have the potential to improve the rate of routine testing among patients with diabetes.

The Telematic Management of Insulin-Dependent Diabetes Mellitus project, funded by the European Union, implemented and evaluated a distributed computer-based system for the management of insulin-dependent diabetes mellitus. The goal was to use Internet technology to support health care providers and patients by providing them with a set of automated services ranging from data collection and transmission to data analysis and decision support (Riva, Bellazzi, and Stefanelli, 1997). The system included a module allowing patients to automatically download their monitoring data from the blood glucose monitoring device and to send them to the hospital information system. The system provided physicians with a set of tools for data visualization, data analysis, and decision support and allowed them to send messages, including therapeutic advice, to the patients (Bellazzi et al., 2002).

Other application domains for web-based systems include congestive heart failure, chronic obstructive pulmonary disease, and wound care. The TeleHomeCare project at the University of Minnesota included a system based on the use of low-cost commercially available monitoring devices and an Internet application designed for patients diagnosed with congestive heart failure or chronic obstructive pulmonary disease or requiring wound care. The system included web pages customized to address the information needs of individual patients and included an online diary with questionnaires to be filled out daily. The daily questionnaire included questions about symptoms, vital signs (such as weight, blood pressure, temperature), overall well-being, and compliance with dietary guidelines. When one or more responses to these questions indicated a situation that required immediate clinical attention, alerts were triggered according to predefined rules and sent to the home care agency staff (Demiris, Speedie, and Finkelstein, 2001).

Oncology patients also often face the challenges of disease management and handling treatment side-effects at home. The National Cancer Institute's Common Terminology Criteria for Adverse Events schema for seven common symptoms was adapted into a web-based patient reporting system, accessible from desktop computers in outpatient clinics and from home computers (Basch et al., 2005). In this study, 80 patients with gynecological malignancies, about to begin standard chemotherapy regimens, were enrolled and encouraged to log into the system and report symptoms at each follow-up visit or, alternatively, to access the system from home.

Numerous toxicities (grades 3 to 4) reported from home prompted clinician interventions. Patients were capable of reporting symptoms experienced during chemotherapy, and their reporting often led to clinical interventions and changes in the care plan—indicating that the use of the Internet can be beneficial for the treatment and monitoring of home patients diagnosed with cancer (Basch et al., 2005).

Finally, care following organ transplant requires an ongoing monitoring of the patient's health status as well as the patient's active involvement in this process. Regular spirometry monitoring of lung transplant recipients, for example, is essential to early detection of acute infection and rejection of the allograft. A prospective study investigated the impact of a web-based telemonitoring system providing direct transmission of home spirometry to the hospital. The study demonstrated that home monitoring of pulmonary function in lung transplant recipients via the Internet is feasible and provides very reproducible data, yet "it has only a mild sensitivity for the detection of acute allograft dysfunction" (Morlion et al., 2002).

As the use of telehealth technologies emerged in the area of home care, most of the earlier studies were either pilot exploratory projects or clinical trials with small sample sizes. One of the earliest clinical trials in the area of telehealth in home care (also referred to as telehomecare) with a large sample size was a study by Johnston and colleagues (2000). This was a quasi-experimental study in which newly referred patients diagnosed as having congestive heart failure, chronic obstructive pulmonary disease, cerebral vascular accident, cancer, diabetes, anxiety, or need for wound care were randomly assigned to either routine home care or a remote video system with peripheral monitoring devices that also allowed nurses and patients to interact in real time. A total of 102 subjects were enrolled in the experimental group and 110 in the control group. The study findings demonstrated no differences in the quality indicators (medication compliance, knowledge of disease, and ability for self-care) or patient satisfaction. Although the average direct cost for home health services was $1,830 in the intervention group and $1,167 in the control group, the total mean costs of care, excluding home health care costs, were $1,948 in the intervention group and $2,674 in the control group.

An extensive recently completed randomized clinical trial of telehomecare, and currently the largest telehomecare randomized study reported in scientific literature, is the Informatics for Diabetes Education and Telemedicine study (Shea et al., 2009). This project compared telehomecare case management with usual care of older, ethnically diverse, medically underserved Medicare beneficiaries with diabetes mellitus residing in medically underserved areas of New York State. The sample included 1,665 Medicare recipients with diabetes, age 55 or older. Findings demonstrate that telehomecare case management resulted in net improvements in blood glucose, cholesterol, and blood pressure levels over 5 years.

Another large (although not randomized) study of home telehealth, carried out by the Veterans Health Administration, introduced a national home telehealth program called Care Coordination/Home Telehealth (Darkins et al., 2008). The purpose of this ongoing initiative is to coordinate the care of veteran patients with chronic conditions in order to avoid or reduce unnecessary admission to long-term institutional care. Routine analysis of data from a cohort of 17,025 patients in 2008 shows the benefits of a 25 percent reduction in number of bed days of care, a 19 percent reduction in number of hospital admissions, and overall high satisfaction rates for patients enrolled in the program (Darkins et al., 2008). The cost of the program was estimated to be $1,600 per patient per year in 2008, which the authors argue is substantially less than other noninstitutional care programs or nursing home care (Darkins et al., 2008).

Rojas and Gagnon conducted a systematic review of the key indicators for assessing telehomecare cost-effectiveness (Rojas and Gagnon, 2008). Their analysis showed that there is fair evidence of cost-effectiveness for many telehomecare applications. However, the heterogeneity among cost-effectiveness indicators in the applications reviewed and the methodological limitations of the studies impede the generalizability of the findings.

These telehealth applications require operation by the patients or their families (including use of a web interface and, in most cases, operation of a monitoring device, such as a glucose reader, a blood pressure cuff, or a spirometer). This obviously has implications for eligibility criteria, as training is often required for patients or families before they can operate the system (requiring the presence and involvement of an informal caregiver when the patient has cognitive or functional limitations). An additional implication for the health care provider at the other end, who receives the collected data sets and, in some cases, conducts videoconference-based consultations, pertains to the training of providers as well as the need for technical support when technical problems arise at either end.

WEB-BASED COMMUNITIES FOR HOME CARE PATIENTS

In addition to web-based applications that follow an institution-centric approach and link home care patients to health care providers, the Internet also supports a consumer-centric model and enables the creation of networks between home care patients diagnosed with the same condition, families or other informal caregivers, communities, and the general public. Such networks are often referred to as virtual communities. A virtual community is a social entity involving several individuals who relate to one another by the use of a specific communication technology that bridges geographic distance (Demiris, 2005). While traditional communities are determined by such factors as geographic proximity, organizational structures, or activities shared by the members of the community, the label "virtual" declares properties that, unlike these of a traditional community, are based on the use of advanced technologies that support interactions and exchange of information between members who may never physically meet (Demiris, 2005).

Virtual communities demonstrate core attributes wherein members have a shared goal, interest, need, or activity that is the primary reason for being part of the community. They engage in repeated, active participation with access to shared resources. Defined policies determine the type and frequency of access to those resources. The sustainability of the community relies on reciprocity of information, support, and services among members (Whittaker, Isaacs, and O'Day, 1997). A virtual community with a health care purpose or focus is a group of people, as well as the social structure that they collectively create, based on the use of telecommunication with the purposes of educating, providing support, discussing issues, sharing resources, consulting with experts, and sustaining relationships beyond or without face-to-face events. Numerous such applications function as self-help groups of individuals diagnosed with the same clinical condition or undergoing similar treatment. As Finn (1999) demonstrated, virtual self-help groups can provide many of the processes used in face-to-face self-help and mutual aid groups. The emphasis in such virtual communities is on mutual problem solving, information sharing, expression of feelings, mutual support, and empathy.

Technologies for virtual communities include, among others, online message boards and automatic mailing list servers for asynchronous communication, videoconferencing, Internet relay chat, group and private chat rooms for synchronous communication, and even social networking platforms, such as Facebook or Twitter. In some cases, communication is not "moderated"; that is, there is no entity responsible for reviewing and filtering posts that are thought to be inappropriate or in violation of any of the rules and terms of the virtual community. In these cases, the community relies largely on the normative processes of its own internal social norms "to define and enforce the acceptable behavior of the community members" (Burnett, Besant, and Chatman, 2001). In other cases, a moderator or group of moderators oversees and facilitates the interaction among members.

In a systematic review of online health care communities in 2004 (Eysenbach et al., 2004), researchers compiled and evaluated the evidence on the effects on health and social outcomes of computer-based peer-to-peer communities and electronic support groups. The authors identified a lack of robust evidence of the effectiveness of consumer-led peer-to-peer communities, partly because most of these communities have been evaluated only in conjunction with more complex interventions or involvement with health professionals (Eysenbach et al., 2004). However, given the great number of unmoderated web-based peer-to-peer groups, further research is needed to assess when and how electronic support groups can be effective (Eysenbach et al., 2004).

Virtual communities can involve patients, family members, informal caregivers, and even researchers. The Comprehensive Health Enhancement Support System (CHESS), developed by the University of Wisconsin, is a platform that provides services designed to help individuals cope with a health crisis or medical concern, but it also invites researchers to use resources and share knowledge and findings (Gustafson et al., 1992). The system provides timely access to such resources as information, social support, and decision-making and problem-solving tools when needed most. This application and its modules and consortia are good examples of a virtual community that serves individual patients' and caregiver needs while also providing an active laboratory for researchers and organizations (Gustafson et al., 1992).

The same advanced telecommunication technologies that can facilitate virtual communities of patients and their families can also enable health care providers to form virtual teams, interacting and collaborating on cases even when separated by large geographic distances. Numerous health care settings lack the interdisciplinary resources required for efficient chronic disease management. Clinicians and researchers at Rush University Medical Center in Chicago developed the Virtual Integrated Practice, a process that creates virtual care teams (Rothschild et al., 2004) that target four strategies: (1) communications, (2) process standardization, (3) group activities, and (4) self-management. The conditions covered are diabetes, chronic obstructive pulmonary disease, and urinary incontinence. Communication among members of the virtual team is both synchronous and asynchronous. Virtual health care provider teams in general can ensure continuity of care as they use a common platform for exchange of messages, opinions, and resources. Such teams can be essential to successful disease management and to providing continuity of care for the patients.

PERSONAL HEALTH RECORDS

A concept emerging from the proliferation of web technologies in people's homes is the personal health record (PHR). The National Alliance for Health Information Technology defines a personal health record as "an individual's electronic record of health-related information that conforms to nationally recognized interoperability standards and that can be drawn from multiple sources while being managed, shared and controlled by the individual" (National Alliance for Health Information Technology,

2008). Specifically, a personal health record is a tool to use in "sharing health information, increasing health understanding and helping transform patients into better-educated consumers of health care" (Kahn, Aulakh, and Bosworth, 2009).

A recent initiative to implement a PHR system was launched in the Veterans Health Administration system (U.S. Department of Veterans Affairs, 2010). Called MyHealtheVet, this system focuses at the moment primarily on appointments, medication requests, protecting the identity of the users, and helping veterans obtain a variety of services. The electronic medical record software vendor, Epic, has also introduced a PHR application currently used by Kaiser Permanente, the Cambridge Health Alliance, and others. These systems are widely used by consumers because they provide important functionality, which could lead to improved health (Mechanic, 2008).

The PHR concept is expected to enable a shift from institution-centric to patient-centric models of care as personal health records can be used for sharing such health information as health finances, diagnoses (problem lists), allergies, immunizations, insurance information, and medications in an easy way that helps people manage their own health (Hassol et al., 2004). In that context, it is the patient and not a health care facility who owns and controls his or her data. For that reason, the industry is showing a growing interest in PHR applications. Such applications introduced recently by Google (Google Health) and Microsoft (HealthVault) can potentially enable consumers to gain access to their health information via the Internet without having to use special hardware or have organizational agreements in place.

Traditional electronic medical record (EMR) systems are controlled and maintained by health care providers, whereas a PHR system is controlled and maintained by the patient. The integration of EMR and PHR systems is envisioned to enable a synergistic model in which PHR data can augment EMR data, allowing for a holistic and collaborative model of care and shared decision making; however, this is not yet a reality. This goal requires addressing several challenges, including technical issues (enabling patient control and authentication, synchronization of records, data encryption, diffusion of interoperability standards), sociotechnical issues (e.g., providers needing to develop trust in PHR data, consumers called on to assume a more active role in the health care delivery process), changes in health care providers' workflow, and education of both consumers and providers, as well as legal and regulatory challenges.

PHR systems potentially can be used in combination with telehealth or other web-based applications, allowing patients to store and process their own data resulting from disease management efforts or communication with health care providers. PHR systems can therefore also be used for disease prevention and wellness promotion, in which consumers who are not necessarily labeled as patients (as they may not have a clinical condition) can manage their lifestyle choices, plans, finances, encounters with the health care system, etc. With their potential to empower consumers and place the patient at the center of decision making and management of his or her own health, PHR tools may in the near future significantly affect home care.

ROBOTIC APPLICATIONS

Robotic applications using artificial intelligence principles and, in some cases, with anthropomorphic features have traditionally been used in the clinical setting, mostly in an experimental mode (e.g., robotic-assisted surgery, including robotic-assisted laparoscopic pyeloplasty, cystectomy, etc.) However, technology advances have introduced robotic applications into the home to address cognitive, functional, and psychological issues.

The Robot/CAMR suite by Johnson and colleagues (2007) includes a robotic application with a conventional force-reflecting joystick, a modified joystick therapy platform, and a steering wheel platform with embedded software to provide extrinsic motivation and outcome assessment for stroke rehabilitation home care patients. Recent reports from a number of laboratories using enhanced sensorimotor training protocols, particularly those with robotic devices, have indicated modest success in reducing impairment and increasing motor power in the exercised limb of patients with stroke when compared with control individuals (Volpe, Krebs, and Hogan, 2001).

The Nursebot project, led by the University of Pittsburgh and Carnegie Mellon University (Montemerlo et al., 2002), focuses on a robot as a platform for intelligent reminding (including reminders of medication or upcoming appointments), telepresence (connecting providers with patients via video), surveillance (to detect emergencies), mobile manipulation (which integrates robotic strength with a person's senses and intellect), and social interaction (with the robot that can take over certain social functions) for older home care patients.

The use of robotic pets has been explored in long-term care facilities, where residents often experience social isolation and loneliness. Banks, Willoughby, and Banks (2008) explored the use of a robotic dog as part of animal-assisted therapy to treat loneliness and compared it with the use of actual living dogs that are in many cases not allowed in these facilities. Findings indicated that the two groups were comparable in terms of outcomes (both groups had statistically significant and comparable improvements in residents' levels of loneliness).

Another robotic application that has been tested in different settings is Paro (Wada and Shibata, 2007), a therapeutic robot baby harp seal that has been designed to create a calming effect on, and elicit emotional responses among, older adults and their caregivers. The robotic application has five kinds of sensors: (1) tactile, (2) light, (3) audition, (4) temperature, and (5) posture sensors, with which it can perceive its environment and people in it. It can recognize light and dark with the light sensor, being stroked and beaten with the tactile sensor, or being held with the posture sensor. Finally, it recognizes the direction of voices and words, such as its name, greetings, and praise with its audio sensor. The system has been tested with encouraging findings for its sociopsychological and physiological influences on older people and their caregivers in homes and assisted living facilities and for both healthy elders and elders with dementia.

SMART HOMES

A "smart home" is a residence equipped with technology installed as an integral part of the infrastructure to facilitate monitoring of residents, or promote independence, and increase residents' quality of life (Demiris, 2008). The technology does not require training of or operation by the resident, thereby distinguishing smart home applications from standalone units that can be used in the home setting and need to be operated by the end-user (e.g., blood pressure cuffs, videophones) or software applications that require end-user initiation and training.

As technology advances, smart home applications are being developed worldwide. The Center for Future Health at the University of Rochester, for example, has developed a Smart Medical Home as a highly controlled environment that includes infrared sensors, biosensors, and video cameras (Marsh, 2002). The Aware Home at the Georgia Institute of Technology explores ubiquitous computing technologies that sense and identify potential crises, assist a senior adult's memory, and track behavioral trends (Kidd et al., 1999). Researchers from five countries (Finland, Ireland, Lithuania, Norway, and the United Kingdom) joined their efforts for the ENABLE project (Cash, 2003), which promotes the well-being of people with early dementia with several features, such as a locator for lost objects, a temperature monitor, and an automatic bedroom light. In Toulouse, France, the PROSAFE project is using a set of infrared motion sensors to support automatic recognition of resident activity and of possible falls (Chan et al., 1999).

Hayes evaluated the use of continuous, long-term in-home monitoring to assess neurological function in healthy and cognitively impaired elders (Hayes et al., 2008). A total of 14 older adults (ages 65 and older) living independently in the community were monitored in their homes by using an unobtrusive sensor system that enabled assessment of walking speed and level of activity. Findings demonstrate the feasibility of this approach and also suggest clear potential advantages to this methodology over conventional episodic testing in a clinic environment. A sensor system was also used to address the challenges of medication adherence. In another study (Hayes et al., 2009), a context-aware reminder system, which generated reminders at an opportune time to take medication, was evaluated with 10 participants age 65 or older, living alone and managing their own medications. Adherence and activity in the home were measured using a system of sensors, including an instrumented pillbox. The study indicates that context-aware prompting may provide improved adherence over standard time-based reminders.

A systematic review of smart home projects identified 114 publications for 21 distinct ongoing smart home projects and initiatives (Demiris and Hensel, 2008). The majority of these projects address safety monitoring and assistance (e.g., use of heat sensors detect environmental hazards, such as fire or gas leaks, and safety features, such as automatically turning on bathroom lights when the resident gets out of bed), security monitoring and assistance (e.g., use of motion sensors that detect intruders), cognitive and sensory assistance (e.g., automated or self-initiated reminders, cognitive aids, such as lost key locators, and technologies that aid users with sensory deficits in vision, hearing, and touch), and overall wellness (e.g., combination of motion sensors, pressure pads, and gait monitors to assess activity levels, use of bed sensors to assess sleep quality).

In spite of the growing number of initiatives in this area, the field is in relatively early stages, focusing on feasibility testing and currently lacking an extensive body of evidence of clinical effectiveness. Most of the identified studies demonstrate the feasibility of the technological solution or describe preliminary evaluation approaches with a limited number of subjects, most commonly in a laboratory setting; only a few present results of testing in actual homes or communities (Elite Care, 2005; Demiris et al., 2006; Rialle et al., 2006).

HUMAN FACTORS CHALLENGES AND CONSIDERATIONS

The use of technology applications and tools in home health care raises a number of issues that human factors expertise is called on to address. The sections below address the issues of privacy and confidentiality; usability; data transmission and interoperability; and policy, economic, and ethical considerations.

Privacy and Confidentiality

Systems that use the Internet or other means to transmit and exchange clinical data call for an examination of how privacy and confidentiality with regard to individuals' health information are protected. Information privacy is the right of care recipients to control the use and dissemination of information that relates to them, and confidentiality is a tool for protecting the patients' privacy. In the United States, the Notice of the Proposed Rule from the Department of Health and Human Services concerning Security and Electronic Signature Standards was introduced in 1998 (U.S. Department of Health and Human Services, 1999) as part of the Health Insurance Portability and Accountability Act (HIPAA) that was passed in 1996. This rule, effective in 2000, proposes standards for the security of individual health information and electronic signature use for health care providers, systems, and agencies. These standards refer to the security of all electronic health information and have a great impact on the design and operation of information technology applications in home care.

The use of the Internet in disease management calls for a clarification and definition of the issues of ownership of and access to monitoring data. In many web-based applications, patients record monitoring data and transmit them daily to a web server, owned and maintained by a private third party that allows providers to log in and access their patients' data. In this context, it is important to determine who is authorized to access part or all of the patient record that is stored on a web server and to control such access rights. This process needs to address not only possible threats to data privacy but also to ethical debates about the restructuring of the care delivery process and introduction of new key players (such as third-party vendors who store and maintain data repositories).

When it comes to personal health records, the privacy issues can be complex. This is because new PHR tools are not necessarily covered by HIPAA regulations. Many PHR developers (e.g., Google, Microsoft) are not covered entities as defined by HIPAA. There is an urgent need to address this gap in the current HIPAA regulations and to establish "additional legal protections to reach these new PHR developers and hosting organizations" (Kahn et al., 2009).

Usability

Usability is critical to the design of information technology applications in home care, as it refers to the accessibility of the design and the specifics of an interface that lead to rapid learning, good skill retention, and low error rates. The implication for IT-based systems in home care is that a usable system is one in which end-users are able to communicate with each other, find information, and navigate the software and hardware with ease (Preece, 2000). A large segment of home care patients are elders and in some cases have functional limitations due to aging, or their diagnosis, or both. A functional limitation describes a "reduced sensory, cognitive or motor capability associated with human aging, temporary injury, or permanent disability that prevents a person from communicating, working, playing or simply functioning in an environment where other people in the population can function" (Electronic Industries Alliance and the Electronic Industries Foundation, 1996, p. 20).

Although information technology can play a great role in disease management, the fastest growing segment of the U.S. population—people over age 50—is often at a disadvantage in spite of emerging innovative tools, because system designers often fail to consider them as a potential user group. Accessibility is a major feature of an interface, but in many cases it is ignored by system designers. Web-based applications targeting home care patients should aim to reach a high level of functional accessibility (Demiris, Finkelstein, and Speedie, 2001) and undergo rigorous usability tests. For that purpose, there are design considerations and guidelines that can inform the implementation of information technology applications in home care (Demiris, Finkelstein, and Speedie, 2001).

Although the opportunities to use human factors methods in designing health IT systems are many, these methods have too seldom been employed in such design efforts. The challenges of usability offer many examples of such opportunities.

Human factors methodologies that can be applied to ensure that end-users' needs and expectations are reflected in the design and implementation of a system include paper prototyping and sketching, scenarios and storytelling, field studies and observations, interviews and focus groups, and simulation and modeling. These methods aim to capture the end-user's perspective, needs, and preferences as well as their current workflow or routine. Paper prototyping, for example, allows designers to create system interfaces on paper and explore numerous options to solicit end-user feedback before developing actual prototypes that can be costly. Similarly, scenarios and storytelling allow the end-user to describe real and hypothetical situations that reveal ways in which an IT system can be used to enhance or redesign the process and information flow. Finally, simulation and modeling allow designers to assess how end-users react to conditions or situations that would be introduced with a new system, without actually developing the finished product.

Arsand and Demiris (2008) propose a framework for user-centered methods for designing patient-centric self-help tools that have implications for home care systems. Specifically, they recommend developing and testing a prototype with real patients who have a need for the tools' functionalities, using scenarios and storytelling as effective ways of explaining how a technical solution works for the patients, as well as of assisting caregivers to gain an understanding of the patient's experience, needs, and expectations. Such a process is dynamic and iterative and requires designers to allocate sufficient time for several meetings with end-users so they can understand the possibilities that the technology provides and let their own creative ideas bloom. Furthermore, they recommend planning for extra iterations on the prototype design and testing with real users, selecting user-centered methods of human-computer interaction that are most relevant for a given context and user group and using the triangulation approach in the process of designing good patient-centric tools.

Ultimately, as design specifications and usability testing become widely diffused and allow for a repository of specifications and standards for commonly used IT tools, it may be possible for clinicians to systematically identify characteristics and conditions of patients, their associated environments, and available resources in order to accurately prescribe the appropriate technology tool that will support their care and disease management at home (or to determine technological approaches that will not work with a given patient's or environment's conditions).

Data Transmission and Interoperability

Technology-based applications in home care require in many cases the secure exchange of clinical data between different systems or data sources to group together the wide range of data required for disease management. In order to facilitate the appropriate transmission and interpretation of information, a semantically sound and technically feasible set of standards to facilitate this information exchange is required. Goossen defined a framework of relevant standards for using clinical data in information technology (Goossen, 2003). These standards include clinical, vocabulary, messages, workflow, and technical standards.

- Clinical standards, such as guidelines indicating evidence-based care, must be clearly reflected in the domain knowledge included in programs for disease management and wellness.
- Vocabulary standards pertain to terminologies in different formats and usually developed for specific purposes, such as clinical documentation, comparison of data, or statistical reporting.
- Standards for messages address the issue of interoperability and focus on the electronic exchange of information within or between health information systems. The classic example is Health Level Seven (HL7) (Aditya et al., 2003), which provides standards for the exchange, management, and integration of data that support clinical patient care and the management, delivery, and evaluation of health care services. Such an interoperability standard is essential when it comes to exchange of data between a home-based application and the electronic medical record of a clinical facility. Current HL7 v3 message models, e.g., for patient care, do allow for the

patient to be "author of health information," thus respecting self-care responsibilities.

- Workflow standards describe the tasks and processes of the care plan, involved stakeholders and timeline, required interactions, and transactions. For example, in home care, there is a detailed care plan that dictates the number of home care visits, their goals, who conducts them (registered nurse, nursing aid, social worker, etc.), and rules for specific processes (e.g., capturing of vital signs).
- Technical standards address infrastructure, networking, and security issues. Particularly relevant for disease management applications are the Internet protocol (TCP/IP) for the infrastructure and Extensible Markup Language (XML) for the technical expression of messages.

Different entities are working toward promoting interoperability among software or hardware applications in home care and disease management. Continua Health Alliance, for example, is a nonprofit, open-industry coalition that aims to establish a system of interoperable personal telehealth solutions (Continua Health Alliance, 2010). Specific objectives of this coalition include the development of design guidelines that will enable vendors to build interoperable sensors, home networks, telehealth platforms, and other services and the establishment of a product certification program pertaining to interoperability across certified products.

Policy Considerations

The public policy issues related to the use of information technology in home health care are the same as those that arise for the use of IT in health care in general and involve several levels (state, federal) as well as numerous stakeholders. Policy considerations include access to care; the quality, safety, and efficacy of the delivered services; and the issues of cost and reimbursement. The issue of access to care is actually a challenging one. At first sight, because information technology bridges geographic distance, it can be seen to increase access to care. However, the widespread use of technology in home care may have the effect of reducing access to care, when its use actually increases the cost of the care.

For example, commercially available devices that function as stand-alone units can often be purchased at a relatively low cost and used by a patient with a chronic condition to monitor that condition at home. A monitoring unit, however, that becomes part of an information technology application, allowing the transmission of the same monitoring data sets through a regular phone line or the Internet to a central server, can often cost 50 times that price or more. Given the limited resources of the health care system and the challenges that home care agencies face, it may be that only a subset of home care patients will have access to such sophisticated and perhaps more beneficial IT-based systems.

In addition, access to care may be affected by the so-called digital divide. In the late 1980s, the term "digital divide" was used to describe the division between people who had a computer and those who did not. Nowadays, however, a similar divide may pertain to infrastructure requirements for the technology. Several web-based home care applications, for example, require high-speed Internet infrastructure in the home, which may not be available in all homes, especially in rural and underserved areas.

Reimbursement becomes an essential component of the planning for maintenance of existing systems and the design of new ones. The Centers for Medicare & Medicaid Services (CMS) states that videoconferencing and related technologies can be used to provide appropriate medical care over geographic distances, but that reimbursement, aside from a small fee paid to the site where the patient is located, will be equivalent to what would have been provided for a face-to-face visit. There is only a token reimbursement for the costs of the associated technologies when used in a rural setting (Center for Drugs and Devices, 1996). Specifically in the field of home care, CMS reimburses for virtual visits (videoconferencing to the home) and remote monitoring at a set amount (prospective payment system) that makes no specific provision for the costs of the technologies (Harris, Gottlieb, and Weiner, 2005). CMS is moving away from reimbursement for services to payments for outcomes (pay for performance) (Hyler and Gangure, 2004), and this will ultimately affect technology-based solutions as well.

A further public policy issue pertains to potential concerns about safety and efficacy of IT devices and systems. The Food and Drug Administration (FDA) has the responsibility for ensuring the safety and efficacy of all such devices marketed in the United States (Hallowell et al., 2003). Devices and tools used for monitoring of disease conditions, such as pulse oximeters, spirometers, and the like are subject to FDA oversight. Embedded IT (and specifically software) is reviewed as an integral device component. It is important in this context to assess FDA's evolving position on software that is used for medical purposes but is not intrinsically bound to a particular device, such as an electronic medical record system, a decision support system, or a web-based disease management program. While the FDA currently defines such systems as tools that provide assistance to health care professionals in the treatment of their patients (thus, these tools themselves have no direct patient impact), this position may change in the near future. In this context, the proliferation of mobile phone devices and computing technologies introduces a new definition for the term "medical device" beyond the traditional standalone appliance that was a "closed" system and served only one clinical purpose. The diffusion of open-source applications and the development of clinical applications for mobile phones and other platforms are creating multipurpose tools that can also function as medical devices. The extent to which mobile phones or other platforms can be validated or tested as medical devices because of specific functions or features they support is currently a fundamental unresolved regulatory issue.

A policy implication well documented in the telehealth literature that applies to the broader use of information technology in home care is the delivery of health care across state borders (Kluge, 2004). For most health care professions, the site of practice is considered to be where the patient (not the practitioner) is located. Health insurance is regulated by the states. Thus, this affects cases in which reimbursement for direct care is sought but technology is used to provide services across state borders.

Finally, policy barriers exist when technology developments are rapid and introduce new realities that have not been appropriately addressed by policy makers, as is the case with personal health records. For example, the financial and clinical data held by provider organizations are not well linked, even within an organization. This limits the kinds of tools that could be developed for personal health records to help consumers understand their treatment options available from their own health plans (Kahn et al., 2009). The policy changes that are likely to lead to improved consumer adoption of personal health records include establishing standards for PHR information, facilitating secure exchange of health information, and improving consumers' access to the records and their understanding of their role and capabilities. The diffusion of PHR systems will also be facilitated by a large body of evidence demonstrating their effectiveness; thus, longitudinal studies and rigorous research initiatives can further this field and provide insight into new paradigms of home care.

Economic Considerations

As Polisena and colleagues (2009) point out, an analysis of the economic impact of home-based IT applications must focus on the incremental costs and health benefits associated with the application of the program to a population of patients. Such economic studies must specify and justify the perspective from which the home-based IT programs and health resource use are measured. Societal, health care system, third-party, and patient/family perspectives have a unique focus that informs the costs that need to be included in the analysis. In addition to direct costs (which include cost of program administration, IT delivery, training and maintenance, health care costs, and patient-borne costs pertaining to disease management), indirect costs (such as patient or caregiver's productivity losses, providers' traveling time to the patient's residence) also need to be considered.

Polisena et al. (2009) developed a framework for the conduct of economic evaluation of home telehealth projects for patients with chronic conditions, calling for the assessment of incremental costs and incremental outcomes of each health care program evaluated. They argue that the majority of published studies are not economic evaluations of home telehealth and cannot assist in determining whether a treatment is justifiable based on the impact on costs and treatment outcomes; often studies interpret a reduced use of health care resources as evidence of improved outcomes (Polisena et al., 2009). Use of health care resources use may be limited, however, due to fewer contacts with home telehealth, meaning reduced frequency of access to other services but not necessarily a reduced need for these services.

This highlights the significance of inclusion of clinical outcomes (which may be surrogate outcomes, such as disease markers or patient's quality of life) in economic evaluations. Introducing technology into the residential setting may initially increase overall costs (by adding costs of software/hardware, training, installation, and maintenance). In these cases, a cost-effectiveness, or cost-utility analysis, can highlight the potential long-term impact of the IT-based application. A cost-effectiveness analysis needs to include data on clinical outcomes associated with the particular disease or condition studied, such as event rates and deaths. Often it is the case that an economic evaluation takes place within a limited time frame that does not facilitate a demonstration of differences in long-term clinical outcomes, as would be the case with longitudinal studies. In these cases, and especially when studying populations with chronic diseases, surrogate markers (such as glycemic control for diabetes, systolic blood pressure for congestive heart failure) can be used to address clinical outcomes. An economic evaluation should include a sensitivity analysis to determine the robustness of the study findings based on the assumptions made (and by varying the underlying assumptions over a range of possible values).

A systematic review of economic evaluations for home telehealth identified a total of 22 studies on home telehealth for chronic diseases published between 1998 and 2008 (Polisena et al., 2009). Home telehealth was found to have cost savings from the health care system and insurance provider perspectives in all but two studies, but, the authors argue, the quality of the studies was generally not high. Current evidence suggests that home telehealth has the potential to reduce costs, but its impact from a societal perspective remains uncertain until higher quality studies become available.

Ethical Considerations

When a system allows stakeholders of health care delivery services to interact while separated by distance, the issue of what has been called "progressive dehumanization" of interpersonal relationships is raised, namely, the conduct not only of the professional but also of the interpersonal aspect of communication online or via communication technologies with a decreasing number of face-to-face interactions. IT-based home care interventions have the potential to bridge geographic distances and in some cases allow for anonymity that might be desired for a specific medical condition; however, such applications might be lacking the sense of touch and interhuman close contact that occurs in face-to-face meetings. Virtual communities represent a physically disembodied social order, and some argue (Winner, 1990) that it will eventually compete with a structure or network of entities that occupy spatial locations. In this context, the argument is that "the fabric of human relationships and communities rests on real presences, real physical meetings and relationships" (Horner, 2001), and their elimination may affect the patient-provider relationship and perhaps even the traditional dimensions of home care.

A theoretical framework for the definition of obtrusiveness in home telehealth technologies was developed by Hensel, Demiris, and Courtney (2006). In this framework, obtrusiveness pertains to the features of information technology that may be perceived as prominently undesirable by an individual user. In all, 22 categories of what may be perceived as obtrusiveness were identified on the basis of a review of the literature and were grouped into 8 dimensions (including, among others, the physical dimension, privacy, usability, human interaction). This effort represents an initial step toward developing measures of obtrusiveness associated with information technology applications in home care and a tool to systematically address ethical considerations involved in such applications.

DISCUSSION

This review highlights the diversity of technology applications and tools in home health care and the promising role they can play for a variety of stakeholders (including patients, families, health care providers, communities, and the general public) and for a multitude of clinical areas (covering physiological, functional, cognitive, social, and psychological parameters as well as holistic aspects of wellness and quality of life). The clear advantages that IT integration in home care carries include the introduction of several stakeholders who can more easily and efficiently communicate in spite of geographic distance and the ability to generate new types of data (e.g., activity levels, sleep quality) and more frequently collect well-established parameters (such as vital signs) without requiring the actual presence of health care providers in the residential setting.

The Use of IT: Shared Decision Making and Patient Empowerment

One of the expectations resulting from the use of IT in home health care is that it will empower patients and their families by providing them with access to information, peers, and other networks and by actively engaging them in the disease management or wellness promotion initiatives. The empirical evidence that involvement in healthcare decisions makes a significant and enduring difference to health care outcomes is not unequivocal (Savage and Armstrong, 1990; Stewart, 1995; Kinmonth et al., 1998), although some studies support this hypothesis. One difficulty (among many) is that the involvement of patients in decisions has been left undefined. It is usually conceptualized as patient-centeredness (Roter, 1989; Stewart et al., 1995), which is a broad and variably interpreted concept that is difficult to assess using current tools (Mead and Bower, 2000a, 2000b). Nevertheless, the ethical need to respect autonomy and respond to home care patients' desire for more involvement in decision making is becoming widely recognized (Richards, 1998; Coulter, Entwistle, and Gilbert, 1999).

A treatment decision-making framework based on information exchange, deliberation about treatment options, and agreement on the treatment to implement has been developed by Charles and colleagues (2003). In this framework, three approaches are presented to label the process and outcome of decision making:

1. The *pure paternalistic approach* is characterized by health care provider control, whereby the provider determines the amount and kind of information that is given to the patient. The information flow is unidirectional. The provider deliberates about the benefits and risks of available options and reaches a decision without patient input (Charles et al., 2003).
2. The *pure informed approach* is characterized by a division of labor and the preservation of patient autonomy. The provider makes available to the patient information on treatment options, challenges, and risks. The patient assesses the situation in the context of her or his own value system and preferences and makes a treatment decision.
3. The *pure shared approach* is characterized by ongoing interaction and information exchange between patient and provider in all stages of the decision-making process. The information flow is bidirectional. The provider offers information about all available options and risks, and the patient discusses personal preferences, his or her value system, lifestyle, and personal preferences. The decision-making process includes an extensive discussion and nego-

> tiations in search of the best option to pursue. The decision-making process is a dynamic one in which both providers and patients may shift away from their initial position (Charles et al., 2003).

Shared decision making is increasingly advocated as an ideal model of decision making about treatment in the clinical encounter in general and in home care specifically. In the shared model, the process by which the interaction is conducted to reach an agreement may be determined at the outset of the encounter or may develop as the encounter unfolds and be shaped dynamically by the ongoing communication. Information sharing is a prerequisite to shared decision making.

It is a challenge to expect all patients to enroll in this process as equal partners, as one may argue that there may often be a power imbalance in the provider-patient relationship. Obviously health care providers have superior knowledge of the options and issues involved, as well as clinical experience, and therefore join the process as experts (Charles, Gafni, and Whelan, 1999). A patient may often participate in the encounter feeling vulnerable due to their illness or fear of the unknown. Additional issues, such as health literacy, income, gender, and cultural barriers, may impede patients and prevent them from expressing their preferences or negotiating with the physician (Charles et al., 1999). As Guadagnoli and Ward point out, it is a challenge for providers who want to practice a shared approach to provide a safe environment for patients, allowing them to be comfortable in exploring information and negotiating options (Guadagnoli and Ward, 1998). The use of information technology (and personal health records specifically) can increase access to information for patients and provide them with options as well as tools to capture their health behaviors and their needs. However, it remains to be explored whether IT use in home health care can indeed support shared decision making and ultimately lead to patient empowerment.

Future Trends

As technology advances, rapid developments in the areas of robotic applications and smart homes are anticipated. Currently, research is under way in Japan to explore the role of humanoids in home health care and nursing homes. The term "humanoid" describes a robotic application with artificial intelligence features that is anthropomorphic. Japan's aging population has ignited efforts to design fully functional robots that can aid elders in their homes or long-term care facilities and address the nursing workforce shortage.

While such developments may not be fully explored in the immediate future but may become long-term trends, there are developments that are anticipated to affect the use of IT in home health care in the very near future. These include Web 2.0 and the proliferation of wireless communications.

Web 2.0 refers to web development and web design that facilitates interactive information sharing, interoperability, and collaboration. A Web 2.0 site allows its users to interact with other users or to change website content, in contrast to noninteractive websites that limit users to the passive viewing of the information provided. Examples of Web 2.0 include web-based communities, social networking sites, and video-sharing sites. The concept of Web 2.0 enables virtual community tools and PHR applications, as well as new and innovative ways for different stakeholders to communicate and collaborate.

Wireless handheld computers and cell phones with expanded computing abilities are widely used and continue their diffusion in the U.S. population. Smart phones and other similar devices can play a role in home care, whether as tools to record daily activities (e.g., nutrition, exercise), to provide reminders, or for even more sophisticated services (e.g., use of global positioning systems to identify health care providers and facilities, built-in sensors to assess amount and type of physical activity and compare with predefined goals).

Unintended Consequences

As is the case with any IT implementation, when exploring options for new and innovative technologies in home health care, one has to predict or prepare for unintended consequences. As new systems are implemented to enhance home care services, one needs to address the possibility of such technologies removing choice and control from users as they learn to rely on automation. There are fears that sophisticated applications, like robotic tools or smart homes, may result in a reduction of social interaction, or that they may provide tools that substitute for personal forms of care and communication (Tetley, Hanson, and Clarke, 2001). Since the technologies are introduced into one's home, the warning by Wylde and Valins (1996) against creating "societies of high-tech hermits" becomes even more relevant.

In addition, the degree to which automated applications lessen the sense of personal responsibility on the part of users or their caregivers must be weighed against associated benefits. Informal caregivers may become less vigilant in monitoring health changes in their loved ones, and the patients themselves may become less vigilant in health self-monitoring or self-management. Further research and dialogue need to address eligibility criteria and user characteristics or clinical conditions that may be more suitable for IT applications in home care. Which populations may benefit the most from telehealth or smart home applications? When do the requirements for infrastructure and training outweigh anticipated benefits? As Stip and Rialle point out (2005), the issues of individual freedom, personal autonomy, informed consent, and confidentiality have to be examined in the context of the target population. They use an example of an IT application for patients with schizophrenia, a condition that causes distortion of reality, often in the form of delusions of persecution and psychosensory phenomena, and highlight the likelihood that surveillance technologies may exacerbate such symptoms. It becomes clear that technology toolkits should be developed and used when appropriate and should demonstrate flexibility to address the profile of every user, including not only clinical (physiological, functional, cognitive) but also psychological and social parameters.

ABOUT THE AUTHOR

George Demiris is associate professor of biobehavioral nursing and health systems in the School of Nursing and Biomedical and Health Informatics, School of Medicine, at the University of Washington. His research interests include the design and evaluation of home-based technologies for older adults and patients with chronic conditions and disabilities, smart homes and ambient assisted living applications, and the use of telehealth in home care and hospice.

REFERENCES

Aditya, B.S., Sharma, J.C., Allen, S.C., and Vassallo, M. (2003). Predictors of a nursing home placement from a non-acute geriatric hospital. *Clinical Rehabilitation, 17*(1), 108-113.

Arsand, E., and Demiris, G. (2008). User centered methods for designing patient-centric self-help tools. *Informatics for Health and Social Care, 33*, 158-169.

Baker, A.M., Lafata, J.E., Ward, R.E., Whitehouse, F., and Divine, G. (2001). A web-based diabetes care management support system. *Joint Commission Journal on Quality Improvement, 27*(4), 179-190.

Banks, M.R., Willoughby, L.M., and Banks, W.A. (2008). Animal-assisted therapy and loneliness in nursing homes: Use of robotic versus living dogs. *Journal of the American Medical Directors Association, 9*(3), 173-177.

Basch, E., Artz, D., Dulko, D., Scher, K., Sabbatini, P., Hensley, M., et al. (2005). Patient online self-reporting of toxicity symptoms during chemotherapy. *Journal of Clinical Oncology, 23*(15), 3,552-3,561.

Bellazzi, R., Larizza, C., Montani, S., Riva, A., Stefanelli, M., d'Annunzio, G., et al. (2002). A telemedicine support for diabetes management: the T-IDDM project. *Computer Methods and Programs in Biomedicine, 69*(2), 147-161.

Burnett, G., Besant, M., and Chatman, E.A. (2001). Small worlds: Normative behavior in virtual communities and feminist bookselling. *Journal of the American Society for Information Science and Technology, 52*, 536-547.

Cash, M. (2003). Assistive technology and people with dementia. *Reviews in Clinical Gerontology, 13*, 313-319.

Center for Devices and Radiological Health, Food and Drug Administration. (1996). *Telehealth related activities.* Available: http://www.fda.gov/AboutFDA/CentersOffices/CDRH/DivisionofCommunicationMediaFDATVStudio/ucm125788.htm [accessed August 2010].

Chan, M., Bocquet, H., Campo, E., Val, T., and Pous, J. (1999). Alarm communication network to help carers of the elderly for safety purposes: A survey of a project. *International Journal of Rehabilitation Research, 22,* 131-136.

Charles, C.A., Gafni, A., and Whelan, T. (1999). Decision-making in the physician-patient encounter: Revisiting the shared treatment decision making model. *Social Science and Medicine, 49,* 651-661.

Charles, C.A., Whelan, T., Gafni, A., Willan, A., and Farrell, S. (2003). Shared treatment decision making: What does it mean to physicians? *Journal of Clinical Ontology, 21,* 932-936.

Continua Health Alliance. (2010). *About the Alliance.* Available: http://www.continuaalliance.org/about-the-alliance.html [accessed June 2010].

Coulter, A., Entwistle, V., and Gilbert, D. (1999). Sharing decisions with patients: Is the information good enough? *British Medical Journal, 318,* 318-322.

Darkins, A., Ryan, P., Kobb, R., Foster, L., Edmonson, E., Wakefield, B., and Lancaster, A.E. (2008). Care coordination/home telehealth: The systematic implementation of health informatics, home telehealth, and disease management to support the care of veteran patients with chronic conditions. *Telemedicine Journal and E-Health, 14*(10), 1,118-1,126.

Demiris, G. (2005). Virtual communities in health care. In B. Silverman, A. Jain, A. Ichalkaranje, and L. Jain (Eds.), *Intelligent paradigms for healthcare enterprises* (vol. 184, pp. 121-137). New York: Springer Verlag.

Demiris, G. (2008). Smart homes and ambient assisted living in an aging society: New opportunities and challenges for biomedical informatics. *Methods of Information in Medicine, 47*(1), 56-57.

Demiris, G., and Hensel, B.K. (2008). Technologies for an aging society: A systematic review of "smart home" applications. *Yearbook of Medical Informatics,* 33-40.

Demiris, G., Finkelstein, S.M., and Speedie, S.M. (2001). Considerations for the design of a web-based clinical monitoring and educational system for elderly patients. *Journal of the American Medical Informatics Association, 8,* 468-472.

Demiris, G., Skubic, M., Keller, J., Rantz, M., Parker Oliver, D., Aud, M., Lee, J., Burks, K., and Green, N. (2006). Nurse participation in the design of user interfaces for a smart home system. In *Proceedings of the International Conference on Smart Homes and Health Telematics* (pp. 66-73), Belfast, Northern Ireland. Amsterdam, the Netherlands: IOS Press.

Demiris, G., Speedie, S.M., and Finkelstein, S. (2001). Change of patients' perceptions of telehomecare. *Telemedicine Journal and E-Health, 7*(3), 241-248.

Electronic Industries Alliance and the Electronic Industries Foundation. (1996). *Resource guide for accessible design of consumer electronics: Linking product design to the needs of people with functional limitations.* A joint venture of the Electronic Industries Alliance and the Electronic Industries Foundation. Arlington, VA: Telecommunications Industry Association.

Elite Care. (2005). Creating an autonomy-risk equilibrium (CARE). Available: http://legacy.lclark.edu/~moss/oatfield%20page.html [accessed May 2010].

Eysenbach, G., Powell, J., Englesakis, M., Rizo, C., and Stern, A. (2004). Health-related virtual communities and electronic support groups: Systematic review of the effects of online peer to peer interactions. *British Medical Journal, 328*(7449), 1,166.

Finkelstein, J., O'Connor, G., and Friedmann, R.H. (2001). Development and implementation of the home asthma telemonitoring (HAT) system to facilitate asthma self-care. *Studies in Health Technology and Informatics, 84*(Pt 1), 810-814.

Finn, J. (1999). An exploration of helping processes in an online self-help group focusing on issues of disability. *Health and Social Work, 24*(3), 220-231.

Goossen, W.T.F. (2003). Templates: An organizing framework to link evidence, terminology and information models in the nursing profession. In *Proceedings of the Eighth International Congress in Nursing Informatics*, Rio de Janeiro, Brazil.

Guadagnoli, E., and Ward, P. (1998). Patient satisfaction in decision making. *Social Science and Medicine, 47*, 329-339.

Gustafson, D.H., Bosworth, K., Hawkins, R.P., Boberg, E.W., and Bricker, E. (1992). CHESS: A computer-based system for providing information, referrals, decision support and social support to people facing medical and other health-related crises. In *Proceedings of the Annual Symposium on Computer Application in Medical Care* (pp. 161-165). Available: http://www.ncbi.nlm.nih.gov/pmc/articles/PMC2248029/pdf/procascamc00003-0178.pdf [accessed June 2010].

Hallowell, N., Foster, C., Eeles, R., Ardern-Jones, A., Murday, V., and Watson, M. (2003). Balancing autonomy and responsibility: The ethics of generating and disclosing genetic information. *Journal of Medical Ethics, 29*, 74-79.

Harris, S.B., Gottlieb, B.L., and Weiner, S. (2005). Regulating broadband. *Communications Lawyer, 23*, 1-10.

Hassol, A., Walker, J.M., Kidder, D., Rokita, K., Young, D., Pierdon, S., Deitz, D., Kuck, S., and Ortiz, E. (2004). Patient experiences and attitudes about access to a patient electronic health care record and linked web messaging. *Journal of the American Medical Informatics Association, 11*(6), 505-513.

Hayes, T.L., Abendroth, F., Adami, A., Pavel, M., Zitzelberger, T.A., and Kaye, J.A. (2008). Unobtrusive assessment of activity patterns associated with mild cognitive impairment. *Alzheimer's and Dementia, 4*, 395-405.

Hayes, T.L., Cobbinah, K., Dishongh, T., Kaye, J.A., Kimel, J., Labhard, M., et al. (2009). A study of medication-taking and unobtrusive, intelligent reminding. *Telemedicine Journal and E-Health 15*, 770-776.

Hensel, B.K., Demiris, G., and Courtney, K.L. (2006). Defining obtrusiveness in home telehealth technologies: A conceptual framework. *Journal of the American Medical Informatics Association, 13*, 428-431.

Horner, D.S. (2001). The moral status of virtual action. In T.W. Bynum (Ed.), *Proceedings of the Fifth International Conference on the Social and Ethical Impacts of Information and Communication Technologies* (vol. 2, pp. 226-235). Gdansk, Poland: Technical University of Gdansk: Ethicomp.

Hyler, S.E., and Gangure, D.P. (2004). Practitioner's corner: Legal and ethical challenges in telepsychiatry. *Journal of Psychiatric Practice, 10*, 272-276.

Johnson, M.J., Feng, X., Johnson, L.M., and Winters, J.M. (2007). Potential of a suite of robot/computer-assisted motivating systems for personalized, home-based, stroke rehabilitation. *Journal of Neuroengineering and Rehabilitation, 4*, 6.

Johnston, B., Wheeler, L., Deuser, J., and Sousa, K.H. (2000). Outcomes of the Kaiser Permanente tele-home health research project. *Archives of Family Medicine, 9*(1), 40-45.

Kahn, J.S., Aulakh, V., and Bosworth, A. (2009). What it takes: Characteristics of the ideal personal health record. *Health Affairs, 28*, 369-376.

Kidd, C.D., Orr, R., Abowd, G.D., Atkeson, C.G., Essa, I.A., MacIntyre, B., Mynatt, E., Starner, T.E., and Newstetter, W. (1999). The aware home: A living laboratory for ubiquitous computing research. Lecture Notes in Computer Science Series, vol. 1670. Available: http://www.springerlink.com/content/d598506140k50v26/fulltext.pdf [accessed June 2010].

Kinmonth, A.L., Woodcock, A., Griffin, S., Spiegal, N., and Campbell, M.J. (1998). Randomized controlled trial of patient-centered care of diabetes in general practice: Impact on current wellbeing and future disease risk. *British Medical Journal, 317*, 1,202-1,208.

Kluge, E.H. (2004). Informed consent to the secondary use of EHRs: Informatics rights and their limitations. *Medinfo, 11*, 635-638.

Marsh, J. (2002). House calls. *Rochester Review, 64*, 22-26.

McKay, H.G., Feil, E.G., Glasgow, R.E., and Brown, J.E. (1998). Feasibility and use of an Internet support service for diabetes self-management. *Diabetes Education, 24*(2), 174-179.

Mead, N., and Bower, P. (2000a). Measuring patient centeredness: A comparison of three observation based instruments. *Patient Education and Counseling, 39*, 71-80.

Mead, N., and Bower, P. (2000b). Patient centeredness: A conceptual framework and review of the empirical literature. *Social Science and Medicine, 51*, 1,087-1,110.

Mechanic, D. (2008). Rethinking medical professionalism: The role of information technology and practice innovations. *Milbank Quarterly, 86*(2), 327-358.

Montemerlo, M., Pineau, J., Roy, N., Thrun, S., and Verma, V. (2002). Experiences with a mobile robotic guide for the elderly. *Proceedings of the Eighteenth AAAI National Conference on Artificial Intelligence.* Cambridge, MA: MIT Press

Morlion, B., Knoop, C., Paiva, M., and Estenne, M. (2002). Internet-based home monitoring of pulmonary function after lung transplantation. *American Journal of Respiratory and Critical Care Medicine, 165*(5), 694-697.

National Alliance for Health Information Technology. (2008). *Defining key health information technology terms.* Available: http://healthit.hhs.gov/portal/server.pt/gateway/PTARGS_0_10741_848133_0_0_18/10_2_hit_terms.pdf [accessed June 2010].

Polisena, J., Coyle, D., Coyle, K., and McGill S. (2009). Home telehealth for chronic disease management: A systematic review and an analysis of economic evaluations. *International Journal of Technology Assessment in Health Care, 25*(3), 339-349.

Preece, J. (2000). *Online communities: Designing usability, supporting sociability.* Chichester, UK: John Wiley and Sons.

Rialle, V., Rumeau, P., Ollivet, C., and Herve, C. (2006). Smart homes. In R. Wootton, S.L. Dimmick and J.C. Kvedar (Eds.), *Home telehealth: Connecting care within the community.* London: RSM Press.

Richards, T. (1998). Partnership with patients. *British Medical Journal, 316*, 85-86.

Riva, A., Bellazzi, R., and Stefanelli, M. (1997). A web-based system for the intelligent management of diabetic patients. *M.D. Computing: Computers in Medical Practice, 14*(5), 360-364.

Rojas, S.V., and Gagnon, M.P. (2008). A systematic review of the key indicators for assessing telehomecare cost-effectiveness. *Telemedicine Journal and E-Health 14*(9), 896-904.

Roter, D. (1989). Which facets of communication have strong effects on outcome: A meta analysis. In M. Stewart (Ed.), *Communicating with medical patients.* Thousand Oaks, CA: Sage.

Rothschild, S.K., Lapidos, S., Minnick, A., Fogg, L., and Catrambone, C. (2004). Using virtual teams to improve the care of chronically ill patients. *Journal of Clinical Outcomes Management, 11*, 346-350.

Salvendy, G. (2006). *Handbook of human factors and ergonomics* (3rd ed.). Hoboken, NJ: Wiley.

Savage, R., and Armstrong, D. (1990). Effect of a general practitioner's consulting style on patient satisfaction: A controlled study. *British Medical Journal, 301*, 968-970.

Shea, S., Weinstock, R.S., Teresi, J.A., Palmas, W., Starren, J., Cimino, J.J., Lai, A., Field, L., Morin, P.C., Goland, R., Izquierdo, R.E., Ebner, S., Silver, S., Petkova, E., Kong, J., and Eimicke, J.P. (2009). A randomized trial comparing telemedicine case management with usual care in older, ethnically diverse, medically underserved patients with diabetes mellitus: 5-year results of the IDEATel study. *Journal of the American Medical Informatics Association, 16*(4), 446-456.

Stewart, M. (1995). Studies of health outcomes and patient-centered communication. In M. Stewart, J.B. Brown, and W.W. Weston (Eds.), *Patient-centered medicine: Transforming the clinical methods.* Thousand Oaks, CA: Sage.

Stewart, M., Brown, J.B., and Weston, W.W. (Eds.). (1995). *Patient-centered medicine: Transforming the clinical method.* Thousand Oaks, CA: Sage.

Stip, E., and Rialle, V. (2005). Environmental cognitive remediation in schizophrenia: Ethical implications of "smart home" technology. *Canadian Journal of Psychiatry, 50,* 281-291.

Tetley, J., Hanson, E., and Clarke, A. (2001). Older people, telematics and care. In A.M. Warnes, L. Warren and M. Nolan (Eds.), *Care services for later life: Transformations and critiques* (pp. 243-258). London: Jessica Kingsley.

U.S. Department of Health and Human Services, Office of the Secretary. (1999). Standards for privacy of individually identifiable health information; proposed rule. *Federal Register, 64*(212), 59,917-60,016.

U.S. Department of Veterans Affairs. (2010). *My HealtheVet.* Available: http://www.myhealth.va.gov [accessed June 2010].

Volpe, B.T., Krebs, H.I., and Hogan, N. (2001). Is robot-aided sensorimotor training in stroke rehabilitation a realistic option? *Current Opinion in Neurology, 14*(6), 745-752.

Wada, K., and Shibata, T. (2007). Living with seal robots: Its sociopsychological and physiological influences on the elderly at a care house. *IEEE Transactions on Robotics, 23,* 972-980.

Whittaker, S., Isaacs, E., and O'Day, V. (1997). Widening the net. Workshop report on the theory and practice of physical and network communities. *SIGCHI Bulletin, 29,* 27-30.

Winner, L. (1990). Living in electronic space. In T. Casey and L. Embree (Eds.), *Lifeworld and technology* (pp. 1-14): Lanham MD: Center for Advanced Research on Phenomenology and University Press of America.

Wylde, M., and Valins, M.S. (1996). The impact of technology. In Valins M.S. and D. Salter (Eds.), *Futurecare: New directions in planning health and care environments* (pp. 15-24). Oxford: Blackwell Science.

10

The Physical Environment and Home Health Care

Jonathan Sanford

There is a direct relationship between health and housing. When an individual is in poor health, is impaired, or has functional declines due to aging, health concerns are virtually indistinguishable from housing concerns, particularly in an aging housing stock (Lawler, 2001). To compensate for and help manage health conditions, the physical environment of homes can be both prosthetic and therapeutic. As a prosthetic environment, the home can compensate for limitations in functional abilities to enable individuals to carry out basic activities associated with daily living safely and independently, participate in social roles, and receive personal assistance from caregivers as needed. Therapeutically, the environment can facilitate health maintenance and management by supporting health-promoting behaviors and provision of health care services.

Many homes are not designed to support either prosthetic or therapeutic needs. They contain potential hazards that can lead to accidents, are deficient in design features that permit safe and independent functioning in daily activities, and lack sufficient space and layout for assistive technologies and personal assistance. Neither is housing designed to accommodate health care equipment, health care providers, or the communications infrastructure necessary to share health information with remote care providers. As a result, there is often a lack of fit between the independent living and health needs of community-dwelling individuals and the places in which they live.

Exacerbating the lack of fit between needs and the design of homes, activity performance and health promotion are typically treated autonomously and with different environmental implications, even though environments that promote independence could reduce health care needs and those that promote health could facilitate independence. In fact, the World Health Organization has suggested that an important goal in health promotion is the creation of environments that support healthy living and well-being (World Health Organization, 1991). Nonetheless, the environment is perceived quite differently by the individuals who function in it and the systems that regulate it. On one hand, a home should provide a prosthetic environment in which individuals can live and function safely as long as they choose to remain there. On the other hand, a number of factors, including the cost of health care and advances in communications and medical technologies, have made the home a preferred environment for health care delivery. Thus, the home has become, not by choice and often in spite of its design, a de facto therapeutic environment. Not surprisingly, the independent living and home health goals that should be mutually supportive—that is, independent living should promote health and home health should promote independent living—often are addressed without consideration for each other.

To engender a more holistic approach to activity and health needs and to provide home environments that are more supportive of those needs, a number of policy, public, and personal constraints must be overcome. These include (1) a reimbursement system that provides only limited coverage for the costs of environmental assessments and modifications for activity limitations only, and particularly lacks incentives for the use of solutions that have broader benefits beyond the specific health-related problems or individuals for whom they were intended; (2) a delivery system that is fragmented, so that the array of health care services, including assistive technologies, health care technologies, environmental modifications, home therapy, and home health, are provided by many different and disconnected providers and funding mechanisms; (3) a regulatory system of building and zoning codes that enables housing to continue to be built as if people will never have activity or health care needs (Pynoos and Regnier, 1997); and (4) a reluctance on the part of homeowners to make changes in their homes due to lack of awareness of, and misperceptions about, the importance of the home environment in effecting engagement, comfort, novelty, and stimulation as well as participation in meaningful activities (Gitlin, 2003).

The success of the home as a health care environment is therefore more complicated than simply modifying the physical environment of the home to fit activity and health care needs. For such interventions to occur, there must be fundamental paradigm shift with regard to the importance of the home environment in promoting activity, health, and health care. To compound the problem, changes must occur in a number of different and mutually exclusive systems that are not particularly aware of the role of the environment in supporting activity and health needs or of each other.

This chapter examines the prosthetic and therapeutic roles of the environment in promoting positive activity and health outcomes, identifies barriers to supportive home environments, and proposes that universal design—the design of products and environments to be usable by all people, to the greatest extent possible, without the need for adaptation or specialized design (Mace, Hardie, and Place, 1991)—be adopted as the conceptual basis for the paradigm shift that is needed to promote independent living and health management. Specifically, the chapter presents (1) a theoretical background to support the role of the environment in independent living and home health care; (2) a discussion of the relationship between prosthetic environmental interventions and improved activity outcomes through facilitating both independence and caregiver assistance; (3) a use of the home as a therapeutic environment in which communication and monitoring technologies can improve health management and treatment through facilitating access to health care; (4) new housing concepts, including smart homes and universal design, that can minimize the impact of prosthetic and therapeutic interventions on the home environment; (5) the barriers to adoption of new housing innovation; (6) the policy changes necessary to improve adoption of housing innovation; and (7) a research agenda that can provide the evidence needed to justify changes in home health policy.

THE ROLE OF THE ENVIRONMENT IN INDEPENDENT LIVING AND HOME HEALTH CARE

Home and community settings are complex environments comprised of physical as well as social, cultural, personal, and temporal environmental factors. For example, social factors might include the impact of other individuals in a home, who may or may not be providing care, as well as the impact of modifications on those individuals (Gitlin, 2003). While a number of environmental factors exist across a variety of contexts (e.g., community, work, school), this chapter specifically focuses on the physical barriers and facilitators (both prosthetic and therapeutic) of positive activity and health outcomes in the home. Other chapters in this volume address social and policy environments.

Physical environmental barriers, such as stairs, lack of toilet and tub grab bars, poor lighting, and poor visual contrast, and lack of space can reduce accessibility; create dangers in the home and community; put community-dwelling individuals with chronic conditions and functional limitations at significant risk for adverse health events (such as falls) and injuries, loss of independence, or difficulty in performing activities of daily living (ADLs); minimize the effectiveness of caregivers, assistive technologies, and health care devices; and even lead to relocation or early institutionalization (Carter et al., 1997; Clemson, Roland, and Cumming, 1997; Cumming et al., 1999, 2001; Oswald et al., 2002; Fange and Iwarsson, 2003; Stark, 2004; Iwarsson, 2005; Lau et al., 2007). Barriers, particularly environmental hazards, are common and pervasive (Gill et al., 1999). For example, one study of factors associated with home environmental problems among older adults reported an average of 13 problems with the environment that posed barriers to safe and independent performance (Gitlin et al., 2001b).

In contrast, environmental facilitators reduce barriers and have positive impacts on functioning of individuals and their caregivers. In fact, one study (Freedman, Martin, and Schoeni, 2002) suggests that gains in functioning of older adults over the past few decades may be the result, in part, of the introduction of facilitators and the reduction of environmental barriers. A second study reviewed 64 studies of environmental interventions for the management of Alzheimer's disease (Gitlin, Liebman, and Winter, 2003) and reported that environmental interventions had some level of success in 90 percent of the studies, resulting in significant improvement in experimental group participants in 10 of 11 randomized clinical trials. More broadly, in a review article of studies on the home environment and disability, Wahl and colleagues (2009) reported that the majority of studies provided supportive evidence that improving the home environment reduces disability-related outcomes.

More broadly, home modifications and assistive and communication technologies have been found to prevent functional decline and disability, promote independent activity and safety, increase task self-efficacy, and enhance health outcomes (Connell and Sanford, 1997, 2001; Mann et al., 1999; Gitlin et al., 2001a; Freedman, Martin, and Schoeni, 2002; Tinetti et al., 2002; Gitlin, 2003; Ferrucci et al., 2004; Oswald and Wahl, 2004; Spillman, 2004; Allen, Resnick, and Roy, 2006; Sanford and Hammel, 2006; Sanford et al., 2006; Oswald et al., 2007) by reducing task demand (Verbrugge and Sevak, 2002). In addition, home modifications have been shown to increase caregivers' effectiveness, well-being, and self-efficacy, as well as to decrease caregiver stress and upset (Gitlin et al., 2001a, 2003). Similarly, research has shown that physical environment facilitators can reduce sedentary behaviors, promote community mobility, and enhance health (e.g., Andersen et al., 2000; Frank, Engelke, and Schmid, 2003; Frumpkin, 2003; Saelens, Sallis, and Frank, 2003).

However, linking specific environmental barriers and facilitators in the home directly to activities is a formidable task (Connell et al., 1993; Connell and Sanford, 1997). Traditional medical models (World Health Organization, 1980) attribute activity performance and health outcomes primarily to an individual's functional abilities. More specifically, these models predict that impairment causes functional limitations, which in turn result in negative performance and health outcomes.

Although the physical environment has long been associated with individual functioning and disability (Rubenstein, 1999; Wahl, 2001; Iwarsson, 2004; Scheidt and Windley, 2006), social models of health have only recently become more accepted. These models suggest that, whereas physiological factors set the threshold on functional ability and health, environmental factors set the threshold on the point at which limitations in ability become a disability (Stineman et al., 2007). Outcomes are therefore situational, the result of the interaction between an individual's abilities (as opposed to limitations) and the demands of the environment, according to the environmental press model (Lawton and Nahemow, 1973). As a result, activity performance, participation, and health are expressions of the fit or misfit between an individual and his or her environment. Optimal person-environment (P-E) fit occurs when an individual's abilities and the demands of the environment are compatible. Conversely, P-E misfit occurs when the environment is either too challenging (i.e., demands exceed abilities) or not challenging enough (i.e., abilities exceed demands). An environment that fits an individual will facilitate positive performance and health outcomes that are manifest in his or her ability to participate in activities when, where, and with whom he or she desires. In contrast, an environment that does not fit an individual will result in negative performance outcomes or performance deficits that may prevent him or her from participating in an activity altogether.

Whereas Lawton's environmental press model suggests the role of the environment in activity and health, the enabling-disabling process model of the Institute of Medicine specifically identifies the environment as a pathway for intervention (Institute of Medicine, 1997). The model suggests that the *disabling process* is the dislocation of an individual from his or her prior integration in an environment due to increasing needs relative to the environment. In contrast, the *enabling process* is either the restoration of the individual's function or environmental modification to remove barriers that limit performance.

Two decades after proposing its medical model, the World Health Organization developed the International Classification of Functioning, Disability and Health (ICF), a new classification system based on a more robust social model (World Health Organization, 2001). The ICF attributes differences between what individuals can do (capacity to engage in activities and participation based on body function and structure) and what they actually do (performance of activities) to the influence of personal and environmental (both social and physical) factors. The classification system not only associates specific environmental factors with positive or negative outcomes but also provides a mechanism for measuring the level of P-E fit or misfit by rating the strength of a particular factor as a facilitator (from 0 to +4) or barrier (from 0 to –4).

Differences between medical and social models have important implications for health and independent living in the home and community. Medical models suggest that achieving positive outcomes involves changing the person (i.e., eliminating or minimizing impairment) or compensating for a functional limitation (i.e., providing assistive technology). In contrast, social models suggest that positive outcomes involve changing either the person or the environmental circumstances or both. Importantly, although the physical environment plays an important role in activity performance and health, it neither dictates nor determines activity performance or health behavior. Rather, the environment simply creates opportunities for activity or behaviors to occur. It is up to individuals and care providers to either take advantage of any opportunities presented by prosthetic and therapeutic environmental facilitators or overcome the demands of any barriers that are present.

PROSTHETIC INTERVENTIONS: HOME MODIFICATIONS TO IMPROVE ACTIVITY OUTCOMES

Reducing environmental demands to improve P-E fit can be accomplished through a variety of home modification strategies (i.e., prosthetic facilitators), including assistive technologies and accessible design features (i.e., specialized equipment and environmental features intended to support people with specific disabilities) and universally designed products and spaces (i.e., environmental features intended to support people regardless of ability), that meet the activity and health needs of individuals and their care providers. Furthermore, the process of environmental intervention is a confluence of activities and delivery of services that begins with assessing needs and includes identification and implementation of solutions, training in the use of solutions, and evaluating outcomes (Sanford, 2004). Of particular relevance here are the following: (1) assessing the demands and needs for eliminating barriers, (2) prosthetic interventions that meet the functional needs of both individual and caregiver, (3) delivery and reimbursement systems to supply and fund best-fit interventions, and (4) choice and impacts of best-fit interventions that must ultimately meet the real-world needs of the situation.

Assessment: Determining Fit, Demands, and Modification Needs

Research suggests that residents' perceptions of their own abilities and environments differ from those of experts and significantly underreport the presence of environmental barriers (Steinfeld and Shea, 1993; Iwarsson and Isacsson, 1996). As a result, a systematic process, performed by skilled specialists, is needed to acquire information about the fit between a person's abilities, activities performed, and environmental attributes; analyze the information; and use clinical reasoning to translate the information into appropriate interventions that will best fit the situation (Steinfeld and Shea, 1993; Pynoos et al., 1997; Anemaet and Moffa-Trotter, 1999; Gitlin and Corcoran, 2000; Niva and Skar, 2006).

To be effective, assessments must produce unbiased, objective information that is both valid and reliable. Yet assessments are conducted by an array of home health service providers—occupational therapists, rehabilitation engineers and technologists, home health nurses, and social workers—and, to a lesser extent, building professionals—remodelers, architects, and interior designers. In addition, some assessments are based on expected abilities and activity performance, and others assess actual activity performance (Sanford and Bruce, 2010). Although both are common and have their benefits, the results of each are subject to different levels of bias, validity, and reliability that can impact the fit between therapeutic interventions and the individual as well as the home environment. Of equal importance, few assessments have proven psychometric properties. In fact, in a review article, Wahl and colleagues (2009) questioned the validity and reliability of assessment procedures of more than half the studies they examined.

Expected Performance: Predicting Needs from Attributes

Assessments that measure a specified set of environmental attributes based on expected rather than actual measures of ability and activity performance result in a prediction of potential, rather than actual, environmental demands. As a result, interventions based on such information are determined irrespective of the actual abilities of the individuals for whom the interventions are intended. This type of assessment is illustrated by a number of instruments, such as the Housing Enabler (Iwarsson, 1999) and the Cougar Home Safety Assessment (Fisher, Coolbaugh, and Rhodes, 2006; Fisher et al., 2008). Both instruments assess the severity of environmental barriers in the absence of an assessment of a client's actual ability or performance. For example, the Housing Enabler, one of the few tools with known psychometric properties, uses a set of typical impairments and functional limitations as a surrogate for individual disability/incapacity. Various environmental attributes are then systematically rated in relation to their expected impact on performance.

Clearly, the measurement of potential demands is helpful when there is no single client whose abilities can be determined (such as for the accessibility of public buildings) or when actual performance of specific activities cannot be determined, such as assessing the home environment for a patient prior to his or her discharge from a clinic. However, measuring potential demands has its limitations. Going back to the discussion of the ICF, contextual factors (including environmental demands and personal factors) account for the difference between an individual's hypothetical capacity to function (i.e., what people can do) and actual performance (i.e., what they actually do) or enacted function (Glass, 1998). If actual ability and activity performance are not assessed, how can one be sure that performance based on expectations of what individuals can do accurately reflects what they actually do and, consequently, the effectiveness of the environmental modifications for a particular client?

Actual Performance: Assessing Needs from Activity

Requiring individuals to demonstrate how they perform routine activities would provide an accurate sense of how the individual interacts with the environment (Pynoos et al., 1997). Thus, when performance outcomes can be determined, as is the case when an individual is living at home, then measurement of actual demands will provide a more accurate picture of environmental demands than will prediction of demand potential. The Canadian Occupational Performance Measure (COPM) (Law et al., 1991) and the Safety Assessment of Function and the Environment for Rehabilitation-Health Outcome Measurement and Evaluation (SAFER-HOME v. 3) (Letts et al., 1998) are two performance-based instruments that can identify actual home modification needs as well as changes in performance after modification interventions. However, these instruments are purely performance-based; they do not assess either environmental attributes or ability. Without a measure of ability, one cannot determine if there is a difference between what an individual can do and what an individual actually does. Moreover, without a measure of environmental attributes, it is not possible to determine what specific changes should actually be made.

Linking the Three A's: Ability, Activity, and Attributes

While assessments of expected demand link environmental attributes to expected levels of ability and activity performance, few assessments examine all three: (1) ability, (2) activity, and (3) attributes. Without all three, it is not possible to determine best-fit interventions for a particular individual. The Comprehensive Assessment and Solutions Process for Aging Residents (CASPAR) is one of the few instruments that measure all three factors (Sanford et al., 2001; Sanford, 2002; Sanford and Butterfield, 2005). It includes a measure of ability under standardized conditions (e.g., turn on a light switch, open a drawer, and turn a doorknob); activity-related problems (e.g., going up steps and stepping over the side of a tub); and detailed measures of activity-relevant environmental attributes, such as the number of steps and the height of the tub. However, CASPAR, like other home assessments, requires a specialist onsite to collect the required information.

Remote Assessment: Overcoming Limitations of Time and Distance

To overcome travel time and distance that increase costs and limit the ability of experts to access clients' homes, a number of studies have demonstrated that real-time, interactive videoconferencing can be used by specialists to successfully identify needs and provide sufficient information to recommend interventions (Sanford et al., 2004, 2007; Sanford and Butterfield, 2005; Hoenig, Sanford, and Griffiths, 2006), thus potentially eliminating the need for a specialist to travel long distances to perform an assessment. These studies suggest that relatively inexpensive videoconferencing technology (e.g., as little as $1,200 for two videophones and a video camera) that uses the telephone system enables specialists to conduct remote assessment in a manner similar to in-home assessments, thus maintaining the integrity of the therapist-patient interaction, and provides a practical alternative to traditional home visits by a therapist for improving task self-efficacy. Nonetheless, to date, teleconferencing technology has been limited to research studies and has not been translated into practice in any ongoing home assessment programs.

Home Modifications: From Needs to Prosthetic Interventions

Providing a facilitating environment in the home is different from providing an accessible environment in community settings. In public places, the Americans with Disabilities Act accessibility guidelines (U.S. Access Board, 2002) are intended to ensure at least basic levels of usability and access for people with acknowledged disabilities. These guidelines apply neither to private residences nor to individuals who have functional losses that do not "qualify" as a disability. Therefore, whether these interventions are assistive technologies, accessible designs, or universal designs, they should be individualized, customized, and personalized to best fit the functional needs of individuals for independent living and their caregivers for providing assistance.

Improving Independent Activity: Prosthetic Modifications for Mobility and Self-Care

Although problems can and do occur throughout the home, research and experience suggest that environmental barriers to the safety and health of individuals in the home are linked to three primary activities: (1) getting into and out of the house, (2) moving around the house, and (3) performing self-care (toileting, bathing, and grooming). Clearly, mobility and transfer tasks are integral to each of these activities. Not surprisingly, therefore, the majority of home environmental interventions have traditionally focused on modifying entrances, circulation paths and stairs, and the bathroom to facilitate mobility and transfer tasks.

Movement into and Out of the Home. Many houses are built above ground level and have a set of steps leading up to a porch, deck, or landing at the door. Not only are stairs a barrier to wheelchair users, they also can become a safety hazard and an obstacle to independence for individuals with gait and balance problems and those who use walking aids. In addition, walkways and stairs frequently are in poor condition and lack handrails for support and adequate lighting at night. To increase safety and mobility, walkways should have smooth, slip-resistant surfaces; steps should be in good repair, with handrails on both sides and with contrasting nosings (the rounded edges of stair treads), or should be replaced with a ramp, sloping walkway, or mechanical lift. In addition, the threshold should be reduced to minimize tripping, doorways should be widened, sufficient space should be provided to maneuver, and an automatic opening system should be installed to eliminate twisting and turning of doorknobs. There should also be adequate lighting operated by motion detectors or timers at all walkways and doors to help maintain independence and ensure the safety of individuals with mobility issues as well as those with vision loss.

Mobility in the Home. Inside the home, people who use mobility aids, such as wheelchairs, frequently lose access to rooms, particularly bathrooms, because hallways or doors are too narrow, furniture obstructs the path of travel, or stairs prevent travel to other floors in the home. Stairs, slippery floors, and obstacles are also potential safety hazards. Stairs, in particular, account for a greater number of falls than any other single location in the home (Kochera, 2002). And the number of multistory homes being constructed has increased precipitously since 1970 (U.S. Bureau of the Census, 1994). For individuals with mobility issues, typical modification strategies to ensure activity, increase safety, and improve health are similar to those for outdoor environments, although stair lifts are commonly used instead of ramps between levels of a home. In addition, for people with vision loss, it is important to control glare by using sheer curtains or translucent shades (as opposed to metal miniblinds that reflect light) to buffer bright sunlight and reduce dark-light transitions between rooms.

Transfer Safety and Self-Care Activities. The bathroom, with its wet, slippery surfaces, small, cramped spaces, and hard surfaces can easily lead to falls and serious injury, even for people without functional limitations.

Bathroom floors are extremely dangerous when wet. For many individuals who have difficulty raising and lowering themselves, including those who use wheeled or ambulatory mobility aids, health, safety, and fall risks are associated with difficulty transferring to the toilet, bathtub, or shower. While individuals who use wheelchairs often lack space to maneuver or get close enough to a fixture, ambulatory individuals with gait and balance problems often lack support (i.e., something to hold onto) to safely lower themselves down onto a toilet or the bottom of a tub or, conversely, to pull themselves back up from these positions. To increase safety and mobility, sufficient space should be available at the toilet, bathtub, shower, and sink for mobility aids and caregiver assistance. In addition, safety can be enhanced by reducing the distance an individual must raise and lower himself or herself (e.g., raising the height of the toilet) or the need to lift one's legs over the side of the tub (e.g., walk-in tub) or the shower curb (e.g., a curbless shower). In addition, safety can be increased and transfers facilitated by adding supports (such as grab bars, safety frame, or floor-to-ceiling pole) or using a fixture with integral supports and increasing the visibility (e.g., contrasting color of the toilet or toilet seat from walls) of all fixtures.

Improving Caregiver Assistance: Prosthetic Devices for Mobility and Transfer

Although mobility and transfer tasks are the most strenuous and difficult activities for caregivers, they are also the most frequent tasks with which both formal and informal caregivers provide assistance (Gershon et al., 2008). Given the strenuous nature of these tasks and the clutter, lack of space, and other safety risks in the home (Gershon et al., 2008), it is not surprising that caregivers experience considerable difficulty and have an increased incidence of injury compared with other health care and human services workers (Myers et al., 1993; Ono et al., 1995; Galinsky, Waters, and Malit, 2001).

To reduce injury and facilitate caregiver assistance, a number of products and devices have been developed to make moving around the home and transferring easier, safer, more efficient, and more dignified, both for the care recipient and the caregiver (see Chapter 8). These include lift systems for moving individuals through the home as well as products that assist with, or eliminate the need for, transfers in bathing and toileting. Regardless of purpose, however, the effectiveness of devices is impacted by and has unique implications for the design of the home environment.

Service Delivery: From Intervention to Implementation

Implementation is somewhat more complex than merely finding someone to install or supply the necessary modifications. Like assessors, there are many providers, who come from different programs and disciplinary backgrounds that can impact what they are able to provide and how they provide it. In addition, the costs of some modifications are reimbursable, while others are not. As a result, providers and payers typically impact decisions about what modifications are actually made. These decisions, in turn, affect not only the effectiveness of modifications in meeting functional needs, but also their impact on the home environment.

Who Provides Home Modifications?

In the United States there is no single model for home modification service delivery. Rather, there is a fragmented system of social service, health service, and construction providers that varies not only by state, municipality, and organization but also by the client's point of entry. Similarly, there is no single profession that provides home modification services; although there are some certification programs, none is recognized beyond its own professional organization.

Home Modification Programs. Many rehabilitation providers include a home modification program as part of the rehabilitation service. However, while individuals who suffer from trauma or chronic illness are placed into the rehabilitation system, others, such as seniors with declining abilities, are typically on their own to find out how and where to enter a complex system of services that could be provided by any number of programs. These include the local area agency on aging (AAA), natural occurring retirement community (NORC) initiative, or center for independent living (CIL); municipal agencies, such as a mayor's office for people with disabilities (MOPD) and department of housing; and state assistive technology programs, departments of veterans affairs, and volunteer organizations like Rebuilding Together. Even more daunting is that the same type of organization may offer different types of services in different locales. For example, in Philadelphia, the local AAA, the Philadelphia Corporation for Aging, provides an extensive in-home modification and repair service from assessment to implementation. In Atlanta, the Georgia NORC initiative provides assessment by an occupational therapist and links homeowners with local nonprofits to provide the modifications. In Chicago, the MOPD offers a complete range of home modification services for people with disabilities up to age 59, and the Department of Housing provides services for people ages 60 and older.

Home Modification Professionals. Like assessments and service programs, home modifications are delivered by a variety of professions. As discussed above, assessments are undertaken primarily by health and other providers of social services and, to a lesser extent, by professionals in the construction industry. However, the scope of modifications differs along professional boundaries. Health professionals typically limit their scope of services to small-scale, off-the-shelf assistive technologies and adaptive products, as well as environmental strategies, such as moving furniture, adding task lighting, and changing the location of activities. In contrast, building professionals focus primarily on changes to the physical environment, ranging from installing grab bars to moving fixtures to adding lifts to full-scale remodeling. However, they may also supply assistive devices and equipment.

A variety of certifications are associated with home modifications, although none is legally binding or affiliated with any professional licensure. For example, the National Association of Home Builders (NAHB) offers a Certified Aging in Place Specialist (CAPS), the American Occupational Therapy Association (AOTA) offers a Specialty Certification in Environmental Modifications, and the Rehabilitation Engineering Society of North America (RESNA) offers an assistive technology practitioner (ATP) certification. While the latter does not specifically focus on home modifications, it is the only certification that is eligible for reimbursement as a clinical service, although occupational therapists can be reimbursed for some home assessments under occupational therapy licensure. In addition, several universities, including the University of Southern California and Georgia Institute of Technology, offer certificates for online programs.

It is important to recognize that there are no national standards for provision of home modification services. Anyone can provide the service, regardless of certification or licensure, although the scope of services that an individual can provide may be restricted by their professional licensure. For example, occupational therapists can perform home assessments, modify products (i.e., use duct tape and Velcro), and provide off-the-shelf products in states in which they are licensed, but they are not permitted to engage in home remodeling as occupational therapists. In contrast, home remodelers are not restricted from providing any of those services, including assessments, regardless of whether they are CAPS certified or not. As a case in point, I am not a licensed therapist, contractor, or architect, yet I not only provide all of these services but also have trained professionals in all three disciplines to do so as well.

Who Pays for Home Modifications?

The majority of home modifications are paid for out of pocket by the homeowner. In fact, less than one-fourth of home modifications are paid for by third-party payers (LaPlante, Hendershot, and Moss, 1992). Of course, most individuals pay for a typical home remodeling, so why shouldn't they pay for home modifications? After all, one could argue that aging or disability is a life event that requires changing one's home just the same as other life changes, such as having children. No one would expect a private or public third-party payer to help modify one's home, such as by adding a nursery, to accommodate such a lifestyle change.

Still, modifications for healthy, independent living in the community should be a public health concern for which funding is made available. Such is the case in many countries where home modifications are considered medical interventions. As part of the Swedish public health program, for example, each municipality provides needed services to individuals with functional limitations, including the modifications necessary (regardless of cost and income level) to continue living in their own homes for as long as possible.

In the United States there is a patchwork of potential funders, ranging from government agencies, to private insurers and workers compensation to social service organizations, such as AAAs and NORCs, to nonprofit volunteer organizations, such as Rebuilding Together. State agencies often have their own programs using tax or bond revenues, often through a housing finance agency. Municipalities often offer tax credits, particularly to developers who build accessible homes. In the federal government, there are at least seven departments that have programs in which funds can be used for home modifications, including Agriculture, Energy, Education, Health and Human Services (HHS), Housing and Urban Development (HUD), Treasury, and Veterans Affairs. Some programs are loans directly to households (e.g., the HOME program of HUD), others are loan guarantees to lenders, and still others are grants, usually to social service organizations. However, regardless of the program, eligibility for services depends on one's situation, unlike Sweden. Some of programs have age restrictions or dollar limits. For example, social services block grants from HHS and home and community care block grants from the Administration on Aging (AOA) are available to social service organizations, but recipients must meet age and income criteria. In addition, many home modification programs in the United States have capped costs from $5,000 to $10,000, which will generally cover only a ramp and some bathroom modifications.

Securing a traditional loan is always an option. For seniors, reverse mortgages, which are based on home equity, are also available, although up-front costs are fairly steep, sometimes amounting to almost 25 percent of the loan. With the fragmentation and restrictions, it is not surprising that in 2000, only half of the 2.1 million older U.S. households that needed home modifications to facilitate aging in place had them (Joint Center for Housing Studies, 2000).

Best-Fit Solutions: From Prosthetic to Practical Interventions

Whereas prosthetic interventions may best fit an individual's or caregiver's functional needs, as the previous discussion suggests, overall best fit is not based simply on functional ability. In addition to provider and payer issues, a large number of other confounding contextual factors impact decisions. These include personal tastes and preferences of a particular individual and others living in the home, social constraints of the living situation, structural limitations of the home, and building and zoning codes. These factors have nothing to do with improving activity outcomes, but they mediate and influence decisions about which interventions should be implemented. While the number of potential mediators is large, cost is by far the most common and most influential. In the end, home modifications that are the best fit for the situation may or may not be an "ideal" fit with the functional abilities of the client or caregiver or with the home environment. For example, assistive devices, such as lifts, tub benches, and toilet seats, are typically more intrusive than structural changes to the home that might provide more space and better performance. Nonetheless, because these devices are less expensive, more often reimbursable, more familiar to health care providers, and more readily obtained, they are much more likely to be installed. Not coincidentally, they also have a much larger impact on the use of space in the home environment.

THERAPEUTIC INTERVENTIONS: TECHNOLOGIES TO IMPROVE HEALTH MANAGEMENT AND TREATMENT

The number of people with chronic conditions is growing rapidly. In fact, 45 percent of the community-dwelling U.S. population have at least one chronic medical condition, and about half of these, 60 million people, have multiple chronic conditions (Wu and Green, 2000). Approximately 83 percent of Medicare beneficiaries have one or more chronic conditions, and 23 percent have five or more chronic conditions (Anderson, 2005). By 2015, an estimated 150 million people in the United States will have at least one chronic condition (Wu and Green, 2000). With the variety of chronic health conditions comes a dramatic increase in the level of care requirements, higher costs (e.g., chronic diseases account for 75 percent of all U.S. health care costs), and the need to integrate multiple physicians, specialists, and formal and informal caregivers (Scheschareg, 2006).

Technology has long been an integral part of health care delivery, primarily in clinical settings to permit diagnosis, intervening treatment, and care of acute or chronic health conditions. New technologies enable active self-management and passive monitoring of safety and activity. Home-based technologies are changing the way health care is provided by "freeing" patients from health care institutions (Sinding, 2003), as well as how the home environment is utilized and conceptualized.

Active Technologies for Self-Management

A variety of standalone and integrated devices are available that enable patients to actively manage their own health and reduce acute episodes. Treatment technologies commonly found in the home are often large pieces of equipment that are used to provide a variety of therapies and to assist bodily functions, including assistance in breathing, medicine delivery, body function, and suction (see Chapter 8).

In contrast to treatment technologies, preventive technologies tend to be smaller portable or mounted electronic monitoring devices that allow individuals or family members to measure and obtain feedback about specific health conditions or physiological status or to facilitate communication with friends, family, and care providers. In addition, several different types of integrated monitoring devices exist. These devices are used by the patient to collect information from multiple peripheral devices (e.g., blood pressure cuff, scale, pulse oximeter) and transmit it to caregivers and care providers. Other systems combine patient monitoring and video that enables patients and providers to interact in real time.

Communication technology to foster social connectedness and prevent deterioration in psychological health, particularly among individuals who have transportation difficulties, is an important, although sometimes overlooked, component of the home-based care system (see Chapter 9). Like home modifications and assistive technologies, medical devices and technologies for self-management can have a large impact on the home environment and on the individuals living there. Large pieces of equipment have obvious space requirements, but smaller items, such as a pulse oximeter or a blood pressure cuff, need to be stored somewhere, as do medical supplies. Disposal of medical supplies, particularly used needles, and a backup generator in case of a power outage are also major considerations. In general, smaller monitoring and communications technologies have little impact on the structure of the home. However, they require space for both the communications hardware as well as any biometric tools (e.g., glucose meters, blood pressure cuff, digital scale) that are needed. Clearly, the larger the number of different systems and biometric tools that are introduced into the home, the more space is required.

Passive Technologies That Monitor Safety and Activity

In contrast to active technologies, there are passive home-based systems that do not depend on active engagement of individuals in the home. These technologies use networks of sensors, transmitters, and receivers embedded in the home environment to (1) monitor activity and location, (2) identify and reduce potential safety hazards, and (3) communicate physiological status to health care providers.

Despite the unobtrusive nature of embedded passive monitoring systems, the installation and potentially the appearance of these technologies will clearly be somewhat intrusive in the home environment. However, simply getting this technology into homes is only part of the problem. Like other technologies, there will be issues with the design of sensor networks that fit unobtrusively in the home environment (e.g., visibility of packaging and antennas), are easy to install and maintain, and are integrated with each other and with other home technology systems.

NEW CONCEPTS IN HOUSING: INTEGRATING PROSTHETIC AND THERAPEUTIC INTERVENTIONS IN A HOME ENVIRONMENT

The large number of home modifications and assistive technologies and medical equipment and health care technologies, combined with the variety of typical personal technologies, such as wheelchairs and walkers, evokes a picture of a home environment cluttered with devices that take up large amounts of space, can potentially get in the way of each other and others in the home, and can themselves become hazards. When these conditions are introduced into homes of older adults or individuals with other chronic conditions, they frequently exacerbate conditions in which many health and safety hazards already exist, including lack of space, clutter, poor lighting, and loose rugs (Gershon et al., 2008).

Unsafe conditions put both home care patients and home health care workers at risk. Among care providers, these conditions contribute to awkward postures lifting and shifting patients that are linked to increased incidence of musculoskeletal injury (Myers et al., 1993; Ono et al., 1995; Galinsky, Waters, and Malit, 2001). Among care recipients, these conditions can increase the risk of falls and other injuries, although the latter issues have not been assessed (Gershon et al., 2008).

To further complicate provision of home health, studies have identified a number of additional concerns about the safety of home environments that can negatively impact care providers and thus the provision of care. These include the location of housing in unsafe neighborhoods, overheated room temperatures, poor indoor air quality, and unsanitary conditions, such as the presence of insects and rodents, mismanagement of medical waste, and lack of standard disinfection practices (Kendra et al., 1996; Fazzone et al., 2000; Manangan et al., 2002; Markkanen et al., 2007; Gerson et al., 2008).

Clearly, maintaining independence and transplanting medical care to the home in the 21st century will have impacts on the physical environment that go well beyond ramps and grab bars. Space is limited, and there are ever-increasing technologies and devices vying for it. Nonetheless, housing is not being designed, and often is not being remodeled, with these needs in mind. In addition, individuals with functional limitations on dexterity, vision, hearing, or cognition may have difficulty manipulating, seeing, hearing, or understanding technology interfaces. To ensure that these technologies can be used by consumers, particularly older adults who make up the majority of home health recipients and who are less familiar with technology, the design of these devices will need to be based on more user-centric principles.

The challenge, however, is to design and incorporate modifications, health care products, technologies, and devices into the home environment without violating two basic principles. First, while space might be the great equalizer, the builder's prime directive is that the home cannot increase in size (i.e., cost). Second, the consumer's prime directive is that products, technologies, and modifications that go into the home must be residential in scale and appearance (i.e., look like they belong). Adherence to these principles will require new approaches to product and housing design that integrate technological systems with each other and in the home environment so that the home remains a home and does not become a hospital.

Woodward and colleagues (2004) argued that home care is dependent on three types of knowledge and skills: (1) those that are appropriate to the client, (2) the care required, and (3) the home. All three have implications for the design of the physical environment, from the standpoint of the design of the home as well as the technologies themselves. As a result, the success of home health care will depend on fundamental changes in the way both homes and technologies are conceived and designed.

To achieve these aims, housing and technology must be appealing to consumers as well as supportive of people with a wide range of functional abilities and health conditions, their caregivers, families, and health care providers. To do this, housing and technology must first work together as a seamless, integrated system. Second, housing should be universally designed, as should the products and technologies themselves. While such solutions are yet to be fully embraced by today's housing market, innovations that embrace smart home technologies and universal design principles offer promise for the future.

Smart Homes

Whereas smart home technologies enable compatible products (e.g., appliances and devices that act as receivers and remote controls or keypads that are transmitters) to talk to each other over a network, the technologies are being developed independently of each other. As a result, there are complex and redundant networks of sensors and hardware that connect care recipients with caregivers and care providers both inside and outside the home. The major difference between a smart home and a smart technology that resides in the home is the integration of systems in the smart home into a controlled network that connects systems and appliances to each other and to the outside world. Not only will such system integration bring together all of the health related information, it will also enable remote care providers to be informed when problems occur, regardless of the nature of the problem.

In the late 1990s and early 2000s, a large number of model smart homes were constructed on many university campuses (e.g., Drexel University, Georgia Institute of Technology, Iowa State University, Massachusetts Institute of Technology, University of Florida) as demonstration homes and laboratories to develop and test new technologies. These homes were designed to monitor daily activities, particularly of older adults, to enable them to have a greater degree of independence and remain at home longer. While many of the technologies had isolated functions, some were integrated systems that worked as a smart home. For example, at Iowa State University, everyday kitchen appliances, including the microwave and the refrigerator, were equipped with sensors. Each appliance had its own capability—the microwave scanned bar codes to calculate cooking times, and the refrigerator calculated the weights of food items to determine when items were running low—and they were also connected to the main computer system that sent a shopping list to the resident's cell phone, which is also integral to the smart home.

As the first decade of the 21st century nears an end, the focus of smart homes is expanding from monitoring activity-based technologies to facilitate aging in place to include home health technologies for a range of care recipients. For example, Matsushita has been developing a variety of health-enabled bathroom products, such as a toilet seat with embedded passive monitoring sensors to monitor and send weight and body fat ratio, heartbeat, blood pressure, and glucose levels to the patient's doctor via the Internet (Brooke, 2009).

Universal Homes

Unlike accessible design, which is an add-on component to support specific types and levels of ability, universal design (UD) is everyday design that supports all types and levels of ability. As a result, the seven principles of universal design (see Table 8-2) define a basic level of usability for everyone.

In contrast to accessible design, which is prescriptive (e.g., a threshold may be no greater than 1/4 inch to allow wheelchair access), UD is performance-based; it describes how and why a design can minimize demands on all users (e.g., a level entrance will enable everyone to safely enter) rather than what the design specification should be. As a result, UD is compatible with the ICF, which suggests that disability is not a single point requiring specialized intervention, but a continuum of ability that would benefit from less demanding design. In so doing, UD, unlike accessible design, makes access the norm, rather than the exception.

An underlying principle in making access and usability the norm is that a home should look like a home, not like an institutional setting. It is therefore important to remember that any products and technologies that are brought into home, regardless of their purpose, should be residential in appearance and tailored to meet the personal needs and tastes of the users. If they are not, users simply will not accept them.

The same rationale applies to traditional medical devices, new assistive products for caregivers, and any new telehealth technologies. These products need to be usable by both health care recipients and providers, and they need to fit into the home environment. Moreover, any home-based technologies will require common interface designs so that users do not need to learn and manage different systems. The technology products need to be easy to use and to learn, and they should take into account declining skills of older adults, such as vision, dexterity, and memory.

While it is unlikely that every design will be usable by everyone, UD can eliminate the need for many adaptive, add-on, specialized accessibility products that are commonly used today. Many home modifications would be unnecessary if homes had originally been designed to better meet people's needs. For example, bathrooms in most homes are inaccessible to people with physical limitations and disabilities because the doors are too narrow, the floor space is too limited, the layout of fixtures is ill conceived, the fixtures themselves are often poorly designed, and there are no supporting features. Better initial design would greatly improve usability for everyone and reduce the need for modifications later on. Ultimately, the universal home sets a baseline from which assistive technologies and accessible design can be introduced when and if they are needed.

A Smart Universal Home: Eskaton's National Demonstration Home

Eskaton is a nonprofit organization headquartered in Carmichael, California, that provides a full spectrum of residential living, health care, and services for more than 14,000 older adults throughout northern

California. The National Demonstration Home, completed in 2008 on the Eskaton Village campus in Roseville, California, provides an innovative approach to healthy, independent living by combining UD, smart home health care technologies, and green living features.

The home combines universal design features, such as wider hallways, stepless entry, curbless showers, and motion sensor lights that minimize hazards, enhance safety, and promote independent activity with a number of technological systems (e.g., monitoring of ADLs, smart appliances, two-way video communication) seamlessly integrated into the design. As a result, technology complements, integrates, and reinforces the physical elements of UD to promote health and wellness, social and health provider connectivity, and safety.

BARRIERS TO ADOPTION OF HOUSING INNOVATION

Even as the home has become a centerpiece of health care in the United States, the lack of supportive housing to promote activity, health, and health care needs is exacerbated by the striking disconnect between these needs and the U.S. health care system (Commission on Affordable Housing and Health Facility Needs for Seniors in the 21st Century, 2002). It comes as little surprise, therefore, that most prosthetic and therapeutic home interventions continue to be designed as medical devices and that UD and smart homes have not yet been adopted on a broad basis.

While the barriers to residentially focused environmental interventions are numerous and varied, they can be traced back to the origins of federally funded health and housing subsidies, which were designed to operate as separate systems, each achieving separate public goods. As a result, the systems through which these services are delivered, as well as the regulations, performance measurements, and implementation guidelines of the two systems, can often conflict and impede coordination. Not surprisingly therefore, there is a general lack of a coordinated and comprehensive system of services that would permit expanded health care and housing options, promote self-sufficiency and independence, and offset social isolation (Lawler, 2001). In its stead, there is a fragmented system of services provided by various public and private health care and social service organizations (Pynoos et al., 1997; Lau et al., 2007) that are hampered by a lack of information, experience, funding, and resources. Similarly, consumers are often uninformed or harbor misperceptions about environmental innovations. Together, these factors have resulted in both a poor supply of and limited demand for environmental innovations. Finally, to compound the problem, the home environment itself is often the source of impediment, inadequately designed or poorly maintained and unable to support the environmental innovations due to disrepair, inadequate systems, and lack of space.

Supply Side Barriers

On the supply side, service providers are typically constrained by resources, the scope and geographical area of support services, their general lack of knowledge of UD and home modifications in general, and a dearth of educational opportunities to learn more about them. As a result there are too few professionals with expertise in environmental interventions to provide services as well as too few of those professionals who have formal training in the area and have a good understanding of universal design. Policy disincentives for UD and a maze of funding resources are also major barriers to acquiring appropriate interventions.

Lack of Providers with Expertise in Environmental Interventions

There is a lack of specialists who can assess both functional abilities and the relevant environmental characteristics (Pynoos, 1993; Pynoos et al., 1996). No single discipline or systematic program provides training that encompasses a comprehensive understanding of the person and the environment sides of the equation, resulting in disciplinary bias that separates the health professions from the building professions (Pynoos et al., 1987). Although some disciplines, such as occupational therapy and architecture, include college-level courses on environmental interventions, these are typically isolated efforts of individual faculty members, not promoted by the program or the profession. Only recently have professional organizations created certification programs, although none is sufficiently comprehensive to ensure a broad knowledge of home environmental interventions.

Provider Biases

Even among specialists, intervention decisions often vary by discipline and level of expertise of the individual delivering services. Each profession tends to have its own disciplinary perspective that influences its understanding of needs and intervention solutions. By virtue of their training and driven by reimbursement systems, health care professionals are understandably more familiar and concerned with impairment and activity performance of the client than with environmental factors, residential construction, or even the range of potential environmental modifications (Pynoos, 1992; Pynoos et al., 1997). As a result, these individuals often underestimate the importance of the physical environment and may not recommend environmental interventions. Yet construction professionals know less about activity and ability than about environmental attributes. As a result, assessments undertaken by construction professionals may overestimate the need for environmental interventions. Similarly, agencies that pay for modifications often introduce system bias by requiring assessments that adhere to their guidelines and result in recommending only interventions that will be reimbursed.

Provider Misperceptions of Universal Design

Despite the widespread acknowledgment and acceptance of the UD principles across many professions and among many manufacturers, application of the principles to the design of housing, as well as to consumer products and technologies, has been slow to take place. Many professionals rely on what they already know rather than try something new (Belser and Weber, 1995). Since many are familiar with accessible design, they often misuse the term "universal design" as a synonym for the former. In addition, misperceptions about the additional cost of UD are manifest in a reluctance to use it as a design strategy. However, if introduced at the beginning of a project, additional costs might be negligible. For example, the cost of a wider doorway is offset by the diminished costs of the wall around it.

Policy Disincentives for Universal Design

UD can have economic advantages for both consumers and providers, particularly if it is part of housing and product design from the beginning. In such cases, everyday housing and products can be used to support health and activity needs without the need for expensive modifications. However, because the reimbursement system is client-centric, it is concerned with meeting the needs of individual clients. In fact, it provides economic disincentives for UD by supporting specialized assistive technology and (to some extent) accessible design solutions, which may have lower initial costs, but greater long-term costs and far less benefit to multiple individuals or society.

Demand Side Barriers

On the demand side, the fragmented delivery system also ensures that consumers are uninformed about the benefits and costs of UD and other environmental modifications. Even making small changes can pose large problems for individuals who are unfamiliar with UD and home modifications and have misperceptions of what they are and what benefits they offer. As a result, studies indicate that the majority of people fail to plan for future needs in their home environment (Filion, Wister, and Coblentz,

1992), and also that people in need often adapt to their current environment, rather than change their home to meet their needs, particularly when the alterations are related to aging or disability (Filion, Wister, and Coblentz, 1992; Gilderbloom and Markham, 1996; Pynoos et al., 1997). This reluctance may explain, in part, why older individuals with disabilities are no less likely to be exposed to environmental hazards in their homes than those without disabilities (Gill et al., 1999). Despite a reluctance to make changes, the strongest predictor of adapting one's home is recognizing the need for environmental interventions (Pynoos et al., 1987). In fact, one study found that when people perceived that environmental interventions would improve performance, they were four times more likely to modify their homes (Gosselin et al., 1992).

Lack of Consumer Awareness of Environmental Interventions

A major reason for the large numbers of individuals with unmet needs for environmental interventions is the lack of awareness of either the interventions themselves or their benefits for activity performance (Pynoos, 1993). Moreover, because UD and other environmental intervention strategies are the exceptions to home design rather than the norm, there are few traditional marketing strategies (e.g., TV advertisements) to inform consumers about their benefits. Even advertisements that feature modifications are often promoting the contractors who specialize in modifications, rather than the modifications themselves, and few include UD features. As a result, consumers may only be familiar with ADA accessibility features that they have seen in public settings or "handicapped" features (e.g., ramps and stainless steel grab bars) in their friends' homes.

One mechanism for creating awareness of the advantages of UD is to try out alternatives to see what works best. This is common practice with most consumer items, as well as in the assessment of individuals with disabilities for modifications needed for the workplace. However, it is not a practice that is used in assessing needs for therapeutic home interventions. Although this is primarily because many home modifications either need to be installed (e.g., grab bars) or are too big to transport (e.g., chair lift), many smaller items, such as tub benches or thermostats, could be included in an assessment. Another option for consumer education is the use of demonstration homes (such as Eskaton), in which people can actually try out different design features (e.g., Mills, Holm, and Christenson, 2001). However, demonstration homes provide only one example of each UD feature, thus restricting comparison across alternatives; they are geographically restricted, which limits their exposure to a broad audience; and, unlike Eskaton, most have been built by local builders and ultimately sold to private individuals, limiting their availability as demonstration homes on a long-term basis.

Consumer Misperceptions of Environmental Modifications

Consumers often associate prosthetic and therapeutic interventions with the stigma of disability and institutional care (Pynoos et al., 1997; Wolford, 2000), which are not perceived to be compatible with the residential appearance and are seen to reduce the market value of their homes (Gilderbloom and Markham, 1996). While these perceptions have a firm basis in the many assistive and health care technologies and accessible design solutions that have an institutional or medical appearance, there are many newer UD products that have been designed specifically for homes.

Consumers also may believe that the costs of environmental modifications are prohibitive, even when they know the benefits. For example, one study (Sohn, 1997) found that older consumers' perceptions of the usefulness and attractiveness of UD features increased after trying them out, although they still believed that the products were too expensive.

Hard-to-Find Funding

The separation of housing and health care in different governmental agencies has created various systems of public subsidies that make it difficult for individuals to find or receive adequate funding. Housing dollars are distributed as a limited subsidy by HUD, which sets income restrictions on who qualifies for housing assistance. In contrast, health dollars are distributed as an entitlement by Medicare at the federal level and by Medicaid at the state level (Lawler, 2001). As a result, funding can come from a number of sources that are hard to categorize and locate. Difficulty finding funds is compounded by eligibility restrictions (e.g., income, age, location, and health status). There is especially limited funding to provide assistance to low-income households, which have a disproportionately high level of need for modifications.

Housing Barriers

The design or the physical condition of the home itself can be a barrier to environmental innovation. Data from the American Housing Survey 1997 suggest that this may well be the case for older adults with functional limitations. Survey data further suggest that homes built after 1980 and multifamily structures are significantly more likely to meet some of the prosthetic needs of older adults than units built in any earlier time period (Louie, 1999). In fact, the data are quite remarkable. For example, elderly households in need of access to the home are about twice as likely to have a ramp (80 versus 41 percent) and a bathroom designed for easier accessibility (77 versus 37 percent) in units built after 1980 than such households in units built before 1940 (Louie, 1999).

In single-family housing, these findings may be attributed in part to changes in home design that occurred around 1980. These included construction of more one-story, slab-on-grade and one- to two-step ranch homes that are more conducive to ramps than older homes, which are often 36 inches or more above grade level; increased size of spaces, such as larger master bedrooms and baths and larger kitchens that facilitate easier wheelchair access; and changes in spatial layout, such as the master bedroom on the main floor and more open floor plans that provide opportunities for easier and safer mobility. In multifamily housing, these improved conditions may be due to governmental regulations for accessibility that went into effect in the 1980s and 1990s (e.g., the Fair Housing Act Amendments and the Americans with Disabilities Act) to prevent discrimination against people with disabilities in housing and public environments.

However, the vast majority of disabled elderly households do not live in newer housing or multifamily units. Instead, most live in older single-family homes built before 1940, of which slightly more than one-third need structural repairs (e.g., new roof) or updated systems (e.g., electric) compared with slightly less than one-quarter of housing units in general (Louie, 1999).

This need for repairs and systems updating is not surprising. Regular maintenance and upkeep of a home, particularly for individuals who are in poor health or have functional declines, may become unmanageable or unaffordable (Lawler, 2001). As a result, these individuals are more likely to shoulder a housing cost burden and live in units with moderately to severely inadequate overall structure and physical systems (Louie, 1999). Whereas structural inadequacy might divert funds for needed environmental interventions (e.g., widening doorways when the roof leaks), system inadequacy may render environmental interventions infeasible due to the costs of upgrading (e.g., adding a curbless shower when the plumbing needs to be replaced). Electrical systems that are outdated and do not meet current building codes are particularly problematic; most local codes require the entire system to be brought up to code when any electrical work is done. Thus, installing a lift could potentially result in having to bring in a new power line from the street, replace the panel box, and rewire the entire house.

POLICY CHANGES TO INCREASE ADOPTION OF HOUSING INNOVATION

On one hand, policy (at the reimbursement level) or lack of it (at the legislative level) bears considerable responsibility for spawning the current system of fragmented services. On the other hand, policy responses to support independent living and home health care, like the system itself, have been piecemeal and fragmented, leaving many people in homes that are unsupportive and in communities that offer them few housing options. This concern is particularly relevant in the current health policy context (Coyte and Young, 1997), in which high-tech home care is increasingly seen as a quick solution to budgetary constraints and a growing elderly population. Not only should public policy encourage health care payers to continue paying for existing equipment and assistive devices, it should also encourage accessible design modifications and, wherever possible, universal design modifications to facilitate safe activity performance and prevent accidents, promote wellness and health management, and ultimately forestall institutionalization. To accomplish this, reimbursement must overcome its "hands-off-the-home" policy, create incentives for universal design, incorporate access into local building codes, make environmental interventions a medical issue, and certify providers of prosthetic and therapeutic interventions.

Overcoming the Hands-off-the-Home Imperative

The greatest obstacle to the success of home-centered health care is ensuring that the government, private insurers, and the public wholly embrace environmental intervention as a necessary component of the health care system, regardless of the real or perceived value it adds to an individual's home. Unlike Sweden and other countries that include home environmental interventions as an option to support independent and healthy living, the U.S. reimbursement system does not. Medicare, for example, will pay for personal assistance, assistive devices, and medical technologies but not home modifications (i.e., accessible design). Medicaid may cover some home modifications, depending on the state. Thus, while willing to spend dollars on medical model interventions, such as caregiving and assistive devices, the system does not generally support the environmental interventions that are necessary to reduce the cost of caregiving and technology or even ensure that they are effective.

Clearly, the reluctance of both public and private agencies to invest in permanent changes that might enhance the value of a private residence is a major barrier to more supportive, universal homes. At the public level, paying for changes to private residences can give the appearance of spending taxpayer dollars on unnecessary remodeling that increases the comfort and wealth of individuals, even if homeowners themselves do not perceive that these changes will increase value. At the private level, third-party payers are reluctant to spend money on environmental interventions that may increase the value of property that they do not own and that could be sold at any time.

Incorporating Access into Local Building Codes

Building codes, which are intended to protect the health, safety, and welfare of the public, should include requirements for accessible or universal housing—but they do not. Even though the building codes use the same requirements as accessibility standards (i.e., ADA accessibility guidelines) for such features as handrails, stairs, and ramps, these requirements are based on safety, not access. There are several reasons for this exclusion of environmental interventions to support independent living and home health care.

First, promoting independence has generally fallen under the purview of civil rights legislation to provide access to public settings, not to improve public health in private housing. As a result, there are few accessibility-focused regulations that cover residential facilities and even fewer that comprehensively regulate the design and modification of private housing specifically for people who have functional or health limitations (Hyde, Talbert, and Grayson, 1997). Nonetheless, there is a growing movement in some countries to extend accessibility regulations to private housing. Moreover, in the absence of specific legislation, accessibility design standards for public buildings are often used as a guide when modifying private homes. In the United States there is a growing movement toward visitable housing, which, while still based on access rather than health, is a step toward broader regulation of private housing.

Second, and perhaps more influential, is that environmental modifications are not considered to be medical interventions under the old medical model. Yet the earliest example of a building law—the New York City Tenement House Act of 1867—was precisely a means to social policy (Davis, 1997). This law was intended to protect society from squalid living conditions that were associated with smallpox and tuberculosis epidemics. The legislation included not only policies to protect the health of the New York's citizens but also enforceable building regulations that mandated design features for cleaner, safer, and better built housing and designated public agencies to carry out those regulations. Similarly, the ICF and the social model of medicine on which it is based reinforce the link between the home environment and health. As a consequence, the ICF provides the impetus and rationale for incorporating environmental interventions for supportive housing into the building codes.

Zoning ordinances must also recognize and support the role of the home as a health care environment. The home may need to support round-the-clock care, which frequently requires live-in caregivers. However, many local zoning ordinances restrict cohabitation by unrelated adults or control multifamily housing (i.e., more than one kitchen) in many communities. Although originally intended to prevent overcrowding and squalid health conditions that were prevalent in late 19th-century cities, such restrictions effectively preclude care providers from living with care recipients. They also restrict the construction of such housing as accessory dwelling units for caregivers or care recipients (e.g., in-law suites) on traditional single-family lots, even though such units can delay the need for institutional care.

Both zoning regulations and building codes restrict the size of dwelling units based on the ratio of unit floor space to lot size. For zoning, this is to maintain the character of a neighborhood, while building codes are designed minimize the amount of impervious (impenetrable) surfaces (e.g., concrete or a roofed structure) to limit water runoff onto adjacent properties. Zoning also restricts where one can locate a structure on a lot, with requirements for front, side, and rear setbacks. The result limits the size of dwelling units and hence the ability to add accessory dwelling units or other housing options that increase the footprint or even size of the original home. Clearly, for the home to succeed as a health care environment, zoning ordinances and building codes must be changed to recognize cohabitation or multifamily units for health reasons.

Creating Incentives for Universal Design

UD is not just a solution for new housing stock. When retrofitting existing housing that must accommodate others in the household (e.g., family members, friends, caregivers, care providers), as it usually does, UD interventions offer more effective solutions overall than home modifications or assistive technologies that benefit only the individual with a functional limitation. In addition, there is a need for products and equipment that work better for everyone and fit better into the home environment. Simply put, better design solutions are needed, and UD provides them. The principles guide both better activity performance (i.e., works better) and better integration (i.e., fits better) in the social and physical context. However, accessible design is perhaps the largest impediment to adoption of universal design. As promulgated and reinforced by codes and standards, accessible design is based on a 20th-century if-you-build-it-they-will-come mentality that is predicated on the belief that enabling independence in activities will beget participation in social roles. UD, in contrast, is a 21st-century model, which, like the ICF, is predicated on the notion that activity and participation, while interconnected, are separate constructs that require their own environmental responses.

In new construction and remodeling, a number of municipalities have changed local building codes to require or offer tax breaks for basic access for wheelchair users. However, these visitability ordinances are by no means "universal design lite." Visitability enables wheelchair users to visit. While it may enable an inhabitant to access the home and live on the first floor, it does not necessarily ensure that the environment will meet the health and activity needs of individuals who occupy the home. Similar policy changes that require or create incentives for UD features, such as curbless showers, bathrooms with a 5-foot turning radius, and wider hallways, through tax breaks or fast-tracked approvals by municipal or state officials, are needed to overcome accessible design mentality.

Nonetheless, with the Americans with Disabilities Act and its mandated accessibility guidelines clearly forging the way (although it has no jurisdiction in home environments), accessible design is inextricably tied to U.S. civil rights legislation. At the same time, assistive technologies in particular, and to a lesser extent accessible design, are reinforced by medical model–based reimbursement policies. These policies focus primarily on improving independence in activity performance rather than participation in social roles. While the former are specific to the individual client, the latter would include environmental interventions that might have additional benefits to the client or others.

In a recent article in the *New York Times*, Ashlee Vance (2009) paints a grim portrait of the reimbursement system as a process so invested in the medical model that specialized medical devices and equipment are preferred over universally designed everyday designs, even when the latter are less expensive, work better, and are preferred by the user. Although the article is based on reimbursement for an assistive device, the same policies hold true for environmental modifications. Regardless of the type of intervention, policies that support specialized technologies over everyday designs may result in increased costs, decreased effectiveness, and poor outcomes. Vance writes:

> Kara Lynn has amyotrophic lateral sclerosis, or A.L.S. . . . A couple of years ago, she spent more than $8,000 to buy a computer . . . that turns typed words into speech. . . . Under government insurance requirements, the maker of the PC, which ran ordinary Microsoft Windows software, had to block any nonspeech functions, like sending e-mail or browsing the Web. . . . Dismayed by the PC's limitations and clunky design, Ms. Lynn turned to a $300 iPhone 3G from Apple running $150 text-to-speech software.

> Medicare and private health insurers decline to cover cheap devices like iPhones and netbook PCs . . . despite their usefulness and lower cost. Instead . . . if Ms. Lynn and others like her want insurance to pay, they must spend 10 to 20 times as much for dedicated, proprietary devices that can do far less. The logic: Insurance is supposed to cover medical devices. . . .
>
> "We would not cover the iPhones and netbooks with speech-generating software capabilities because they are useful in the absence of an illness or injury," said Peter Ashkenaz, a spokesman for the federal Centers for Medicare & Medicaid Services.

Medicalizing Environmental Interventions

The American Medical Association should support and promote environmental interventions as a health care issue. If, as the ICF suggests, the environment is an intervention in both health treatment and prevention, then one should expect that the professionals responsible for people's health and well-being (i.e., physicians) would be aware of, if not somewhat knowledgeable about, these types of health interventions. After all, preventive medicine and clinical intervention are dependent on environmental modification. However, it is a rare physician who considers environmental interventions as part of a care plan. Nonetheless, while no one really expects physicians to prescribe home modifications, they should be knowledgeable enough to suggest them, just as they would suggest diet and exercise as an intervention, and recommend a consultation with an expert in the area, such as an occupational therapist, which could be reimbursable.

Primary care clinicians, including physicians, physician assistants, and nurse practitioners, should be instrumental in recommending home interventions of any kind, including those in the physical environment. Not only are these clinicians most likely to be seen by the majority of people, but because they are expected to be knowledgeable about medical interventions and they are generally well respected, it is also likely that their advice will be followed. However, to be the first line of defense in educating the American public, primary care clinicians need to recognize how the home environment might affect their treatment plans. This will require policy changes in the American Medical Association, medical and nursing schools, and training hospitals to adopt a social model of medicine and seek out experts in environmental intervention to train the clinicians of the future.

Certifying Service Providers

Professional organizations should focus on developing practitioner expertise by designing certification programs that promote uniform and accurate assessments, ensure appropriate intervention recommendations, and result in successful and efficacious interventions. However, educating the range of professionals involved in home health interventions, including health care professionals, social service personnel, and workers in the building industry will require policy change not only at the level of the professional organizations but also at the regulatory level. At the organizational level, it will require a change in the laissez-faire policy that acknowledges the need for training but does not proactively apply a comprehensive program to ensure that professionals are adequately trained. At the regulatory level, it will require change in the way the Centers for Medicare & Medicaid Services (CMS) reimburses. Although CMS already requires licensure/certification for some services (e.g., licensed occupational therapists can perform functional assessments, certified assistive technology practitioners can perform assistive technology assessments), certification for all of the various types of home intervention services (e.g., assessment, medical remodeling, training) should be included. In addition, certification should be more stringent than that currently offered and should be designed specifically for the home environment (e.g., neither occupational therapist licensure nor assistive technology practitioner certification ensures a knowledge of either the client's housing needs or the home environment). Where CMS leads, private insurers will follow.

TOWARD AN AGENDA FOR RESEARCH ON THE PHYSICAL ENVIRONMENT AND HOME HEALTH CARE

Everyone who has an impact on the quantity and quality of housing—from consumers to builders to clinicians to regulators and legislators—needs evidence that environmental modifications can improve functioning and health outcomes, are cost-effective, and reduce the need for future modifications. However, the gaps in the knowledge base related to state of the physical environment and home health are wide enough to drive a truck through. Most of what people think they know is based on practice rather than evidence. After three decades of debate, there are few empirical data and a general lack of psychometrically sound measures (Gitlin, 2003). Research is still needed to identify the best methods of service delivery; adequacy of training; types of interventions that work for whom, where, and when; environmental impacts of various interventions; value added by UD; and effectiveness and cost benefits of interventions for care recipients, care providers, and society.

If the goal of research is to inform and affect practice both directly and through legislation and regulatory policy, then it is imperative that research create an evidence base that demonstrates not only the efficacy and effectiveness of interventions (i.e., what works and for whom) but, more importantly, their cost-effectiveness and benefits. In fact, the evidence base for UD is extremely weak, although this is not surprising given the current regulatory environment that denies reimbursement for everyday design. As a result, there are few published cohort studies that have described and compared the types of UD interventions used by people within and across user groups or have evaluated the effectiveness of specific ones in meeting needs across individuals.

At the heart of the problem is a lack of understanding and consensus about both independent and dependent variables. On one hand, there is a need to understand the environment as an independent variable: What are the salient environmental factors that affect activity and health? On the other hand, there is a need to identify key performance measures and appropriate outcome (dependent) measures—such as the physical and mental health of individuals and their caregivers as well as their acceptance of health technologies in the home. In addition, there is a need to continue to pull together the research that has been done (e.g., Wahl et al., 2009) and to identify the types of research designs that can be appropriately undertaken to answer relevant human factors questions, including: (a) benchmarking of environmental effects on ADLs, health, and injury; (b) environmental impacts based on individual and subgroup differences; (c) effectiveness of specific environmental interventions as they relate to home health; and (d) barriers to and facilitators of social participation.

Environment as an Independent Variable

Environmental research has suffered from studies, many firmly entrenched in epidemiological models, that lacked a basic understanding of the key environmental factors that impact activity and health outcomes. Such studies have focused on associating outcomes with the presence or absence of specific environmental barriers or facilitators (e.g., presence or absence of a grab bar or handrail) rather than the measurable attributes (e.g., height and diameter) of those features, the demands they exert, and valid measures of those demands (Stark and Sanford, 2005; Sanford and Bruce, 2010). As a result, many studies have used inappropriate and invalid environmental measures that have underestimated the contribution of environmental factors to health outcomes.

This underestimation is particularly evident in many studies of falls, which may account, in part, for findings reported by Wahl and colleagues (2009) that support for environmental influences on fall-related outcomes was less favorable than for functional ability-related outcomes. For example, in a prospective cohort study to determine whether the prevalence of environmental hazards increased the rate of nonsyncopal (i.e., not from fainting) falls among older adults, Gill, Williams, and Tinetti (2000) had a trained research nurse assess home hazards using a standard instrument that included 13 potential slip and trip hazards. Based on falls reported over a 3-year period, the risk of a nonsyncopal fall was only significantly elevated for 1 of the 13 hazards. Although the investigators concluded that there was no support for an association between environmental hazards and nonsyncopal falls, an alternative would be to question whether the 13-item assessment instrument, which, despite its widespread use, has never been actually validated, accurately measured fall risk. In addition, the list of hazards, such as throw rugs, lack clear definition of the attributes that actually are associated with falls. Clearly, throw rugs can be differentiated from each other by such a wide range of attributes—e.g., thickness, size, contrast, location—each of which could potentially induce a fall (or not). There is nothing inherent in rugs themselves that would make them a potential hazard. As a consequence, the researchers were perhaps misled to an overgeneralized conclusion at the expense of understanding perhaps the more salient environmental factors that impact falls.

Defining Appropriate Outcome Measures

Environmental research has also suffered from a lack of a set of mutually agreed-upon health outcomes. To date, studies have used traditional rehabilitation outcomes, such as improved activity performance, to evaluate the effectiveness of assistive technologies and home modifications (e.g., Mann et al., 1999; Gitlin et al., 2001a; Gitlin, 2003; Sanford and Hammel, 2006; Sanford et al., 2006). While these measures may be appropriate to evaluate individualized interventions for people with specific functional limitations, without assessing activity outcomes of others they say little about the UD implications of these interventions. However, defining activity performance is not as simple as it seems. Difficulty and dependence are common outcomes that can measure performance either directly, through observations or self-report (e.g., Connell et al., 1993; Connell and Sanford, 2001), or indirectly, through self-efficacy (Tinetti, Richman, and Powell, 1990; Sanford et al., 2006). Although these two outcomes measure different constructs (e.g., problems encountered with or without assistance versus level of assistance required, respectively), they often are used interchangeably. Time (e.g., time to transfer on/off a toilet) is also frequently used as an outcome measure (see Sanford and Megrew, 1995; Sanford, Story, and Jones, 1997; Sanford, Echt, and Malassigne, 1999). Generally the assumption is that the faster one can perform a task, the better. However, it is not always clear that increased speed of performance is a positive outcome. For example, enabling an individual to perform a controlled versus an uncontrolled transfer to a toilet will not only decrease speed of transfer but also increase safety.

The inability to measure critical outcomes has too often resulted in studies in which the effectiveness of environmental interventions lacks statistical significance. However, the most critical consideration in defining positive health outcomes is identifying ones that are important to the target group of individuals for whom the only issue is simple: Does it make a difference in my life? In fact, small changes in measurable health outcomes, even if they are not statistically significant, may equate to big gains in the quality of people's lives. This suggests that clinical significance may be important regardless of whether statistical significance can be demonstrated.

Defining measures of cost-effectiveness is equally complicated and is determined by the cost of the benefits of an intervention. However, it is not clear who benefits. If, like health benefits, cost benefits are consumer driven, they can involve a number of factors, such as added value, aesthetic value, functional value, and emotional value. If, instead, benefits are defined by society, then societal value is clearly important. Finally, when defined by the reimbursement system, initial and life-cycle costs would also be important.

Experimental Designs

Although environmental studies are easy to identify, they are not easy to undertake in real-world environments in which contextual factors are impossible to control. As a result, there are critical methodological challenges for studies in this field (Wahl et al., 2009). Of particular relevance and importance is the applicability, or lack thereof, of randomized controlled trials and longitudinal studies (Wahl et al., 2009). These types of studies are considered to be the gold standard of clinical research and produce the type of data that are required to justify policy change, but their validity for environmental research is difficult to defend. In contexts in which interventions cannot be randomly assigned nor the environment controlled, randomized controlled trials, and blinded studies in particular, are based more on an inappropriate research paradigm than one that is likely to produce valid and generalizable results.

Randomized controlled trials have been used for interventions that have introduced assistive technologies and environmental strategies into the home (e.g., Gitlin et al., 2001a) when the physical environment is the intervention, but most real-world circumstances make it difficult to use these and other experimental intervention designs (e.g., random/

nonrandomized, or controlled/uncontrolled pre-post). There are many practical and ethical concerns, such as the high initial costs of many physical environmental interventions, the costs of changing interventions in crossover designs, the disruption of installing or constructing environmental interventions, and the ethics of withholding intervention/treatment in the control group if the intervention is the only alternative or of exposing patients to an inferior intervention when an alternative is deemed more appropriate. As a result, the field is dominated by studies of convenience. These include cohort studies of assistive technologies, evaluations of environments in use (e.g., postoccupancy evaluations), and case study evidence from practice that benefitted from programs that were already implementing environmental interventions. While these studies help to understand the effects of environmental features, set precedents, and suggest trends, there is a basic lack of the critical evidence about the benefits of environmental interventions and their effect on health outcomes that is necessary for policy change.

Clearly, a myriad of issues confound environmental studies. However, these issues further complicate research when the physical environment is the intervention. As such, the most practical approach is to use quasi-experimental pretest and posttest designs that leverage the naturally occurring context rather than creating or altering it. The most likely design, and probably the most commonly used quasi-experimental design in social research, is the nonequivalent groups design, which requires a pretest and posttest for a treated and a comparison group. It is structured like a pretest-posttest randomized experiment but lacks random group assignment.

Although the lack of random assignment complicates statistical analyses in quasi-experimental designs, the experimental approach permits the research to fit seamlessly into and capitalize on naturally occurring situations. This suggests that funders and programs with vested interests in effecting positive activity and health outcomes must be more proactive in supporting the evaluation of intervention effectiveness. However, unlike clinical drug trials, there are rarely prescribed dosages of environmental attributes that can be varied and tested for efficacy, safety, and level across individuals. Rather, prescriptions for environmental interventions must be individualized and context-specific. As a result, it is imperative that research endeavors to understand what works, for whom, and under what circumstances. To do so, measures of efficacy must be defined that are relevant to individuals, programs, and government agencies on both the supply and demand sides of the equation. Therefore, in addition to experimental and quasi-experimental designs, relevant environmental factors should be included as a health covariate in standardized longitudinal studies, such as future versions of the National Long Term Care Survey, the Survey of Income and Program Participation, and other annual health surveys, such as the National Health Care Disparities

Report. Finally, to ensure that the appropriate and relevant environmental factors are being examined in contextually meaningful ways, it is of utmost importance that experts in environmental assessment, analysis, and intervention are involved in these research efforts.

CONCLUSIONS

While health programs and housing programs in the United States operate independently of each other, the needs of individuals would suggest they should not. For individuals with functional limitations and chronic conditions, housing and health are inextricably intertwined and, with innovations in design and technology, are likely to become even more so. These interconnections are bolstered by the public health community itself, as embraced by the model of health embodied in the World Health Organization's International Classification of Functioning, Disability and Health, in which the environment is seen as both a therapeutic health care milieu and a prosthetic health intervention.

Although decisions about the most effective environmental intervention (assistive technologies, accessible design, or UD) are context specific, UD is the intervention that is most compatible with the ICF model. However, a variety of interconnected barriers have limited the adoption of universally designed products, technologies, and spaces as environmental interventions. Limited information contributes to a lack of consumer demand; limited demand for home modification services results in few experienced providers and remodelers; inexperienced providers and remodelers produce poorly crafted, ill-suited modifications; small, scattered, little-known, and underutilized funding sources produce a patchwork of public service programs and make it hard for low-income households to undertake projects. Consumers are often frustrated by the process of obtaining and making home modifications and are discouraged by the results.

The most conspicuous barrier to adoption of this innovation is the policy paradigm that rewards specialized technology and personal assistance with limited and calculated benefits rather than everyday universal design, which has potential for multiple and far-reaching benefits. While the increased application of universal design principles requires changes in consumer and provider behavior, it most significantly requires fundamental changes in regulatory policy, from building and zoning codes to reimbursement. This includes allowances in the codes to permit health-related environmental interventions that are necessary for people to remain in their homes. It also requires changes in reimbursement that recognize and support environmental assessments and interventions as part of discharge planning and continue to support them on an ongoing basis as conditions change and throughout the life span. Nonetheless, to overcome biases entrenched in the medical model, policy decision makers must also recognize that non-randomized, pre-post designs undertaken by experts in the environment will produce the most valid and reliable data regarding the effectiveness of physical environmental interventions.

Demonstration programs, such as the Money Follows the Person (MFP) Program, can also provide valuable evidence. The MFP Program provides a mechanism for monies to follow the person into the community at levels equitable to those allocated for institutional/nursing home care. In addition, the MFP Program requires the coordination of information, supports, services, and funding across systems, as well as the need for consumer direction and control throughout the process. As of 2010, funding in 31 states enabled more than 27,000 people to transition out of nursing homes and other institutions to community housing (National Council on Disability, 2010).

While the MFP Program is demonstrating that the home environment can function in lieu of institutional care, it does not specifically allocate funds for environmental interventions, nor does it designate the home as a health care setting. As a result, the MFP Program is more of a paradigm adjustment than a fundamental change in thinking. As long as housing and health remain separate, decisions about the allocation of monies from each will be driven by bureaucratic rules rather than by the needs of individuals and their health care providers. Ultimately, the adoption of the physical environment, and UD in particular, as a broad-based intervention strategy will require fundamental paradigm shifts in both housing and health that recognize the home environment and everything in it as an integral part of the medical milieu.

Today, most UD products and homes are generally more expensive than other consumer products. Typically that is because universally designed products are designed better, are easier to use, and are more desirable. An example is a $300 smart phone compared with other cell phones, many of which are given away. However, the cost of specialized design for a few individuals is even more expensive. Going back to the case of Kara Lynn, when the cost of the $300 iPhone is compared with an $8,000 augmentative communication device that didn't work as well, the cost savings for the American public per device can be significant. Taken to another level, the cost of new UD housing—or even of retrofitting existing housing with UD modifications that will benefit those who occupy the home now as well as those in the future—will be small compared with the costs of institutional care or having to repeatedly modify the same home to meet the activity and health needs of each occupant over the life span of the residence. The question, therefore, is not about the costs of housing if UD is made a health care intervention, but about the costs of care if nothing is done.

ABOUT THE AUTHOR

Jonathan Sanford is director of the Center for Assistive Technology and Environmental Access in the College of Architecture at the Georgia Institute of Technology and a research architect at the Rehabilitation Research and Development Center of the Atlanta Department of Veterans Affairs. He is an architecturally trained researcher engaged in universal design and the design of accessible environments for older adults.

REFERENCES

Allen, S., Resnik, L., and Roy, J. (2006). Promoting independence for wheelchair users who live alone: The role of home accommodations. *Gerontologist, 46*(1), 115-123.

Andersen, L., Schnohr, P., Schroll, M., and Hein, H. (2000). All-cause mortality associated with physical activity during leisure time, work, sports, and cycling to work. *Archives of Internal Medicine, 60*, 1,621-1,628.

Anderson, G.F. (2005). Medicare and chronic conditions. *New England Journal of Medicine, 353*(3), 305-309.

Anemaet, W.K., and Moffa-Trotter, M.E. (1999). Promoting safety and function through home assessments. *Topics in Geriatric Rehabilitation, 15*(1), 26-55.

Belser, S.H., and Weber, J.A. (1995). Home builders' attitudes and knowledge of aging: The relationship to design for independent living. *Journal of Housing for the Elderly, 11*(2), 123-137.

Brooke, J. (2009, September 15). Japanese masters get closer to the toilet nirvana. *New York Times*. Available: http://www.nytimes.com/2002/10/08/international/asia/08JAPA.html [accessed June 2010].

Bruce, C., and Sanford, J.A. (2009). Assessment for workplace accommodation. In T. Oakland and E. Mpofu (Eds.), *Assessment in rehabilitation and health* (pp. 205-221). Upper Saddle River, NJ: Prentice Hall.

Bureau of Labor Statistics. (2006). *Career guide to industries, 2006-2007 edition*. Washington, DC: U.S. Department of Labor. Available: http://www.bls.gov/oco/cg/cgs035.htm [accessed June 2010].

Carter, S.E., Campbell, E.M., Sanson-Fisher, R.W., Redman, S., and Gillespie, W.J. (1997). Environmental hazards in the homes of older people. *Age and Aging, 26*, 195-202.

Center for Technology and Aging. (2009). *Technologies for remote patient monitoring in older adults*. Draft position paper, December.

Center for Universal Design. (1997). *The principles of universal design, version 2.0*. Raleigh: North Carolina State University. Available: http://www.design.ncsu.edu/cud/about_ud/udprincipleshtmlformat.html [accessed February 2010].

Clemson, L., Roland, M., and Cumming, R.G. (1997). Types of hazards in the homes of elderly people. *Occupational Therapy Journal of Research, 17*(3), 200-213.

Commission on Affordable Housing and Health Facility Needs for Seniors in the 21st Century. (2002). *Seniors commission report*. Final Report to Congress, June 28. Available: http://govinfo.library.unt.edu/seniorscommission/pages/final_report/sencomrep.html [accessed September 2009].

Connell, B.R., and Sanford, J.A. (1997). Housing needs of older people to facilitate independence and safety. In S. Lanspery and J. Hyde (Eds.), *Staying put: Adapting the places instead of the people*. Amityville, NY: Baywood.

Connell, B.R., and Sanford, J.A. (2001). Difficulty, dependence, and housing accessibility for people aging with a disability. *Journal of Architectural and Planning Research, 18*(1), 3-18.

Connell, B.R., Sanford, J.A., Long, R.G., Archea, C.K., and Turner, C.S. (1993). Home modifications and performance of routine household activities by individuals with varying levels of mobility impairment. *Technology and Disability,* 2(4), 9-18.

Coyte, P., and Young, W. (1997). Applied home care research. *International Journal of Health Care Quality Assurance, 10*(1), i-iv.

Cumming, R.G., Thomas, M., Szonyi, G., Frampton, G., Salkeld, G., and Clemson, L. (2001). Adherence to occupational therapist recommendations for home modifications for falls prevention. *American Journal of Occupational Therapy, 55*, 641-648.

Cumming, R.G., Thomas, M., Szonyi, G., Salkeld, G., O'Neill, E., Westbury, C., and Frampton, G. (1999). Home visits by an occupational therapist for assessment and modification of environmental hazards: A randomized trial of falls prevention. *Journal of the American Geriatrics Society, 47*, 1,397-1,402.

Davis, S. (1997). *The architecture of affordable housing.* Berkeley: University of California Press.

Fange, A., and Iwarsson, S. (2003). Accessibility and usability in housing: Construct validity and implications for research and practice. *Disability and Rehabilitation, 25*, 1,316-1,325.

Fazzone, P.A., Barloon, L.F., McConnell, S.J., et al. (2000). Personal safety, violence, and home health. *Public Health Nursing, 17*, 43-52.

Ferrucci, L., Guralnik, J.M., Studenski, S., Fried, L.P., Cutler, G.B., Jr., and Walston, J.D. (2004). Designing randomized, controlled trials aimed at preventing or delaying functional decline and disability in frail, older persons: A consensus report. *Journal of the American Geriatrics Society, 52*, 625-634.

Filion, P., Wister, A., and Coblentz, E.J. (1992). Subjective dimensions of environmental adaptation among the elderly: A challenge to models of housing policy. *Journal of Housing for the Elderly, 10*(1 and 2), 3-32.

Fisher, G.S., Coolbaugh, K. and Rhodes, C. (2006). A field test of the Cougar home safety assessment for older persons, version 1.0. *Californian Journal of Health Promotion, 4*(2), 181-196.

Fisher, G.S., Kintner, L. Bradley, E., Costulas, D., Kozlevcar, J. Mahonski, K, McMenamin, K., Rompilla, A. Woods, J., Stine, J., and Ewonishon, K. (2008). Home modification outcomes in the residences of older people as a result of Cougar home safety assessment (version 4.0) recommendations. *Californian Journal of Health Promotion, 6*(1), 87-110.

Frank, L., Engelke, P.O., and Schmid, T.L. (2003). *Health and community design: The impact of the built environment on physical activity.* Washington, DC: Island Press.

Freedman, V.A., Martin, L.G., and Schoeni, R.F. (2002). Recent trends in disability and functioning among older adults in the United States. *Journal of the American Medical Association, 288*, 3,137-3,146.

Frumpkin, H. (2003). Healthy places: Exploring the evidence. *American Journal of Public Health, 93*(9), 1,451-1,456.

Galinsky, T., Waters, T., and Malit, B. (2001). Overexertion injuries in home health care workers and the need for ergonomics. *Home Health Care Service Quarterly, 20*, 57-73.

Gershon, R.M., Pogorzelska, M.T., Qureshi, K.A., Stone, P.W., Canton, A.N., Samar, S.M., Westra, L.J., Damsky, M.M., and Sherman, M. (2008). *Home health care patients and safety hazards in the home: Preliminary findings.* Available: http://www.ahrq.gov/downloads/pub/advances2/vol1/Advances-Gershon_88.pdf [accessed September 2009].

Gilderbloom, J.L., and Markham, J.P. (1996). Housing modification needs of the disabled elderly: What really matters? *Environment and Behavior, 28*(4), 512-535.

Gill, T.M., Williams, C.S., Robison, J.T., and Tinetti, M.E. (1999). A population-based study of environmental hazards in the homes of older persons. *American Journal of Public Health, 89*, 553-556.

Gill, T.M., Williams, C.S., and Tinetti, M.E. (2000). Environmental hazards and the risk of nonsyncopal falls in the homes of community-living older persons. *Medical Care, 38*(12), 1,174-1,183.

Gitlin, L.N. (2003). Conducting research on home environments: Lessons learned and new directions, *Gerontologist, 43*, 628-637.

Gitlin, L.N., and Corcoran, M. (2000). Helping homes be safe: Environmental adaptations for people with dementia. *Alzheimer's Care Quarterly, 1*(1), 45-54.

Gitlin, L.N., Corcoran, M.A., Winter, L., Boyce, A, and Hauck, W.W. (2001a). A randomized, controlled trial of a home environmental intervention to enhance self-efficacy and reduce upset in family caregivers of persons with dementia. *Gerontologist, 41*, 15-30.

Gitlin, L.N., Liebman, J., and Winter, L. (2003). Are environmental interventions effective in the management of Alzheimer's disease and related disorders? A synthesis of the evidence. *Alzheimer's Care Quarterly, 4*, 85-107.

Gitlin, L.N., Mann, W., Tomita, M., and Marcus, S.M. (2001b). Factors associated with home environmental problems among community-living older people. *Disability and Rehabilitation, 23*(17), 777-787.

Gitlin, L.N., Winter, L., Corcoran, M., Dennis, M., Shinfeld, S., and Hauck, W. (2003). Effects of the home environmental sill-building program on the caregiver-care reciepient dyad: Six-month outcomes from the Philadelphia REACH initiative. *Gerontologist, 43*, 532-546.

Glass, T.A. (1998). Conjugating the tenses of function: Discordance among hypothetical, experimental and enacted function in older adults. *Gerontologist, 38*(1), 101-112.

Gosselin, C., Robitaille, Y., Trickey, F., and Maltais, D. (1992). Factors predicting the implementation of home modifications among elderly people with loss of independence, *Physical and Occupational Therapy in Geriatircs, 12*(1),15-27.

Hoenig, H., Sanford, J.A., and Griffiths, P. (2006). Development of a tele-technology protocol for in-home rehabilitation. *Journal of Rehabilitation Research and Development, 43*(2), 287-298.

Hyde, J., Talbert, R., and Grayson, P.J. (1997). Fostering adaptive housing: An overview of funding sources, laws and policies. In S. Lanspery and J. Hyde (Eds.), *Staying put: Adapting the places instead of the people* (pp. 223-236). Amityville, NY: Baywood.

Institute of Medicine. (1997). *Enabling America: Assessing the role of rehabilitation science and engineering*. J. Brandt and A.M. Pope (Eds.). Committee on Assessing Rehabilitation Science and Engineering. Division of Health Sciences Policy. Washington, DC: National Academy Press.

International Longevity Center-USA. (2006). *Caregiving in America*. The Caregiving Project for Older Americans. Available: http://www.ilcusa.org/media/pdfs/Caregiving%20in%20America-%20Final.pdf [accessed June 2010].

Iwarsson, S. (1999). The housing enabler: An objective tool for assessing accessibility. *British Journal of Occupational Therapy, 62*(11), 491-497.

Iwarsson, S. (2004). Assessing the fit between older people and their home environments: An occupational therapy research perspective. In H.-W. Wahl, R. Schiedt, and P. Windley (Eds.), *Annual review of the Gerontological Society of America 2003, vol. 23: Focus on aging in context: Socio-Physical environments* (pp. 85-109). New York: Springer.

Iwarsson, S. (2005). A long-term perspective on person-environment fit and ADL dependence among older Swedish adults. *Gerontologist, 45*, 327-336.

Iwarsson, S., and Isacsson, A. (1996). Housing standards, environmental barriers in the home, and subjective general apprehension of housing situation among the rural elderly. *Scandinavian Journal of Occupational Therapy, 3*(2), 52-61.

Joint Center for Housing Studies. (2000). *The state of the nation's housing 1999*. Cambridge, MA: Author.

Kendra, M.A., Weiker, A., Simon, S., Grant, A., and Shullick, D. (1996). Safety concerns affecting delivery of home health care. *Public Health Nursing, 13*, 83-89.

Kochera, A. (2002). *Falls among older persons and the role of the home: An analysis of cost, incidence and potential savings from home modification*. AARP Public Policy Institute. Available: http://assets.aarp.org/rgcenter/il/inb49_falls.pdf [accessed June 2010].

LaPlante, M.P., Hendershot, G.E., and Moss, A.J. (1992). Assistive technology devices and home accessibility features: Prevalence, payment, need and trends. *National Center for Health Statistics Advance Data, 217*, 1,012.

Lau, D.T., Scandrett, K., Jarzebowski, M., Holman, K., and Emanuel, L. (2007). Health-related safety: A framework to address aging in place. *Gerontologist, 47*(6), 830-837.

Law, M., Baptiste, S., Carswell-Opzoomer, A., McColl, M.A., Polatajko, H., and Pollock, N. (1991). *Canadian Occupational Performance Measure*. Toronto, ON: CAOT.

Lawler, K. (2001). *Aging in place: Coordinating housing and health care provision for America's growing elderly population*. Cambridge, MA: Joint Center for Housing Studies of Harvard University's Neighborhood Reinvestment Corporation.

Lawton, M.P., and Nahemow, L. (1973). Ecology and the aging process. In C. Eisdorfer and M.P. Lawton (Eds.), *The psychology of adult development and aging* (pp. 619-674). Washington, DC: American Psychological Association.

Lehoux, P. (2004, October 5). Patients' perspectives on high-tech home care: A qualitative inquiry into the user-friendliness of four interventions. *BMC Health Services Research, 4*(28). Available: http://www.biomedcentral.com/1472-6963/4/28 [accessed June 2010].

Lehoux, P., Richard, L., Pineault, R., and Saint-Arnaud, J. (2006). Delivery of high-tech home care by hospital based nursing units in Quebec: Clinical and technical challenges. *Nursing Leadership, 19*(1), 44-55. Available: http://120.72.90.83/longwoods/content/18048 [accessed June 2010].

Letts, L., Scott, S., Burtney, J., Marshall, L., and McKean, M. (1998). The reliability and validity of the safety assessment of function and the environment for rehabilitation (SAFER Tool). *British Journal of Occupational Therapy, 61*(3), 127-132.

Louie, J. (1999). *Housing modifications for disabled elderly households*. Cambridge, MA: Joint Center for Housing Studies of Harvard University.

Mace, R.L., Hardie, G.J., and Place, J.P. (1991). *Accessible environments: Towards universal design*. In W.E. Preiser, J.C. Vischer, and E.T. White (Eds.), *Design intervention: Toward a more humane architecture*. New York: Van Nostrand Reinhold.

Manangan, L.P., Pearson, M.L., Tokars, J.I., Miller, E., and Jarvis, W.R. (2002). Feasibility of national surveillance of health care associated infections in home care settings. *Emerging Infectious Diseases, 8*, 233-236.

Mann, W.C., Ottenbacher, K.J., Fraas, L., Tomita, M., and Granger, C.V. (1999). Effectiveness of assistive technology and environmental interventions in maintaining independence and reducing home care costs for frail elderly: A randomized controlled trial. *Archives of Family Medicine, 8*, 210-217.

Markkanen, P., Quinn, M., Galligan, C., et al. (2007). There's no place like home: A qualitative study of the working conditions of home health care providers. *Journal of Occupational and Environmental Medicine, 49*(3), 327-337.

Mathews, J.T. (2006). Existing and emerging healthcare devices for elders to use at home. *Generations Journal of the American Society on Aging, 30*(2), 13-19.

Mills, T., Holm, M.B., and Christenson, M.A. (2001). Public opinion of universal design in housing. *Proceedings of the Annual RESNA Conference.* Washington, DC: RESNA Press.

Myers, A., Jensen, R.C., Nestor, D., and Rattiner, J. (1993). Low back injuries among home health aides compared with hospital nursing aides. *Home Health Care Services Quarterly, 14*, 149-155.

National Council on Disability. (2010). *The state of housing in America in the 21st century: A disability perspective.* Washington, DC: Author.

Niva, B., and Skar, L. (2006). A pilot study of the activity patterns of five elderly persons after a housing adaptation. *Occupational Therapy International, 13*(1), 21-34.

Ono, Y., Lagerstrom, M., and Hagberg, M., et al. (1995). Reports of work related musculoskeletal injury among home care service workers compared to nursery school workers and the general population of employed women in Sweden. *Occupational and Environmental Medicine, 52*, 686-693.

Oswald, F., and Wahl, H.-W. (2004). Housing and health in later life. *Reviews of Environmental Health, 19*(3-4), 223-252.

Oswald, F., Schilling, O., Wahl, H.-W., and Gang, K. (2002). Trouble in paradise? Reasons to relocate and objective environmental changes among well-off older adults. *Journal of Environmental Psychology, 22*, 273-288.

Oswald, F., Wahl, H.-W., Schilling, O., Nygren, C., Fange, A., Sixsmith, A., Sixsmith, J., Szeman, Z., Tomsone, S., and Iwarsson, S. (2007). Relationships between housing and healthy aging in very old age. *Gerontologist, 47*, 96-107.

Pynoos, J. (1992). Strategies for home modification and repair. *Generations: Journal of the American Society on Aging, 16*(2), 21-25.

Pynoos, J. (1993). Toward a national policy on home modification. *Technology and Disability, 2*(4), 1-8.

Pynoos, J., and Regnier, V. (1997). Design directives in home adaptation. In S. Lanspery and J. Hyde (Eds.), *Staying put: Adapting the places instead of the people* (pp. 171-191). Amityville, NY: Baywood.

Pynoos, J., Angelleli, J., Tabbarah, M., and De Meire, M. (1996). *Improving the delivery of home modifications.* Los Angeles: National Resource Policy Center on Housing and Long Term Care.

Pynoos, J., Cohen, E., Davis, L., and Bernhardt, S. (1987). Home modifications: Improvements that extend independence. In V. Regnier and J. Pynoos (Eds.), *Housing the aged: Design directives and policy considerations* (pp. 277-303). New York: Elsevier.

Pynoos, J., Liebig, P., Overton, J., and Calvert, E. (1997). The delivery of home modification and repair services. In S. Lanspery and J. Hyde (Eds.), *Staying put: Adapting the places instead of the people* (pp. 171-191). Amityville, NY: Baywood.

Rubenstein, L.Z. (1999). The importance of including the home environment in assessment of frail older people. *Journal of the American Geriatrics Society, 47*, 111-112.

Saelens, B., Sallis, J., and Frank, L. (2003). Environmental correlates of walking and cycling: Findings from the transportation, urban design, and planning literature. *Annals of Behavioral Medicine, 25*(2), 80-91.

Sanford, J. (2002). Development of a comprehensive assessment for delivery of home modifications. *Physical and Occupational Therapy in Geriatrics, 20*(2), 43-55.

Sanford, J.A. (2004). *Home modifications: Assessment, implementation and innovation.* Presented at the American Occupational Therapy Association Annual Conference, May 19, Minneapolis, MN.

Sanford, J.A. (2010). Assessing universal design in the physical environment. In T. Oakland and E. Mpofu (Eds.), *Rehabilitation and health assessment* (pp. 255-278). New York: Springer.

Sanford, J., and Bruce, C. (2010). Measuring the impact of the physical environment. In T. Oakland and E. Mpofu (Eds.), *Rehabilitation and health assessment* (pp. 207-228). New York: Springer.

Sanford, J.A., and Butterfield, T. (2005). Using remote assessment to provide home modification services to underserved elders. *Gerontologist, 45*, 389-398.

Sanford, J., and Hammel, J. (2006). Impact of accessibility modifications to the home environment on community living and activity. *Gerontological Society of American Annual Conference,* Dallas, TX.

Sanford, J.A., and Megrew, M.B. (1995). An evaluation of grab bars to meet the needs of elderly people. *Assistive Technology, 7*(1), 36-47.

Sanford, J.A., Echt, K., and Malassigne, P. (1999). An E for ADAAG: The case for accessibility guidelines for the elderly based on three studies of toilet transfer. *Journal of Physical and Occupational Therapy in Geriatrics, 16*(3/4), 22-23.

Sanford, J.A., Griffiths, P.M., Richardson, P., Hargraves, K., Butterfield, T., and Hoenig, H. (2006). The effects of in-home rehabilitation on task self efficacy in mobility impaired adults: A randomized clinical trial. *Journal of American Geriatrics Society, 54*, 1,641-1,648.

Sanford, J.A., Griffiths, P.M., Richardson, P., Hargraves, K., Butterfield, T., and Hoenig, H. (2007). A comparison of televideo and traditional in-home rehabilitation in mobility impaired older adults. *Journal of Physical and Occupational Therapy in Geriatrics, 25*(3), 1-18.

Sanford, J.A., Jones, M.L., Daviou, P., Grogg, K., and Butterfield, T. (2004). Using telerehabilitation to identify home modification needs. *Assistive Technology, 16*(1), 43-53.

Sanford, J.A., Pynoos, J., Gregory, A., and Browne, A. (2001). Development of a comprehensive assessment for delivery of home modifications. *Physical and Occupational Therapy in Geriatrics, 20*(2), 43-55.

Sanford, J., Story, M., and Jones, M. (1997). An analysis of the effects of ramp slope on people with mobility impairments. *Assistive Technology, 9*, 22-33.

Scheidt, R., and Windley, P. (2006). Environmental gerontology: Progress in the post-Lawton era. In J.E. Birren and K.W. Schaie (Eds.), *Handbook of the psychology of aging* (6th edition, pp. 105-125). Amsterdam: Elsevier.

Scheschareg, R. (2006). *Gaining access to the $300 billion+ consumer out-of-pocket spending market.* Intuitive Care Advisors Advanced Home Healthcare Products and Services 2005 channel Report. Available: http://www.agingtech.org/documents/Advanced_Home_Healthcare_P&S.pdf [accessed June 2010].

Sinding, C. (2003). Disarmed complaints: Unpacking satisfaction with end-of-life care. *Social Science and Medicine, 57*, 1,375-1,385.

Sohn, J. (1997). *Older consumers' pre- and post-trial perceptions of residential universal design features.* Unpublished master's thesis. Kansas State University, Manhattan.

Spillman, B.C. (2004). Changes in elderly disability rates and the implications for health care utilization and cost. *Milbank Quarterly, 82*, 157-194.

Stark, S. (2004). Removing environmental barriers in the homes of older adults with disabilities improves occupational performance. *Occupation, Participation and Health, 24*, 32-39.

Stark, S.L., and Sanford, J.A. (2005). Environmental enablers and their impact on occupational performance. In C. Christiansen and C.M. Baum (Eds.), *Occupational therapy: Performance, participation, and well-being* (pp. 298-337). Thorofare, NJ: Slack, Inc.

Steinfeld, E., and Shea, S. (1993). Enabling home environments. *Technology and Disability,* 2(4), 69-79.

Stineman, M.G., Ross, R.N., Masilin, G., and Gray, D. (2007). Population-based study of home accessibility features and the activities of daily living: clinical and policy implications. *Disability and Rehabilitation, 8*(2), 34-45.

Tinetti, M.E., Baker, D., Gallo, W.T., Nanda, A., Charpentier, P., and O'Leary, J. (2002). Evaluation of restorative care vs. usual care for older adults receiving an acute episode of home care. *Journal of the American Medical Association, 287*, 2,098-2,105.

Tinetti, M.E., Richman, D., and Powell, L. (1990). Falls efficacy as a measure of fear of falling. *Journal of Gerontology, 45*(6), P239-P243.

U.S. Access Board. (2002). *ADA accessibility guidelines for buildings and facilities (ADAAG)*. Available: http://www.access-board.gov/adaag/html/adaag.htm [accessed June 2010].

U.S. Bureau of the Census. (1994). *Statistical abstract of the United States*, 114th edition. Washington, DC: U.S. Department of Commerce.

Vance, A. (2009, September 15). Insurers fight speech impairment remedy. *The New York Times*. Available: http://www.nytimes.com/2009/09/15/technology/15speech.html [accessed June 2010].

Vebrugge, L., and Sevak, P. (2002). Use, type and efficacay of assistance for disability. *Journal of Gerontology. Series B. Psychological and Social Sciences, 57*, S366-S379.

Wahl, H.-W. (2001). Environmental influences on aging and behavior. In J.E. Birren and K.W. Schaie (Eds.), *Handbook of the psychology of aging, 5th edition* (pp. 215-237). San Diego: Academic Press.

Wahl, H.-W., Fange, A., Oswald, F., Gitlin, L.N., and Iwarsson, S. (2009). The home environment and disability-related outcomes in aging individuals: What is the empirical evidence? *Gerontologist, 49*(3), 355-367.

Wolford, N. (2000). *Universal design standards for single-family housing*. Unpublished doctoral dissertation, Oregon State University.

Woodward, C.A., Abelson, J., Tedford, S., and Hutchison, B. (2004). What is important to continuity in home care? Perspectives of key stakeholders. *Social Science and Medicine, 58*, 177-192.

World Health Organization. (1980). *The international classification of impairment, disability and health* (p.143). Geneva: Author.

World Health Organization. (1991). *Action for public health: Sundsvall statement on supportive environments*. Sundsvall, Sweden: Author.

World Health Organization. (2001). *International classification of functioning, disability and health*. Geneva: Author.

Wu, S., and Green, A. (2000). *Projection of chronic illness prevalence and cost inflation*. Santa Monica, CA: RAND Corporation.

11

Impact of Cultural, Social, and Community Environments on Home Care

Steven M. Albert

The home environment is critical for maintaining health and well-being among the medically ill and people living with disabilities. Access to appropriate supportive care technologies and home health care services depends in part on where homes are located, what sorts of spaces are available for care in the home, and whether basic services (such as utilities) are reliable. These aspects of home environments are difficult to measure, even when features of homes are narrowly defined and only a single attribute, such as safety, is considered (Gitlin, 2003). Measurement challenges become more complex when considering that each of these environmental features also has a cultural or social component. Homes are located in *neighborhoods*, where home health care providers may not feel welcome or safe because of crime in a low-income neighborhood and discrimination or suspicion in a higher income one. Homes differ in their spaces available for care but also in the willingness of *families* to make these spaces available, adapt them as needed, and work with home health staff to provide care. Also, utilities, telephone service, and access to services differ by *community*, with some communities well serviced and others shortchanged. Thus, the home environment is nested in social and cultural layers that may lead to different home care outcomes, even with similar patients and common home environments (Barris et al., 1985).

The cultural component is immediately visible in family adaptation to home care. Families differ in the degree to which they reorganize themselves and their living spaces to accommodate care for the disabled or medically unstable (Albert, 1990), with different tolerance for disorder and different strategies for reducing such disorder (Rubinstein, 1990).

Consider the family facing end-of-life care for a medically unstable older person or child. For some families, hospice and death in the home is unthinkable (or perhaps not possible if home hospice services are unavailable). For other families, hospice and death in the home is the preferred outcome. The same may apply to other medical technologies, such as home infusion technologies, or to different types of care, such as managing the demented or incontinent patient at home. In the broadest sense, what kind of home care a patient receives depends to some degree on the meaning of "home"—that is, whether families consider these sorts of adaptations appropriate, along with more obvious home and community environmental constraints.

In this sense, cultural, social, and community environments must also be considered as human or ergonomic factors relevant to the adoption and successful use of home care technologies. Consider one model of technology adoption that has been applied to the use of consumer health information technology, the patient technology acceptance model (Or et al., 2006; Or and Karsh, 2009). In this approach, key determinants of acceptance of Internet monitoring of health status among patients with cardiac disease included perceived usefulness of the technology (performance expectancy), perceived ease of use (effort expectancy), and the perceived sense that others would use such a technology in similar circumstances (subjective norm). Each of these determinants has a cultural, social, or community component. Perceived usefulness depends in part on contact with providers, which is affected by features of a patient's community. Perceived ease of use depends on social support from families, whether families will help maintain technologies, and how receptive they are to instruction from home health care providers. Finally, subjective norms involve social influence and clearly depend on the kinds of social contact families have, where they live, and how insular they are in culture or language.

The significance of this dimension of home care should not be underrated. One middle-aged African American caregiver followed in our research had adapted her home to accommodate advanced dementia care of her mother. The hospital bed was centrally placed in the living room. She had attached a crib mobile to the bed and replaced its objects with photographs of family members and other keepsakes important to her mother. A commode was placed near the bed, and she herself slept in an adjacent room to monitor her mother at night. The bookcases and closet served as storage spaces for medical supplies and adult diapers. Guests who visited had to pass by the elder as they entered the house and were expected to engage her in conversation. The caregiver said her mother was "the best looking and best cared-for person with Alzheimer's disease in Philadelphia." Not every family is willing or able to make these accommodations, as in the case of another caregiver in this case series, who removed a similarly impaired person from her home because of strain with her husband and fear of the effect of such care on her children.

This kind of variation suggests a need to consider the full spectrum of social-ecological factors in home care. The social-ecological approach considers the interplay among individual factors, social relationships, and community environments (McElroy et al., 1988). Visually, it can be imagined as a series of concentric circles, with the individual in the smallest circle at the center. Progressively expanding circles radiate outward that first include social relationships and then community environments. Beyond the community sphere is a larger circle encompassing public policies and laws that regulate provision of home care. The value of this approach is its ability to show how actions in one domain depend on, or may influence, actions in another domain; thus, changes in the individual domain may depend on changes in family or social relationships. More particularly, how families think about the meaning of a home or household may affect decisions to bring certain medical technologies or services into the home. How families think about these issues will depend on cultural factors (shared ideas about what's appropriate in a household or living space) and social norms, such as community accommodation of home care.

To examine the effect of cultural, social, and community environments on home care, I begin with a brief treatment of the social-ecological model as it applies to these home care environments. I focus particularly on culture as it may be relevant to home care, the least studied of these elements.

HOME CARE AND THE SOCIAL-ECOLOGICAL MODEL

The social-ecological model emerged from ecological systems theory (Bronfenbrenner, 1979), which explicitly sought to examine transactions between persons and their environments. The model stresses cross-level influences, in which community or organizational environments can shape individual behavior (top-down effects), but also examines how individuals form groups or take actions that may affect higher level organizational or community spheres (bottom-up effects). The Centers for Disease Control and Prevention has incorporated social-ecological models into a number of its health promotion and disease prevention efforts.

The simple onion or Russian doll rendering of social-ecological relations as concentric circles is not in itself very informative. However, flowchart models based on such relationships can be useful for specifying hypothesized cross-level influences. One such flow diagram for decisions to adapt homes for advanced medical technology is shown in Figure 11-1.

The figure shows the four levels mentioned earlier: (1) individual, (2) family social relations, (3) community-neighborhood effects, and (4) the policy domain. At each level, the relevant agent faces a challenge. At the

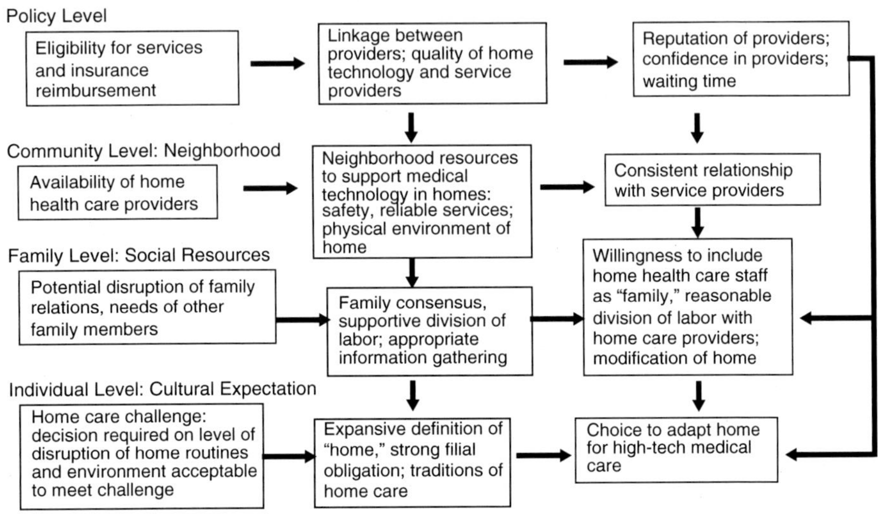

FIGURE 11-1 Social-ecological model adapted for home care research: Adaptation of homes for advanced medical technologies.

level of the individual is a home care challenge, in which a family caregiver must decide what level of disruption of home routines and environments is acceptable and whether to adapt a home for an advanced medical technology, such as home infusion or ventilator support. At the level of the family and social relations, the challenge is potential disruption of family relations and reconciling the demands of home care with the needs of other family members. At the level of the community, the challenge is the availability of home health care providers for a neighborhood. The policy level includes constraints on home care involving program eligibility and insurance.

Each of these challenges is addressed by resources (or ineffectively managed because of particular obstacles) specific to that level of social ecology. At the individual level, cultural expectations, such as an expansive definition of "home" that includes medical care, a strong sense of filial obligation, and traditions of home care, may allow families to decide in favor of adapting homes for advanced medical technologies. At the level of family social relations, family consensus, a supportive division of labor, and appropriate information gathering respond to the challenge of potential disruption of family relations. Similarly, community factors, such as neighborhood resources to support medical technology in homes, may lessen the impact of low availability of home health care agency services.

Most significant for the social-ecological approach are cross-level influences shown by arrows that cut across levels indicated in the figure. Thus, family consensus, a supportive division of labor, and appropriate information gathering at the level of social relations may support individual cultural expectations about home care. Likewise, a consistent relationship with service providers at the level of the neighborhood may reinforce pro-adaptation resources at the level of the family, such as willingness to include home health care staff as "family," and a reasonable division of labor with home care providers. These in turn will support cultural expectations for adapting homes to provide care.

Few studies have examined the full range of determinants of home care specified in the social-ecological framework. Most studies cover only a few of the levels or paths linking levels. I turn now to features of each level in the social-ecological model relevant to home care.

THE CULTURAL CONTEXT OF HOME CARE

Culture affects the day-to-day organization of care. Consider the idea of partnership between families and nurses sought by home health care agencies. Agencies rightly recognize that optimal self-management of disease and a person's return to function depend on a reasonable division of labor, shared information, and the willingness of family caregivers to learn rehabilitation and nursing protocols, medication administration, the use of assistive technologies, and the like (Wolff et al., 2009). But a family's involvement may depend on how they define this partnership and, in particular, whether or not the home health care provider is considered part of the family (Knox and Thobaben, 1997; McGarry, 2009). Similar effects of culture may be evident in the willingness of families to accept telehealth technology, express their degree of burden or need for help, or seek hospice care at the end of life.

By culture anthropologists refer to shared beliefs, knowledge, feelings, and objects that have a "directive force" or motivational quality (D'Andrade, 1995). Culture leads people to categorize and assign meanings, expect certain behaviors, and act in particular ways. A simple example can be seen in ideas about gender and height. Americans for the most part prefer that husbands be taller than wives. People notice when this expectation is violated. Some may even make this a consideration in the choice of a spouse. This gendered approach to height may reflect other asymmetries between men and women, such as disparities in wages. While the strength of this cultural expectation may be waning (and may vary across groups defined by socioeconomic status), it gives a feel for the subtle but powerful influence of culture.

How do people identify these cultural expectations, and how might they be relevant for decisions about home care? One productive approach is to elicit concepts using techniques from cognitive anthropology. Essentially, this approach extends investigation of folk taxonomies (e.g., colors, plants, pottery, kinship, emotions), the stock-in-trade of cognitive anthropology, into broader domains. Early on, in such an investigation I conducted for caregiver tasks, I determined that caregivers distinguished among emotional, cognitive, and physical disability support (Albert, 1991). More recently, the same technique has been used to elicit expectations regarding more abstract cultural domains, such as what makes success in life, leisure activity, social support, and family relationships (Dressler et al., 2005). For the latter, Dressler and colleagues asked a sample of Brazilians to list the goods or possessions people need to lead a good life, or the activities people typically engage in during their free time, or who they typically turn to for different kinds of support and subjected these lists to formal analysis designed to examine the degree of consensus across respondents. As evidence of shared culture, they found a single shared "cultural answer key," along with individual variation. Notably, people whose lists or ratings were not consonant with the dominant cultural pattern were more likely to have poorer mental and physical health and even higher blood pressure.

In the cultural domain of home care, it would be valuable to conduct a similar investigation. Some potential elicitation frames might include the following:

- What changes in your home would be appropriate when a family member is seriously ill and may die?
- What changes in your household would you need to make in order to provide quality care for a family member receiving home health care services?
- What aspects of a home make it hard or easy for a home health care worker to do his or her job?

Family members with experience of home care would be likely to generate a long list of answers to the first elicitation, which might include hospice services, infusion technologies, a hospital bed, a commode, smart home telemonitoring, more reliable telephone or utility service, modifications to the home to increase access, a place to store medical supplies, a separate place for visitors or other family members, and perhaps others. Some caregivers would produce shorter lists, some longer, but it is likely that a single cultural consensus would emerge. This elicitation would allow a first look at the cultural domain of home care. A reasonable hypothesis would involve less efficient decision making (and perhaps poorer outcomes for patients) by caregivers who do not express the consensus view.

This approach to culture does not involve differences among ethnicities or people who speak different languages but rather the operation of culture in a population. Family caregivers and health care professionals in a single culture may differ in expectations for care or home accommodation, but these differences may be less salient than cross-cultural differences associated with ethnicity, race, country, or language. A growing body of research suggests that expectations regarding care differ across cultures (Sommer et al., 1999). For example, cultures differ in the degree to which pain, limitation in activity, or cognitive impairment is considered an appropriate cause for medical intervention. In the United States, minorities are less likely to use skilled nursing facilities and perhaps more likely to tolerate dementia and old-age disability at home (Hinton and Levkoff, 1999; Whitehouse et al., 2005).

The elicitation of home care culture described above can be used to identify subcultures and also differences across cultures. We turn now to some cross-cultural differences identified for expectations of home care.

Commitment to Family Care

Ethnic and cultural groups differ in their commitment to family care. African Americans are more likely than whites to endorse the primacy of family care (Dilworth-Anderson et al., 2005) and accordingly are less likely to make use of formal long-term care, including respite, home care, adult day programs, skilled nursing facilities, and hospice. Similarly, Latinos delay institutionalization relative to whites; a higher cultural value assigned to family care leads to more positive views of family caregiving, which in turn leads to a negative evaluation of skilled nursing facilities as an option for dementia or end-of-life care (Mausbach et al., 2004).

Differences in commitment to family care are based on cultural norms of filial piety or obligation. The concept of *xiao*, or filial piety, is a well-developed element in Chinese culture. However, it is strongly gendered, so that the burden of such care falls on adult daughters or daughters-in-law, not sons (Zhan, 2004). Caregiving in American families shows a more variegated pattern, both in underlying concepts and in the division of labor (although caregiving remains mostly women's work). Norms of filial obligation are heavily influenced by education, with greater acceptability and use of skilled nursing home care evident among more highly educated people. As minorities advance through the educational and occupational ladders, these differences in recourse to skilled care may lessen.

Little information is available for differences among cultural groups in receptivity to home adaptation. Given differences in recourse to institutional placement, as described earlier, cultures with a strong bias toward home care may be *more* receptive to adaptation of homes to accommodate medical technologies. However, these households may face other social or community constraints that make it difficult to deliver such technologies. I return to these points below.

Caregiving Burden and Satisfaction

With norms of filial obligation and positive appraisals of caregiving demands, ethnic and cultural minorities are more likely to report satisfaction in caregiving. Latina caregivers report lower appraisals of stress and greater perceived benefits of caregiving; they also make greater use of religious coping than white caregivers (Coon et al., 2004). Similarly, African American caregivers report lower anxiety, greater well-being, and more perceived benefits of caregiving than white caregivers (Haley et al., 2004). More generally, cultures differ in how well reciprocity between care receivers and caregivers is maintained after the onset of caregiving (Becker et al., 2003).

Communication with Health Professionals

A central finding in medical anthropology is the difference between illness and disease (Kleinman, Eisenberg, and Good, 1978). Clinicians diagnose and treat disease (abnormalities in body structure or function), but patients suffer *illness,* in which symptoms carry social significance and force changes in social function. Illness depends on social status and systems of meaning used to understand symptoms. Thus, families and health professionals may start with completely different premises when they collaborate to ameliorate disease or manage disability.

A striking example is a culture-bound syndrome, *susto*. *Susto*, sometimes translated as "fright disease" or "separation of body and soul," is a prevalent condition throughout Latin America. It is a folk or culture-bound syndrome to the extent that it is not associated with a particular abnormality in body structure or function recognized by Western medicine. Although it involves fatigue, anxiety, and withdrawal from social roles, it is not simply a psychological disorder. People suffering *susto* do not differ in psychological profiles from a matched sample and they benefit from antibiotic treatment (Rubel, O'Nell, and Collado-Ardon, 1984). The person with *susto* views the condition as a spiritual affliction triggered by negative social interaction, speaks of it this way, and as a result seeks treatment from a traditional healer rather than a physician.

Clearly, how people understand symptoms affects how they speak about a condition, to whom they disclose symptoms, when they seek treatment, and who they think can help them. In the case of home care, if expectations for rehabilitation are low or people view disability as inherent to aging, or if they consider incontinence, muscular dyscontrol, or agitation shameful, they may be less likely to involve health care professionals or paraprofessionals. They may seek to deny or hide the condition. Arranging optimal home care in this case may be complicated and require exquisite skill in bridging cultures.

Patient and family willingness to seek help, to disclose symptoms, or simply to cooperate in care depends in part on the personal relationships that patients develop with home care providers. Patients are more or less comfortable with different providers (and providers are similarly more or less comfortable with different patients, families, or home settings). Concordance in race or ethnicity may not be the most important factor in such comfort. One systematic review did not find concordance in race or ethnicity a significant predictor of receipt of services or satisfaction with care (Meghani et al., 2009). Such concordance may be more important for more generalized trust in communication with physicians or satisfaction with health services overall (Sohler et al., 2007).

Still, the role of cultural differences and lack of concordance between patients and health care providers should not be underestimated. In urban centers, such as New York City, it is very common for home health care providers and patients to speak different languages, come from different neighborhoods, and have very different expectations for care. Yet home care paraprofessionals are expected to work in patient homes, to serve to some extent as surrogate family, and to help disabled or critically ill patients function on their own terms. The potential for misunderstanding and frustration is high, as described below.

Health Decision Making

Culture may be relevant for decisions to seek treatment or receive clinical preventive services. For example, ethnic and racial minorities are less likely to take advantage of preventive health services, such as vaccinations and cancer screening, even when these are available (Chen et al., 2005). However, it is hard to know how much of this difference in service use is related to aspects of culture (such as a different understanding of prevention in late life or differences in the degree to which people view health as a matter of personal agency) and how much may be due to the cultural insularity that characterizes many ethnic enclaves. "Cultural insularity" in this context refers to restrictions in access to health information related to culture, such as not speaking English, but also to religious proscriptions against contact with mainstream culture, for example, watching television or reading English-language newspapers.

This kind of insularity may have an important significance for health in ethnic communities organized around religious beliefs. For example, in an orthodox Jewish sample of older women in New York City, the prevalence of mammography, Pap smears, and colorectal cancer screening was low compared with other women of similar age and education. Use of these preventive services was lowest in the orthodox women who reported least exposure to mainstream sources of health information (Albert, Harlap, and

Caplan, 2004). For ethnic and cultural communities that wish to maintain traditions yet participate in effective disease prevention or home care, it is important that they mobilize community resources, perhaps in partnership with service providers, to develop appropriate delivery of information in culturally acceptable ways.

The Stigma of Disability

Tolerance of disability in families appears to be linked to socioeconomic status (SES), with greater tolerance associated with lower SES (Murphy, 1990). More broadly, consider cultural attitudes toward aging. With each additional decade of life, adults will see not only declines in strength and walking speed and slowing in reaction time but also declines in addictive behaviors and crime, reduction in severe psychiatric disorders, and increased contact with close family (Albert and Freedman, 2010). American culture stresses the negative features of aging, something to be fought or covered up. In other cultures, the stress may be on the more positive elements, as among the Samia of Kenya, who boast of aging as a time to sit by the fire and be fed (Albert and Cattell, 1994). Americans, by contrast, may consider dependence and need for help in old age worse than death (Clark, 1972).

INTERPERSONAL RELATIONSHIPS

The second level in the social-ecological model is family and social relationships. Social relationships differ across cultures in the relative priority assigned to individual and family interests. When family concerns are placed above those of the individual, sociologists speak of "familism." A consistent body of research has documented the greater familism among non-U.S.-born and U.S.-born Latinos, and the greater tendency of minority groups to receive social support from family members rather than friends (Almeida et al., 2009). African American caregivers who endorsed family-based justifications for caregiving showed better health outcomes and reported less caregiving stress than caregivers not endorsing these justifications (Dilworth-Anderson, Goodwin, and Williams, 2004). However, other research suggests that familism can also intensify the stresses and mental health consequences of home care (Kim, Knight, and Longmire, 2007; Rozario and DeRienzis, 2008).

When an individual's interests are subordinated to family interests, families may be more likely to adapt the home for medical care. That is, the disruption of the home and restrictions on other family members inherent in complex home care (in which family members may have to maintain equipment, not have friends visit, not be able to leave the home, etc.) may be more acceptable if home care is considered a dominant family obligation that trumps individual interests. In the social-ecological framework described earlier, familism at the level of social relationships may reinforce individual cultural expectations for home care.

Families and Receptivity to Use of Home Care Services and Medical Technologies

Whether minority groups use home care services and home-based medical technologies more or less than nonminorities use them depends in part on how these services are defined, how available they are in particular localities (and often what kind of state Medicaid waiver policy is in play), and whether differences in SES are adequately controlled. Because of these differences, studies differ in estimates of the independent role of cultural group or ethnicity in home care utilization. This line of research is most developed for aging services. One review through the 1990s found no differences in home care utilization by race (Kadushin, 2004). Other studies report lower utilization, for example, among Mexican Americans (Crist et al., 2009). In New York City, where home care for seniors is generously supported by state and city, Medicaid home care utilization did not differ among whites, African Americans, and Caribbean Latinos (Navaie-Waliser et al., 2001; Albert et al., 2005).

The absence of differences in home care service use by cultural group may or may not mean equal likelihood of use of medical technologies in the home. Here higher levels in the social-ecological framework may become more relevant (see Figure 11-1). Even if families in different cultural groups are equally receptive to adaptation of homes for medical technologies, minority families in less resourced neighborhoods or communities may be less likely to gain access to these technologies. Likewise, smaller homes or neighborhoods with less reliable infrastructural support may pose additional challenges to adapting homes, even when families are receptive. Again, this suggests a need for social-ecological approaches that consider cross-level influences on health care decision making.

What about family relationships or culture would lead to potential differences in home care utilization or the adaptation of homes? Despite some thought that ethnic or cultural minorities may differ in the recognition of medical symptoms, such as dementia in elders (e.g., finding dementia behaviors more acceptable), such differences in fact appear to be an artifact of knowledge about dementia or access to dementia care (Mahoney et al., 2005). Similarly, while poorer mental health (anxiety, depressive symptoms, panic syndromes) has been reported for a number of different cultural groups in the United States, the greater prevalence is probably due to the challenges of assimilating to a new and often very different society and not to features of culture per se (Gonzalez, Haan, and Hinton, 2001). Many differences attributed to culture may actually be artifacts of low access to services or limited knowledge of a disease process.

Confidence in Home Care Services

One study of home care service use by Mexican Americans showed that familism was related to confidence in the services; elders and caregivers who endorsed familism more highly were less convinced of the value of home care and were accordingly less likely to use such services (Crist et al., 2009). In this analysis, confidence in home care services was an independent predictor of service use and directly related to familism. Interestingly, Crist and colleagues in this study defined home care use as two or more visits from a provider, not just a single one. One reason for this approach was the observation that "elders or family caregivers agree to an initial visit, out of politeness or feeling pressured while in the hospital, but refuse return visits" (Crist et al., 2009, p. 30).

Discrimination

Discrimination in experiences with medical providers (or more generally) may affect receptivity to home care. In the Mexican American sample mentioned earlier, experiencing discrimination was associated with less confidence in home care services and lower usage (Crist et al., 2009). Another question is whether minority and nonminority families receive the same services at home. One study found higher use of physical and occupational therapy among whites and Asians relative to black and Hispanic home health recipients, but this difference was no longer significant with adjustment for case mix (Peng, Navaie-Waliser, and Feldman, 2003). Here, too, it is difficult to tell whether differences are based on insurance coverage status (which is often associated with socioeconomic status and race/ethnicity) or on differences in culture. In a study of home health care of elders discharged from hospitals after a stroke or traumatic brain injury, elders who had private insurance in addition to Medicare were more likely to receive occupational and physical therapy. Minority families were less likely to have private insurance and for this reason were less likely to receive rehabilitative care (Levine et al., 2006). Similar factors may be at work for adaptation of homes for medical technologies.

Psychosocial Preferences for Care: Dignity, Privacy, Comfort, Trust

Cultural "hot button" issues, which include feeding, personal assistance and privacy, and end-of-life care, are surprisingly understudied. A recent qualitative study did not find differences in care preferences across African American, Chinese, Hispanic, Native American, and non-Hispanic white families (Mullan et al., 2009). These ethnically diverse caregivers were much more concerned with access to appropriate care, avoiding unmet need, and navigating challenging bureaucracies. They did describe cultural differences between family and agency staff concerns, but these were less salient in their experience of receiving home care. Similarly, privacy concerns and receptivity to telemedicine technologies do not appear to differ across cultural groups, at least in initial pilot studies (Dang et al., 2008; Demiris et al., 2009). More research is required to establish psychosocial preferences for care among families providing home care and patients with different disabilities and medical needs.

The social-ecological approach may help explain the absence of differences at the level of families and social relationships in psychosocial preferences for care. Given the overwhelming need to access services and the key position of community resources in gaining such access, families may need to accept greater flexibility or standardization of services, whatever their own preferences. The potential for conflict between families and providers in such cases is clear.

It is also important to recognize that the boundaries of families are not always obvious. As mentioned earlier, families differ in the degree they allow outsiders, such as home care providers or therapists, to become "family." It may also be complicated for a home care provider to discern who belongs in a patient's family and how the family defines its functions, which in turn may be relevant for communication and clear expectations regarding care (Knox and Thobaben, 1997). If home care providers must become family to have reasonable access to patients and support from families, then establishing appropriate professional boundaries may also be difficult.

Finally, patient groups differ in the trust they place in medical providers and medical care. Research suggests different kinds of trust: in one's personal physician, in the competence of a physician's care, and in formal and informal sources of health information. One study found that African American adults had less trust in their physicians and greater trust in informal health information sources than whites (Musa et al., 2009). Greater trust in one's own physician was associated with use of preventive health care. Trust may also be relevant for adoption of home care technologies, but little research is available in this area. If informal sources of health information are more important for some cultural groups for the adoption of home health care technologies, then it will be important to work through these informal networks for changing social norms regarding acceptability.

COMMUNITY AND NEIGHBORHOOD FACTORS

Community factors represent the third level in the social-ecological model. These clearly affect access to home care and perhaps also outcomes of home care. For example, in a neighborhood with a high crime rate, it may be difficult to attract agency care, and home care paraprofessionals may be reluctant to make home visits. Home care equipment and technologies brought into a home may make it a target for theft or attract attention a family may not want. Homes in these neighborhoods may not have local providers, making it more complicated to replenish supplies or monitor effective use of technologies.

Also, physical characteristics of homes may complicate the delivery of home care. For example, a home in a low-income neighborhood may not have reliable telephone service. Intermittent telephone service may affect the ability of health providers to contact clients and conduct appropriate follow-up. Similarly, inability to pay electric bills may affect the use of home care technologies, especially nasal ventilation devices for neuromuscular disease, oxygen devices, and telemedicine devices. Even devices that automatically upload device readings require access to wireless networks. More generally, families struggling to maintain a home may have difficulty providing the kind of stability and security needed for effective home care. Chapter 10 presents an extensive discussion of the physical environment and its effects on home care.

The American Geriatrics Society recognizes the importance of home and neighborhood in the effective delivery of home care: "In some cases, the home environment itself may be a barrier to continuing home care. Unsafe neighborhoods, household disruptions from alcohol or drug use, and inadequate room for equipment or environmental modifications may make home care a poor or risky option" (see http://www.healthinaging.org/aginginthe know).

Neighborhoods and personal risk factors in some cases travel together and increase the risk of adverse outcomes in the use of home care technologies. Consider the case of long-term oxygen therapy. About 1 million people in America use oxygen in the home, mostly for the treatment of smoking-related respiratory illness, such as chronic obstructive pulmonary disease. The risk of fire is high if users smoke because oxygen saturates clothing, fabric, and hair and serves as a fire accelerant. Thus, a cigarette will burn faster and hotter in an oxygen-rich setting. As many as 43 percent of oxygen users smoke. Because the prevalence of smoking is higher in low-income neighborhoods, adverse effects of oxygen therapy are more likely in these settings. Fire-related mortality and injury with oxygen use is rare but significant enough for the U.S. Public Health Service to issue warnings (*Mortality and Morbidity Weekly Review*, 2008).

The role of neighborhoods in shaping health and well-being more generally has also become increasingly clear. To take only one example, an important study by Klinenberg (2004) shows the critical role of neighborhoods in the risk of death from extreme summer heat. Isolation, usually thought of as a problem for individuals, turns out to be heavily dependent on features of communities. In this study of the July 1995 heat wave in Chicago, similarly impoverished communities did not bear the same brunt of heat mortality. For example, North and South Lawndale, contiguous communities with equal proportions of both elderly and elderly living below the poverty level, differed by a factor of 10 in heat deaths. The difference, Klinenberg argues, was in their community social capital, that is, health resources related to social ties. South Lawndale's predominantly Latino community was economically vibrant, less crime-ridden, more densely populated, with active civic organizations. North Lawndale, predominantly African American, stood out among Chicago communities for its loss of population over the prior 30 years, crime, decaying housing stock, and, most critically, absence of economic activity and civic organizations. Isolated elders in North Lawndale were most at risk of heat death. They lived in fear of crime and nailed windows shut. They feared opening doors to city social workers sent to check up on them. Even if they ventured outside, they had no place to go because there were few stores, parks, or community gathering places to seek cooler air or information about services. Most critically, they had no one to check up on them as part of the normal course of daily life.

Social capital may be involved in quite distal health processes, such as likelihood of recovery from coronary disease (Scheffler et al., 2008). Similarly, measures of community integration that appear quite remote from health processes, such as the proportion of people in a community performing volunteer service, may turn out to be critical resources for health. Even more striking, what is apparent in the risk of heat death or other extreme health events may also apply to a far more general range of health behaviors and outcomes. Wight et al. (2006) used data from the Health and Retirement Survey, merged with community ecological indicators (i.e., census tract indicators of median levels of education or income) to show that community status and individual cognitive health are related.

Home Care in Dangerous Places

In a study of home care in New York City, home care paraprofessionals were asked how they handled assignments in buildings they felt were unsafe because of crime or gang violence (Albert, 2002). They suggested a number of strategies for potentially dangerous assignments. First, they stressed the need in some cases not to accept an assignment. "We have a choice. If we are sent on a case, you stay the first day. If you don't like it, call your supervisor and say, 'The client is OK, but the neighborhood is dangerous and I don't want to go back there.'"

A second strategy is to make clear one's position as a home attendant or therapist, a neutral party, and to enlist neighbors as supporters or protectors. As one reported, "When I go into a project, when I see the people there, the first thing I do is introduce myself. Whoever I meet downstairs, the first time, I introduce myself. I say I am here to work, and I ask if I can count on them to help me do my job."

Home care paraprofessionals in this study often felt a need to call agency supervisors. Many stressed the necessity of a cell phone (actually prohibited by some home care agencies in the 1990s) and the need to call 9-1-1 and seek police interventions: "If it's a dangerous situation where you are going to be hurt, you take yourself out of there. [But] you don't go away. If you're in danger, you call the agency, you call the family; you take yourself out of there and call 9-1-1." Home attendants are required to stay with clients even in situations of danger (and many did so in the neighborhoods surrounding the World Trade Center following the 9/11 terror attacks). They stressed that they would leave a home or apartment only in a situation of immediate danger and even then would call their agencies on the way out, as they are required to do.

Violence against home care workers is not well documented. In the Minnesota Nurses Study, violence directed at nurses was actually lower among home care nurses than nurses working in hospitals. It was highest among nurses working in skilled nursing settings (Gates, 2004; Gerberich et al., 2004). The study, however, cannot be considered definitive. Only 10 percent of the nurses worked in home care agencies, and these were grouped with school and public health nurses. Also, the study stressed violence directed at nurses by patients. The potential for other forms of violence outside the hospital and skilled nursing home setting is likely to be much higher. For example, in the New York City study of home attendants providing personal assistance care, many reported thefts, pressure if not overt threats from family members, and great concern for personal safety (Albert, 2002).

Home Care in Inhospitable Places

Home attendants also described difficult home situations, and these descriptions often included physically difficult environments (Albert, 2002). Surprisingly, homes in the winter were said to be too warm for the most part, rather than cold and drafty. Home care paraprofessionals were well aware of dangerous home conditions, such as loose floor boards, inadequate windows, obstacles to mobility, and antiquated kitchens. These impressions accord with a recent survey in the United Kingdom. The prevalence of "nondecent" homes among vulnerable families was surprisingly high and linked to residence in older structures, one unintended consequence of otherwise desired household stability and aging in place (Donald, 2009). The same situation prevails in the United States. Golant (2008) draws attention to low-income elderly homeowners living in the oldest housing stock in the country. These seniors were vulnerable, living in housing that put them at great risk of having unmet health care needs. This, in turn, had spillover effects on neighborhoods, once these elderly were unable to maintain their homes. For this reason, geriatric care managers have begun to look for alliances with community developers to help ensure adequate access to services and repairs (Austin, McClelland, and Gursansky, 2006).

The aging housing stock may also make it difficult to provide adequate home care. Home and community environmental facilitators and barriers are relevant for rehabilitation outcomes (Keysor et al., 2006), and they are likely to be relevant as well for effective delivery of home care, although few studies address the topic.

Access to Home Health Care Workers and Technologies: A Social Capital Perspective

Access to home care may be affected by more subtle community effects, apart from the environmental limitations of homes and barriers posed by the low SES of communities. Weak neighborhoods mean weak social ties, with fewer neighbors to check in on elders, absence of common safe areas (such as stores or parks) that allow people to seek refuge or make contact with others, and less support for home care personnel seeking to deliver services to shut-in elders. Thus, social networks can have properties that are protective of health, and their absence or weakness may make it quite difficult to deliver services to homes. Strong networks allow people with disabilities or health concerns to obtain direct support (both instrumental and emotional) and also enable people to obtain the information they need to access services.

The value of these sorts of community support for home care is clear. They shore up families, allow home care personnel to do their jobs more effectively, and keep people connected to communities even when they face serious illness.

Other evidence suggests more diffuse benefits for social capital. Communities that are well served by medical facilities and home care agencies indirectly provide high-quality, timely information about services and new technologies. They link families in search of such information and thus promote more effective use of resources (and also indirectly promote greater health differentials between high- and low-income neighborhoods).

One study examining child care resources suggests that differences in these social capital effects may be responsible for poorer outcomes in low-income neighborhoods even when they are adequately served (Small and Jacobs, 2008). Provider agencies in higher income communities in this study were more closely linked than agencies in lower income communities. Thus, the flow of information is more efficient in high-income communities and allows greater efficiencies in service delivery.

GAPS AND DIRECTIONS FOR RESEARCH

The social-ecological approach suggests that improvement in home care outcomes will depend on adequate recognition of the role of culture, family and social relationships, and communities in the delivery of care. Interest in the first and second areas is long-standing. Attention to community factors and linkages across levels is more recent, and research in this area is much less developed. I conclude with a series of recommendations derived from the social-ecological approach, as well as a series of hypotheses suggested by this inquiry.

Cultural Assessment in Home Care

A first need is better tools for the assessment of cultural expectations for home care and psychosocial preferences for care delivery. Transcultural nursing has taken the lead in developing methodologies for assessing cultural differences among patients as well as the receptivity of health care providers to these differences (Narayan, 1997; Davidhizar and Bechtel, 1998; Heineken and McCoy, 2000). These approaches recognize the necessity of seeing the world through a patient's eyes and point out the need for "cultural synergy" between nurse and patient, that is, mutual recognition of different cultures in the service of care.

Campinha-Bacote (2002) has developed a screening instrument for the assessment of cultural competence in nursing. This approach includes three key elements: cultural awareness ("Am I aware of my personal biases and prejudices towards cultural groups different than mine?"), cultural skill ("Do I have the skill to conduct a cultural assessment in a culturally sensitive manner?"), and cultural knowledge ("Do I have knowledge of the client's worldview?"). As an example of the utility of this approach, Campinha-Bacote notes that hypertension treatment may have a very different meaning among African American elderly, for whom hypertension implies emotional pressure or tension and not just a stiffening of arterial walls. Explanations to patients must take these different understandings into account if patients are to adhere to medication regimens and adopt lifestyle prescriptions.

The challenge of crossing cultural boundaries obviously becomes more difficult when home care personnel and patients do not speak the same language. Family or other translators become critical. My research with home care in New York City suggests that differences in language are quite common—not surprising when one notes that New York City's fastest growing populations include Mandarin, Russian, and Spanish speakers. One home health care agency director suggested that 80 percent of her agency's clients and home attendants differed in culture. The agency had to develop guidelines for cases in which clients and home care workers do not speak the same language or share a common culture. As one home attendant stated, "You go into their homes. You have to learn to cook their food, their way. We are all from different cultures. You have to learn to respect different things." These home attendants reported that the best way to cross cultures was to try to learn key words from a different language. This in itself becomes a bond between clients and workers and a bridge across cultures.

Despite the concern for cultural competence and its assessment, it is difficult to identify studies that examine the relationship between cultural competence and home care outcomes. One would expect a host of better outcomes to follow from culturally sensitive home care: for example, greater adherence to medication, quicker return to function, greater consumer satisfaction, and lower rates of rehospitalization. But at this point empirical data are unavailable. A recent systematic review of home nursing interventions is notable for the absence of any cultural variables in assessing home care outcomes (Liebel et al., 2009).

Including Families in Home Care

A second need suggested by the social-ecological approach is investigation of better ways to include families in home care. As indicated earlier, the bedrock of home- and community-based services is family care (Levine et al., 2006). Studies of the actual work of family caregivers, how these tasks relate to "formal" or paid care, and the impact of such tasks on caregivers' own lives are critical for understanding the kinds of services that will be needed to allow patients with extensive needs to remain in their homes. Yet despite extensive research on family caregiving, it is surprising how little research examines interactions between families and home care providers. Since the combination of family and paid formal care is increasingly common (and modal in service-rich urban areas, such as New York City), this gap is doubly surprising. Also, the challenges of agency handoffs to families, as when home health care coverage ends (and cases are closed), remain mostly unexplored. Few studies follow family caregivers through the process of beginning and ending formal home care or training and continued recalibration of home medical technologies.

By all indications, families are extremely active even when patients are receiving paid home care services. In our study of patients discharged with stroke and traumatic brain injury (Levine et al., 2006), we found that family caregivers provided about three-quarters of the weekly care (32 of 43 total hours) while families received weekly insurance-based home health care services, regardless of type of insurance coverage. About three-quarters of the families were providing personal care, and most were delivering nursing services, including dispensing medications, monitoring symptoms, checking blood pressure, and other tasks performed by nurses on their visits. A smaller proportion was managing equipment and providing physical/occupational therapy, speech therapy, and cognitive remediation.

Thus, families are by no means passive and must be considered active partners in care. Yet home care agencies do not, for the most part, treat them this way. Our study showed that families in some cases are barred from seeing complete medical information or care plans (because of Health Insurance Portability and Accountability Act regulations), even in their own homes. Nor are they always alerted in advance of the date of case closings. Only about half the family caregivers in our study were notified of case closing in time to make adequate preparations.

A key gap in research and policy, then, is to understand how families and formal home care providers interact: what the points of friction are and how coordination between the two can be enhanced. A randomized trial of greater inclusion of families in the home care process might be very informative for improving outcomes.

One such experiment is currently being assessed—a form of consumer-directed care. The Cash and Counseling Demonstration and Evaluation allowed families eligible for personal assistance home care services in Arkansas, Florida, and New Jersey to take greater control of the hiring, training, and use of aides for people with severe disabilities, including mental illness, across the life span.[1] As part of the evaluation of the program, a comparison group receiving traditional agency-directed care was identified in each state. Results from a number of the programs suggest that greater inclusion of families in care planning and management results in positive outcomes, including satisfaction with care arrangements, reliability of paid caregivers, meeting patient needs, caregiver stress, and patient quality of life. Notably, risks of adverse events and new health problems did not differ between control and treatment groups, suggesting that greater family inclusion is at least as safe as agency-directed care (Shen et al., 2008). Direct-care workers in the experimental condition also reported better

[1]As of 2009, the Cash and Counseling program had been renamed and extended to at least 12 additional states (see http://www.bc.edu/schools/gssw/nrcpds/meta-elements/pdf/NewCenterReleaseDraf.pdf).

work conditions and greater satisfaction with their jobs (Foster, Dale, and Brown, 2007).

The Cash and Counseling Demonstration and Evaluation suggests that greater inclusion of families and due recognition of cultural expectations for care may improve home care. The demonstration focused mainly on personal assistance services, but it would be valuable to determine if families in the intervention arm also used medical technologies more effectively or were better able to adapt homes for the use of such technologies.

Recognizing the Key Role of Neighborhoods and Communities

The role of neighborhoods in home care is perhaps the least well researched of the three elements in the social-ecological framework. Many studies report an independent effect of neighborhood on access to primary care, emergency care, hospice services, and specialist services; but I was not able to identify studies that examine neighborhood factors in access to home care. As mentioned earlier, even when low-income communities are adequately serviced by home care agencies, the effectiveness of such services may be lower than in other communities because of poor housing stock, unreliable access to electricity or telephone service, crime, and lack of community supports. More subtle effects of social capital are likely to be relevant as well, with fewer linkages between agencies and poorer integration of agencies with other community-based institutions. The result is less efficient exchange of information and slower diffusion of innovations. The latter may be particularly important for the use of new home care technologies.

A key gap in research in this domain is a multilevel analysis of neighborhood factors in home care outcomes. Such research would determine if outcomes for home care are poorer in lower income communities after appropriate control for case mix and service delivery. Positive findings would be a strong argument for the relevance of social capital in individual health outcomes and would support other studies that have shown such neighborhood effects as, for example, the recurrence of coronary syndromes and risk of rehospitalization (Scheffler et al., 2008).

Finally, in keeping with the social-ecological approach, it is important to conduct analyses that examine cross-level relationships among culture, social relationships, and communities. These will be difficult until further studies, as suggested here, are conducted in each of the component areas.

Workforce Training

Training the home care workforce in cultural differences and the complexities of family relationships is critical. As mentioned earlier, many home health care agencies have begun such efforts. The Cash and Counseling program suggests that families themselves can train the workforce in such sensitivity, with benefits to both consumer and provider.

Personal assistance paraprofessionals, respiratory technicians, physical and occupational therapists, home health care nurses, and social work case managers all bring their own cultural expectations to home care. These expectations are drawn from personal experience as well as professional training and socialization.

Among home care paraprofessionals, differences in culture of origin between providers and consumers are likely to be large. This is low-income work, with minimal training and little opportunity for career advancement. In urban areas, home care paraprofessionals are likely to be minorities or immigrants. In our research, these workers reported discrimination and often exploitation from patient consumers. The home attendants we interviewed were frankly embarrassed by the lack of compassion some families showed for their clients and had much higher expectations for care than these families. This, in itself, made for some tension, as when home care attendants stayed longer than required to address a need that should have been a family's responsibility. Home attendants had to be resocialized in some cases as caregivers not to give out their telephone numbers, not to accept gifts, and not to buy food for a neglected client. They had to learn that some home situations were unsuitable for home care and required agency intervention.

Professional organizations have begun to develop appropriate training for home care workers, particularly in social work, paraprofessional home care, and nursing. But similar programs are not available for the growing group of technicians who train families in respiratory care, the use of communication assistance devices, or new and emerging technologies. This is an area ripe for development, and professional licensing organizations would do well to learn from other clinical specialties and consider requiring such training for certification.

HYPOTHESES FOR FUTURE RESEARCH

This inquiry suggests a number of hypotheses for future research, some of which were mentioned earlier, all drawing on the social-ecological framework developed for home care. I conclude with a list of hypotheses relevant to the adaptation of homes to accommodate advanced medical technologies. These may help guide future research in the area:

- Family caregivers who do not express the consensus view on home adaptation for medical or supportive care will be less efficient in decision making regarding home care and perhaps risk poorer outcomes for patients.

- Families with a more expansive meaning of the home as a site for care will be more receptive to adapting homes for advanced medical technologies.
- Cultures with a strong bias toward home care and away from institutional care will be more receptive to the adaptation of homes.
- Greater subordination of an individual's interests to those of the family (familism) will be associated with greater adaptation of homes.
- Even if families in different cultural groups are equally receptive to the use of medical technologies, minority families in less resourced neighborhoods or communities may be less likely to gain access.
- Families in resource-poor communities will accept greater flexibility or standardization of services to obtain home care, whatever their own preferences, with potential for conflict between families and providers.

Interventions in which families exert greater control over vendors and providers, like the Cash and Counseling Demonstration and Evaluation, may promote more effective home use of emerging medical technologies.

How to Enhance Home Health Care with What Is Known Now

This review suggests that successful adoption of home care technologies depends on individual human factors but also the context in which individuals live, including the social, cultural, and community resources available to them. One implication of the social-ecological approach to home health care, then, is the need to consider these factors in adoption decisions, which implies an expanded approach to human factors. By way of conclusion, it is worth highlighting two approaches to enhancing home health care, currently available, suggested by this approach.

First, the focus on social factors suggests that patients may adapt technologies in ways unanticipated by designers. People fit the technologies into their daily lives and in ways that accommodate culture and family dynamics. For example, patients seek ways to use the technologies but also to be free of them (Fex, Ek, and Soderhamn, 2009). They may begin with attention to instruction but then innovate and improvise as they fit the use of the technologies into the rhythms of family life. When possible, patients find ways to make technologies less bulky, noisy, clumsy, and heavy. These innovations could suggest changes in design.

Second, social and community factors can also be seen as resources rather than constraints in the adoption of technologies. For example, low self-efficacy is an important obstacle to successful adoption. It may be possible to harness social and community factors to promote self-efficacy. In fact, community self-help organizations organized around home health care technologies already go a long way toward this end. Many patient support groups seek to develop patient self-efficacy in this area. These groups invite vendors or therapists to demonstrate equipment and often introduce new patients to patients who have already adopted it. These efforts represent important enhancements to home health care that emerge from a social-ecological perspective.

ABOUT THE AUTHOR

Steven M. Albert is professor in the Graduate School of Public Health at the University of Pittsburgh. His research focuses on the assessment of health outcomes in aging and chronic disease, including physical and cognitive function, health service use and the cost of care, quality of life, and clinical decision making.

REFERENCES

Albert, S.M. (1990). The dependent elderly, home health care, and strategies of household adaptation. In J.F. Gubrium and A. Sankar (Eds.), *The home care experience: Ethnography and policy* (pp. 19-36). Newbury Park, CA: Sage.

Albert, S.M. (1991). Cognition of caregiving tasks: Multidimensional scaling of the caregiver task domain. *Gerontologist, 13*(6), 726-734.

Albert, S.M. (2002). *Home attendants speak about home care: A guide to home care, spoken by the women who provide personal assistance/home attendant care to frail elders in New York City.* New York: Fan Fox and Leslie R. Samuels Foundation.

Albert, S.M., and Cattell, M.G. (1994). *Old age in global perspective: Cross-cultural and cross-national views.* New York: G.K. Hall.

Albert, S.M., and Freedman, V.A. (2010). *Public health and aging: An introduction to maximizing function and well-being.* New York: Springer.

Albert, S.M., Harlap, S., and Caplan, L. (2004). Cancer screening among older women in a culturally insular community. *Preventive Medicine, 39,* 649-656.

Albert, S.M., Simone, B., Brassard, A., Stern, Y., and Mayeux, R. (2005). Medicaid home care services and survival in New York City. *Gerontologist, 45,* 609-616.

Almeida, J., Molnar, B.E., Kawachi, I., and Subramanian, S.V. (2009). Ethnicity and nativity status as determinants of perceived social support: Testing the concept of familism. *Social Science and Medicine, 68,* 1,852-1,858.

Austin, C.D., McClelland, R.W., and Gursansky, D. (2006). Linking case management and community development. *Care Management Journal, 7,* 162-168.

Barris, R., Kielhofner, G., Levine, R.E., and Neville, A. (1985). Occupation as interaction with the environment. In G. Kielhofner (Ed.), *A model for human occupation* (pp. 42-62). Baltimore: Williams and Wilkins.

Becker, G., Beyene, Y., Newsom, E., and Mayen, N. (2003). Creating continuity through mutual assistance: Intergenerational reciprocity in four ethnic groups. *Journal of Gerontology: Social Sciences, 58,* S151-S159.

Bronfenbrenner, U. (1979). *The ecology of human development.* Cambridge, MA: Harvard University Press.

Campinha-Bacote, J. (2002). The process of cultural competence in the delivery of healthcare services: A model of care. *Journal of Transcultural Nursing, 13*, 181-184.

Chen, J.Y., Diamant, A., Pourat, N., and Kagawa-Singer, M. (2005). Racial/ethnic disparities in the use of preventive services among the elderly. *American Journal of Preventive Medicine, 29*, 388-395.

Clark, M. (1972). Cultural values and dependency in later life. In D.O. Cowgill and L.D. Holmes (Eds.), *Aging and modernization* (pp. 263-274). New York: Appleton-Century-Crofts.

Coon, D.W., Rubert, M., Solano, N., Mausbach, B., Kraemer, H., Arguelles, T., Haley, W.E., Thompson, L.W., and Gallagher-Thompson, D. (2004). Well-being, appraisal, and coping in Latina and Caucasian female dementia caregivers: Findings from the REACH study. *Aging and Mental Health, 8*, 330-345.

Crist, J.D., Kim, S.-S., Pasvogel, A.,and Velazquez, J.H. (2009). Mexican American elders' use of home care services. *Applied Nursing Research, 22*, 26-34.

D'Andrade, R.G. (1995). *The development of cognitive anthropology*. Cambridge, UK: Cambridge University Press.

Dang, S., Remon, N., Harris, J., Malphurs, J., Sandals, L., Cabrera, A.L., and Need, D. (2008). Care coordination assisted by technology for multiethnic caregivers of persons with dementia: A pilot clinical demonstration project on caregiver burden and depression. *Journal of Telemedicine and Telecare, 14*, 443-447.

Davidhizar, R., and Bechtel, G.A. (1998). Assessing the patient from a cultural perspective. *Journal of Practical Nursing, 48*, 16-21.

Demiris, G., Oliver, D.P., Giger, J., Skubic, M., and Rantz, M. (2009). Older adults' privacy-considerations for vision-based recognition methods of eldercare applications. *Technology and Health Care, 17*, 41-48.

Dilworth-Anderson, P., Brummett, B.H., Goodwin, P., Williams, S.W., Williams, R.B., and Siegler, I.C. (2005). Effect of race on cultural justifications for caregiving. *Journal of Gerontology: Psychological Sciences, 60*, S257-S262.

Dilworth-Anderson, P., Goodwin, P.Y., and Williams, S.W. (2004). Can culture help explain the physical health effects of caregiving over time among African American caregivers? *Journal of Gerontology: Social Sciences, 59*, S138-S145.

Donald, I.P. (2009). Housing and health care for older people. *Age and Ageing, 38*, 364-367.

Dressler, W.W., Borges, C.D., Balieiro, M.C., and Dos Santos, J.E. (2005). Measuring cultural consonance: Examples with special relevance to measurement theory in anthropology. *Field Methods, 17*, 331-355.

Fex, A., Ek, A-C., and Soderhamn, O. (2009). Self-care among persons using advanced medical technology at home. *Journal of Clinical Nursing, 18*, 2,809-2,817.

Foster, L., Dale, S.B., and Brown, R. (2007). How caregivers and workers fared in Cash and Counseling. *Health Services Research, 42*, 510-532.

Gates, D.M. (2004). The epidemic of violence against healthcare workers. *Occupational and Environmental Medicine, 61*, 649-650.

Gerberich, S.G., Church, T.R., McGovern, P.M., Hansen, H.E., Nachreiner, N.M., Geisser, M.S., Ryan, A.D., Mongin, S.J., and Watt, G.D. (2004). An epidemiological study of the magnitude and consequences of work related violence: The Minnesota Nurses' Study. *Occupational and Environmental Medicine, 61*, 495-503.

Gitlin, L.N. (2003). Conducting research on home environments: Lessons learned and new directions. *Gerontologist, 43*, 628-637.

Golant, S.M. (2008). Commentary: Irrational exuberance for the aging in place of vulnerable low-income older homeowners. *Journal of Aging and Social Policy, 20*, 379-397.

Gonzalez, H.M., Haan, M.N., and Hinton, L. (2001). Acculturation and the prevalence of depression in older Mexican Americans: Baseline results of the Sacramento Area Latino Study on Aging. *Journal of the American Geriatrics Society, 49*, 948-953.

Haley, W.E., Gitlin, L.N., Wisniewski, S.R., Mahoney, D.F., Coon, D.W., Winter, L., Corcoran, M., Schinfeld, S., and Ory, M. (2004). Well-being, appraisal, and coping in African-American and Caucasian dementia caregivers: Findings from the REACH study. *Aging and Mental Health, 8*, 316-329.

Heineken, J., and McCoy, N. (2000). Establishing a bond with clients of different cultures. *Home Healthcare Nurse, 18*, 45-51.

Hinton, W.L., and Levkoff, S. (1999). Constructing Alzheimer's: Narratives of lost identities, confusion, and loneliness in old age. *Culture Medicine Psychiatry, 23*, 453-475.

Kadushin, G. (2004). Home health care utilization: A review of the research for social work. *Health and Social Work, 29*, 219-245.

Keysor, J.J., Jette, A.M., Coster, W., Bettger, J.P., and Haley, S.M. (2006). Association of environmental factors with levels of home and community participation in an adult rehabilitation cohort. *Archives of Physical Medicine and Rehabilitation, 87*, 1,566-1,575.

Kim, J.H., Knight, B.G., and Longmire, C.V. (2007). The role of familism in stress and coping processes among African American and white dementia caregivers: Effects on mental and physical health. *Health Psychology, 26*, 564-576.

Kleinman, A., Eisenberg, L., and Good, B. (1978). Culture, illness, and care: Clinical lessons from anthropologic and cross-cultural research. *Annals of Internal Medicine, 88*, 251-258.

Klinenberg, E. (2004). *Heat wave: A social autopsy of disaster in Chicago*. Chicago: University of Chicago Press.

Knox, C., and Thobaben, M. (1997). Partnerships between home care providers and client families. *Home Care Provider, 2*, 57-59.

Levine, C., Albert, S.M., Hokenstad, A., Halper, D., Hart, A.Y., and Gould, D.A. (2006). "This case is closed": The transition in family caregiving when home health care services end. *Milbank Quarterly, 84*, 305-331.

Liebel, D.V., Friedman, B., Watson, N.M., and Powers, B.A. (2009). Review of nurse home visiting interventions for community-dwelling older persons with existing disability. *Medical Care Research Review, 66*, 119-146.

Mahoney, D.F., Cloutterbuck, J., Neary, S., and Zhan, L. (2005). African-American, Chinese, and Latino family caregivers' impressions of the onset and diagnosis of dementia: Cross-cultural similarities and differences. *Gerontologist, 45*, 783-792.

Mausbach, B.T., Coon, D.W., Depp, C., Rabinowitz, Y.G., Wilson-Arias, E., Kraemer, H.C., Thompson, L.W., Lane, G., and Gallagher-Thompson. D. (2004). Ethnicity and time to institutionalization of dementia patients: A comparison of Latina and Caucasian female family caregivers. *Journal of the American Geriatrics Society, 52*, 1,077-1,084.

McElroy, K.R., Bibeau, D., Steckler, A., and Glanz, K. (1988). An ecological perspective on health promotion programs. *Health Education Quarterly, 15*, 351-377.

McGarry, J. (2009). Defining roles, relationships, boundaries and participation between elderly people and nurses within the home: An ethnographic study. *Health Social Care Community 17*, 83-91.

Meghani, S.H., Brooks, J.M., Gipson-Jones, T., Waite, R., Whitfield-Harris, L., and Deatrick, J.A. (2009). Patient-provider race-concordance: Does it matter in improving minority patients' health outcomes? *Ethnicity and Health, 14*, 107-130.

Mortality and Morbidity Weekly Review. (2008). Fatal fires associated with smoking during long-term oxygen therapy: Maine, Massachusetts, New Hampshire, and Oklahoma, 2000-2007. Reported by T. Wendling and A. Pelletier. *Mortality and Morbidity Weekly Review, 57*(31), 852-854. Available: http://www.cdc.gov/mmwr/preview/mmwrhtml/mm5731a3.htm [accessed June 2010].

Mullan, J.T., Grossman, B.R., Hernandez, M., Wong, A., Eversley, R., and Harrington, C. (2009). Focus group study of ethnically diverse low-income users of paid personal assistance services. *Home Health Care Services Quarterly, 28,* 24-44.

Murphy, R.F. (1990). *The body silent: The different world of the disabled.* New York: W.W. Norton.

Musa, D., Schulz, R., Harris, R., Silverman, M., and Thomas, S.B. (2009). Trust in the health care system and the use of preventive health services by older black and white adults. *American Journal of Public Health, 99,* 1,293-1,299.

Narayan, M.C. (1997). Cultural assessment in home healthcare. *Home Healthcare Nurse, 15,* 663-670.

Navaie-Waliser, M., Feldman, P.H., Gould, D.A., Levine, C., Kuerbis, A.N., and Donelan, K. (2001). Experiences and challenges of informal caregivers: Common themes and differences among whites, blacks, and Hispanics. *Gerontologist, 41,* 733-741.

Or, C.K.L., and Karsh, B-T. (2009). A systematic review of patient acceptance of consumer health information technology. *Journal of the American Medical Informatics Association, 16,* 550-560.

Or, C.K.L., Karsh, B-T, Severtson, D.J., and Brennan, P.F. (2006). *Patient technology acceptance model (PTAM): Exploring the potential characteristics of consumer health information technology acceptance by home care patients with chronic illness.* Santa Monica, CA: Human Factors and Ergonomics Society.

Peng, T., Navaie-Waliser, M., and Feldman, P.H. (2003). Social support, home health service use, and outcomes among four racial-ethnic groups. *Gerontologist, 43,* 503-513.

Rozario, P.A., and DeRienzis, D. (2008). Familism beliefs and psychological distress among African American women caregivers. *Gerontologist, 48*(6), 772-780.

Rubel, A.J., O'Nell, C.W., and Collado-Ardon, R. (1984). *Susto: A folk illness.* Berkeley: University of California Press.

Rubinstein, R.L. (1990). Culture and disorder in the home care experience: The home as sick room. In J.F. Gubrium and A. Sankar (Eds.), *The home care experience: Ethnography and policy* (pp. 19-36). Newbury Park, CA: Sage.

Scheffler, R.M., Brown, T.T., Syme, L., Kawachi, I., Tolstykh, I., and Iribarren, C. (2008). Community-level social capital and recurrence of acute coronary syndrome. *Social Science and Medicine, 66,* 1,603-1,613.

Shen, C., Smyer, M., Mahoney, K.J., Simon-Rusinowitz, L., Shinogle, J., Norstrand, J., Mahoney, E., Schauer, C., and del Vecchio, P. (2008). Consumer-directed care for beneficiaries with mental illness: Lessons from New Jersey's Cash and Counseling program. *Psychiatric Services, 59,* 1,299-1,306.

Small, M.L., and Jacobs, E.M. (2008). Why organizational ties matter for neighborhood effects: Resource access through childcare centers. *Social Forces, 87,* 387-414.

Sohler, N.L., Fitzpatrick, L.K., Lindsay, R.G., Anastos, K., and Chinazo, O.C. (2007). Does patient-provider racial/ethnic concordance influence ratings of trust in people with HIV infection? *AIDS and Behavior, 11,* 884-896.

Sommer, B., Avis, N., Meyer, P., Ory, M., Madden, T., Kagawa-Singer, M., Mouton, C., Rasor, N.O., and Adler, S. (1999). Attitudes toward menopause and aging across ethnic/racial groups. *Psychosomatic Medicine, 61,* 868-875.

Whitehouse, P.J., Gaines, A.D., Lindstron, H., and Graham, J.E. (2005). Anthropological contributions to the understanding of age-related cognitive impairment. *Lancet Neurology, 4,* 320-326.

Wight, R.G., Anechensel, C.S., Miller-Martinez, D., Botticello, A.L., Cummings, J.R., and Karlamanga, A.S. (2006). Urban neighborhood context, educational attainment, and cognitive function among older adults. *American Journal of Epidemiology, 163*, 1,071-1,078.

Wolff, J.L., Roter, D.L., Given, B., and Gitlin, L.N. (2009). Optimizing patient and family involvement in geriatric home care. *Journal of Healthcare Quality 31*, 24-33.

Zhan, H.J. (2004). Through a gendered lens: Explaining Chinese caregivers' task performance and care reward. *Journal of Women and Aging, 16*, 123-142.

12

Effects of Policy, Reimbursement, and Regulation on Home Health Care

Peter A. Boling

Human factors in home health care involve many stakeholders: those receiving care, families and friends, paid workers of various kinds and skill levels, employers, and communities in a broad sense, because tens of millions of individuals rely on home care each day. Despite excellent workers and advanced technology, people experience inconsistent quality, fragmented care, and poorly aligned payments. Home care remains a stepchild while health policy centers on hospitals and other facilities, physicians, pharmacies, and insurers. Despite a holistic culture, a large, dedicated workforce, and care valued by recipients, home care remains poorly understood, sometimes mistrusted, and abstract for many decision makers, and as currently organized it has limited proven ability to control overall costs. This all can change.

THE LANDSCAPE OF HOME HEALTH CARE

Societal Context, Costs, and Care Silos

There is a growing sense of crisis. Medicare cost about $500 billion in 2009 and the Medicare Hospital Insurance fund balance will be zeroed in seven years. Without a plan to "bend the cost curve," corrective options include reduced provider payments, reduced coverage, higher copayments, or taxes to raise revenues equal to about 4 percent of gross domestic product 10 years hence. The larger frame is over $2 trillion annually spent on health care, or one-sixth of the economy, impacting the nation's ability to compete internationally. Nearing the brink, people debate about the numbers of uninsured (45 million) or underinsured (80 million), public and private insurance options, regional cost variation, poor public health metrics, and financing for potential solutions while spending 30 percent more per capita than any other industrialized nation on health care.

At $57 billion in 2007 including all payers, home care is only 3 percent of U.S. health care (National Association for Homecare & Hospice, 2009) (see Figure 12-1). And like health care generally, home care is organized into separately funded categories, called silos: home health agencies, hospices, medical equipment, home health aides, pharmacy managers, medical providers, and thousands of private bureaucracies. Two key referral sources, hospitals and nursing homes, are in fiscal and regulatory silos of their own. Thus, financing promotes discontinuous care. Rules that govern the care of people with heavy chronic illness burdens result in an uncoordinated, overly costly, and hazardous delivery system that is far from patient-centered and is known for its failings (Schoen et al., 2008) (see Figure 12-2).

Some financing models, including Medicare Part C, offer opportunities to break down silos using financial risk. However, only 11.4 million people, or about a quarter of Medicare beneficiaries, are in such payment models (Henry J. Kaiser Family Foundation, 2009, 2010). And there are

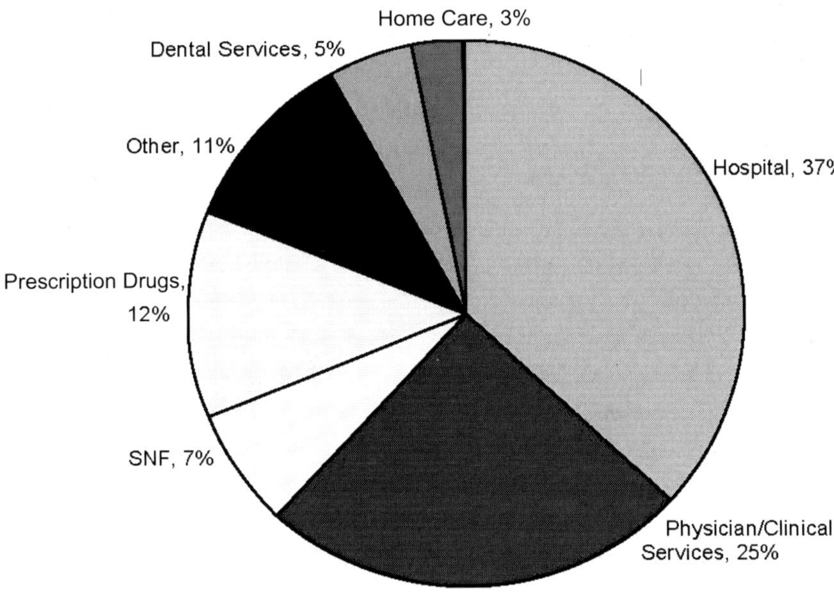

FIGURE 12-1 Personal health care expenditures, 2006.
NOTE: SNF = skilled nursing facility.
SOURCE: National Association for Homecare & Hospice (2009).

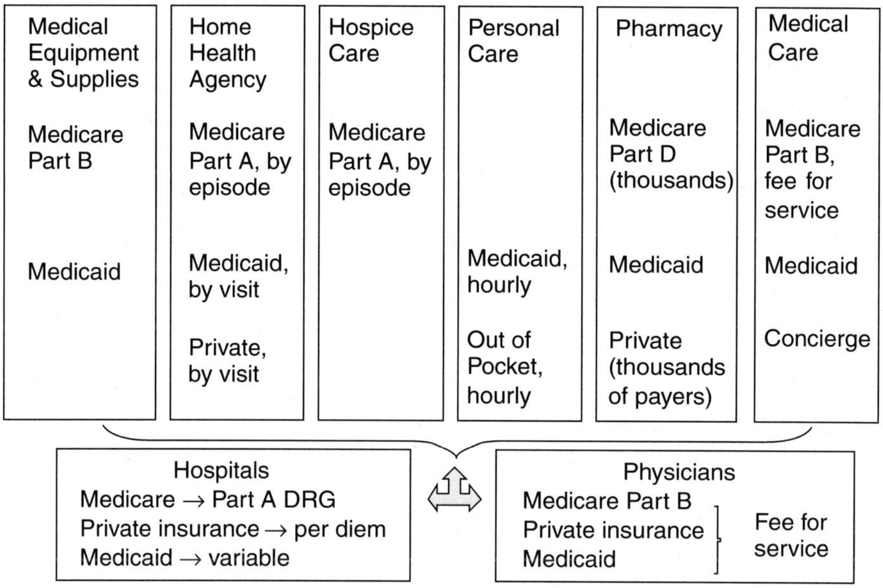

FIGURE 12-2 Home care silos and payment sources.

other concerns. Importantly, managed care enrollees are disproportionately healthy, and most high-cost seniors rely on standard Medicare benefits. Even in risk-bearing entities, integrated at-home care with a strong medical component is rare. Reasons for this lack of emphasis include the origins of managed care models in conventional settings and finance systems, competing corporate interests for the insurer, and lack of senior management familiarity with what advanced home care can provide.

However, portable technologies and experiences with caring for sick patients in the community are now lighting new paths in which fully developed and integrated interdisciplinary home care teams, which include physicians and other medical providers, work together with other providers of care and community resources to produce better care at lower cost.

Population Need for Home Care

Individual needs for community-based care vary. Although it is simplified, and acknowledging that some patients fall into more than one of these categories, for the purposes of framing, I divide the general population into subsets based on typical care needs (see Figure 12-3). Their needs vary by group, as do the human factors impacts of policy, regulation, and available care options.

Group A contains healthy, predominantly younger persons who are functional and independent but might be considered home care users if one includes public health measures deployed at home to promote healthy living, such as reminder systems to lose weight or stop smoking and web-based self-help tools for episodic illness (flu, ankle sprain, rash).

Group B members are mobile and can readily visit physician offices but have chronic diseases, such as high blood pressure, diabetes, asthma, or sleep apnea. Home modification, diet, exercise, and monitoring are routinely used at home, and in-home care improves outcomes (Ogedegbe and Schoenthaler, 2006; Shelledy et al., 2009). Examples are blood pressure monitors (if accurate) (Akpolat et al., 2009), glucose monitors, peak flow meters, asthma action plans, machines for maintaining continuous positive airway pressure, air filters, and removal of mold-bearing items. Individuals use the Internet to send data to physicians from home or to receive medical advice. Broadly construed, they are home care users.

Group C members either have conditions from birth, like cerebral palsy or other chronic conditions—which are often neurological or mus-

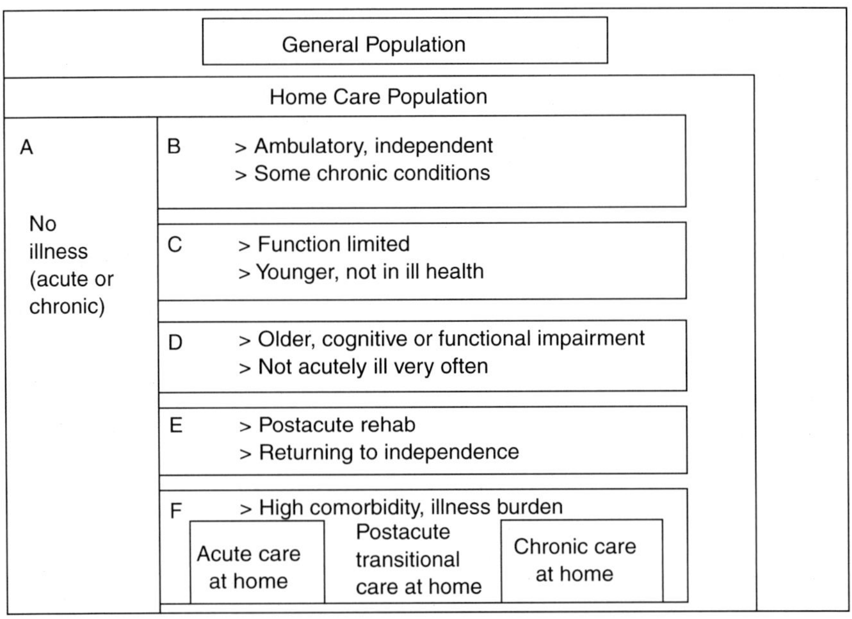

FIGURE 12-3 The home care population and its typical care needs.

culoskeletal and severely limit function but are not progressive—or disabling permanent injuries acquired in childhood or adult life. An example is paraplegia. With assistive technologies, many such individuals function independently, are infrequently ill, and are rarely hospitalized. Group C members use home care for support of activities of daily living (ADLs) and instrumental activities of daily living (IADLs), often in the form of medical devices plus personal assistance with bathing, dressing, and mobility. Group C members fall through cracks in insurance coverage or are harmed by bureaucracy used to control cost and fraud. For example, a 50-year-old quadriplegic man, free of wounds for decades, now has a deep, dangerous Stage 4 pressure wound that will take months to heal because of a 2-week administrative delay in replacing a damaged support surface.

Group D members are generally older, frail, and functionally impaired but medically stable. Many have dementia or inborn cognitive impairment that requires supervision and standby help to prevent injury or to remain in the community. Also prevalent are advanced stages of disabling conditions, like arthritis or prior stroke, that mandate physical support each day from equipment and other persons. However, because these illnesses do not cause frequent acute medical crises, Group D individuals use limited skilled home care. Care plans do not change from month to month. Group D members have difficulty accessing office-based medical care because of immobility. However, in Group D money cannot be readily saved through case management, other than in a small subset whose eventual nursing home placement can be deferred by socially oriented caregiver support. Group D needs long-term home care. Third-party coverage is largely limited to those in poverty (Medicaid) or those who are affluent (long-term care insurance).

Group E members of all ages are in postacute care, recovering from an acute episode like major surgery, acute illness, or trauma. Return to independence is expected, and baseline health is fairly good. Some may receive intravenous therapy at home or at work for a curable infection. Technically advanced home care may be extensive, but its use is temporary. Current Medicare and private insurance payment designs best suit the episodic needs of Group E.

Group F includes most of the need for what typically comes to mind when thinking about home health care. Users vary in age from infants to very old adults, carry heavy chronic illness burden, often with end-stage organ system failure (heart, lung, liver, kidney, brain), have multiple concurrent conditions, and have significant persistent functional deficits, often three or more, and in many cases five or six, ADL deficits.

In Group F, infants might be premature with resultant home ventilator dependence or a condition requiring artificial feeding. Imagine the mother, caring for three other children and a household, trying to manage these daily responsibilities and also bring such a technology-dependent child to the doctor's office. Younger adults in Group F might have complications of childhood diabetes or cystic fibrosis.

Older adults, however, make up the majority of Group F. They have a mix of diseases, with no one predominant. This mix is shaped by conditions that are most prevalent: stroke, vascular disease, emphysema, complicated diabetes, and more. The variety and complexity of conditions challenge clinicians and require diverse skills. Illness acuity and stability fluctuate. Individuals rapidly get sick enough to be hospitalized. Group F members move frequently between health care silos and have multiple changes in condition that require revised care plans and active, longitudinal coordination among providers. Errors are made in as many as half of the transitions between settings. Most of the 2 to 3 million Group F members deteriorate with time and die, with an average life expectancy of 3 to 4 years.

Functional Dependency, Chronic Illness, and Service Use

Activity limitation due to chronic conditions occurs in 7 percent of children and 42 percent of people ages 75 and over. ADL limitations (walking, transferring, bathing, dressing, eating, or toileting) increase with age, and severe deficits (three or more ADLs) occur in 1.9 million community-dwelling U.S. adults (see Table 12-1) (Centers for Disease Control and Prevention, 2009).

Among community dwellers ages 65-74, the National Health Interview Survey revealed that 912,000 out of 17.4 million people (5 percent) cannot sit for 2 hours (are bedfast) (Centers for Disease Control and Prevention, 2009), and about 15 to 20 percent need help to walk. Such people often have difficulty leaving home for health care. These functional deficits are on the final common path, where the combination of severe illness and incapacity drive health care costs.

Sorting the Medicare population by cost, the top 5 percent used 43 percent of resources, with average costs of $63,000 in 2002 (Holtz-Eakin, 2005).

TABLE 12-1 Community-Dwelling Adults with Three or More ADL Deficits

Age Group	Percent with 3+ ADL Deficits	Number of Persons Affected
18-44	0.2	276,000
45-54	0.5	228,000
55-64	0.9	272,000
65-74	1.6	299,000
75-84	3.2	439,000
85+	9.7	378,000

NOTE: ADL = activities of daily living.

Some were catastrophic cases, some fully recovered, and some died. Those who lived 5 years (the majority) were intermittently high-cost users from month to month. In 2005, the top 10 percent of Medicare beneficiaries used 63 percent of resources, with average annual costs in the top 10 percent bracket of $44,000 (Potetz and Cubanski, 2009). A similar pattern is seen in younger (Medicaid) and employer-based insured groups.

Impaired physical function itself predicts high costs. In 2004, simply having three or more ADL deficits conveyed average costs of $32,000 per person (Medicare Beneficiary Survey) compared with $15,000 with one or two ADL deficits and $7,000 with no ADL deficits.

Along with function, the presence of multimorbid conditions drives cost. People with five or more chronic conditions use two-thirds of the resources, receive far more prescriptions, see a multitude of doctors, and have exponentially more hospital stays, including many that are preventable (Goldfield et al., 2008). Cost-containment strategies based on a single disease or on a nurse care coordinator who is not a core health care team member are unlikely to succeed, as most recently shown in the failed Medicare Health Support demonstration (Linden and Adler-Milstein, 2008) and the Coordinated Care Demonstration (Brown et al., 2008).

No published national analysis directly links ADL deficits, home health use, and overall costs at the individual level. However, because of the close link with hospital use, home care users probably do include most of the costliest beneficiaries. In Medicare Part A, for example, each year about 3 million people meet the homebound and skilled care criteria and receive skilled home health care at some point, totaling about 7 million discrete episodes each year.

Summing up, there are 3-4 million relatively immobile people in U.S. communities who span all ages, are sick with multiple concurrent illnesses, and have intermittently high health care costs. Many are not terminally ill (i.e., will not die in 6 months or less) and do not qualify for hospice; these people regularly fall through the cracks of the formal care system.

Finally, every discussion of home care must include unpaid family caregivers, who do most of the work. Caregiving falls to people who are not trained as clinicians yet are required to do technical clinical work along with basic daily care. Learned skills include intravenous therapy, tracheostomy and ventilator support, wound care, catheter changes, and medication oversight, work that in other care settings is restricted to licensed nurses. Most caregivers are women, their average duration exceeds 4 years, and they average 25 hours per week (Giovannetti et al., 2009). In this role, they lose time from work, lose employment, and develop health problems, with adverse economic consequences for worker and employer (Coe and Van Houten, 2009). Employers' cost for full-time employees with caregiving roles is $17.1 billion ($2,441 per employee), and total cost to employers for full-time, employed caregivers is $33.6 billion (Metlife, 2006). This is a significant part of the human factors equation. Chapter 7 of this volume discusses informal caregivers in detail.

FIVE SERIOUS PROBLEMS OF LONG-TERM HOME HEALTH CARE

Problem 1: Human ADL Support, Medicaid, and Long-Term Care Coverage

The lack of a consistent national policy on long-term care or of a systems approach to care at home is a major overarching problem for home care that daily affects paid providers, care recipients, and their families, who are trying to solve these problems.

In patient Groups C and D, most paid home care is long-term care, financed through Medicaid or out of pocket. Medicare does not cover long-term care, and most U.S. citizens cannot afford or have not purchased long-term care insurance. This leaves no options for millions of older persons or for younger functionally impaired persons without property or income. It leaves professional care providers daily scrambling to help find resources from a polyglot of local charities and other programs that have inadequate scope, wax and wane, and are difficult to find.

Care recipients who qualify for Medicaid and their families depend heavily on paid, unskilled caregivers who may be in the home from 4 to 16 hours per day for ADL support and standby assistance. Even when they can find work, low-income care recipients and family members avoid seeking employment (income) because they risk losing coverage for needed equipment, medication, and personal assistance. People even divorce to secure Medicaid coverage. Long-term care is not covered by most employer-based insurance. Moving across state lines to be near other family members who can help with care can be problematic, since state Medicaid benefits vary greatly. In addition, states cannot carry deficits and may abruptly reduce services when fiscally stressed, whereas federal programs like Medicare are more protected.

Along with impacts on care recipients and families who need the services, health care providers and case managers spend many frustrating hours each week on securing coverage. Medicaid is often the key. Medicaid requires a comprehensive means test, with a threshold near the federal poverty level that varies from state to state.

Medicaid approval and access to services depends on review of detailed information about personal finances and often takes months. Once coverage is approved, weeks more may pass before services start—which can be a long time during a sociomedical crisis. Coverage often lapses due to failure to receive or complete annual update forms, wrong addresses, changes in regulation, or small changes in household finances. All these policy and regulatory gaps affect both families and home care workers in terms of burden and care outcomes.

Once coverage is in place, medical providers who have little training in or knowledge of long-term care are deluged with volumes of documents to review and sign for supplies, equipment, and services—such as identical forms every 6 months for diapers, disposable pads, or feedings. The paperwork, with the invisible rules behind it, is a de facto throttle on the system. The work, uncompensated and tedious, is an inefficient, ineffective way to manage resource use. Overburdened providers may sign papers to "clear the stack" without scrutiny or fail to sign important forms. The administrative burden derives from the limited financing of long-term care, which generates regulatory demands to document need and use. The lack of incentives for clinicians to engage in oversight has led to a dearth of qualified clinical managers who know what services are needed and what is superfluous or fraudulent.

Because Medicaid long-term care financing is a key theme, it is important to consider the impact of state payment policy on care. States vary fivefold in Medicaid funding for community-based care, which averages 2.3 percent of gross state product (GSP): in 2004, the range was from less than 1 percent in the Dakotas and Nebraska to 4.1 percent in Massachusetts and 4.8 percent in New York. By contrast, nursing home care averaged 7.4 percent of GSP, ranging from 1.9 percent in Alaska and 3.2 percent in Nevada to 12.2 percent in Connecticut. New York and Massachusetts are also above average in nursing home spending, consistent with relatively generous Medicaid programs in those states (see http://www.kff.org/). Some argue that targeted and well-managed Medicaid community-based services meet needs more effectively (Kemper et al., 2008) and reduce state nursing home bills by more than the home care cost. However, state policy has evolved slowly, despite much expert concurrence with such concepts.

The quality of home health aide and personal care also is a recognized national issue (Stone and Newcomer, 2009). There is minimal required training, and caregivers are paid near minimum wage. Commonly reported problems include rapid turnover and aides failing to appear, being rude, stealing, or doing poor work. Of the typical hourly cost of $18, half goes to agency overhead. Conversely, in many cases aides are trusted like family members; donate their own time, money and possessions to the household of the care recipient; and are invaluable. A new survey called Consumer Assessment of Healthcare Providers and Systems (CAHPS) for home and community-based care services has been created to systematically measure quality. The CAHPS program is a family of standardized surveys that ask consumers and patients to evaluate health care experiences, covering issues like provider communication skills and service accessibility.

Individual home care agreements are made by private individuals with other private individuals. With no agency overhead, these workers are paid more. Such arrangements are treasured by those who find reliable help and are difficult to count. Initiatives such as the Cash and Counseling Demonstration and Evaluation (Foster, Dale, and Brown, 2007), in which care recipients or families manage home care using public funds, have succeeded in improving quality and afford insight into the human factors dimensions of long-term care in the community (Foster, Dale, and Brown, 2007; Kemper, 2007; Wiener, 2007).

Between CAHPS and creative new models like Cash and Counseling, plus the increasing affluence of baby boomers, the personal care component of home health care is moving forward, but it will have to contend with the increasing ratio of older persons needing care to younger persons available to deliver it and will increasingly depend on an international workforce.

Problem 2: Assistive Technology and ADL Support

A second core feature of long-term care at home is assistive technology, including durable medical equipment (DME). Financing is less problematic in this area than for personal care, since devices are funded by both Medicaid and Medicare Part B (with a 20 percent copayment for some). Equipment includes basic items, like wheelchairs, walkers, commodes, and hospital beds, and advanced items, like pneumatic patient lifts and powered personal vehicles (Brummel-Smith and Dangiolo, 2009). Key human factors principles include recognizing clinical need, selecting the right device for the person and care setting, training the user, and ensuring maintenance. Although a new era is on the horizon with technical capacity for "smart houses," the nation is far from ready to disseminate this costly technology to the broad population in need.

Financing approaches include rental (for high-cost devices), monthly fees, rent-to-own, and direct purchase. A Medicare issue arises under rent-to-own: when rental ends in ownership, service support often stops. Items wear out or break. Some repairs are covered; other items are replaced. Too often, bureaucratic delays have serious human clinical consequences.

Historically, profits from high-end items have fed durable medical equipment providers' bottom lines. These profits paid for customer services (trained support staff who deliver equipment and teach users) and charity care (forgiveness of unattainable copayments). With reduced Medicare payments, support services are shrinking. In most locations, competition and regulatory oversight still ensure new or newly refurbished equipment, but the quality of training and support is uncertain. Further Medicare cuts could weaken support because of the cost of expert respiratory and occupational therapists. Other human factors impacts include fear and risks associated with the equipment: some devices frighten users and families. Risk of injury or death comes with improper use, so training and support are important. Mandatory oversight of quality is provided by external accrediting bodies and Medicare program surveyors, but it is limited.

Unfettered direct-to-consumer marketing for high-end durable medical equipment, like scooters and lift chairs, plus low-cost items, like moist heating pads that lack proven benefit but feel good, is another problem. Individuals are told "all you need is an order from your doctor" without knowledge of whether they meet coverage criteria. This puts physicians in an awkward position. Informing consumers may relieve unmet needs, yet marketing creates both overuse and inherent resistance among physicians to approve even the legitimate services that are lost in the background of overuse.

Oversight of durable medical equipment is complex. Some is managed under contracts through Medicare Part A organizations, like hospices and nursing homes. This secondary arrangement was devised to prevent duplication and target services, but it complicates physicians' and discharge coordinators' roles and alters patient choice. Ordering durable medical equipment requires specialized knowledge. Regulations are opaque; a physician cannot see what is covered when doing paperwork. Overall, misdirected use of durable medical equipment is modest compared with excessive and redundant diagnostic tests and procedures performed by medical specialists and readily accepted by patients and payers.

As technology advances, it will be increasingly vital to educate consumers about selecting the right device and about safe use. I recall recently talking with a young woman now caring for her ventilator-dependent 50-year-old mother at home. The daughter is bright and has learned a lot about highly technical clinical care in a short time. Yet she cannot cope with this challenge without substantial ongoing professional support.

Problem 3: Inadequate Postacute Care Model for Complex Patients

The transition from hospital to home and the immediate posthospital interval are vital. Unacceptable rates of serious errors are well documented, affecting perhaps half of cases: wrong medicines, no medicines, no follow-up plans, and little or no clinical information for postacute providers are common rather than exceptional (Boling, 2009). Postacute home health care is delivered by teams of nurses, therapists, aides, and social workers employed by home health agencies. The care plan is reconstructed at home with limited data. Physician involvement is minimal, making home care the only setting in which seriously ill individuals are cared for almost entirely without active physician input.

Medicare Part A has the largest influence on this home care silo. Cost-based financing in the 1980s and 1990s was associated with exponential growth and evolution into chronic care rather than the postacute care specified by the 1965 Medicare legislation. The 1997 Balanced Budget Act abruptly transformed the industry (Murkofsky and Alston, 2009). Although gradual modulation was reportedly intended, a regressive Interim Payment System (1997), followed 3 years later by at-risk prospective payment (2000), caused a 50 percent drop in service within 2 years. This affected care recipients and families and caused major losses in the industry talent pool. Agencies rebounded under the Prospective Payment System (PPS) and its defined payments for 60-day episodes. Payment is adjusted for case mix and ranges fivefold in about 80 categories, averaging about $2,400. Visits per 60-day interval dropped sharply (from 50 to 20) with renewed emphasis on postacute care and efficiency. After initial comprehensive assessment, care focuses on defined goals. Episodes are shorter and families feel pressure from the first day to assume responsibility for care, including wound care and other newly learned technical skills.

Unlike Medicare, the private insurance sector has thousands of payers and no central data source to help evaluate quality or impact. Generally, home care is a small budget item, paid by the visit and approved a few visits at a time. Home care can be used effectively as an integrated feature in some large health systems (Suter et al., 2008), and technologies like telemedicine have been used to augment home care. However, these exemplars are notable for their scarcity.

The quality of Medicare home health agency postacute care is measured nationally using OASIS data. Risk-adjusted outcome data, (Home Care Compare), publicly reported by the Centers for Medicare & Medicaid Services (CMS), are used to improve quality (Schade et al., 2009), modulate payment, and compete. Most agencies are accredited by either the Joint Commission or the Community Health Accreditation Program (CHAP). All are subject to Medicare audits. These rigorous evaluations focus on regulatory compliance and the care process within the silo, not on outcomes across time and settings. Despite instances of excessive or inappropriate care, most fraud and abuse were weeded out in the 1990s by the Office of the Inspector General.

Current home health care models perform well for individuals on a trajectory back to full recovery after an acute illness (Group E), but there are problems in Group F when individuals have advanced chronic illness that waxes and wanes. Hospitalization was frequent under cost-based reimbursement and has increased under PPS: the national risk-adjusted rate in a 60-day Medicare episode is 29 percent (National Association for Home Care and Hospice, 2009). Notably, in 2004 the best 1,750 Medicare agencies averaged 17 percent, while the worst 1,750 averaged 47 percent, showing both high acuity (the best hit only 17 percent) and opportunity for improvement in others. Similarly, in the final 2 years of life, marked geographic variation in home care spending and a positive correlation between home health care cost and hospitalization argue against the case for effective substitution (Wennberg et al., 2008). Finally, 1 in 7 Medicare home health episodes ends in hospitalization within 2 weeks; this highlights the need to engage immediately and actively.

This overall mediocre record relates to operating in silos, poor communication, lack of aggressive medication reconciliation, absence of medical care and skilled case management in the early weeks, and thus inability to respond to changes in condition. In 35 percent of cases, there is no medical encounter during the home health episode, showing limited physician participation (Wolff et al., in press). Even when there are encounters, they are not timely and not provided to individuals who need them most. However, the exemplars show what is possible when there is a systematic approach to home-based care as a defined focus.

The value of integrating active medical management with home health agency work is supported by transitional care research. In rigorous clinical trials, advanced practice nurses were assigned to selected, high-risk cases in the hospital, and the cases were followed closely at home for a month (Naylor et al., 1999), producing significant cost savings (50 percent). Issues remain of "scalability" and who will care for graduates of a new "transitional care" silo when they can't return to a clinic. Savings in 2004 were about $5,000 per case.

Less intensive but perhaps more scalable are "guided care" (Leff et al., 2009) or transition coach strategies (Coleman et al., 2006), which rely more on the health record and the care recipient or caregiver. In this model, busy office-based physicians with many competing responsibilities are expected to address medical management needs. It is unclear whether this approach is robust enough to alter outcomes for complex, unstable patients. Savings are about $500 to $1,000 per patient.

Problem 4: No Longitudinal Care in Complex Cases with High Comorbidity

Ultimately, home care for Group F members with high comorbidity suffers greatly from intermittency and lack of medical continuity. Frail individuals move into and out of skilled care and lack consistent physician contact over time and during critical intervals; one-third of the time there is no billed physician service during a home health care episode (Wolff et al., in press). This burdens the care recipients, families, and the nonphysician home care professionals who need physician guidance on the complex medical issues that are prevalent.

When home health agency care starts, the agency team performs extensive data gathering and then provides care. If care recipients don't die, they improve or they go to a hospital or nursing home and are discharged from home health care. Many different physicians are involved only tangentially, and there is little continuity. At home, individuals and their families lack access to trusted medical advice when having trouble and receive little in-person medical care until they are sick enough to visit an emergency department. Functional deficits hinder physician office visits. If they make the trip, they need advance notice and expensive transportation, while worsening health may afford little warning time to schedule appointments. Family members must take time off work to attend physician encounters. Born of financing mechanisms, this is an expensive care model that is ill suited to population needs. The care model adversely affects care recipients, their families, the home health care staff, and the physicians involved.

Physicians started fading from home care 40 years ago, as they became busy with other roles and house call fees failed to keep pace with costs. When the 1992 Resource-Based Relative Value Scale (RBRVS) sought to level the playing field between procedural and cognitive services in Medicare payment, house calls were rare and were never addressed. House calls were formally valued in 1998 through advocacy by the American Academy of Home Care Physicians and secondarily supported by family physicians and geriatricians. In 2001, visits to group homes and assisted living facilities were also upgraded so that margins were thin but adequate for those with a passion for this work to form new practices. In 2007, proposed payment cuts of 20 percent on house call codes again threatened new mobile practices. Urgent advocacy reduced the cuts, reinforcing need for constant vigilance and the human impact of public policy on care providers.

Unsolved problems also remain for house calls in the Medicare fee-for-service arena. The practice expense component (about half of the total service code value) omits travel time, and cost inputs are based on an office scenario. Furthermore, since 1997 state Medicaid programs are not obliged to pay Medicare Part B copayments; most pay below Medicare's 80th percentile, forcing a 20 percent loss on those who serve low-income populations. Case management, which occupies about 30 percent of work time in home medical care, is underrepresented in the fee schedule. New codes for reviewing and signing home health agency care plans and overseeing complex agency cases were added in 1995 and 2001. Although well meant, the oversight codes require too much fine-grained documentation of minutes spent and apply only to select patients. Overall costs, including travel, phone calls, and paperwork, exceed Medicare revenue, requiring home-based medical programs to seek other revenue sources to create a sustainable business plan, rather than concentrating on those with the greatest needs for home care and medical attention.

With few exceptions, private payers have expressed little interest in home medical care, preferring to concentrate on other issues. This disadvantages younger adults and low-income (Medicaid) individuals, who again lack access unless their physicians choose to accept financial burdens by seeing them for payment that is below cost, if they are paid at all.

Finally, regulatory oversight of house calls by some Medicare carriers has burdened providers. Audits for all billed claims, which cause payment delays and restricted cash flow, have bankrupted high-quality house call programs, leaving the people they served with no recourse. Audits are a side-effect of mistrust and automated fraud prevention systems. House call providers exhibit high-frequency use of house call codes that are used rarely by office-based peers, thus flagging house call providers' profiles as outliers. Those with the stamina and the cash to fight find most or all denials overturned on appeal, but many have given up and sought other lines of work. Audit abuse has not been addressed by CMS management, perhaps due to competing priorities. Senior CMS administrators deny intent to discourage house calls as a matter of national policy.

Payment and compliance regulation are often linked with quality measurement. In home medical care, formal evaluation of quality is offered by the Joint Commission. Only large health systems can afford the considerable cost and the loss of efficiency associated with data gathering, and there is no economic value from accreditation. Other attempts have been made to develop measures that are suited to the role, but these are not in general use. An expert panel identified appropriate quality benchmarks for home care using Assessing Care of Vulnerable Elders (ACOVE) indicators as a platform (Smith, Soriano, and Boal, 2007). There also is a house call provider exam offered by the American Academy of Home Care Physicians. Most standard quality benchmarks, like diabetic control and cancer screening rates, are meaningless in the care of people in the final years of life and advanced states of ill health (Boyd et al., 2005). One thing does stand out in virtually every home care study: care recipients prefer it.

On balance, facing significant disincentives and lower income potential has caused all but the most committed champions to avoid home medical practice. This fact stands in contrast to the growing evidence of economic and clinical benefit from a home medical care model that includes transitional care.

Problem 5: The Hidden Costs of Privatizing Public Benefits

Budgeting only 2.5 percent for administration, in contrast to the lowest cost private payers at 7 percent, Medicare runs lean and almost all Medicare funds pay for actual care. Critics argue that more administrative controls would reduce overuse and fraud. Providers complain about low payments compared with the private sector. Economists note that lack of competition leads to inefficiency and poor quality. Still, it is instructive to consider two decades of experience with private-sector diversification of Medicare, including explosive growth as Part D and the 2003 Medicare Modernization Act have resulted in 4,000 additional private-sector plans. This experience should teach caution when considering human factor implications.

Among new options, prescription drug plans (PDPs) offer only drug coverage, whereas Medicare Advantage plans offer one-stop shopping for all health care. Two positive results are notable: consumers are more aware of drug costs and willing to accept generic alternatives, and half of the 6 million "Medicare poor" have newly attained drug coverage, along with 20 million others who had less need of the expensive new government benefit (Zhang et al., 2009).

Problems with human factors implications counterbalance the positive results. The new plans have created much unfunded work and frustration for physicians, pharmacists, and consumers, as hours are spent every week navigating a forest of new formularies and sluggish preauthorization processes for drug or service coverage, which can take an hour for a single item and regularly cause delays in care. Many beneficiaries do not know what plan they have or what it covers. Health plans sell policies to unwitting individuals with low health literacy or dementia. The plans restrict care and disrupt established relationships without recipients' being aware of the impacts. Marketers create favorable selection bias (outside Walmart, not in senior centers, where frail people congregate). Some plans employ care management for enrollees with higher comorbidity, but most focus on maximizing enrollment. MedPAC now advises reduced incentives for private insurers. Finally, patients often change plans, further complicating matters.

When debating administrative efficiency, some consider the private insurance industry better suited than government. However, recall that the main drags on current public payment systems relate to defining eligibility (means testing) and providing care with limited resources (de facto rationing), not to administrative inefficiency once services are adequately funded. Experience with services actively regulated by private payers shows those processes to be more burdensome and expensive than government. Experts (Kronick, 2009; Zarabozo and Harrison, 2009) have found that cost shifting in Medicare managed care has increased overall cost by 13 percent, with fewer services rendered and reduced consumer perception of care quality among sicker beneficiaries who most need care (Keenan et al., 2009).

EVIDENCE OF VALUE FROM MEDICALLY LED HOME CARE TEAMS

Evidence is mounting that medically managed home care can produce outcomes far superior to 1-2 percent improvements in major endpoints (e.g., hospitalization) that are routinely accepted in drug trials and other clinical research.

One source of data is the Department of Veterans Affairs (VA) health system, in which systematic implementation of standardized home-based primary care (HBPC) produced a 24 percent decrease in overall costs for care of these ailing veterans (now over 11,000). These programs now adhere to national standards for patient selection, care process, and quality, producing greater homogeneity and a more comprehensive approach than the HBPC model tested at 16 sites in the 1990s. At that time, there was improved satisfaction, but variable model adherence and no cost savings. Current national VA data show that although home care costs increase with HBPC, much lower hospital costs (–62 percent) and nursing home costs generate overall savings. While the data are limited to the VA, the results are impressive and the sample is large (Beales and Edes, 2009).

The Program of All-Inclusive Care for the Elderly (PACE) model, a permanent federal benefit since 1997, also offers insight. PACE teams serve frail low-income older persons with Medicare and Medicaid coverage who live in the community but meet criteria for nursing home care. The care model is organized around a community day health center. Financing is a global risk agreement, funded by monthly capitation from Medicare based on projected costs (using Hierarchical Condition Category scoring) plus Medicaid costs. PACE now has 65 sites and 17,000 enrollees. The program has grown slowly, in part due to stringent enrollment requirements, substantial capital and escrow needs (now around $4 million per site), and low capacity (150-200 per site). Analyses show that change in care financing and delivery can reduce dependence on inpatient settings for sick, disabled populations (Kane et al., 2006). PACE participants and providers consider this an excellent model.

Another option for frail Medicare beneficiaries is the Special Needs Program (SNP) offered since the late 1990s, now with about 775 programs and 1 million enrollees. This is a Medicare managed care risk contract for persons with multimorbidity and higher costs. Success has varied. Core issues are patient selection and recruitment, plus clinical team makeup and fiscal management. Most of the programs arise in traditional care systems and conventional provider groups that may not be ready for this work.

Hospital at Home, which provides acute home care for patients who meet criteria for inpatient hospital care, has also shown improved satisfaction and fewer in-hospital complications, though as yet no definite cost savings (Cheng, Montalto, and Leff, 2009).

Office Without Walls (OWW) is a special program developed in one Nevada geriatric managed care organization. Unpublished data compare its enrollees (n = 437) with 875 comparably old (age 86) and ill persons managed by office practices. OWW members received 3,365 home visits but no office visits and had much less hospital use (33 percent less emergency department use and 50 percent fewer bed days), saving $1.5 million per year ($1,500 per person) if adjusted to an enrolled population of 1,000 individuals.

A recent randomized clinical trial of an at-home geriatric assessment and consultation program for low-income seniors in Indianapolis called GRACE showed marked improvement in clinical care. There was also a 40 percent reduction in hospital use during the second year of operation (Counsell et al., 2007) among higher risk participants, even though this was not a case management or primary care model and did not include urgent response capacity.

In sum, comparing current usual home health care to office, hospital, or even nursing home settings, one finds a model that is largely missing one key ingredient: an active medical presence. Yet substantial evidence and common sense both suggest that combining medical care with other home health services will improve outcomes, will save money, and is preferred. Financial incentives are a key reason for this striking incongruity. As a matter of health policy, for the benefit of both users and providers, a new, integrated home care model is needed, free of the cost of bricks and mortar and empowered by portable technology.

FUTURE POLICY DIRECTIONS

In considering people with functional loss and advanced chronic illness (Groups C through F), there are two main policy priorities. One is a national policy for financing long-term care in support of activities of daily living that incorporates a broad vision with the home as the preferred locus and center for care. To achieve this, a systems approach must be employed, with careful consideration of the many contributing elements: living space design, technology applications of a variety of types, workforce development and training, financing mechanisms with incentives aligned to attain objectives, and community support services, like delivered food and other necessary amenities.

The other priority is redesign of medical care for people who are frequent users of costly services, again using a broad conceptualization of what home care can deliver. This requires changes in both delivery systems and regulation and financing, with incentives aligned to produce desired results and the use of setting-specific quality measures, like those discussed earlier. Payment reform alone is inadequate, as managed care experiments have shown. Because home care has been a stepchild in health care policy, it is necessary to put new home care models into the spotlight—models that are patient-centered and focus on population needs—rather than starting with the needs of the health care system and its funding sources.

The serious health problems of community-dwelling elderly persons cannot be addressed in silos or by managing one condition at a time.

Certain systemic conditions (like vascular disease, either alone or with diabetes) underpin much of the most costly care but produce multiple ailing body systems: a person with coronary disease, peripheral vascular disease, ischemic stroke, chronic kidney disease, congestive heart failure, atrial fibrillation, peripheral neuropathy, visual impairment, and diabetes has many conditions. Most of these diagnoses involve vascular pathology, but the key to optimal management is a core team of advanced generalists who can concurrently treat all of the conditions, with help as needed from organ-specific specialists, rather than having each of several different specialized teams manage one condition, or "care by committee." Going to the care recipient's home is also the only way to really know what is going on in many such cases. Focusing on these costly, immobile individuals with enhanced, medically led, interdisciplinary care delivered in the home can reduce resource use by up to 50 percent while improving safety and satisfaction.

Payment models must be addressed simultaneously. Seasoned administrators and noted analysts write about strategies to control runaway Medicare and Medicaid costs (Hsiao, 2007; Rosenthal, 2009; Wilensky, 2009). Options are few: fee-for-service, per-episode (short-term risk-bearing arrangement), capitation (longer-term risk-bearing arrangement that may include global or partial risk), salary with defined responsibilities (VA or staff model health maintenance organization), and gain-sharing based on predicted costs. Ultimately providers must be either placed at risk or rewarded differentially on the basis of desired outcomes. Quality must be part of the final formula, linking results to payment. Pay for performance is a way of modifying payment based on specific process measures. Gain-sharing is a results-based form of pay for performance.

For physicians, fee-for-service payment incentives foster high-volume service in efficient practice settings; they maximize encounters and procedures rather than care coordination and focused management of a few high-cost individuals. And fees for home visits and for care coordination are inadequate to generate sustained interest and growth. However, studies show that alternate modes of financing can attract physicians (Devlin, 2008).

Risk-bearing strategies require capital reserves and large organizations. To date, many risk-bearing mechanisms were subverted by recruiting low-cost individuals. Risk-bearing arrangements for complex patients have either enrolled small numbers (PACE) or failed due to their care model. In any organization, unless senior management is committed to innovation, advanced home care is unlikely to evolve. Pay for performance in conventional financing models offers little incentive for the arduous case management work needed to improve patterns of use. Gain-sharing in conjunction with restructured care delivery systems remains largely untested.

One new idea is Independence At Home (IAH), a gain-sharing strategy introduced in Congress in 2009 (H.R. 2560 and S. 1131) and included in the final health reform bill as Section 3024. It is based on using a technology-enhanced, medically led mobile team to care for small numbers (150 minimum) of high-risk Medicare beneficiaries. Leaving Medicare Parts A and B intact, IAH teams would share in savings from prevented hospitalizations, creating an incentive to work hard and to be responsive. Savings would be calculated based on predicted costs of the population served. IAH teams would follow vulnerable, medically complex, function-limited persons for years, probably for life in most cases, providing prompt access to holistic, comprehensive care, and a one-stop shop. IAH teams would gradually expand, "building out" the problems in the current system.

PACE has shown that CMS can estimate cost at the individual level well enough for its sites to succeed despite small size and wide variance around mean per-person costs. With protections against inadequate service that include measures of satisfaction, easy voluntary withdrawal, and selected evidence-based chronic care process measures that are meaningful to patients with multimorbidity, IAH offers improved care plus cost savings. It is designed for low-cost, local start-up to speed implementation, without having large risk contracts or physical plants. Electronic health records are essential and expected to improve quality and safety and enhance efficiency, but they are also costly. IAH teams will invest in health information technology from the margins created by gain-sharing.

It is difficult to precisely calculate potential cost savings from wide-scale adoption of an IAH model or others like it, which focus care on the people at greatest risk, aligning incentives while changing primary care delivery, but it can be estimated. Ranking Medicare beneficiaries by cost, in the top 10 percent (4 million people) the average 2009 cost is about $50,000. Reducing average cost 25 percent would save $50 billion per year. And the 4 million is also the number of persons in the center of the target using functional status as the primary selection criterion.

A low-end estimate could be based on home health agency Part A rehospitalizations. Using the 29 percent national rate and 7 million episodes yields 2 million hospital admissions. A 25 percent improvement would avert 500,000 hospitalizations; if these averaged $15,000, Medicare savings would be $7.5 billion. This is a low estimate, as some at-risk persons are either not referred or are in and out of Part A care.

The VA Home-Based Primary Care Program is another frame. In 2002 dollars, annual home care cost per person was $11,000 more after HBPC than before it. This was offset by reduced hospital costs ($11,000) and nursing home costs ($10,000). Total costs were lowered from $38,000 to $29,000 (24 percent). Adjusting for inflation at 5 percent and applying this math to 4 million Medicare beneficiaries who cost $50,000 each in 2009, home care would cost $62 billion more but hospital and nursing home use would be $116 billion lower, saving $54 billion overall.

To satisfy critics, it is important to address concerns about workforce and the impact of an IAH "carve-out" on other stakeholders and other new health care designs.

The baby boom will change the shape of health care. If the current path continues, hospitals can anticipate more Medicare volume and the prospect of providing those services at a discounted rate relative to current payments, which are often at or below cost. Thus, hospitals should support IAH in order to focus on what they do best: advanced surgery, intensive care, and complex inpatient management using lots of high technology.

Typical primary care physicians already coordinate care with 117 other practices (Pham et al., 2009), and they also have more than enough clients. Furthermore, the frail IAH population is not ideal for office practice, since these persons require more time during encounters and much more time between encounters. High-volume physician offices will always struggle to meet the needs of this complex and immobile population. Although a large enough office practice can structure a support system that will accommodate the care management requirements of this population, the physician owners or business managers must intentionally choose to set aside time to care for the immobile patients and the payment system must support that, or these patients will always be marginalized as they are now. None of the other health care reform options will achieve this, except for the most advanced medical homes, after many years of substantial investment.

IAH can be viewed as a specialized patient-centered medical home (PCMH) without bricks and mortar. Taking a frail, sick older person out of bed and forcing them to travel to the physician's office, often requiring a family member to take time off work to make sure key issues are addressed, does not seem patient-centered. An office-based PCMH strategy of using telemedicine and delegating direct care to professionals with less training, in lieu of physician care, would create a lower standard of care for some of the sickest persons in society. Finally, the PCMH financial model is inadequate to cover the extra care costs of this population.

Specialty physicians likewise will have more than enough Medicare business and would not miss seeing the IAH population subset who require more time and bring more risk-benefit issues and more complex decisions to procedural care. Specialists face the same risk as hospitals—of working harder for lower rates unless ways can be found to target resources and lower overall Medicare costs.

The accountable care organization (ACO) model is designed to compensate large health systems for care of a population that includes frail, complex cases. An IAH program would help an accountable care organization deliver care and control costs, just as it would for a Medicaid Advantage plan that serves large numbers of high-cost elders or a special needs program. An IAH program matches the financial needs of accountable care organizations and special needs programs. The question remains whether most such large entities will ever develop home-based care models. Historically, most have not done so.

It is likely that varied approaches will emerge for managing patients with advanced chronic illness. Some will use more telemedicine, more smart technology, more specialized consultation by pharmacists, more fully developed interdisciplinary teams. Some will purchase additional social work, personal care, community care managers, and other support services.

PROFESSIONAL WORKFORCE DEVELOPMENT AND OTHER POSSIBLE BARRIERS

Critics of the home care model for advanced chronic illness care have focused on the lack of sufficient experienced medical providers (physicians, nurse practitioners, other advance practice nurses, physician assistants). Although rarely noticed, a few thousand medical providers nationally have focused their efforts on mobile medical care using Part B payments and contract roles. Care of 300 very sick older persons at home might require a team with two nurse practitioners, a physician, and a small staff. To reach 4 million patients under these assumptions would require 13,000 physicians and 26,000 nurse practitioners supported by a team. Much of the team exists in home care, except for the medical component. The question is: How long would it take to grow such a workforce?

Consider hospital medicine, in which a "hospitalist" employed by the hospital assumes the responsibilities of attending physician and case manager for the duration of an in-patient's stay. This rapidly growing field with 30,000 workers arose in a decade from only 500 in 1997 due to a reliable payment source (the hospital) and a defined clinical role that is appealing to young physicians. Hospitalists work hard, with defined schedules and strong infrastructure supports. One can imagine medical home care teams emerging quickly given suitable incentives and supports, particularly within the established framework of home health agencies. Young physicians are inherently altruistic. Many would welcome the challenge and personal rewards of this work, for which care recipients and families are very grateful. The IAH teams in turn will attract more talented nurses and other workers to the field.

After 10 years, a successful gain-sharing model might contend with insufficient numbers of persons in usual care against which to calculate savings as well as statistical regression to the mean, which would impact estimated cost savings. Recalibration and possibly even a revised payment model would be needed. By then, the market and provider workforce would be ready for risk-based care for frail elders living in the community.

The biggest barriers to effective change in home care will come from lack of vision, entrenched systems, and interests that seek to maintain current revenue streams, to their own detriment. Change must come, and early adopters will prosper. Horizontal and vertical integration must be expected, much as was predicted during the "failed" national experiment with for-profit managed care, which has worked best for people who are not ill.

In order to meet the needs of the sickest individuals in the home, those delivering care need flexible and efficient designs while promoting high-quality care and proper rewards and allowing patients to move between settings, as suggested in Figure 12-4.

Importantly, incentives are needed for members of an interdisciplinary home-based team to engage in the difficult aspects of this work for the members of Group F:

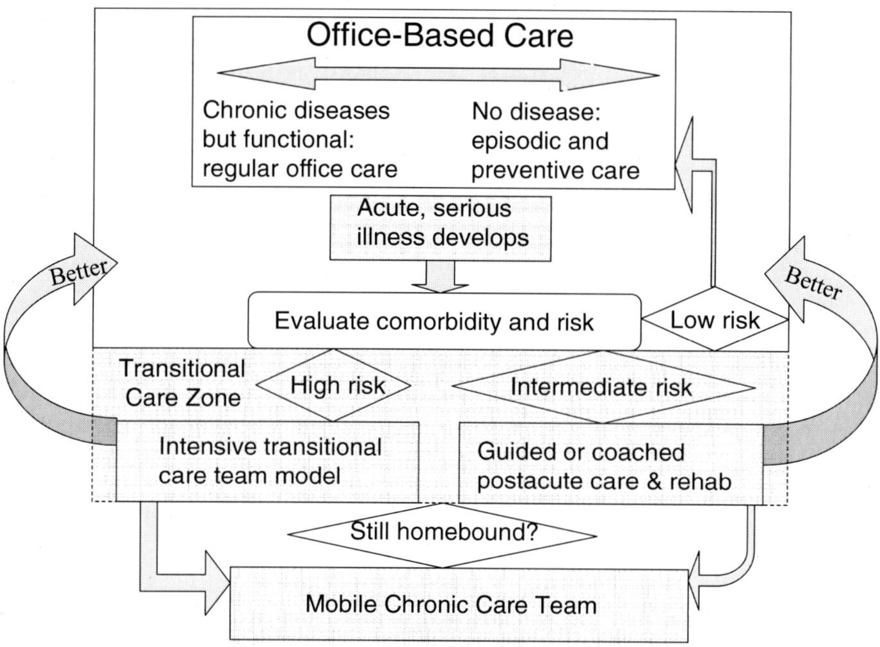

FIGURE 12-4 Movement of at-risk persons between care settings.
SOURCE: Reprinted from Boling (2009). With permission from Elsevier.

- Selecting appropriate persons for intensive team care; suitable candidates are much sicker than the average person seen by office physicians or home health.
- Making and implementing complex medical decisions for ongoing care of individuals with multiple active problems, often several problems that are unstable or meta-stable, and for which treating one impacts several others.
- Timely, effective response to urgent situations in complex patients.
- Interacting with hospitals and specialty physicians in complicated cases.
- Care coordination involving multiple services and multiple sources of support.
- Addressing unrealistic expectations of the care recipient and the family for what health care can deliver and compassionately making difficult decisions.
- Disentangling social from medical issues; a line must be drawn when people seek to use medical resources to address social needs that are sometimes limitless.
- Finding or creating community resources to solve complex problems.

The complex scenarios in which advanced medical home care providers, care recipients, and their families find themselves remind one of surgery, played out in slow motion over years. Care recipients depend heavily on a trustworthy physician-led interdisciplinary team who will see them through their entire course of care. Serious consequences attach to ill-advised decisions. Care providers must know how to prepare, what to cut, what not to cut, and how to manage the recuperative period. It takes considerable knowledge, training, skill, and experience to do this well. And each case is a deeply personal human drama that leaves indelible lifelong memories in all who are involved.

In summary, home care has an extensive workforce at varying levels of skill and has developed a much enhanced range of technical capability that is needed by people of all ages. By having a broad vision that has its foundation in population needs and a willingness to restructure health care so that it is intentionally organized around the home and in the community and is thus truly patient-centered, people can achieve greater user satisfaction, better outcomes, and lower cost. Care and support should be targeted and proportionate to need. Robust quality measures have been developed that are appropriate to home care models and can be used to ensure value-based purchasing. Much can be learned from other nations that have invested in community-based care as society moves forward. A systems-based approach with prominent consideration of human factors will be vital to the proposed and much-needed redesign of payment, regulation, and care delivery in the home.

ABOUT THE AUTHOR

Peter A. Boling is professor of medicine at Virginia Commonwealth University, where he heads geriatrics and is interim chair of general internal medicine, which includes geriatrics, ambulatory care, hospitalists, and women's health, medical education, and research. He has a longstanding interest in health policy and has published and spoken widely on home care.

REFERENCES

Akpolat, T., Dilek, M., Aydogdu, T., Adibeli, Z., Erdem, D.G., and Erdem, E. (2009). Home sphygmomanometers: Validation vs. accuracy. *Blood Pressure Monitoring, 14*, 26-31.

Beales, J.L., Edes, T. (2009). Veteran's Affairs home based primary care. *Clinics in Geriatric Medicine, 25*(1), 149-154.

Boling, P.A. (2009). Care transitions and home health care. *Clinics in Geriatric Medicine, 25*(1), 135-148.

Boyd, C.M., Darer, J., Boult, C., Fried, L.P., Boult, L., and Wu, A.W. (2005). Clinical practice guidelines and quality of care for older adults with multiple co-morbid diseases: implications for pay-for-performance. *Journal of the American Medical Association, 294*(6), 716-724.

Brown, R., Peikes, D., Chen, A., and Schore, J. (2008). 15-site randomized trial of coordinated care in Medicare FFS. *Health Care Financing Review, 30*(1), 1-25.

Brummel-Smith, K., and Dangiolo, M. (2009). Assistive technologies in the home. *Clinics in Geriatric Medicine, 25*(1), 61-79.

Centers for Disease Control and Prevention. (2008). *Vital and health statistics series 10, Number 242: Summary health statistics for U.S. adults*. National Health Interview Survey, 2008. Available: http://www.cdc.gov/nchs/data/series/sr_10/sr10_242.pdf [accessed September 2009].

Centers for Disease Control and Prevention. (2009). *National Health Interview Survey, 2003-2007*. Table 1: Frequency Distributions of Numbers of Limitations in Activities of ADL and IADL from 2003 to 2007. Available: http://www.cdc.gov/nchs/health_policy/ADL_IADL_tables.pdf [accessed September 2009].

Cheng, J., Montalto, M., and Leff, B. (2009). Hospital at Home. *Clinics in Geriatric Medicine, 25*(1), 79-82.

Coe, N.B., and Van Houten, C.H. (2009). Caring for mom and neglecting yourself? The health effects of caring for an elderly parent. *Health Economics, 18*, 991-1,010.

Coleman, E.A., Parry, C., Chalmers, S., and Min, S.J. (2006). The care transitions intervention: results of a randomized controlled trial. *Archives of Internal Medicine, 166*, 1,822-1,828.

Counsell, S.R., Callahan, C.M., Clark, D.O., Tu, W., Buttar, A.B., Stump, T.E., and Ricketts, G.D. (2007). Geriatric care management for low-income seniors: A randomized controlled trial. *Journal of the American Medical Association, 298*(22), 2,623-2,633.

Devlin, R.A. (2008). Do physician remuneration schemes matter? The case of Canadian family physicians. *Journal of Health Economics, 27*, 1,168-1,181.

Foster, L., Dale, S.B., and Brown, R. (2007). How caregivers and workers fared in Cash and Counseling. *Health Services Research, 42*(1, Part II), 510-532.

Giovannetti, E.R., Wolff, J.L., Frick, K.D., and Boult, C. (2009). Construct validity of the Work Productivity and Activity Impairment Questionnaire across informal caregivers of chronically ill older patients. *Value in Health, 12*(6), 1011-1017.

Goldfield, N.I., McCullough, E.C., Hughes, J.S., Tang, A.M., Eastman, B., Rawlins, L.K., and Averill, R.F. (2008). Identifying potentially preventable readmissions. *Health Care Financing Review, 30*(1), 75-91.

Henry J. Kaiser Family Foundation. (2009). *Medicare Advantage.* Website publication #2052-12. Available: http://www.kff.org/Medicare/upload/2052-12.pdf [accessed September 2009].

Holtz-Eakin, D. (2005). High-cost Medicare beneficiaries. Congressional Budget Office report to Congress. May. Available: http://www.cbo.gov/ftpdocs/63xx/doc 6322/05-03 [accessed September 2009].

Hsiao, W.C. (2007). Why is a systemic view of health financing necessary? More money is a necessary but insufficient condition for better health. *Health Affairs, 26*(4), 950-961.

Institute for Health Policy and Clinical Practice. (2008). *The Dartmouth atlas of health care.* Available: http://www.dartmouthatlas.org/atlases/2008_Chronic_Care_Atlas.pdf [accessed September 2009].

Kane, R.L., Homyak, P., Bershadsky, B., Flood, S. (2006). *Journal of Gerontology, 61A*(7), 689-693.

Keenan, P.S., Elliott, M.N., Cleary, P.D., Zavlavsky, A.M., and Landon, B.E. (2009). Quality assessments by sick and healthy beneficiaries in traditional Medicare and Medicare managed care. *Medical Care, 47*, 882-888.

Kemper, P. (2007). Commentary: Social experimentation at its best: The Cash and Counseling demonstration and its implications. *Health Services Research, 42*(1, Part II), 577-586.

Kemper, P., Weaver, F., Short, P.F., Shea, D., and Kang, H. (2008). Meeting the need for personal care among the elderly: Does Medicaid home care spending matter. *Health Services Research, 44*(1, Part II), 344-362.

Kronick, R. (2009). Medicare and HMOs—the search for accountability. *New England Journal of Medicine, 360*(20), 2,048-2,050.

Leff, B., Reider, L., Frick, K.D., Scharfstein, D.O., Boyd, C.M., Frey, K., Karm, L., and Boult, C. (2009). Guided care and the cost of complex healthcare: A preliminary report. *American Journal of Managed Care, 15*(8), 555-559.

Linden, A., and Adler-Milstein, J. (2008). Medicare disease management in policy context. *Health Care Financing Review, 29*(3), 1-11.

Murkofsky, R.L., and Alston, K. (2009). The past, present and future of skilled home health agency care. *Clinics in Geriatric Medicine, 25*(1), 1-18.

National Association for Home Care & Hospice. (2009). *Home care and hospice facts and stats.* Available: http://www.nahc.org [accessed September 2009].

Naylor, M.D., Brooten, D., Campbell, R., Jacobsen, B.S., Mezey, M.D., Pauly, M.V., and Schwartz, J.S. (1999). Comprehensive discharge planning and home care follow-up of hospitalized elders. *Journal of the American Medical Association, 281*(7), 613-620.

Ogedegbe, G., and Schoenthaler, A. (2006). A systematic review of the effects of home blood pressure monitoring on medication adherence. *Journal of Clinical Hypertension, 8*(3), 174-180.

Pham, H.H., O'Malley, A.S., Back, P.B., Salontz-Martinez, C., and Schrag, D. (2009). Primary care physicians' links to other physicians through Medicare patients: The scope of care coordination. *Annals of Internal Medicine, 150*, 236-242.

Potetz, L., and Cubanski, J. (2009). A primer on Medicare financing (pages 1-22). Henry J Kaiser Family Foundation. July. Available: http://www.kff.org/medicare/7731.cfm [accessed September 2009].

Rosenthal, M.B. (2009). Beyond pay for performance—emerging models of provider-payment reform. *New England Journal of Medicine, 359*(12), 1,197-1,200.

Schade, C.P., Esslinger, E., Anderson, D., Sun, Y., and Knowles, B. (2009). Impact of a national campaign on hospital readmissions in home care patients. *International Journal for Quality in Health Care, 21*(3), 176-182.

Schoen, C., Osborn, R., How, S.K.H., Doty, M.M., and Peugh, J. (2008). In chronic condition: Experiences of patients with complex health care needs, in eight countries. *Health Affairs, 28*(1), w1-w16.

Shelledy, C.D., Legrand, T.S., Gardner, D.D., and Peters, J.I. (2009). A randomized, controlled study to evaluate the role of an in-home disease management program provided by respiratory therapists in improving outcomes and reducing the cost of care. *Journal of Asthma, 46*, 194-201.

Smith, K.L., Soriano, T.A., and Boal, J. (2007). Brief communication: National quality of care standards in home-based primary care. *Annals of Internal Medicine, 146*, 188-192.

Stone, R., and Newcomer, R. (2009). Advances and issue in personal care. *Clinics in Geriatric Medicine, 25*(1), 35-60.

Suter, P., Hennessey, B., Harrison, G., Fagan, M., Norman, B., and Suter, W.N. (2008). Home-based chronic care: An expanded integrative model for home care professionals. *Home Healthcare Nurse, 26*(4), 222-229.

Wennberg, J.E., Fisher, E.S., Goodman, D.C., and Skinner, J.S. (2008). Tracking the care of patients with severe chronic illness: The Dartmouth atlas of health care. pp. 180. Available: http://www.dartmouthatlas.org/downloads/atlases/2008_Chronic_Care_Atlas.pdf [accessed May 2010].

Wiener, J.M. (2007). Commentary: Cash and Counseling in international context. *Health Services Research, 42*(1, Part II), 510-532.

Wilensky, G.R. (2009). Reforming Medicare's physician payment system. *New England Journal of Medicine, 360*(7), 653-655.

Wolff, J.L., Meadow, A., Boyd, C.M., Weiss, C.O., and Leff, B. (in press). Physician evaluation and management of Medicare home health patients. Submitted to *Medical Care.*

Zarabozo, C., and Harrison, S. (2009). Payment policy and the growth of Medicare Advantage. *Health Affairs, 28*(1), 55-67.

Zhang, Y., Donohue, J.M., Lave, J.R., O'Donnell, G., and Newhouse, J.P. (2009). The effect of Medicare Part D on drug and medical spending. *New England Journal of Medicine, 361*, 52-61.

Appendix

Workshop Agenda and Participants

Workshop on the Role of Human Factors in Home Health Care

THURSDAY, OCTOBER 1, 2009

8:15 am Workshop Check-In

8:30 **Welcome and Introductions**
- *Barbara Wanchisen*, Director, Committee on Human-Systems Integration
- *David Wegman*, Chair, Committee on the Role of Human Factors in Home Health Care

8:45 **Remarks on the Sponsor's Objectives for the Workshop**
- *Kerm Henriksen*, Human Factors Advisor for Patient Safety, Agency for Healthcare Research and Quality (AHRQ)
- *Teresa Zayas-Caban*, Senior Manager, Health Information Technology, AHRQ

Workshop Plan and Procedures
- *Susan Van Hemel*, Study Director, NRC

- **Session 1: People Who Receive and Provide Home Health Care**

Moderators*: Sara Czaja and Judith Matthews, Committee Members

---

*Each presentation will be 35 min. long, followed by 10-15 min. Q&A period led by moderators.

9:00 People Receiving Care and/or Managing Their Own Health
- *Neil Charness*, William G. Chase Professor of Psychology, Florida State University

9:50 Informal Caregivers: Family, Friends, Others
- *Richard Schulz*, Professor of Psychiatry and Director of the University Center for Social and Urban Research, University of Pittsburgh (co-author: Connie A. Tompkins)

10:40 Break

10:50 Formal Caregivers: Professionals, Paraprofessionals, Direct-Care Workers
- *Carolyn Humphrey*, Independent Consultant and *Paula Milone-Nuzzo*, Pennsylvania State University

11:40 Session 1 Discussion
- *Margaret Quinn*, Professor, Department of Work Environment; Director, Sustainable Hospitals Program, University of Massachusetts–Lowell, discussant

12:30 pm Lunch

- **Session 2: Home Health Care Tasks and Tools**

Moderators: Daryle Gardner-Bonneau and Misha Pavel, Committee Members

1:30 Home Caregiving Tasks
- *Colin Drury*, Distinguished Professor Emeritus, State University of New York, Buffalo

2:20 Medical Devices and Equipment
- *Molly Story*, President, Human Spectrum Design

3:10 Break

3:20 Information Technology
- *George Demiris*, Associate Professor, Biobehavioral Nursing and Health Systems, University of Washington

4:10 Session 2 Discussion
- *R. Paul Crawford*, Director of Research, Product Research and Incubation, Digital Health Group at Intel, discussant

5:00 Adjourn for the day

6:00 Working dinner

FRIDAY, OCTOBER 2, 2009

8:15 am Workshop Check-In

- **Session 3: The Environments of Home Health Care**

Moderators: Jon Pynoos, Laura Gitlin, and K. Eric DeJonge, Committee members

8:30 Physical Environment
- *Jonathan Sanford*, Director and Senior Research Scientist, Center for Assistive Technology and Environmental Access, Georgia Institute of Technology

9:20 Culture, Community, and Social Environments
- *Steven Albert*, Professor and Associate Chair for Research and Science, Department of Behavioral and Community Health Sciences, University of Pittsburgh

10:10 Break

10:20 Policy, Reimbursement, and Regulation Environments
- *Peter Boling*, Director of Long-Term Care and Geriatrics, Virginia Commonwealth University, Medical College of Virginia Hospital

11:10 Session 3 Discussion
- *Carol Raphael*, Chief Executive Officer, Visiting Nurse Service of New York, discussant

12:00 pm **General Discussion**
Moderator: David Wegman

12:30 Closing Remarks
- *David Wegman*, *Kerm Henriksen*, and *Teresa Zayas-Caban*

12:45 Adjourn Workshop

NOTE FOR PUBLIC MEETINGS: This meeting is being held to gather information to help the committee conduct its study. This committee will examine the information and material obtained during this, and other public meetings, in an effort to inform its work. Although opinions may be stated and lively discussion may ensue, no conclusions are being drawn at this time; no recommendations will be made. In fact, the committee will deliberate thoroughly before writing its draft report. Moreover, once the draft report is written, it must go through a rigorous review by experts who are anonymous to the committee, and the committee then must respond to this review with appropriate revisions that adequately satisfy the Academy's Report Review Committee and the chair of the National Research Council before it is considered a National Research Council report. Therefore, observers who draw conclusions about the committee's work based on today's discussions will be doing so prematurely.

Furthermore, individual committee members often engage in discussion and questioning for the specific purpose of probing an issue and sharpening an argument. The comments of any given committee member may not necessarily reflect the position he or she may actually hold on the subject under discussion, to say nothing of that person's future position as it may evolve in the course of the project. Any inferences about an individual's position regarding findings or recommendations in the final report are therefore also premature.

PARTICIPANTS AND REGISTRANTS

Committee:
David H. Wegman, *Chair*, University of Massachusetts–Lowell
Sara Czaja, University of Miami Miller School of Medicine
Eric DeJonge, Washington Hospital Center, Washington, DC
Daryle Jean Gardner-Bonneau, Bonneau & Associates, Portage, Michigan
Michael Christopher Gibbons, Johns Hopkins University
Laura N. Gitlin, Thomas Jefferson University
Judith Tabolt Matthews, University of Pittsburgh School of Nursing
Misha Pavel, Oregon Health and Science University
P. Hunter Peckham, Case Western Reserve University
Jon Pynoos, University of Southern California
Robert M. Schumacher, User Centric, Inc., Oakbrook Terrace, Illinois
Mary Weick Brady, Food and Drug Administration, Rockville, Maryland
Jennifer L. Wolff, Johns Hopkins University

Speakers:
Steven Albert, University of Pittsburgh
Peter Boling, Virginia Commonwealth University Medical Center

Neil Charness, Florida State University
R. Paul Crawford, Intel Corporation
George Demiris, Washington State University
Colin Drury, University of Buffalo
Carol Humphrey, C.H. Humphrey Associates
Paula Milone-Nuzzo, Penn State University
Margaret Quinn, University of Massachusetts–Lowell
Carol Raphael, Visiting Nurse Service of New York
Jonathan Sanford, Georgia Institute of Technology
Richard Schulz, University of Pittsburgh
Molly Follette Story, Human Spectrum Design

Project Sponsors:
Teresa Zayas Cabán, Agency for Healthcare Research and Quality
Kerm Henriksen, Agency for Healthcare Research and Quality

Invited Guests:
Sheila Arbury, Occupational Safety and Health Administration
Sandy Berman, Center for Devices and Radiological Health
Meryl Bloomrosen, American Medical Informatics Association
Deborah Boehm-Davis, George Mason University
Jeff Brady, Agency for Healthcare Research and Quality
Randall Carson, Smith & Nephew
Trish Dawidczyk, Covidien
Thomas Edes, U.S. Department of Veterans Affairs
Elena Fazio, Federal Interagency Forum on Aging-Related Statistics
Dominic Furniss, University College, London
Robyn Gershon, Columbia University, Mailman School of Public Health
Erwin Gianchandani, National Science Foundation
Elise Handelman, Occupational Safety and Health Administration
Suzi Iacono, National Science Foundation
Kate King, Centers for Medicare & Medicaid Services
Jane Lipscomb, University of Maryland
Amber Mason-Dixon, U.S. Department of Veterans Affairs
Kelly Mingle, U.S. Department of Veterans Affairs
Wendy Nilsen, National Institutes of Health
Marcia Nusgart, Coalition of Wound Care
Mary Parker, MKHP Associates, LLC
Pat Patterson, Agilis Consulting Group, LLC
Dena Puskin, Health Resources and Services Administration
Louis Quatrano, National Institutes of Health
Deborah Randall, Aging Services and Telehealth Consulting
Carol Regan, Paraprofessional Healthcare Institute

Carrie Rich, Perkins+Will/Georgetown University
Emily Rosenoff, U.S. Department of Health and Human Services, Office of the Assistant Secretary for Planning and Evaluation
Judith Sangl, Agency for Healthcare Research and Quality
Mitali Sen, U.S. Census Bureau
Abha Shrestha, Agency for Healthcare Research and Quality/Contractor National Opinion Research Center
Rosie Sood, National Institute on Aging
Michelle Washko, U.S. Administration on Aging
Sandy Weininger, U.S. Food and Drug Administration, Center for Devices and Radiological Health
Bernadette Wright, The Lewin Group

National Research Council Staff:
Barbara Wanchisen, Director, BBCSS and Interim Director, COHSI
Mary Ellen O'Connell, Associate Director, BBCSS
Susan Van Hemel, Study Director, BBCSS
Renée L. Wilson Gaines, Senior Program Assistant, BBCSS
Michael J. Feuer, Executive Director, DBASSE
Patricia Morison, Associate Executive Director, DBASSE
Miron Straf, Deputy Executive Director, DBASSE
June Heidemann, Program Assistant, BBCSS
Steve Olson, Workshop Rapporteur